Stochastic Finance with Python

Design Financial Models from Probabilistic Perspective

Avishek Nag

Apress®

Stochastic Finance with Python: Design Financial Models from Probabilistic Perspective

Avishek Nag
Bangalore, Karnataka, India

ISBN-13 (pbk): 979-8-8688-1051-0 ISBN-13 (electronic): 979-8-8688-1052-7
https://doi.org/10.1007/979-8-8688-1052-7

Copyright © 2024 by Avishek Nag

This work is subject to copyright. All rights are reserved by the Publisher, whether the whole or part of the material is concerned, specifically the rights of translation, reprinting, reuse of illustrations, recitation, broadcasting, reproduction on microfilms or in any other physical way, and transmission or information storage and retrieval, electronic adaptation, computer software, or by similar or dissimilar methodology now known or hereafter developed.

Trademarked names, logos, and images may appear in this book. Rather than use a trademark symbol with every occurrence of a trademarked name, logo, or image we use the names, logos, and images only in an editorial fashion and to the benefit of the trademark owner, with no intention of infringement of the trademark.

The use in this publication of trade names, trademarks, service marks, and similar terms, even if they are not identified as such, is not to be taken as an expression of opinion as to whether or not they are subject to proprietary rights.

While the advice and information in this book are believed to be true and accurate at the date of publication, neither the authors nor the editors nor the publisher can accept any legal responsibility for any errors or omissions that may be made. The publisher makes no warranty, express or implied, with respect to the material contained herein.

    Managing Director, Apress Media LLC: Welmoed Spahr
    Acquisitions Editor: Celestin Suresh John
    Development Editor: James Markham
    Coordinating Editor: Gryffin Winkler

Cover designed by eStudioCalamar

Cover image by Freepik.com

Distributed to the book trade worldwide by Apress Media, LLC, 1 New York Plaza, New York, NY 10004, U.S.A. Phone 1-800-SPRINGER, fax (201) 348-4505, e-mail orders-ny@springer-sbm.com, or visit www.springeronline.com. Apress Media, LLC is a California LLC and the sole member (owner) is Springer Science + Business Media Finance Inc (SSBM Finance Inc). SSBM Finance Inc is a **Delaware** corporation.

For information on translations, please e-mail booktranslations@springernature.com; for reprint, paperback, or audio rights, please e-mail bookpermissions@springernature.com.

Apress titles may be purchased in bulk for academic, corporate, or promotional use. eBook versions and licenses are also available for most titles. For more information, reference our Print and eBook Bulk Sales web page at http://www.apress.com/bulk-sales.

Any source code or other supplementary material referenced by the author in this book is available to readers on GitHub (https://github.com/Apress). For more detailed information, please visit https://www.apress.com/gp/services/source-code.

If disposing of this product, please recycle the paper

Table of Contents

About the Author ix

About the Technical Reviewer xi

Introduction xiii

Part I: Foundations 1

Chapter 1: Introduction 3

What Is Quantitative Finance 3

Why Stochastic 5

    What Is Special About Stochastic Methodologies 6

Numerical Implementation 9

    Why Python 10

    The Approach of Pythonic Implementation 10

    Probabilistic and Numerical Programming 11

Summary 13

Chapter 2: Finance Basics and Data Sources 15

Different Financial Assets 15

    Stocks 15

    Options 16

    Portfolio 17

Basic Interest Theory 18

    Simple Interest 19

    Discrete Compound Interest 19

    Continuous Compound Interest 20

Data Source Adapters for Financial Data 21

    Yahoo Financials 22

    Market Stack 26

TABLE OF CONTENTS

> Returns 30
>> Simple Return 31
>> Multiperiod Simple Returns 33
>> Log Returns 34
>> Multiperiod Log Returns 34
>
> Summary 35

Chapter 3: Probability 37
> The Inception of the Idea for Probability Theory 37
> Probability Space and Basic Definitions 38
>> Definition of Probability 39
>> Why Study Probability for Finance 40
>> Set-Theoretic View of Probability 41
>
> Random Variable 43
>> Discrete Random Variable 44
>> Continuous Random Variable 47
>
> Probability Distributions 48
>> Joint and Marginal Distribution 50
>> Likelihood and Parameters 51
>> Moments, Expectation, and Variance 52
>
> Poisson Distribution 55
> Uniform Distribution 57
> Exponential Distribution 58
> Gaussian/Normal Distribution 60
> Characteristic Function 62
> Parameter Estimation 67
>> Frequentist Method 68
>
> Method of Moments 79
>> Bayesian Method 82
>
> Summary 93

Chapter 4: Simulation 95

Random Variable Generation 95
Inverse Transform Method 96
Inverse Method for PMF 100
Acceptance/Rejection Method 102

Monte Carlo Simulation 115
Variance Reduction 124

Summary 130

Chapter 5: Stochastic Process 131

Inception of Stochastic Process 131
Random Walk Model 133
Statistical Metrics of Symmetric Random Walk Model 134
Quadratic Variation of Symmetric Random Walk Model 135

Scaled Random Walk Model 136

Brownian Motion 140
Stochastic Calculus and Integrals – A Brief Introduction 141
Stochastic Differential Equation – Financial Asset Dynamics 142

Poisson Process 150

Summary 153

Part II: Basic Asset Price Modeling 155

Chapter 6: Diffusion Model 157

Modeling Financial Asset Price with SDE 157
SDE-Based Model-Building Steps 158
Formation of SDE – Log-Asset Price and Ito Lemma 159

Risk-Neutral Settings 164
Estimation of PDF and Its Parameters 164

Inference 172
Monte Carlo Simulation of Diffusion Model 173
Time Unit Transformation 176
Average Forecast – Mean Path 177

v

TABLE OF CONTENTS

    Uncertainty Bounds 178

    Backtesting and RMSE Score 178

  Change of Frequency 180

    Computing Distributions of the Mean Path 181

  Comparison and Improvement... 185

  Summary.. 187

Chapter 7: Jump Models... 189

  General Formation of Jump Model... 189

    Ito Lemma for Jump Model 190

    Templates in Python for Parametric Jump-Diffusion Process 192

  Merton Model.. 195

    Path Generation for Merton Model 196

    Parameter Estimation of Merton Model.. 198

    Forecasting with Merton Model 213

  Kou Model 219

    Sampling Jumps from Asymmetric Double Exponential Distribution 219

    Stochastic Process for Kou Model and Path Generation 221

    Parameter Estimation of Kou Model 225

    Forecasting with Kou Model 228

  Nonparametric Models.. 231

    Brief Review of the Kernel Method 234

  Summary.. 256

Part III: Financial Options Modeling 257

Chapter 8: Options and Black- Scholes Model 259

  Options – Basics and Formulations 260

    Option Nomenclatures 260

    Payoff Function... 262

    Put-Call Parity... 263

Black-Scholes Model	264
Risk-Neutral Probability Method	265
Summary	308

Chapter 9: PDE, Finite Difference, and Black-Scholes Model ... 309

PDE – A Short Introduction	309
Solution of PDE – Finite Difference Method (FDM)	311
Explicit Method	314
Implicit Method	328
Crank-Nicolson Method	337
Black-Scholes PDE	343
Implicit FDM for the Black-Scholes Model	345
Integration with Diffusion Model and Python Implementation	346
Summary	350

Part IV: Portfolios ... 353

Chapter 10: Portfolio Optimization ... 355

Brief Idea About Portfolios	355
The Mean-Variance Analysis	356
Portfolio Simulation	363
Minimum Variance Portfolio	369
Additional Constraints	377
Efficient Frontier	381
Efficient Frontier Simulation	382
Summary	385

Bibliography ... 387

Index ... 389

About the Author

Avishek Nag has been an analytics practitioner for more than 17 years, specializing in statistical methods, machine learning, NLP, and Quantitative Finance. He has experience in designing end-to-end machine learning systems and driving data science/ML initiatives from inception to production in multiple organizations (Cisco, VMware, MobileIron, etc.). A few years of experience in the commodity trading domain inspired him to write this book. He has also authored other books on machine learning and survival analysis, respectively. His data science and ML-related blogs can be found on Medium (@avisheknag17). Besides his work, he is also a passionate artist who loves to explore architectural drawings through pencil and ink. Samples of his artwork can be found on Instagram (/avisheknag17), Artquid.com (artquid.com/avishekarts), and many other art platforms.

About the Technical Reviewer

Sonal Raj is a data scientist, engineer, mathematician, and Python evangelist from India, who has carved a niche in the financial services domain. He is a Goldman Sachs and D. E. Shaw alumnus who currently serves as a vice president for a leading high-frequency trading firm heading their data management and research division.

Sonal holds dual masters in computer science and business administration and is a former research fellow of the Indian Institute of Science. His areas of research range from image processing and real-time graph computations to electronic trading algorithms and platforms. Sonal is the author of the titles *The Pythonic Way* (BPB, 2021) and *Neo4j High Performance* (Packt, 2015). His career milestones include creating low latency trading algorithms, trading strategies, market signal models, and components of electronic trading systems. He is also a community speaker and a Python and data science mentor to young minds in the industry.

When not engrossed in reading fiction or battling it out in chess, he spends far too much time watching rockets lift off.

Introduction

Who Should Read This Book?

This book is for you if you belong to any of these categories:

- You are a financial investment professional who uses no external tools for various reasons. This book can be a guideline for you. It can inspire you to be more tech-savvy and build your small tool to manage your investments and portfolio free of cost. Prerequisites like probability and statistics are well covered here.

- You are a data scientist/machine learning Scientist. Then it is a de facto choice for you. You may be interested to learn topics like the modeling of stochastic processes, Monte Carlo simulations, estimating density functions, the Bayesian method of Portfolio optimization, etc., and how to use Python to do all these kinds of stuff. Design patterns used in this book may inspire you to follow a clean coding practice and boost the reusability aspects of the solutions.

- You are a quantitative researcher. From a domain perspective, you can learn how to hedge the volatility of a portfolio, estimate the risk of a security, estimate option values as well as Option Greeks, etc.

- You are a software engineer working in the finance domain. It can work as a handbook if you are responsible for developing some financial models without any support from your organization's data science team. Are you afraid of probability and stats? Do not worry. Chapters 3 and 4 will help you cover those gaps.

- Is probabilistic programming bothering you? You do not have connections with the finance domain but want to learn stochastic modeling. Design patterns and Python code discussed in this book will guide you to learn topics like implementing Monte Carlo simulation, stochastic portfolio optimization, estimating a probability density function, and many more.

INTRODUCTION

What Do You Need to Get Started?

Stochastic Finance is a heavily interdisciplinary subject, and especially for this book, you will deal with multiple topics parallelly – probability and statistics, linear algebra, calculus, optimization, programming with object-oriented Python, and some finance basics. Not everything in that list has equal weightage. The two most important topics are probability and statistics and, to some extent, object-oriented Python. The first one will be covered in Chapters 3 and 4, respectively.

For Python components design, I will explain necessary design patterns and programming styles in the respective sections as and when it is necessary. If you need further assistance, I recommend *Practical Python Design Patterns* by *Wessel Badenhorst (Apress; ISBN: 978-1-4842-2679-7)*.

For linear algebra, calculus, and optimization, I recommend *Linear Algebra and Optimization for Machine Learning* by Charu C. Aggarwal (Springer; ISBN: 978-3-030-40343-0).

For any professional programming, an IDE is good, and so is Python. I prefer using VS code. However, there is no limitation here. Feel free to use whatever dev editor you are comfortable with.

PART I

Foundations

CHAPTER 1

Introduction

Stochastic Finance comes under the more extensive umbrella of Quantitative Finance, which includes all numerical methods and their computational implementations from purely probabilistic perspectives targeted to solve problems in finance and economics. It shows how to model instruments of financial systems leveraging the randomness present there. The terms *stochastic* and *probabilistic* may sound intimidating to many readers. That is natural, especially for people from not-so-good mathematical/statistical backgrounds. However, do not worry; we will delve into these details stepwise. This book talks about different techniques used in Stochastic Finance from theoretical (mathematical details) and practical perspectives – programming and component design examples with Python should give you a 360-degree view of the subject. In addition, despite the availability of ready-made financial modeling systems (mostly, they are not free of cost), it always makes sense to have a transparent idea of their generic working principles. This could be useful when financial investors have limited access/resources to acquire such modeling systems or lack trust.

Knowing about *Quantitative Finance* is essential before jumping to its stochastic counterpart. In this chapter, we will discuss at a high level what Quantitative Finance is and how stochastic methodologies and implementation with Python help here. This should give you an essential high-level context of the main topic.

What Is Quantitative Finance

Quantitative Finance is all about managing money, and of course, finance itself is about that. However, with quant finance, we get a solid numerical foundation on top of it. Moreover, managing money leads to putting your money in some form of financial instrument that can give some returns (we will discuss returns later, but for now, assume that it is related to profit in layman's terms). According to *Investopedia (https://www.investopedia.com)*, "*Financial instruments are assets that can be traded, or they can*

CHAPTER 1   INTRODUCTION

also be seen as packages of capital that may be traded." Assets can be in the form of cash or another financial instrument. Different categorization schemes exist for these instruments. Among them, we will be interested in discussing *securities*, which can be liquidated easily on a public exchange. *Investopedia* says, *"The term 'security' refers to a fungible, negotiable financial instrument that holds some monetary value."*

Securities can be broadly classified into the following:

> **Debt**: These are risk-free instruments and "secure" in the true sense, such as bank deposits and bonds. You keep getting a fixed interest as a return throughout the period once you make a fixed deposit in a bank.
>
> **Equity**: Company shares as stocks.
>
> **Derivatives**: It is a delayed delivery contract agreement between two parties whose value depends on another instrument. Examples of this are options, futures, swaps, etc. In this book, we will be discussing options only.

Finance is about allocating funds for business with an assessment of risk and profits. You can make a profit just by putting a bulk amount of money as fixed deposits in any public sector bank that always gives you a fixed return, or else you may choose to put it in the share market that may give you a higher return but with chances of sudden loss. That is why the correct estimation of the investment is super important. Ultimately, it is your choice. However, something should be there to guide you, especially if you are a naïve investor. With debt-based securities, the calculation of profits is crystal clear as they provide a fixed interest. You might already know this as almost everyone (at least whoever can afford to read this book) has a savings bank account, and we keep our money there. It is a sort of investment. Expert guidance may not be essential for this case. But what about the stock market? Can you tell me what will be the value of the stock after one week? It is challenging to compute, unlike simple interest formulae studied in the 10th standard. However, knowing that is important to compute your profit or loss from there. Their values may not follow a known deterministic pattern. That is why the estimation of values of securities like stocks, options, and futures involves complex statistical modeling. With those models in place, you can manage your investment and get ideas on how much benefit you will get from it. Investment in securities involves risk. It is often said that risk assessment is more important than profit assessment while dealing with securities.

Moreover, here is the difference with the debt-based instrument. Later, one is much safer as it involves zero risk but may not make you rich. As an investor, you choose where you want to put your money. However, that decision should come after a detailed analysis of risk and profit assessment.

Why Stochastic

Let us first look at the publicly available security value, i.e., the stock price value of some organization. Figure 1-1 shows such an example – the stock values of Airbnb.

Figure 1-1. *Stock values of Airbnb from June 2022 to February 2023*

You can go to `https://finance.yahoo.com/lookup/` and see there a list of stock symbols. Selecting ABNB from there will show you a consolidated summary page, and clicking the Full-Screen link will take you to a page, as shown in Figure 1-1. Yahoo Finance only shows a handful of trending symbols on the home page. You must search for other symbols not directly shown in the Quote Lookup search box on the page's middle-right side.

Figure 1-1 shows a series of ups and downs plotted against time. That is a widespread way of visualization of stock prices. Now you must have the big question: *where is the stochastic part here? Stochastic* is a technical word associated with random probability distributions and nondeterministic (refer to Chapter 3). It means that something is there whose value(s) cannot be determined precisely, and there are some uncertainties around it. Stock values are potential examples of such things. By "*determined,*" we mean forecasting future values to help you plan your investments. For example, knowing the stock values of Airbnb for November 2023 (November 2023 is the future date considering the time this book is being written) will guide you about the investments you plan to do that time or something you are doing now and expecting some return around that timeframe. It is a widespread practice taken by investors and stock traders.

What Is Special About Stochastic Methodologies

Knowing the future values of stocks or security involves fair amount of mathematical modeling. Stock values depend on time (as shown in Figure 1-1) and resemble a stream. That gives the idea of modeling them with *stochastic processes*. Readers familiar with probability and statistics must know it, but for others, a very short definition should work for now – "*stochastic process is a stream of random values without a particular state.*" We will study all of these in Chapters 3 and 4 as they need a handful of concepts in probability and statistics.

Many moving factors make the values of security random. For example, political, socioeconomic, and any current emergencies all influence the stock market, but knowing how many of such factors are there and to what extent they influence is quite tricky. There are no such readily available formulae that give us the answer. Even if we can craft some potential factors from experience and domain knowledge and try using those in the model, we will still not have all the answers. Suppose three factors are denoted by x_1, x_2, and x_3, representing a political situation, socioeconomic condition, and current emergencies, respectively. Do not worry too much about their magnitude, scale, range, and any other details. Of course, all factors should adhere to these, but for now, assume that it has already been taken care of in x_1, x_2, and x_3. Another significant factor could be time. With time, stock values go up or down, which is a well-known fact. So, we have four factors, and now the question is how they relate to stock values. If we denote stock price as S, then the relation would be something like this:

$$S = time + b_1 x_1 + b_2 x_2 + b_3 x_3$$

Or rather like this:

$$S = time * b_1 x_1 * b_2 x_2 * b_3 x_3$$

The first one is additive, and the second one is multiplicative. Moreover, they are exclusive rather than inclusive, as there can be many more permutations and combinations. Crafting such forecasting models needs a detailed understanding of the physics of the stock market. Even after thorough analysis, some hidden factors or complex mathematical operator that binds them together may be left out to be included. Ultimately, we are back to the same question: *How much information is sufficient?* The inability to answer this question causes uncertainty – the most discussed phrase in the statistics study. It is the presence of uncertainty that makes a system nondeterministic. In simplest terms, uncertainty can be defined as effects on any system due to the lack of knowledge about hidden parts.

On the contrary, a system becomes deterministic if you know everything inside and how they relate to each other to form a response. Two of the closest examples from Quantitative Finance would be the returns from fixed-rate govt bonds and interests from savings bank accounts. They work on simple interest formulae (refer to Chapter 2). If you know your principal amount, time, and the interest rate, you can quickly compute the return and the final amount. Unlike a stock market, here you know the physics of the system. Unfortunately, most of the things we see around us follow nondeterminism. Then how is it possible to forecast things? Researchers around the world have made it work. This statement may sound very simple, but the task is complex. Capturing the uncertainty is the major challenge in modeling nondeterministic system. Moreover, it is never foolproof, as some information will always be left out. That is why acquiring as much information as possible is the primary goal so that we can infer the best output from there.

Figure 1-2 shows a comparison of behaviors between deterministic and nondeterministic systems. For better understanding, we encapsulate these two systems as functions – $f_{D(x)}$ and $f_{ND(x)}$, respectively. Observe that for the same input x, $f_{D(x)}$ always produces the same output y, but that is not true for $f_{ND(x)}$ as it produces variable outputs – y_1, y_2, y_3, etc. Isn't it weird? Does that at all happen in reality? Well, the reason for the existence of $f_{ND(x)}$ is our lack of universal knowledge about any system. An example from finance will make it more clear to you. Suppose time is denoted by x, and $f_{ND(x)}$ represents a hypothetical function that returns the stock price of company A at a given time. As we never know how many factors influence stock value, $f_{ND(x)}$ can only give us a range of possible stock values denoted by y_1, y_2, y_3, etc. It means that upon multiple invocations of $f_{ND(x)}$, it will return different values. The objective of $f_{ND(x)}$ is to be as accurate as possible so that when the given time occurs, the realized stock price is close enough to the

CHAPTER 1   INTRODUCTION

forecasted one. On the contrary, simple interest calculated on the principal amount is an excellent example of $f_{D(x)}$. For a given time, its value will always be the same, i.e., for a given interest rate, time, and principal amount, you will get the same total amount (interest plus principal).

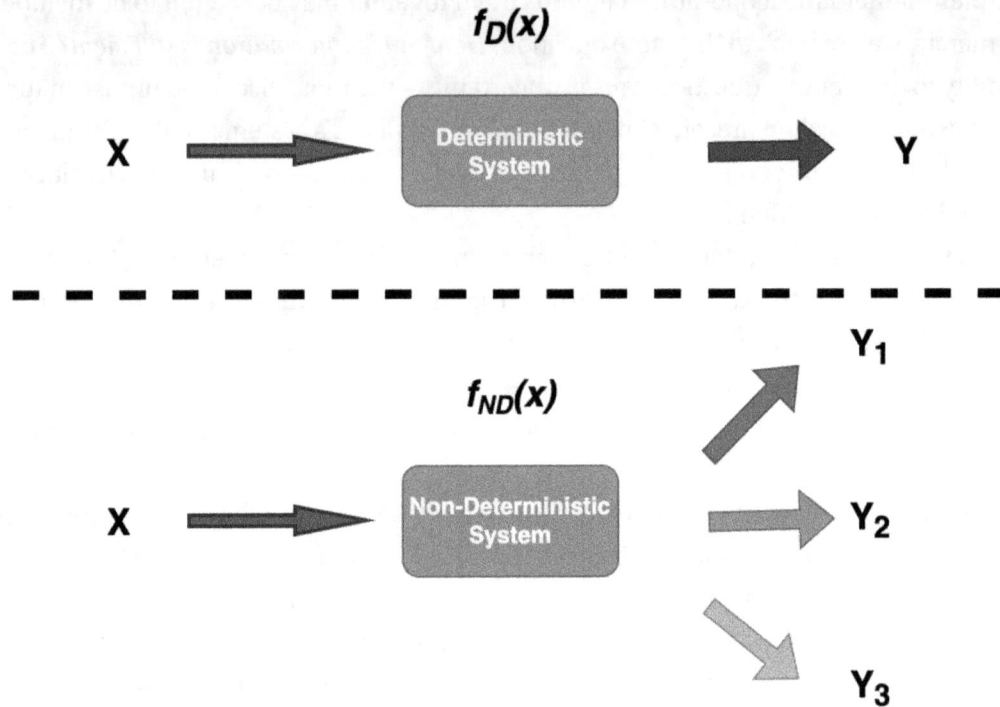

Figure 1-2. *Deterministic vs. nondeterministic workflow*

You may still have one question: How do we handle many possible output values for $f_{ND(x)}$? At ground level, any nondeterministic function returns a distribution of values, and the correct estimated value is a computed statistic from there. It could be mean, median, or some other. You will learn more about it in Chapters 3 and 4 while discussing probability distributions.

Stochastic models, also described as random process or probability-based models, are used for modeling any nondeterministic system that involves probabilistic analysis of the system's states. The term *"stochastic"* describes the phenomenon of not being in a particular state, and the probability theory quantifies it. In the present case, system states could be values of stocks or other securities. If the same theory is applied to model the path of a storm instead of security prices, the basic principles will not change, but its interpretation will be different.

This book will discuss methods to explore these system states and capture uncertainties through simulation, backed by *stochastic differential equations (SDE)*. You might be thinking – is it the only way to do this? Of course not. To model securities, other methods based on traditional machine learning and, more specifically, deep learning also have their dominant footprint. Although their foundations are also based on probability theory, unlike those, stochastic simulation methods explicitly use stochastic processes. They have a few advantages over other methods:

- They consume less data for modeling.

- They have better maintainability.

- They have better uncertainty quantification capabilities.

If "uncertainty quantification" sounds unfamiliar, hold yourself until you cover Chapter 3. However, for now, think of it as a tool to know the probable errors beforehand once you get some forecasts of the security price. To make it simpler, for example, assume that some forecasting model tells you that the stock value of a hypothetical company XYZ will rise to $100 in the next four days with an uncertainty bound of ±$20. $100 is still an average forecast that may not be entirely accurate. Its actual interpretation is as follows: "Estimated average price of XYZ stocks would be $100, and it may vary from $80 to $120." So, it would be best to plan your investment accordingly to hedge against this low value of $80. In this case, uncertainty is quantified as a range between $80 and $120. The biggest advantage of stochastic simulation methods for finance is that they generate uncertainty estimates as a by-product unlike other methods which can also support that but with some tweaks.

Numerical Implementation

You might have already built an intuition about what could be the form of models we will be discussing in the subsequent chapters. However, we need to touch upon mathematical formulae or derivations in detail. Any topic in data analytics does not only stop in theory; instead, the end goal is to implement and release it as a piece of software. For the current scenario, we need probabilistic programming and will use Python for that.

CHAPTER 1   INTRODUCTION

Why Python

Being very flexible, developer friendly, easily maintainable, and deployable, Python has moved up the ladder quickly, especially for numerical programming. Python makes it easy to modify and play with different ideas quickly. Python and another language, Ruby, became very popular around 2005 timeframe for web development. At that time, it was still considered just as another "scripting language" for quick prototyping and web framework-based UI. It had limited scope for developing severe, large-scale applications. Later, it started gaining popularity in scientific computing, and after that, it almost became a de facto standard in the data analytics community. Python is comparable in data visualizations and interactive programming with other commercial programming languages and tools like R, SAS, Tableau, etc.

Python shows its flexibility while leveraging and integrating other programming languages like C. As for numerical computation, C has the performance advantage, so few Python libraries like numpy and scipy have leveraged by having Pythonic wrappers on top of them instead of competing with C. So as a developer, you will have the performance of C and the flexibility of Python.

Python's most significant advantage is its ability to be a full-scale programming language and provide end-to-end solutions. Earlier, many organizations used to have particular languages or tools like R and SAS for doing any data analytics-related R&D and then port the entire stuff to Java or C++ to give it a final shape in the production environment. A significant effort was needed for the porting activity, which, of course, used to come with many challenges – missing out on something crucial while conversion, incompatibility between the paradigm of two different languages, etc. Python has done exceptionally well in covering both two aspects. Of course, it also has its challenges, but still more and more companies are accepting Python for prototyping, researching, and building production-grade systems.

The Approach of Pythonic Implementation

Reusability and maintainability are key quality attributes for any healthy software system running in the production environment. Object-oriented principles and programming often help us to achieve these attributes. Python strongly supports OOPs though it is not fully object-oriented like Java. Object orientation is a choice rather than a compulsion in Python. However, as said earlier, it is recommended for a healthy system. I have followed OOPs principles for financial and probabilistic computing in this book as much as possible. Most publicly available resources in this area are focused on just discretely solving the problem, and only some of them cover the end-to-end picture, i.e., starting from theory, mathematical derivations, code, and a workable design. By design, here we mean component design. Discussing the entire architecture is out of scope as this is not a software architecture handbook. Python components in this book are designed so that even if you remove the finance part from there, they should be ready to be used in other domains. For example, while discussing the stochastic process, I have provided one base component that can be fully/partially leveraged in any other area that uses the stochastic process as an underlying modeling methodology.

Probabilistic and Numerical Programming

Traditional programming has precise answers to the questions or problems it tries to solve; hence, it is deterministic. Think about the checkout systems of an e-commerce portal. The number of items added by the user, their price, and shipping charges to the specified address are all used to calculate the total bill amount to be paid. Each of these is predefined; they are just added and multiplied together to produce the final amount. Let us not consider how price and shipping charges are decided. They are already provided, like $f_{D(x)}$ in Figure 1-2. Most of the business logic you write while developing commercial applications at your organization is deterministic. There is nothing special about it, and you know this programming style.

Nondeterministic programming is tricky. Multiple invocations of $f_{D(x)}$ with the same input will produce the same output, but that is not true for $f_{ND(x)}$ and hence for any stochastic system. While writing probabilistic software components, you must keep this in mind and need to handle it in such a way that ensures stable output. The generation of output distribution is often considered a fundamental working principle there. Figure 1-3 shows such an example. It is a realization of different outputs from a stochastic simulation model – they represent stock price paths over a fixed period. You must estimate the distribution at first and then simulate it to achieve this.

CHAPTER 1 INTRODUCTION

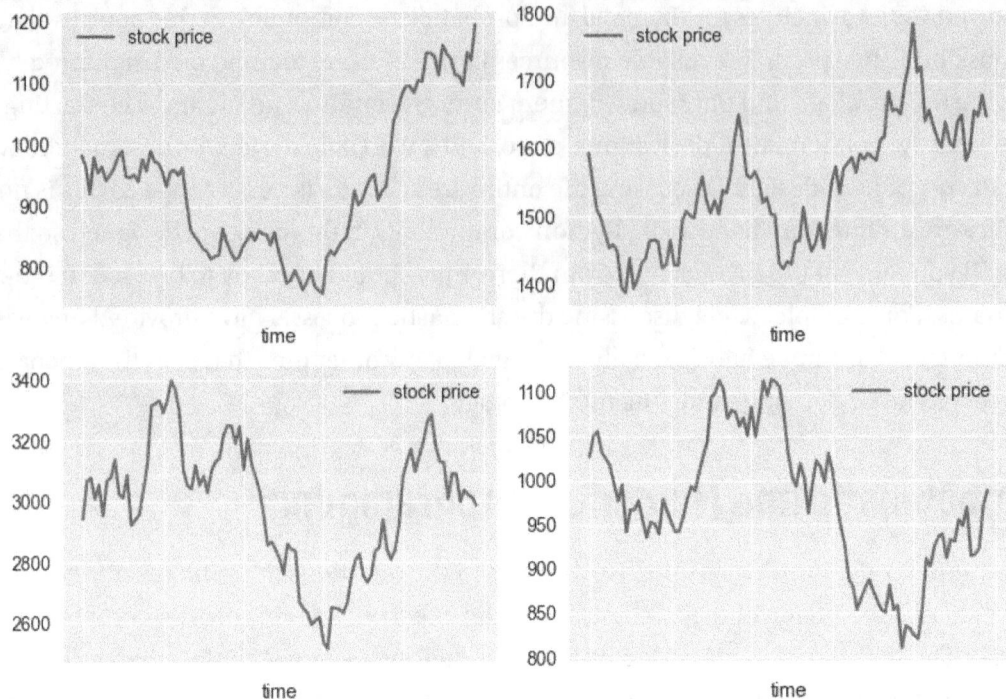

Figure 1-3. *Example of output distribution from a nondeterministic system – realizations of the stock price paths*

Figure 1-4 shows the flow of a stochastic simulation system. As said earlier, the objective is to capture the inherent uncertainty in the system as much as possible. The estimated output is obtained by a simulation activity that runs the system with the same set of inputs and aggregates them at the end. Ideally, the aggregation operation can be numerical integration or summation (or even average).

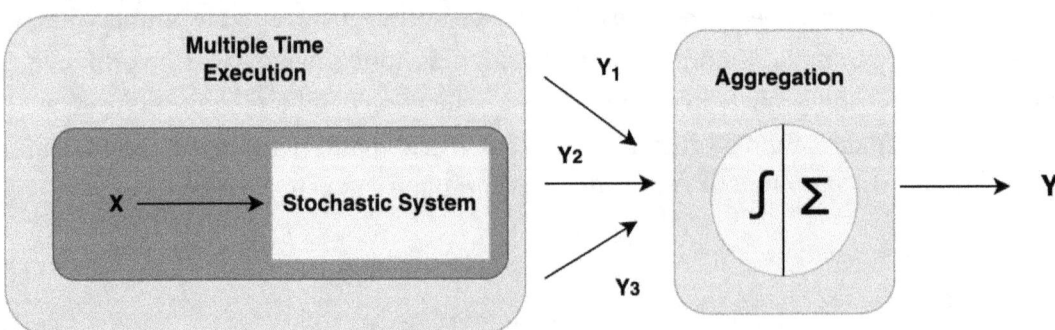

Figure 1-4. *Flow of simulated output generation from a stochastic system*

Path simulation and forecasting mean path are excellent examples to demonstrate Figure 1-4. The left-hand side box of Figure 1-4 would explore various possible paths of a stock asset within a timeframe, whereas the box on the right-hand side gives an average of those paths as the final forecast result. In this book, we exactly follow this approach for forecasting financial asset prices.

In my opinion, numerical programming, and that too with reusability, is fun – it is a marriage between software engineering and mathematics. Numerical programming shows the way to implement abstract mathematical ideas in a language that a computer understands. Ultimately, probability calculation, which is mainly needed for this book, is a set of numerical procedures. For that, we must make many approximations to break the abstract nature of mathematical formulas. For example, to find a derivative w.r.t. x, we repetitively compute $\Delta f/\Delta x$ – a numerical equivalent of a derivative function. It becomes more useful when you cannot find that derivative analytically and are left with only numerical options. In this book, you will find a similar approach in many sections that may not directly relate to derivative computation but follow the idea in some sense. You will also learn how to translate a procedural-styled mathematical calculation into an object-oriented style to boost reusability and maintainability.

Summary

- Stochastic Finance is a subpart of Quantitative Finance that provides methodologies to model financial instruments mainly using stochastic processes and simulation.

- Stochastic systems showcase nondeterminism – a phenomenon that causes a system not to have a particular state.

- Most systems around us are nondeterministic – financial instruments are just one of them.

- Python is a de facto choice for implementing stochastic systems as it has both flavors – ease of use and support for an object-orientated approach for promoting reusability.

CHAPTER 2

Finance Basics and Data Sources

In the first chapter, we discussed a very short introduction to financial instruments. But, to model those instruments successfully, we need to know more about financial theory fundamentals – time value of money, interest details, computing returns, etc. These concepts are commonly needed to understand whatever instrument we plan to model – stocks, options, or portfolios. This chapter will discuss all of these, along with a design of financial data source adapters.

Different Financial Assets

Continuing the discussions done in Chapter 1 about different financial assets, we are primarily interested in three nondeterministic assets: *stocks*, *options*, and *portfolios* for this book. In this section, we briefly familiarize three asset types, as these are frequently mentioned in the rest of the book.

Stocks

The birth of stock price happens through a company's **initial public offering (IPO)** upon registration in a publicly traded exchange. A *stock price* is the indicator of the popularity and demand of the company's shares in the market – more precisely, a market evaluation of the company's value per share. The movement of stock prices in a seemingly random fashion results from the fact that the market, consisting of the key investors, speculators, and common people, is not very certain about a company's profits and future earnings, which affects its valuation. Moreover, a stock is a specified portion of the company's ownership, giving the shareholder several rights, such as participating in general body meetings (at least on paper). As the stock price is random and dependent on time, investors make money by buying and selling them at different times. Such behavior makes stock prices suitable to be modeled by a stochastic process. In this book, we study stochastic processes, such as the *diffusion process, jump-diffusion process*, etc., to forecast stock prices and explain the current uncertainties.

Options

Over the past 45 years, derivatives have been increasingly popular in the financial market. Futures and options are the two most popular derivates traded in regulated exchanges. But many others, like forwards, swaps, and exotic-type options, entered the OTC (over-the-counter) market, which is not so well regulated. Of course, there are risks and losses, and who doesn't know about the crisis of 2008 due to the OTC market crash? So, understanding derivatives' nature through stochastic methods is the best policy that we can take to mitigate potential risks. Researchers worldwide have already devised a handful of such methods – in this book, we discuss a few.

Formally, a *derivative* is a financial instrument whose value depends on other, more basic, underlying assets. We only discuss here stock *options*, which is a derivate that depends on the underlying stock price. In vanilla stock trading, buying and selling happen based on the stock's market value at the time of the transaction. But, in options, a contract lies between the buyer and the seller. This contract is formally known as the *options*, which can be bought by the option buyer with a paid premium. This allows the buyer to exercise their right to buy or sell when the underlying stock price moves in their favor. Note that doing this exercise is a *right* and *not an obligation*. It is the buyer's choice to do that.

There are two types of option contracts:

a) A *call* option gives the option buyer the right to buy the underlying asset by a certain date for a certain price.

b) A *put* option gives the option seller the right to sell the underlying asset by a certain date for a certain price.

The price in the contract is known as the *exercise price* or the *strike price*, and the exercise date is known as the *expiration date* or *maturity*. Options let you buy or sell assets at a much lower or higher price than the market value at maturity – both benefit you. But, still, it is your choice to do that, as you can always step back. In exchange, you need to pay a premium to buy the right, and the advantage is twofold – avoiding loss and making a profit. The *payoff* is the value of the option, which is the difference between strike price and stock price at that time, assuming that paid premium will not return, irrespective of your decision to exercise the option.

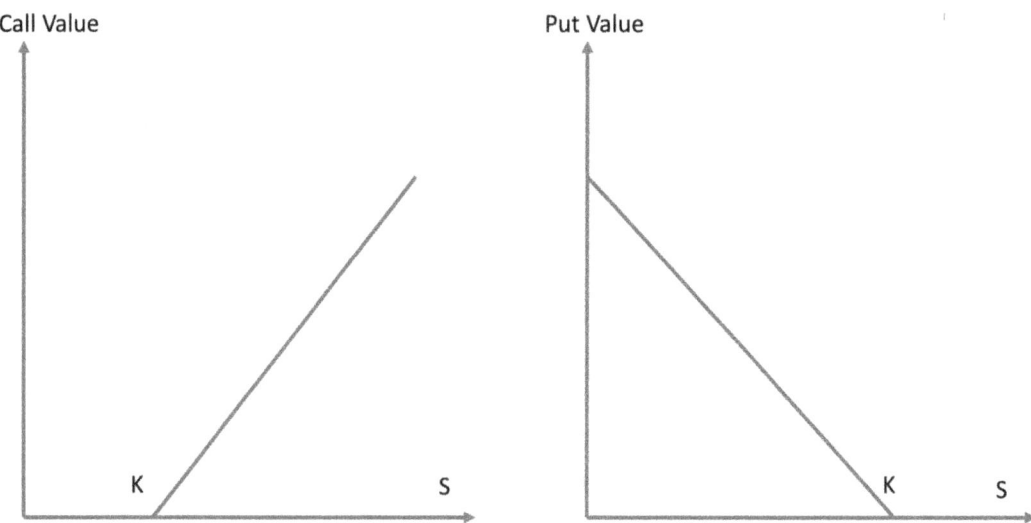

Figure 2-1. *Payoff of both call and put options as a function of stock price S*

Figure 2-1 shows the payoff curve for both call and put options where K is the strike price. In short, options let you leverage your speculative view of the market and hedge against big losses.

From a statistical perspective, estimating a good value of the option premium is the core problem, i.e., how much premium you should pay to buy an option that will hedge against a potential loss. As the function of underlying assets and time, options are a stochastic process, a function of another stochastic process, making it a complex problem to solve. We discuss further details in Chapter 8, including two methods to solve the option premium evaluation problem – the *risk-neutral probabilistic method* and *stochastic partial differential equation (SPDE)* – based on the *Black-Scholes* model.

Portfolio

A *portfolio* is a collection of assets – both deterministic and nondeterministic. You can form a portfolio with stocks, options, government bonds, and other derivatives. Risks and returns from the portfolio will also have flavors according to their compositions. Investors prefer to use portfolios rather than individual assets to better hedge against uncertainties. For example, portfolio risk comprising stocks A and B may be much less than each stock's risk. But the total return you seek from your investments can be obtained by distributing the total amount between two stocks, hence getting double benefits – reducing risk while getting the same return.

A well-balanced portfolio can perfectly depict the market's situation, giving investors a unified holistic view. They don't have to look at different company's stock prices and do repeated estimations about their returns. A *stock index* is a live example of a readily available portfolio. A few such stock indices of different countries are the following:

a) **NIFTY 50 by NSE Indices:** A collection of 50 stocks of companies impacting the Indian economy

b) **S&P 500 by S&P Dow Jones Indices:** A collection of 500 stocks of leading US companies

c) **Nikkei 225 by Nihon Keizai Shimbun:** A collection of 225 highly liquid stocks listed under the Tokyo Stock Exchange reflecting the state of Japan's economy

d) **CSI 100 by China Securities Index:** A collection of 100 influential Chinese companies' stocks reflecting the state of the Chinese economy

All indices mentioned above and any other one outside these are mostly based on computing the weighted average of stocks. The assignment of weights happens through some predefined criteria or optimization algorithm. Chapter 10 discusses portfolio theory in detail and this weight estimation scheme.

Basic Interest Theory

One of the fundamental concepts in finance is the time value of money. Today's money does not have the same numerical value as tomorrow's. Many complex reasons can be quoted from the theory of economics for this. But, without even going into that much detail, we can see two primary apparent reasons – inflation and market movement. Suppose you want to borrow $200 and promise to repay it to the bank after two days. Do you have to repay the same amount, or is something extra to be added there? It is a straightforward scenario – interest must be paid, and that's the extra. Another example would be interest earned from the savings bank account. In both cases, interest adjusts the asset's (the loan amount or savings account balance) past and present monetary value.

If somebody gives you two choices, getting $200 right now or after one year, which one will you choose? Are both options equivalent? Of course not. If you had put that amount in a savings bank account, you would have gotten $210 after one year. So, you prefer to get $200 now rather than anytime later because of its time-dependent monetary value. $200 and $210 are the present and future values of the asset, respectively. This will be helpful while evaluating *options.*

Simple Interest

You might have studied this in tenth standard, but still, for our convenience, let's recap once. Consider the example of interest earned from a savings bank account for a starting amount (i.e., initial asset value) P (called the principal) on which the interest earned throughout a period T with a rate of interest r. Denote A as the final asset value after period T; P, T, r, and A are related by

$$A = P(1+Tr)$$

Other than savings bank accounts, fixed deposits and govt bonds are good examples of simple interest-based assets.

Discrete Compound Interest

The interest amount is added to the principal in the simple interest model at the last stage. But what if it is added after each unit period? We call it a discrete compound interest model. In the simple interest case, just after one period, asset value A becomes

$$A = P(1+r)$$

In the second period, P(1 + r) serves as the principal, so the asset value becomes

$$A = P(1+r)(1+r) = P(1+r)^2$$

With mathematical induction, we get the expression for T period as

$$A = P(1+r)^T$$

CHAPTER 2 FINANCE BASICS AND DATA SOURCES

The above one is the compound interest formula, and adding the interest back is known as interest compounding. But there is a variation to it, and that's more useful in our case. Most of the time, the interest rate period and interest compounding frequency differ. For example, if r is defined as the yearly interest rate and compounding are scheduled for each month, then there is a mismatch, and the above formulae fail. As r is defined for the year, the compounding rate would be r/12. In general, if compounding happens m times per interest period, then A is given by

$$A = P\left(1 + \frac{r}{m}\right)^{mT}$$

If m interest payments happen in T, the time between two payments would be 1/m, and each interest will increase the principal by a factor $1 + \frac{r}{m}$. This model is also known as periodic compounding.

Continuous Compound Interest

It is an asymptotic version of periodic compounding. If the compounding frequency is too high, i.e., $m \to \infty$, then we can deduce an asymptotic form. First, recall the definition of Euler number e:

$$e = \lim_{x \to \infty} \left(1 + \frac{1}{x}\right)^x$$

Then, putting $x = \frac{m}{r}$ and taking the limiting value of A,

$$A = P\left[\lim_{m \to \infty}\left(1 + \frac{r}{m}\right)^{\frac{m}{r}}\right]^{rT}$$
$$= Pe^{rT}$$

The above formulae approximate continuous compounding well when the frequency m is large.

In practice, continuous compounding estimates the time value of money invested in assets. In other words, it approximates the "what if" condition – what if the money was invested in a bank account with an interest rate r? This hypothetical measurement compares the monetary value of an asset's price movements. Observe that from the above formulae, operators e^{rT} and e^{-rT} can be used interchangeably to get the future and past value of money invested in an asset:

$$S_T = S_0 e^{rT}$$

and

$$S_0 = S_T e^{-rT}$$

r is often called risk-free interest rate. This relation does not quantify the asset's price directly as that follows different dynamics, which will be discussed in Chapter 4. It instead tries to tally the value of money invested in assets. You will see its importance in Chapter 6 while discussing options.

Data Source Adapters for Financial Data

Now it's time to do some serious Python coding and start designing the first reusable component. Whatever model we try to build, data is the utmost important aspect, without which we can't even take a single step. For that, this component will be all about accessing the data. Later chapters will show leveraging this to feed data into core financial models.

In our discussions, we will be dealing primarily with stock price data, so we define an adapter interface named *StockPriceDatasetAdapter* as given in Listing 2-1.

Listing 2-1. Adapter interface for stock price data source

```
class StockPriceDatasetAdapter(metaclass=ABCMeta):
    """
    Interface to access any data source of stock price quotes. Multiple
    implementations can be made to support different data sources.
    """
    DEFAULT_TICKER = 'PFE'
    @property
    @abstractmethod
    def training_set(self, ticker=None): ...
    """
```

```
    Property to get training dataset for a given stock symbol (ticker).
    This dataset can be used to train a stock price model. Although there
    are no such restrictions on using it elsewhere.
    Returns
    ----

    A data frame. Each data frame has two columns: stock price & time
@property
@abstractmethod
def validation_set(self, ticker=None): ...
"""
        Property to get validation dataset for a given stock symbol
        (ticker). This dataset can be used to validate a trained stock
        price model. Although there are no such restrictions on using
        it elsewhere.
    Returns
    ----

    A data frame. Each data frame has two columns: stock price & time """
```

We rely on the freely available public data source throughout the book, though you will also know about another one that needs a license.

Yahoo Financials

It has a handful of ticker symbols (a ticker indicates a short form of any stock name). You can have a look at those by going to *https://finance.yahoo.com/trending-tickers/*. Figure 2-2 shows the Yahoo Finance portal with all trending stock symbols on the leftmost side.

CHAPTER 2   FINANCE BASICS AND DATA SOURCES

Symbol	Name	Last Price	Market Time	Change	% Change	Volume	Market Cap
MSFT	Microsoft Corporation	330.53	4:00PM EDT	+1.21	+0.37%	28.098M	2.456T
GOOG	Alphabet Inc.	140.12	4:00PM EDT	+2.22	+1.61%	25.416M	1.748T
GOOGL	Alphabet Inc.	138.81	4:00PM EDT	+2.31	+1.69%	42.239M	1.748T
SNAP	Snap Inc.	9.71	4:05PM EDT	+0.22	+2.32%	48.399M	15.757B
VZ	Verizon Communications Inc.	34.30	4:00PM EDT	+2.91	+9.27%	61.433M	144.199B
^NSEI	NIFTY 50	19,167.60	2:13PM IST	-114.15	-0.59%	0	N/A
V	Visa Inc.	234.65	4:00PM EDT	+3.12	+1.35%	6.572M	488.025B
META	Meta Platforms, Inc.	312.55	4:00PM EDT	-1.46	-0.46%	17.068M	804.241B
^NSEBANK	NIFTY BANK	42,969.30	2:13PM IST	-181.90	-0.42%	0	N/A
DBK.DE	Deutsche Bank Aktiengesellschaft	10.16	10:28AM CEST	+0.66	+6.92%	10.984M	20.678B
TXN	Texas Instruments Incorporated	146.92	4:00PM EDT	+0.60	+0.41%	6.35M	133.403B
TDOC	Teladoc Health, Inc.	18.12	4:00PM EDT	+0.11	+0.61%	8.128M	2.989B
TYRES.HE	Nokian Renkaat Oyj	6.31	11:43AM EEST	-1.05	-14.28%	2.045M	870.492M
WLN.PA	Worldline SA	10.39	10:28AM CEST	-12.71	-55.02%	5.838M	3.075B

Figure 2-2. *Trending tickers as shown on Yahoo Financials page*

Yahoo Finance hosts a collection of REST APIs to get all the information, which is free. Fortunately, Python already has a library with the same name *yahoofiancials*, which saves you from writing all the boilerplate code. However, we may need some customization on top of the API response. Hence, first, we create a base component *BaseStockPriceDatasetAdapter* irrespective of the data source, as given in Listing 2-2.

Listing 2-2. Base component class to be used by all data source adapters

```
class BaseStockPriceDatasetAdapter(StockPriceDatasetAdapter, ABC):
    def __init__(self, ticker:str=None):
        self._ticker = ticker
        self._training_set = None
        self._validation_set = None

    @abstractmethod
    def _connect_and_prepare(self, date_range: tuple): ...
    '''
    The implementing data source adapter should override this function.
    It should connect to the stock price data source and return records
    within the specified date range
    '''
```

23

CHAPTER 2 FINANCE BASICS AND DATA SOURCES

```python
    @property
    def training_set(self):
        return self._training_set.copy()

    @property
    def validation_set(self, ticker=None):
        return self._validation_set.copy()
```

The next task is to create an adapter specific to *Yahoo Financials* that extends *BaseStockPriceDatasetAdapter* as shown in Listing 2-3 (only *__init__* is shown there).

Listing 2-3. YahooFinancialsAdapter (only __init__ is shown)

```python
import pandas as pd
from yahoofinancials import YahooFinancials

class YahooFinancialsAdapter(BaseStockPriceDatasetAdapter):
    """
    Dataset adapter for Yahoo Financials (https://finance.yahoo.com/).
    """

    def __init__(self,
                 # Name of ticker for which stock values are to be fetched.
                 # The default value is PFE i.e. for Pfizer
                 ticker=StockPriceDatasetAdapter.DEFAULT_TICKER,

                 # YahooFiancials support different time intervals.
                 # Frequency is an enum to hold that value to be sent via
                 # request. Values can be: 'daily', 'weekly', 'monthly'

                 frequency=Frequency.DAILY,

                 # Stock values to be fetched for the given date range
                 training_set_date_range=('2020-01-01',
                                          '2021-12-31'),
                 validation_set_date_range=('2013-07-01',
                                            '2013-08-31')):
        super().__init__(ticker=ticker)
        self._frequency = frequency
```

CHAPTER 2 FINANCE BASICS AND DATA SOURCES

```
        self._yf = YahooFinancials(self._ticker)
        self._training_set = self._connect_and_prepare(training_set_
                            date_range)
        self._validation_set = self._connect_and_prepare(validation_set_
                            date_range)
```

Function *_connect_and_prepare* does the actual work of connecting to the API and extracting the results as shown below:

```
def _connect_and_prepare(self, date_range: tuple):
    stock_price_records = None
    records = self._yf.get_historical_price_data(date_range[0],
                                                 date_range[1],
                                                 self._frequency.value)
                                                [self._ticker]
    stock_price_records = pd.DataFrame(
                                    data=records['prices'])\
                                    [['formatted_date', 'close']]
    # Rename columns for convenience
    stock_price_records.rename(columns=
                                    {
                                    'formatted_date':'time',
                                    'close': 'stock price'},
                                inplace=True)
    return stock_price_records
```

Yahoo Financials, by itself, provides options to set the granularity of the result. We define a Python enum *Frequency* to set that value while making a request. Other details should be self-explanatory from the documentation given in Listing 2-3.

We can test *YahooFianancialsAdapter* like below:

```
import visualization as vs

def test_actual_stock_price_visualizer():
    yf_adapter = YahooFinancialsAdapter()
    records = yf_adapter.training_set
    vs.plot_actual(records, 'Pfizer')
```

25

CHAPTER 2   FINANCE BASICS AND DATA SOURCES

By default, it gets all *Pfizer* stock prices with a time range between *January 1, 2020*, and *December 31, 2021*. Figure 2-3 shows the dataset plot (refer to *chapter2/test/test_stock_price_data_sources.py*).

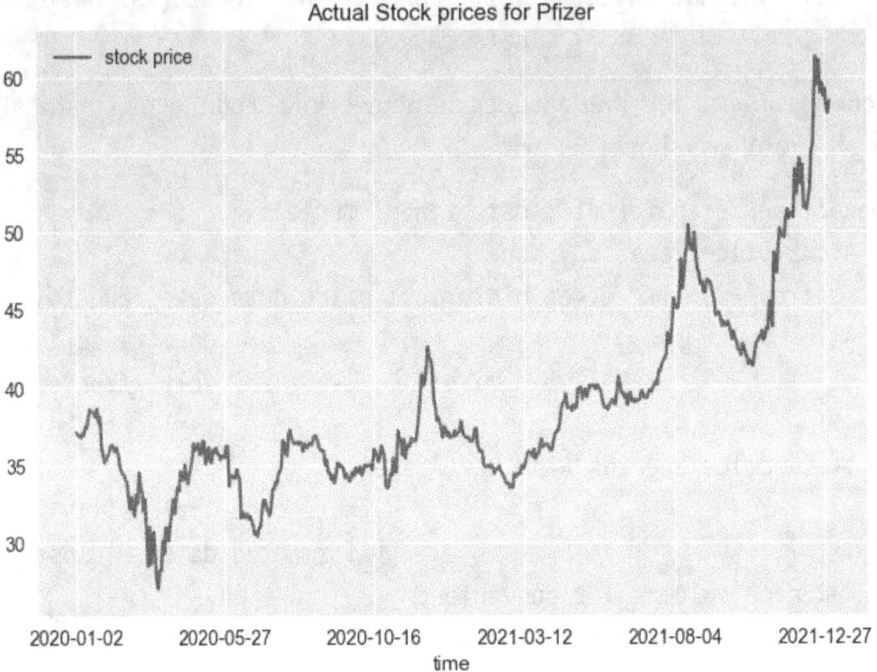

Figure 2-3. *Pfizer stock prices*

Market Stack

It is also a public API provider of stock data for organizations and developers. But it is licensed, hence requires registration. Only 100 requests per month are free over there. This free option may be good for experimental activities (that too not confirmed and depends on the situation), but to use it in the production setup, you need to choose among different subscription plans. I also took one to get full access. Upon buying the subscription, they provide one API key that needs to be passed in each request. For more details, go through the Market Stack portal `https://marketstack.com/`.

Market Stack offers services to fetch all available symbols from the stock market, which *Yahoo Financials* doesn't. We discuss leveraging that while simulating portfolios in Chapter 10. Unlike Yahoo Financials, there is no available Python library support for Market Stack, so we must build one. One sample API response looks like that shown in Figure 2-4.

CHAPTER 2   FINANCE BASICS AND DATA SOURCES

```
{
    "pagination": {
        "limit": 100,
        "offset": 0,
        "count": 100,
        "total": 2517
    },
    "data": [
        {
            "open": 151.19,
            "high": 151.47,
            "low": 148.56,
            "close": 150.43,
            "volume": 95939200,
            "adj_high": null,
            "adj_low": null,
            "adj_close": 150.43,
            "adj_open": null,
            "adj_volume": null,
            "split_factor": 1,
            "dividend": 0,
            "symbol": "AAPL",
            "exchange": "XNAS",
            "date": "2022-09-23T00:00:00+0000"
        },
        {
            "open": 152.38,
```

Figure 2-4. *API response from Market Stack*

Response from the Market Stack API provides pagination parameters that must be handled. Let's start defining the *MarketStackAdapter* class and put some constants needed for API communication as shown in Listing 2-4.

Listing 2-4. MarketStackAdapter and its defined constants

```
class MarketStackAdapter(BaseStockPriceDatasetAdapter):
    """
    Dataset adapter for Market Stack (https://marketstack.com/).
    It can be used for symbols not supported by Yahoo Financials.
    """
```

27

CHAPTER 2 FINANCE BASICS AND DATA SOURCES

```
    # Dictionary of request parameters
    _REQ_PARAMS = {'access_key': '###',
                   'limit': 500}
    # REST API url to get end-of-day stock quotes
    # supported by marketstack.com
    _EOD_API_URL = 'http://api.marketstack.com/v1/eod'
    # REST API url to get list of all stock symbol
    # supported by marketstack.com
    _TICKER_API_URL = 'http://api.marketstack.com/v1/tickers'
```

The access key is masked there for security reasons.

Now, let's do the big part – pagination support. We create an inner class within *MarketStackAdapter* named *_PaginationRecords,* which is a duck-typed iterable (for details about duck-typing, go through `https://docs.python.org/3/glossary.html`). It is shown next in Listing 2-5.

Listing 2-5. _PaginatedRecords inner class to support pagination for Market Stack API

```
class _PaginatedRecords:
    """
        Market stack API sends a paginated response with offset,
        limit & total records. Inner class _PaginatedRecords
        provides a stateful page navigation mechanism to
        iterate over records.
    """
    def __init__(self, api_url, req_params):
        self._req_params = req_params
        self._offset = 0
        self._total_records = sys.maxsize
        self._api_url = api_url

    def __getitem__(self, index):
        """
        Duck typed function to get the current page records &
        increment the offset accordingly
        """
```

CHAPTER 2 FINANCE BASICS AND DATA SOURCES

```
    if (self._offset + self._req_params['limit']) >= self._total_
    records:
        raise StopIteration()

    self._req_params['offset'] = self._offset
    api_response = requests.get(self._api_url, self._req_
    params).json()
    self._total_records = api_response['pagination']['total']
    self._offset = self._offset + self._req_params['limit'] + 1
    return api_response['data']
```

Function *_connect_and_prepare* leverages above *_PaginationRecords* to iteratively go through the returned records and build a customized response as shown in Listing 2-6.

Listing 2-6. Function _connect_and_prepare under MarketStackAdapter that builds the response

```
def _connect_and_prepare(self, date_range: tuple):
    def _extract_stock_price_details(stock_price_records, page):
        """
        Inner function to extract fields: 'close', 'date', 'symbol'
        of current element obtained from json response.
        """
        ticker_symbol = page['symbol']
        stock_record_per_symbol = stock_price_records.
        get(ticker_symbol)
        if stock_record_per_symbol is None:
            stock_record_per_symbol = pd.DataFrame()
        entry = {'stock price':[page['close']],
                 'time':[page['date'].split('T')[0]]}

        stock_price_records[ticker_symbol] = pd.concat([
                                            stock_record_
                                            per_symbol,
                                            pd.DataFrame(entry)],
                                            ignore_index=True)
    return stock_price_records
```

```python
        if self._tickers is None: return None

    req_params = MarketStackAdapter._REQ_PARAMS.copy()
    req_params['symbols'] = ','.join(self._tickers)
    req_params['date_from'] = date_range[0]
    req_params['date_to'] = date_range[1]
    stock_price_records = {}
    # Iterate over response and fetch records to populate a custom
      data frame
    for records in MarketStackAdapter._PaginatedRecords(
                    api_url=MarketStackAdapter._EOD_API_URL,
                    req_params=req_params):
        for page in records:
            stock_price_records = _extract_stock_price_details(stock_
                                price_records, page)
    return stock_price_records
```

Response from *MarketStackAdapter* will be the same as *YahooFinancialsAdapter*, as both follow a single interface contract – plotting the records will also look the same, as shown in Figure 2-3. That's the advantage of using this design template, irrespective of underlying API or physical data store, interfacing with them will remain unchanged.

Returns

As discussed in Chapter 1, we seek comfortable returns when investing in any asset, whether it is stock, options, futures, or physical property. Going by simple meaning, *returns* are nothing but how much money you make from your investments. It is the percentage growth of an asset for a specific period and is given by the following expression:

$$\text{Return} = \frac{\text{Present Value of asset} - \text{Past Value of asset}}{\text{Past Value of asset}}$$

As shown, it is expressed in a percentage scale and, hence, an excellent tool to compare the profitability of assets with different measurement units. That's why the return is often considered instead of actual asset value while modeling any financial

CHAPTER 2   FINANCE BASICS AND DATA SOURCES

instrument. For example, suppose the stock values of the fictional company XYZ were at $100 and $110 on the 24th and 31st of January 2023, respectively. So, the calculated return is 0.1 (= (110−100)/100) or 10% for seven days. In other words, buying the asset on the 24th of January and selling it on the 31st will give you a 10% return. Again, suppose the stock price reached $103 on the 26th of January, and then for a two-day period, you will get 0.03 or 3% return. Both are examples of positive return, i.e., you are making a profit here, but things can go wrong when the asset's present value becomes lower than the past value, which makes the return negative, and you are at a loss then. Using stochastic methods, we try to find a reasonable estimate of future returns, which will help you streamline your investment decisions.

Simple Return

Let's now focus on some mathematical formulation about returns. As you know from the discussions, asset value is time-dependent, and hence, it's best to denote it consistently by attaching a time index. Following that convention, suppose S_t and S_{t-1} are the asset prices at time t and t−1, respectively, and then the simple return R_t is given by

$$R_t = \frac{S_t - S_{t-1}}{S_{t-1}} = \frac{S_t}{S_{t-1}} - 1$$

An alternative expression is

$$R_t = \frac{S_{t+1} - S_t}{S_t} = \frac{S_{t+1}}{S_t} - 1$$

The difference between the two lies in the way the return is defined – backward or forward direction. Return can also be defined as a function of period τ:

$$R_t(\tau) = \frac{S_t}{S_{t-\tau}} - 1$$

τ indicates what frequency is maintained when we compute returns – daily, monthly, weekly, or any custom one. It also depends on the scale of time t. If t denotes the present week, then t−1 is the previous week, and the same goes for days and months. You can compute different types of returns by setting an appropriate τ. For example, τ should be 3 to have quarterly returns, where t indicates months.

CHAPTER 2 FINANCE BASICS AND DATA SOURCES

Nondeterministic assets like stocks or options must go through this return computation as profits are uncertain. But what about bonds, fixed deposits, or savings bank interest? Let's put the simple interest formulae into the expression of returns:

$$R_t^{Simple\ Interest} = \frac{P(1+rt)}{P} - 1 = rt$$

From the expression, you can see that the total return at time t is easy to compute, as you know, interest rate r before investing. Unlike their nondeterministic counterparts, returns are known to you precisely before investment.

To see returns computation in action, we need actual asset price data. Now it's also a good opportunity to test our data source adapters and use their output. We pick up stock price data of *Pfizer* at monthly, weekly, and daily frequency. Function *compute_returns* does that all for us as shown in Listing 2-7.

Listing 2-7. Function to compute returns for monthly, weekly, and daily frequency

```
def compute_returns():
    monthly = YahooFinancialsAdapter(
                frequency=Frequency.MONTHLY).training_set
    #   R_t = S_t/S_(t-1) - 1
    monthly['Return'] = monthly['stock price']/monthly['stock price'].
                shift(1) - 1
    weekly = YahooFinancialsAdapter(
                frequency=Frequency.WEEKLY).training_set
    weekly['Return'] = weekly['stock price']/weekly['stock price'].
                shift(1) - 1
    daily = YahooFinancialsAdapter(
                frequency=Frequency.DAILY).training_set
    daily['Return'] = daily['stock price']/daily['stock price'].
                shift(1) - 1
    periodic_returns = [('Daily', daily), ('Weekly', weekly), ('Monthy',
                monthly)]
    return periodic_returns
```

CHAPTER 2 FINANCE BASICS AND DATA SOURCES

Notice that Listing 2-7 uses backward-defined formulae to compute returns. Output from this will appear as shown in Figure 2-5 once plotted.

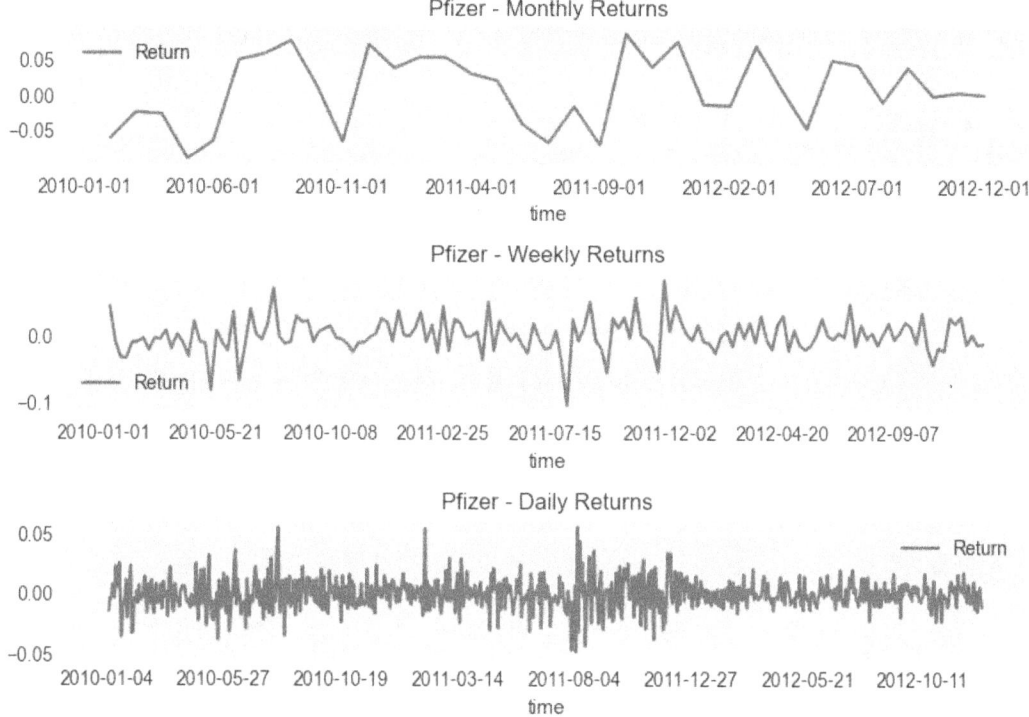

Figure 2-5. *Returns of Pfizer stock*

We didn't use any formal design template to write that function for *return* computation, as we plan to do that formally in Chapter 9 while discussing *portfolios* and incorporating returns there.

Multiperiod Simple Returns

A simple τ period return expression can be split into a product of multiple one-period returns like the below:

$$\begin{aligned} R_t(\tau) + 1 &= \frac{S_t}{S_{t-\tau}} \\ &= \frac{S_t}{S_{t-1}} \cdot \frac{S_{t-1}}{S_{t-2}} \cdots \frac{S_{t-\tau+1}}{S_{t-\tau}} \\ &= (1+R_t) \cdot (1+R_{t-1}) \cdots (1+R_{t-\tau+1}) \end{aligned}$$

33

CHAPTER 2   FINANCE BASICS AND DATA SOURCES

It means we can decompose a big period's returns into smaller chunks. For example, a 25-day return can be split into multiplied forms of 1-day, 2-day, and up to 24-day simple returns. This factorization helps to find any big period's returns without calculating the entire series, provided we know the single period ones.

Log Returns

The simple return has a lower bound: −100% or −1. It happens when the asset price becomes very low (close to zero) at any point due to adverse interest or willingness of shareholders to exhale all cash out in the market. It is a problem for mathematical modeling as a shorter bound limits the power of optimization algorithms. As a workaround, we prefer the logarithm of the payoff ratio, which is, in turn, the differences between adjacent log-asset prices:

$$r_t = \log \frac{S_t}{S_{t-1}}$$
$$= \log S_t - \log S_{t-1}$$

Investors/share buyers may get tempted to put money in assets that give sudden high returns (considering simple returns), which may not be a rational decision for gaining profits in the long run. Log returns can cut down the effect of very high/low returns and present a much more stable view to investors. Anyway, log and simple returns are related by

$$r_t = \log(1 + R_t)$$

Multiperiod Log Returns

It is a logarithm of multiperiod simple returns. Applying the same on $R_t(\tau) + 1$, we get

$$r_t(\tau) = \log(1 + R_t(\tau))$$
$$= \log(1 + R_t) + \log(1 + R_{t-1}) + \ldots + \log(1 + R_{t-\tau+1})$$
$$= r_t + r_{t-1} + \ldots + r_{t-\tau+1}$$

Unlike simple returns, multiperiod log returns are a summation of single-period log returns, which are easier to handle and work as a better input to any optimization algorithm.

Summary

This chapter introduced basic financial nomenclatures, interest theory, and the designing data source adapters. Short descriptions of different financial instruments are needed to grasp the mathematical modeling done in this book, and the same goes for interest theory. We learned how money's value changes over time, affecting the overall asset price. Discussions on *return* computation showed us how to measure the target objective of our investments, i.e., the profit and loss. And the one vital topic is data sources – as no matter what models we build in this book, we need data for that, and to access financial data sources, we need adapters. Design templates for data sources like *Yahoo Financials* and *Market Stack* will be useful as we move through different chapters.

In the next chapter, we will review the *theory of probability* both from the theoretical and practical perspectives that will work as a solid base for learning applied concepts of *Stochastic Finance*.

CHAPTER 3

Probability

Uncertainty is a part of life – be it stock price movement or a common natural phenomenon like the movement of a cyclone, tossing a coin, or even analysis of an engineering component. From sixteenth-century mathematicians to modern-day data scientists, everyone has tried and is continuously doing the same to decode *"uncertainty"* and give a stable shape to systems. *Probability theory* is the tool that helps them to do so. Despite having umpteen books, papers, and articles, this topic is still a gray area for many. This chapter introduces *probability* with examples in Python, and it is a *must-have* for a deep understanding of modeling financial instruments. A plethora of reference materials on this is already available both in online and physical form. You will get enough ideas on formulations and mathematical details from those. This chapter intends not to deluge you that much with the same stuff again but rather discuss interpretations of the different topics from the financial modeling perspective. Of course, theory and derivations are integral parts of our discussion, but we focus on discussing more *why* than *what*.

The Inception of the Idea for Probability Theory

You will be surprised to know that decoding the "uncertainty" can help in saving lives and property. For example, if we can foresee the chances of calamities like seismic events or cyclones and estimate their uncertainty, we can at least take some precautionary measures. Methods of *probability*, of course, become essential in computing the uncertainty and chance of any such event. Beyond its applications to natural sciences and engineering, this theory has emerged as a strong tool in analyzing the stock market, which is the area of interest of this book. Before going into the details of definitions and other mathematical rigors, let us discuss why probability analysis is needed in general. What situation forces us to use probability estimation? Recall what you learned in Chapter 1 about a nondeterministic system.

Wind movement of seasonal cyclones can be a good example of that. Do we know what physical factors inside the cyclone eye drive its wind direction? A meteorologist can answer that question, but a naïve person cannot. Scientists must have built numerous models to forecast wind/storm direction. But, as said earlier, if you are naïve about weather science, then knowing these factors would be impossible for you. So there is no question of forming a deterministic model if the same job of modeling a storm is assigned to you. Tossing a coin is another one and possibly the best example. We do not know exactly what factors influence coin flipping. To the best of my knowledge, nobody has ever built a magical deterministic model with all the factors that can tell the outcome, like an Oracle. Even though that list of golden factors is missing, we can guess there must be many such granular ones influencing the outcome of the toss. Some probable list: position of the fingers tossing the coin, wind direction, and the surface on top of which it would fall, and this must be inclusive. Knowing all these beforehand at a very detailed level could have helped us determine the outcome, i.e., head or tail. But, unfortunately, be it coin tossing or determining the direction of a cyclone, none of these are known in detail if you have to model them, and as a result, we must rely only on the previous outcomes of the experiments to forecast any such future events.

On the other hand, computing simple interest (discussed in Chapter 2) is fully deterministic. Given an interest rate *(r)*, initial amount *(P)*, and time *(t)*, we will be able to compute the total amount A precisely without any uncertainty present in the output. So, in short, when we don't know the influential factors of any event, we cannot forecast any value for that event precisely; hence, probability analysis helps us there. Recall discussions from Chapter 1 – some magical formula was thought there for forecasting stock price with factors x_1, x_2, etc., though it doesn't exist. Had it been deterministic, things would be smooth, and computation would proceed without producing any uncertainty, but unfortunately, our roads are not covered with roses like these. As a solution, we need analysis of outcomes generated from previous experiments, be it coin tossing or stock price forecasting, to model a nondeterministic system – probability theory is the starting point of that solution.

Probability Space and Basic Definitions

Random experiment is probably the first term people become familiar with when learning probability. Performing any activity of uncertainty, as discussed in the previous section, can be defined as a random experiment. A few examples are tossing

CHAPTER 3 PROBABILITY

a coin, throwing a dice, and capturing stock market data. The outcomes of any random experiment are known as *events*. In the coin tossing experiment, head and tail are two possible events.

Similarly, numbers from one to six and captured stock market prices are outcomes from the other two experiments. In general, events don't exhibit any visible pattern that can be determined beforehand, unlike deterministic ones.

Before discussing the definition of probability, we need to know a few things from a set-theoretic angle:

> **Sample space**: The set of all possible outcomes is known as sample space, denoted by Ω. In the coin tossing experiment, head and tail form the sample space as *{head, tail}*. But if you toss two coins simultaneously, then it should look like this: *{(head, head), (head, tail),(tail, head),(tail, tail)}*. *Pfizer* stocks shown in Figure 2-2 are another sample space of the random experiment "Capture Pfizer stocks for a given time."
>
> **Event**: Any subset of Ω is an event E. For the two-coin tossing example, (tail, head) is an event. For financial instruments, things would be a little different. Unlike toss output, they have continuous values rather than discrete, so there will be infinite number of possible events.

Generally, events are associated with a criterion, and that's the foundation of computing the probability. Consider sample space for the three-coin tossing experiment. Valid events would be *{(head, head, head), (head, tail, head), … (tail, tail, tail)}*. Now, if I say, identify events that have two *tails*. You can easily do that and reply with the answer: *{(head, tail, tail), (tail, head, tail)*, and *(tail, tail, head)}*. How did you find that? Very simple, right? You just iterated over the sample space and picked up events that satisfy the "having two tails" criterion. We can say that one filter is applied over a set that does the job. The number of events that satisfy the criteria builds the base of probability. Let's now define it formally.

Definition of Probability

If c is the number of outcomes supporting an event E and N is the total number of different outcomes (cardinality of Ω), then the probability of event E is given by

CHAPTER 3   PROBABILITY

$$P(E) = \frac{c}{N}$$

More formally, under set-theoretic notation,

$$P(E) = \frac{n(E)}{n(\Omega)}$$

In practice, if N is unknown to us, we must run the random experiment as often as possible. That makes $P(E)$ a limiting ratio like

$$P(E) = \lim_{N \to \infty} \frac{c}{N}$$

where $P(E)$ lies between 0 and 1. The expression $N \to \infty$ has experimental rather than mathematical significance as the true probability would be found only by repeating the trials of random experiment an infinite number of times (at least in theory). For example, writing down the full sample space is difficult for a random experiment of tossing 50 coins at a time, though analytically, with the help of combinatorics, you can compute $n(\Omega)$. But, sometimes, analytic methods for exploring sample space don't work or even impossible, especially for uncountable continuous data. For example, do you know how many possible values can a stock index take? Of course not, because it is infinite in theory. Hence, we must repeat the random experiment as trials and record the supporting events. In short, $n(\Omega)$ should be estimated by N, i.e., $N \approx n(\Omega)$.

Why Study Probability for Finance

Everything discussed so far should look fine to you. But one question might be haunting if this topic sounds very alien to you, i.e., you are a first-timer reading about probability – "What is end goal of studying probability especially for Finance?". Although Chapter 1 has touched upon this one while covering nondeterministic systems, formally, it can be said that to know the chances of future events and estimate an unknown nondeterministic system's output, we must know the theory of probability. For finance, to invest in the stock market and know the estimated profit from the portfolio, knowing the chances of a security price reaching some good point is essential and the probability analysis comes there to rescue us. Though the earlier statement is too high level and much detailed computation is needed to reach the target objective, still, this should sound like a good summary.

Set-Theoretic View of Probability

In set theory, a *measure* is defined as a mapping from a set to a real number. For example, a mapping that counts the number of elements of a set is a measure. Hence, on the same line, probability is nothing but a measure.

Probability Space

Probability space is defined as a tuple $(\Omega, \mathbb{F}, \mathbb{P})$ where

> **Sample space** Ω: Set of all possible basic outcomes. An event E is a subset of Ω, i.e., $E \in \Omega$.
>
> **Event space** $\mathbb{F}$: A *field* that defines all possible subsets of events. This helps combine multiple events and compute their probability. For example, {(head, tail),(tail, tail)} is an element of the event space for the two-coin toss experiment.
>
> **Probability law** $\mathbb{P}$: It is a measure $\mathbb{P}: \mathbb{F} \to [0, 1]$ of an event E. It gives the relative size of the event set compared to the sample space.

One very important rule to be mentioned, the total probability over sample space is 1, i.e.,

$$P(\Omega) = 1$$

As Ω consists of many $E \in \Omega$,

$$\sum_E P(E) = 1, \quad \forall E \in \Omega$$

Other rules of set theory also apply to probability space, such as

$$P(A \cup B) = P(A) + P(B) - P(A \cap B)$$
$$P(A \cap B) = P(A).P(B); \textit{ if events } A \& B \textit{ are indpendent}$$
$$= P(A).P(B|A); \textit{ if events } A \& B \textit{ are dependent}$$

CHAPTER 3   PROBABILITY

Independence and Conditional Probability

If the occurrence of one event before another changes the probability of the other, the one depends on the other – this is the fact of dependence and independence of events. For example, if today's stock index influences tomorrow's, the probability of the stock index reaching some point tomorrow will depend on today's value. That happens in real, and we will see that in detail while discussing the *stochastic process* in Chapter 5. Let's take another example of drawing red and blue balls from a bucket to further elaborate on event dependence. Suppose the bucket has three red and four blue balls, and you are asked to draw five balls in two times – two at first time and three at second time. But the bucket is kept at a dark room so you can't see color of the balls while drawing. You can only see them once you come out from that room. In this setup, can you compute the probability that you end up drawing two red and three blue balls? Let X and Y be the two events representing drawing two and three balls, respectively. Probability of X is easy to compute and is given by

$$P(X) = \frac{^3C_2}{^7C_2}$$

Now, after this, things will be a little different when you are about to draw three balls. Event Y here depends on X because drawing two red balls has reduced the sample space, making the number of balls now five. Event Y is given as Y | X as it depends on X, and the corresponding probability is

$$P(Y|X) = \frac{^4C_3}{^5C_3}$$

The probability of the combined event, $X \cap Y$, is given by

$$P(X \cap Y) = P(X).P(Y|X)$$
$$= \frac{^3C_2}{^7C_2} \cdot \frac{^4C_3}{^5C_3}$$
$$\approx 0.057$$

Let's explore the sample space of two events and validate the analytical computation above. Suppose balls are numbered, and we write those on the surface in this fashion – red_1, blue_2, red_3, blue_4, etc. Sample space of drawing first event, i.e., drawing 2 balls at a time, looks like this:

{(red_1,blue_1),(red_1,blue_2),(red_1,blue_3),..(red_1,red_2),(red _2,red_3),(red_1,red_3)..(blue_1, blue_2).. }

There is a total of 21(=$^7C_2$) combinations in this sample space, out of which 6(= $^3C_2$) contains two red balls. It clarifies the event X. The bucket is now left with five balls (one red and four blue) before facing the event Y, which is conditional on X. As we don't know precisely which red ball is left there, the filtered sample space for event Y conditional on X (drawing three balls at a time) looks like this:

{(red_1,blue_1,blue_2), (red_2, blue_2, blue_3),(blue_1, blue_3, blue_4),(blue_2, blue_4, blue_1)..}

Now, combining two sample spaces, keeping the fact in mind that balls drawn at the first time will be missing while drawing at the second time, we get

{(red_1,blue_1, red_2, blue_, blue_3), (red_1,blue_2, blue_1, blue_3, blue_4),…(red_1,red_2, blue_1, blue_3, blue_4),(red_1, red_3, blue_1, blue_2, blue_3)..}

Notice that two of the combined events supporting $X \cap Y$ are (red_1,red_2, blue_1, blue_3, blue_4) and (red_1, red_3, blue_1, blue_2, blue_3), and there are many such which ultimately gives the resultant probability as 0.057. It means that on average, 5.7 times, at the end, you have the combination of two red and three blue balls upon drawing five balls 100 times. We established through this example that with the help of combinatorics, probability can be computed by avoiding full exploration of large sample spaces and filtering them with events (another example is discussed next in the "Random Variable" section).

Although discussing the set-theoretic view is essential to have a solid foundation in probability theory, the functional view of probability is more useful for the topics of Stochastic Finance discussed in this book. That's why covering further details on this is not so relevant and out of scope. Interested readers can refer to [1].

Random Variable

When we talk about *events*, we mean statements based on some phenomenon; for example, *Google* stocks reaching $138.49, getting a three in dice throw, raining tomorrow, and many more. From the set-theoretic view of probability, these descriptions are delicate but practically difficult to manage and quantify. That's why we need some quantification scheme to give it full numerical shape. Random variables solve that purpose.

CHAPTER 3   PROBABILITY

RANDOM VARIABLE – DEFINITION

Random variables provide a well-defined quantification scheme for mapping from events to numbers.

Numbers represented by random variables should be chosen judiciously to have meaningful representation; and in some cases, events themselves can guide in doing that. This book deals with security prices, so they all will be real nonnegative numbers, i.e., the random variables will have values as real numbers. It is far easier than the set-theoretic notation. Under pure theoretical settings, a random variable X is a function that maps descriptive events to numbers. Formally,

$$X(\omega):\Omega \to \mathbb{R}, \qquad \omega \in \mathbb{F}$$

where X is defined as a function over event ω.

Few examples are as follows:

- The event of *Google* stocks reaching $135 can be written as $X = 138.49$, and $P(X=138.49)$ can be as high as 0.90. We can ignore ω while writing if F contains continuous real numbers, as $X(\omega)$ also outputs the same for that case.

- Events like getting *head* or *tail* in a toss can be interchangeably encoded as 1 or 0. Following this, $P(\{Head\})$ and $P(\{Tail\})$ can be written as $P(X=1)$ and $P(X=0)$, respectively. This encoding is mostly a probability modeler's choice rather than the result of any rule for $\mathbb{F}$ with discrete items.

The two examples discussed above are the basis of two classifications of random variables – continuous and discrete, as discussed next.

Discrete Random Variable

Let's take a fresh random experiment of *throwing three dice* at a time. As each dice can produce a number between 1 and 6, we can have $216(=6^3)$ possible combinations. The sample space looks like this:

CHAPTER 3   PROBABILITY

$$\Omega = \{(1,1,1),(1,1,2),\ldots(3,2,4),\ldots(6,6,5),(6,6,6)\}$$

The probability of having any single combination is 1/216, for example,

$$P(\{1,4,3\}) = \frac{1}{216}, P(\{5,4,2\}) = \frac{1}{216}$$

Instead of writing in set-theoretic notation, we can name these combinations like $A_1, A_2, \ldots A_{216}$ and assign a random variable Z for them, i.e., each combination is an *event* now. Hence, rewriting probability expressions,

$$P(Z = A_1) = \frac{1}{216}, P(Z = A_2) = \frac{1}{216}, \ldots, P(Z = A_{216}) = \frac{1}{216}$$

Z is a perfect example of a discrete random variable that takes countable discrete values. A more complex event description would be "always having 4 from the third dice." The valid events for this should look like this:

$$\{(1,1,4),(1,2,4),..(3,4,4),\ldots(6,5,4)\}$$

By theory, we should perform a sufficient number of trials (close to infinity) and count how many times any element of $\mathbb{F}$ appears there. The ratio of the two gives us the probability. This one may sound infeasible. As we learned while discussing conditional probability, using *combinatorics* is a more convenient way of computing probability. Same goes here also. To elaborate, we can always have four from the third dice in $30 (= {}^6P_2)$ possible ways, and that makes the probability of an event ξ_1.

$$P(\{\xi_1 = (3,2,4)\}) = \frac{30}{216} \approx 0.138 \; , \xi_1 = (1,3,4) \in \Omega$$

Denoting the random variable for E for this, we can write $P(E = \xi_1) = 0.138$.

A more relevant example for this book is the random experiment of analyzing jumps in financial security prices, and discrete random variables best represent them. A diagrammatic view of the phenomenon can be shown in Figure 3-1.

CHAPTER 3   PROBABILITY

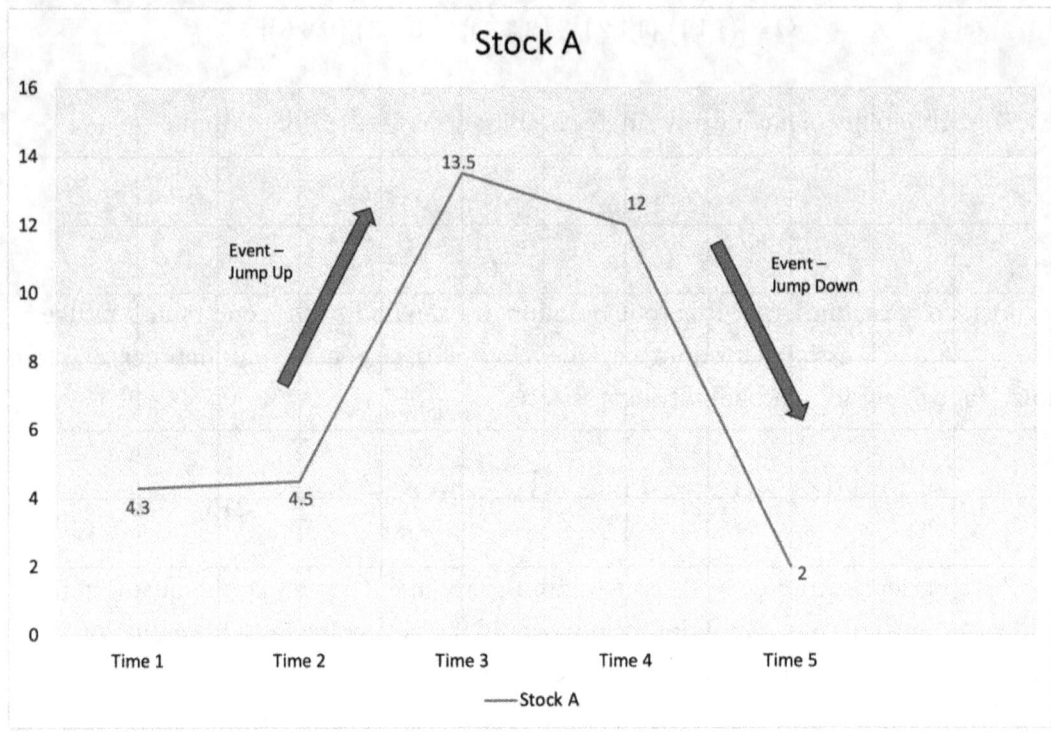

Figure 3-1. *Security price jumps as discrete random variable*

There are two significant jumps as given by

$$\left|S_{T_2} - S_{T_3}\right| = |4.5 - 13.5| = 9 \text{ and } \left|S_{T_4} - S_{T_5}\right| = |12 - 2| = 10$$

Denote S_{T_i} as security price at time *i*. A *jump* is considered a significant price difference within a given time interval. However, this *significant difference* is user defined rather than always being a fixed value. The number of jumps between a given timeframe can be considered a discrete random variable. In Figure 3-1, considering five as a minimum significant difference, we get two jumps between timeframe T_1 to T_5. We can write

$$P(J=2) = \frac{2}{4} = 0.5 \text{ (there are 4 time differences)}$$

where *J* is the discrete random variable indicating number of jumps. Although this computation is extremely crude, it shows the foundation of jump estimation, which will be discussed in the subsequent chapters.

In short, discrete random variables should be used for countable events, which can be represented by categorial or integer values.

Continuous Random Variable

Figure 3-1 shows us a stock's time and price changes – all changes can be discretely identified. What if I say what you see is a partial picture; there are further details inside it? That may sound strange, but that's reality. Can I say that the price changed from 4.5 to 4.500001, then 4.500002, and this way reached 13.5? I think I can. Or is it far granular – 4.5 to 4.50000001, then 4.50000002, and so on? How do you count jumps, then? Which change would you consider? Is it at all countable? Continuous random variable is the answer here. They represent continuous values, and within a given range, there can be an infinite number of possible values, at least in theory. For them, sample space Ω and event space $\mathbb{F}$ both contain continuous elements. Everything we discussed under the "Discrete Random Variable" section also applies here, but with an exception – things cannot be counted. We must make it countable by converting it into discrete groups or using ready-made distributions (discussed next). The price of financial security is the example most suitable for this book as a continuous random variable. In general, any measurement that supports floating point arithmetic is a good candidate to be a continuous random variable.

Being continuous, it is never possible to know $n(E)$ and $n(\Omega)$ in a conventional way, i.e., knowing the size of the sets just by counting. But one possible way is to know the set's length and area (for multidimensional variables) by integration. We can write

$$P(X = x \in E) = \frac{\int_E dx}{\int_\Omega dx}.$$

The probability for a continuous random variable is a ratio of two integrals. In theory, for the discrete cases, at last, we can compute the counts of events either by experiment and observation or else by combinatorics, but for the continuous cases, analytical evaluation is needed for direct computation. As said earlier, one indirect alternative method exists by continuous to discrete conversion with the help of small-sized bins. But being very error-prone, that's not a viable option. We must need a solid analytical framework to compute the integral ratio. Probability distributions help us there, as discussed next.

CHAPTER 3   PROBABILITY

Probability Distributions

The basic requirement for computing the probability of an event is the repetition of trials under identical conditions. Satisfying the conditions mentioned by these words – "repetition" and "identical" – is practically infeasible. For example, suppose you are performing the random experiment of capturing the stock values for a fictional company A from January 2018 to January 2019. Theoretically, you should be able to repeat it for the same period. But is that possible, i.e., going back to January 2018 and again capturing the data with the same environmental conditions? Of course not. Secondly, naïve counting of events is any way not possible for continuous variables. So, we need some mechanism as discussed in the previous section – should work for both discrete and continuous. Being a *measure,* probability anyway behaves like a function that takes the state of the random variable (random variate) as input and returns a value between 0 and 1. Hence, the problem boils down to finding an appropriate function $f(x)$ where x is the random variable (both continuous and discrete). This $f(x)$ should somehow estimate the true probability of events.

For discrete random variable x, $f(x)$ is known as *probability mass function (PMF)*, and by *probability law,*

$$0 \leq f(x) \leq 1 \text{ and } \sum_{x} f(x) = 1$$

For continuous random variable x, $f(x)$ is known as the *probability density function (PDF)*, and then

$$f(x) \geq 0 \text{ and } \int_{x} f(x) dx = 1$$

This is the functional view of the probability. Note that the total probability for all possible values of random variable is 1 as the all possible values of x forms the sample space.

Once $f(x)$ is defined, we can get a list of x and $f(x)$ paired values for the entire x range. That list is known as the *probability distribution* (we repeatedly use the term "Distribution" to refer to the probability distribution in this book). Note that, for PDF, there is no restriction on $f(x)$ to be less than 1, i.e., probability can be greater than 1. Doesn't that sound weird? No, it is not. But why? We will discuss it in short. But before that, we need to know what a *cumulative distribution function (CDF)* is.

$F(x)$, a.k.a. known as the *cumulative distribution function (CDF)*, sums up all probabilities of different values less than current x. It is given by

$$F(x) = \sum_{-\infty}^{x} f(x), \quad x \text{ is discrete}$$

$$= \int_{-\infty}^{x} f(x) dx, \quad x \text{ is continous}$$

So, for continuous variable only we can write

$$f(x) = F'(x) = \frac{d}{dx} F(x)$$

By the definition of derivative,

$$f(x) = F'(x) = \lim_{h \to \infty} \frac{F(x+h) - F(x)}{h}$$

So, rather than being pure measure of probability, $f(x)$ is the rate of probability or the probability per unit length. Its value depends on how h is chosen. By theory of derivatives, h should be infinitesimal and a division by it may cause $f(x)$ to be greater than 1. By law of *physics*, we may say that resulting value is a *density of probability* which is true for continuous variables. Theoretically, $P(X = x) = 0$, i.e., probability at any point is zero for them. This may sound surprising but that's a fact for PDF. Then how to find out valid probability? Well, by integration as usual. From PDF, we can find out probability of a random variable lying between a and b as

$$P(a \leq X \leq b) = \int_a^b f(x) dx$$
$$= \int_a^b dF(x)$$
$$= F(b) - F(a)$$

But that's still between a and b and not exactly at a fixed point. The fact is that probability computed from PDF is an area formed between a and b. Applying the same for infinitesimal increment δ on a instead of b,

$$P(X = a)$$
$$= P(a \leq X \leq a + \delta)$$
$$= \int_a^{a+\delta} f(x) dx$$
$$\approx f(a).\delta$$

where $f(a).\delta$ is approximation for $P(X = a)$.

Figure 3-2 shows a comparative view of $f(x)$ for both PMF and PDF.

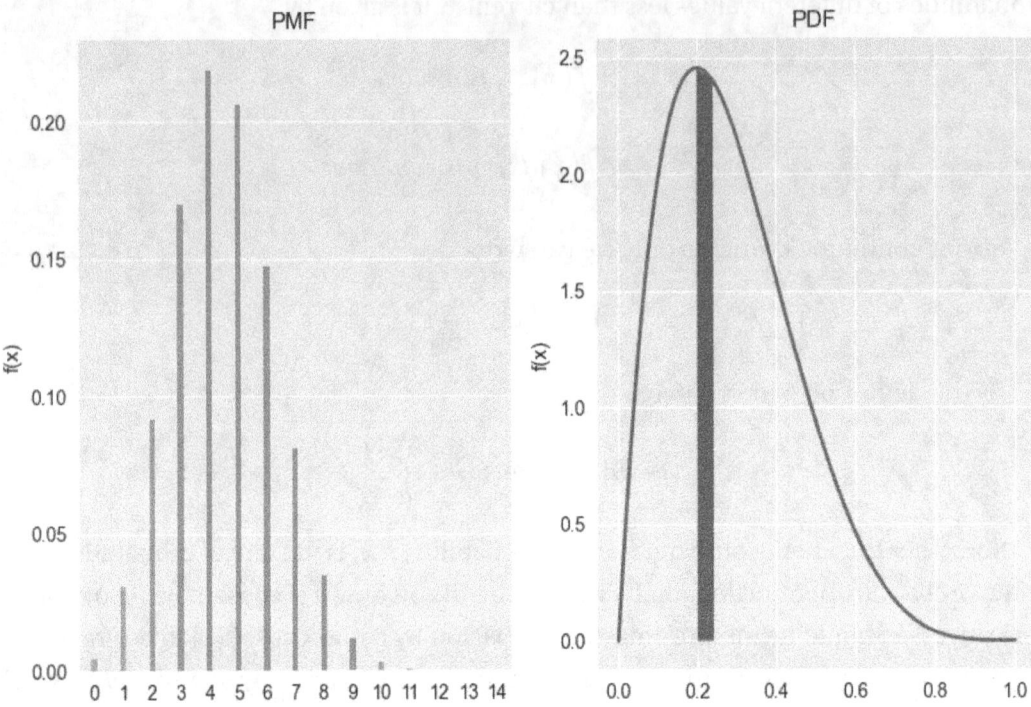

Figure 3-2. *PDF vs. PMF shapes. The shaded area in PDF shows probability of a data point.*

Being discrete, $f(x)$ looks like a bar diagram for PMF, whereas it forms a curve for PDF. Notice the shaded area under the PDF curve – equal to the $f(a)$. δ at point $a = 0.2$, where δ is the width of the area. This is true for any PDF. You can find the required code for this under /chapter3/dist_shapes.py, but there is nothing to worry about that much, as we won't discuss it here. For now, please focus on the output shapes generated by it.

Joint and Marginal Distribution

We know the probability of the intersection of two events is given by

$$P(A \cap B) = P(A).P(B|A), \quad A \& B \text{ are not independent}$$
$$= P(A).P(B), \quad A \& B \text{ are independent}$$

The set-theoretic view of probability gives it. But, by replacing events with two separate random variables, we get the ***joint distribution***, which is almost equivalent to the intersection of separate events:

$$f(X,Y) = f(X).f(Y|X)$$
$$= f(X).f(Y)$$

where $f(Y|X)$ is the conditional distribution of Y given X.

If we sum/integrate one random variable over another from a joint distribution, we get ***marginal distribution***, which is given by

$$f_{Marginal}(X) = \sum_y f(X,y), \text{ if } f(X,Y) \text{ is a PMF}$$

$$f_{Marginal}(X) = \int_y f(X,y), \text{ if } f(X,Y) \text{ is a PDF}$$

Likelihood and Parameters

In practice, $f(x)$ is defined as $f(x; \theta)$, where θ is known as the distribution parameters. θ represents the population or the data, and it is the factor that determines the shape of the distribution. For PDF, the curve shown in Figure 3-2 was generated by a density function known as *beta distribution*:

$$f_{Beta}(x; \alpha, \beta) = \frac{x^{\alpha-1}(1-x)^{\beta-1}}{B(\alpha, \beta)}$$

where

$$B(\alpha, \beta) = \frac{\Gamma(\alpha)\Gamma(\beta)}{\Gamma(\alpha+\beta)}, \qquad \Gamma(a) = (a-1)!$$

Both α and β are the distribution parameters, and we used $\alpha = 2$ and $\beta = 5$. It boils down the function into this form, $f(x) = 30x(1-x)^4$. Using a different α and β would have produced a different curve. The same goes for the PMF.

This $f(x; \theta)$ with a given value of θ is known as *likelihood*. In practice, we always seek the likelihoods instead of the true probabilities. For example, from the beta distribution, the likelihood of a data point $x = 0.2$ is given by $f_{Beta}(0.2; 2, 5)$. True probability is hard to find because of the limitations of performing the trials. Hence, *density* and *mass* functions help us estimate the probability with the set of handy parameters. You might be thinking about how to know the exact values of θ. Yes, that's the objective of a big discussion known as *parameter estimation,* and we will cover it later.

But to have some high-level idea for now, first, we need to know what *observations*, a.k.a. *random variates*, are. These are realizations of random variables, i.e., the output produced by the random variable from one or more trials. For example, trials of the random experiment *throwing three dice* produced observations like (1, 1, 1), (1, 1, 2), etc. Figure 2-3 from Chapter 2 shows the real stock prices. They are the observations produced by random variable(s) representing stock price. Though we didn't model anything based on stock price, nothing stops the variables from doing their job as they exist within the data.

The parameter (s) represents the domain of the observations. There are specific methods to find out their approximate value from the observations. That makes parameters dependent on them, i.e., using a different set of observations will end up the distribution having different parameters. The reason for this is intuitive – different domains have their footprint on the random variables. For example, parameters representing two sets of observations – one for Apple stocks and another for Google stocks – will differ as their price movements behave differently.

Moments, Expectation, and Variance

Expectation is the average value, a.k.a. *mean* of random variable when drawn from its probability distribution. It is given by

$$E(X) = \sum_x xf(x), \qquad \text{if } f(x) \text{ is PMF}$$

$$E(X) = \int_x xf(x)dx, \qquad \text{if } f(x) \text{ is PDF}$$

It is taken over all possible values of X. For continuous variables, the expectation is computed over all available realizations of X if the integration shown above cannot be computed in closed form.

CHAPTER 3   PROBABILITY

Variance

Variance is the expected value of the square of the distance of the random variable from the mean. It is given by

$$Var(X) = E\left[(X - E(X))^2\right] = \sum_x (x - E(X))^2 f(x), \quad \text{if } f(x) \text{ is PMF}$$

$$Var(X) = E\left[(X - E(X))^2\right] = \int_x (x - E(X))^2 f(x)dx, \quad \text{if } f(x) \text{ is PDF}$$

Variance is the measure of dispersion and uncertainty present within the distribution. Recall the short descriptions on "uncertainty quantification" from Chapter 1. Variance is the metric for that. On the same note, from the *Stochastic Finance* perspective, variance is the indicator of risk present in a financial asset. In Listing 2-7, we computed returns for various periods as these can be treated as realizations of the underlying random variable representing *return*. So, from there, variance can be computed using a probability distribution and the *Var(X)* expression given above. Variance computation is like a litmus test for investors as a higher resulting variance, either from returns or directly from asset values, indicates ups and downs that can lead to potential loss. This is treated like a fundamental theorem in Stochastic Finance. In Chapter 6, we will discuss how to compute realized and estimated variance from stock prices, and in Chapter 10, while discussing portfolios, we will learn how to gain maximum return from our investments by setting a fixed risk parameter.

Moments

Moment is a generic version of *expectation* and v*ariance* as it is taken for a random variable raised to a specific power and w.r.t a base as shown below:

$$m_r^c = E\left[(X - c)^r\right] = \sum_x (x - c)^r f(x), \quad \text{if } f(x) \text{ is PMF}$$

$$m_r^c = E\left[(X - c)^r\right] = \int_x (x - c)^r f(x)dx, \quad \text{if } f(x) \text{ is PDF}$$

where c is the base and r is the power and m_r^c is known as *r*th order moment about c. Any moment with base zero, i.e., c = 0, is known as a *raw moment* denoted by m_r', whereas the same with base mean (c = E(X)) is the *central moment* denoted by μ_r.

53

Notice that the *mean* and *variance* are nothing but the *first-order raw moment and second-order central moment*, i.e., m_1' and μ_2, respectively.

Moments indicate how the mass of the distribution is spread across. Higher moments (higher values for r) give the expected high values in the distribution whereas m_1' is the center of mass. They can be considered as junction points of the distribution exhibiting certain statistical properties. One informal way of comparing two probability distributions is by comparing their moments of several orders, especially for PDFs. We can try matching certain junction points to check the equality of two distributions instead of comparing the whole distribution pointwise; hence, moments have a role to play. Moments can be used to model security prices with jumps – such examples will be covered in Chapter 8.

Moments Approximation

Moments of a large unknown population can be approximated from a set of realized samples without even knowing the distribution $f(x)$ used in moments formulae. The expectation operator E can be replaced by $\dfrac{1}{n}$ in the following way, irrespective of $f(x)$ being PDF or PMF.

$$m_r^c \approx \frac{1}{n}\sum_{i=1}^{n}(x_i - c)^r$$

$$m_1' \approx \frac{1}{n}\sum_{i=1}^{n} x_i$$

$$\mu_2 \approx \frac{1}{n}\sum_{i=1}^{n}(x_i - m_1')^2$$

The above three expressions are known as *sample moment, sample mean,* and *sample variance*, respectively, giving the basic statistical properties of the underlying distribution. We can apply the above expression to compute the same for returns obtained from Listing 2-7. Sample moments are used to estimate distribution parameters (θ) by *method of moments* to be discussed later.

Next, we discuss a few distributions relevant for the topics covered in this book.

Poisson Distribution

We saw in Figure 2-1 what financial instruments look like. Observe that there are lots of ups and downs. The stock market behaves in a random fashion – sometimes, we see bullish behavior, and sometimes, the bear dominates the market. These two are integral parts of the stock market as they provide gentle trends. But what if stocks of fictional company A jump from $100 to $180 in one day? It is observed that this much change is very unusual for A. Or what if the reverse happens, i.e., from $180 to $100? That's also a significant change and a bit uncommon. Both phenomena may be considered some form of big change events and are technically called *jumps*. Figure 3-3 is a demonstration for that. *Poisson* distribution is suitable for modeling such events where we seek how many times a *jump* happens for financial instrument price within a timeframe, and of course, it is a discrete distribution of positive integers. Some other good examples are the number of passengers on a bus, the arrival of customers in a store, the number of text messages on your cell phone, etc. In general, Poisson distribution can be used to model any *counts*.

PMF of Poisson distribution is given by

$$f_{Poisson}(x) = \frac{\lambda^x}{x!} e^{-\lambda}, \quad \lambda > 0, x = 0,1,2..$$

where λ is the parameter of the *Poisson* PMF.

Listing 3-1 shows how to plot Poisson distribution with a fixed interval, and Figure 3-3 shows the output.

Listing 3-1. Function to compute PMF of Poisson distribution with a set of different parameters

```
import chapter3.visualization as vs3
from scipy.stats import poisson

def poisson_distribution():
    # a set of different λ values
    lamdas = [1, 4, 10, 40]

    # generate a sample of input x (positive integers only) that work as
    random variates
    x = np.arange(0, 15)
```

CHAPTER 3 PROBABILITY

```
# Get probabilities of input x for different λ values
prob_x = {
    lamda: (
        x,
        # pmf returns the probability of input x from poisson PMF
        poisson(lamda).pmf(x),
    )
    for lamda in lamdas
}
# plotting x vs probabilities for different λ values
vs3.poisson_plot(prob_x)
```

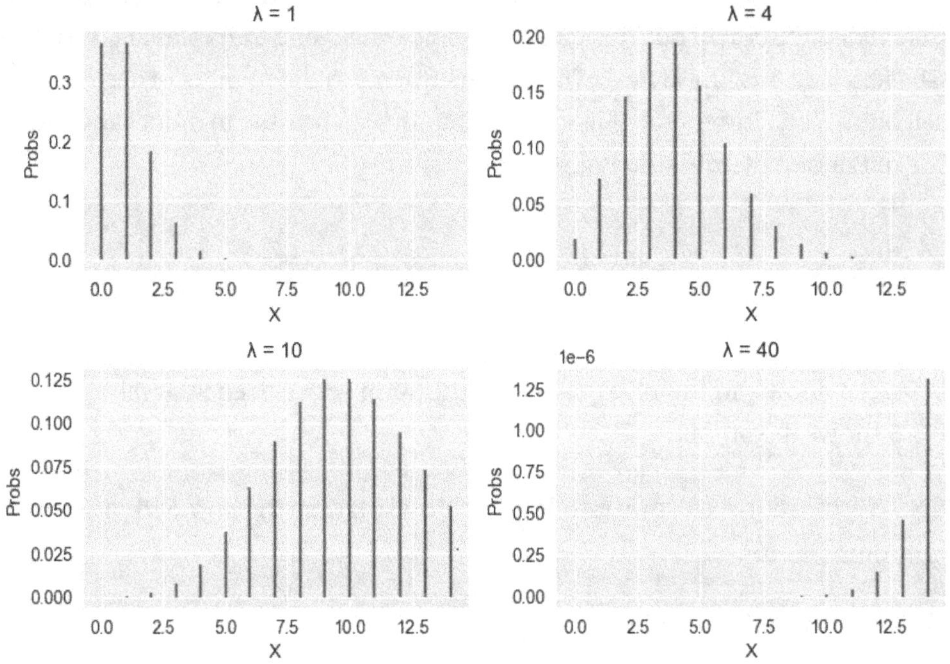

Figure 3-3. *PMF plots of Poisson distribution for different λ values*

CHAPTER 3 PROBABILITY

Uniform Distribution

Uniform distribution is probably the simplest of all distributions. It is nothing but a constant probability over a given interval. Its PDF is given by

$$f_{Uniform}(x) = \begin{cases} \dfrac{1}{b-a}, & a \leq x \leq b \\ 0, & \text{otherwise} \end{cases}$$

It may not look very sensible, but it is the foundation of other random variables. With the support of a uniform random variable, we can generate any random variables and their distribution. We will discuss this in detail in the next chapter. Listing 3-2 shows how to plot uniform distribution with a fixed interval, and Figure 3-4 shows the output.

Listing 3-2. Function to compute PDF of uniform distribution with fixed interval

```
from scipy.stats import uniform

def uniform_distribution():
    # generate a sample of input x  that work as random variates
    x = np.linspace(start=-500, stop=500, num=100)

    # Get probabilities of input x for a given range a & b (denoted by loc
    & scale)
    probs = uniform.pdf(x, loc=100, scale=200)
    # plotting x vs probabilities
    vs3.uniform_plot(x, probs)
```

CHAPTER 3 PROBABILITY

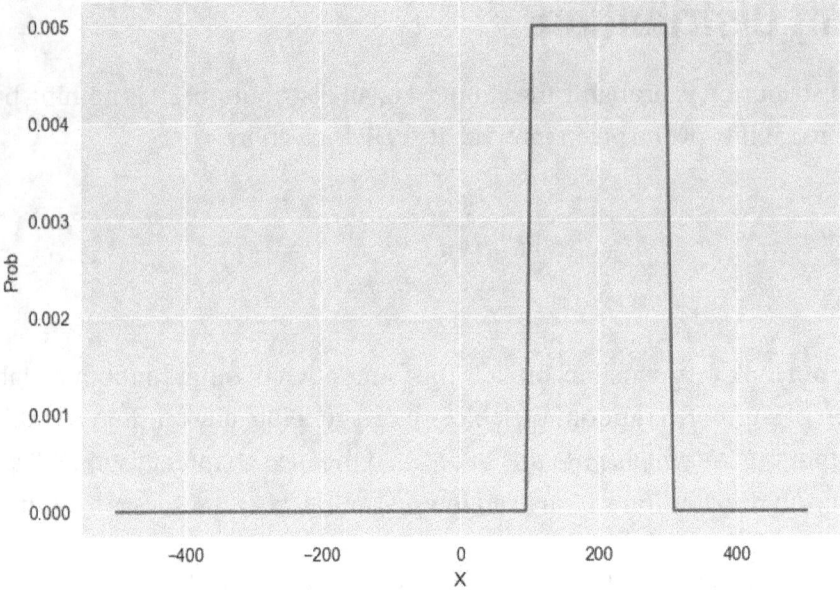

Figure 3-4. *PDF plots of uniform distribution*

Exponential Distribution

Exponential distribution is very closely related to the Poisson distribution. In *Poisson*, we take the specific number of events during a period as random variables, whereas in *exponential*, time is the random variable. It is the distribution of time intervals between two consecutive events.

PDF of the exponential distribution is given by

$$f_{Exponential}(x;\lambda) = \lambda e^{-\lambda x}, \quad x > 0, \lambda > 0$$

where λ is the parameter known as the rate of decay.

Listing 3-3 shows how to plot exponential distribution with various parameters, which produces output as shown in Figure 3-5.

Listing 3-3. Function to compute PDF of exponential distribution with a set of different parameters

```python
from scipy.stats import expon

def exponential_distribution():
    # a set of different λ values (should be positive)
    lamdas = [0.5, 1.3, 0.9, 2]
    # generate a sample of input x (only positive) that works as random
    variates
    x = np.linspace(start=0, stop=5, num=100)
    # Get probabilities of input x for different λ values
    prob_x = {
        lamda: (
            x,
            # pdf returns the probability of input x from poisson PDF
            expon.pdf(x, loc=0, scale=1 / lamda),
        )
        for lamda in lamdas
    }
    # plotting x vs probabilities for different λ values
    vs.exponential_plot(prob_x)
```

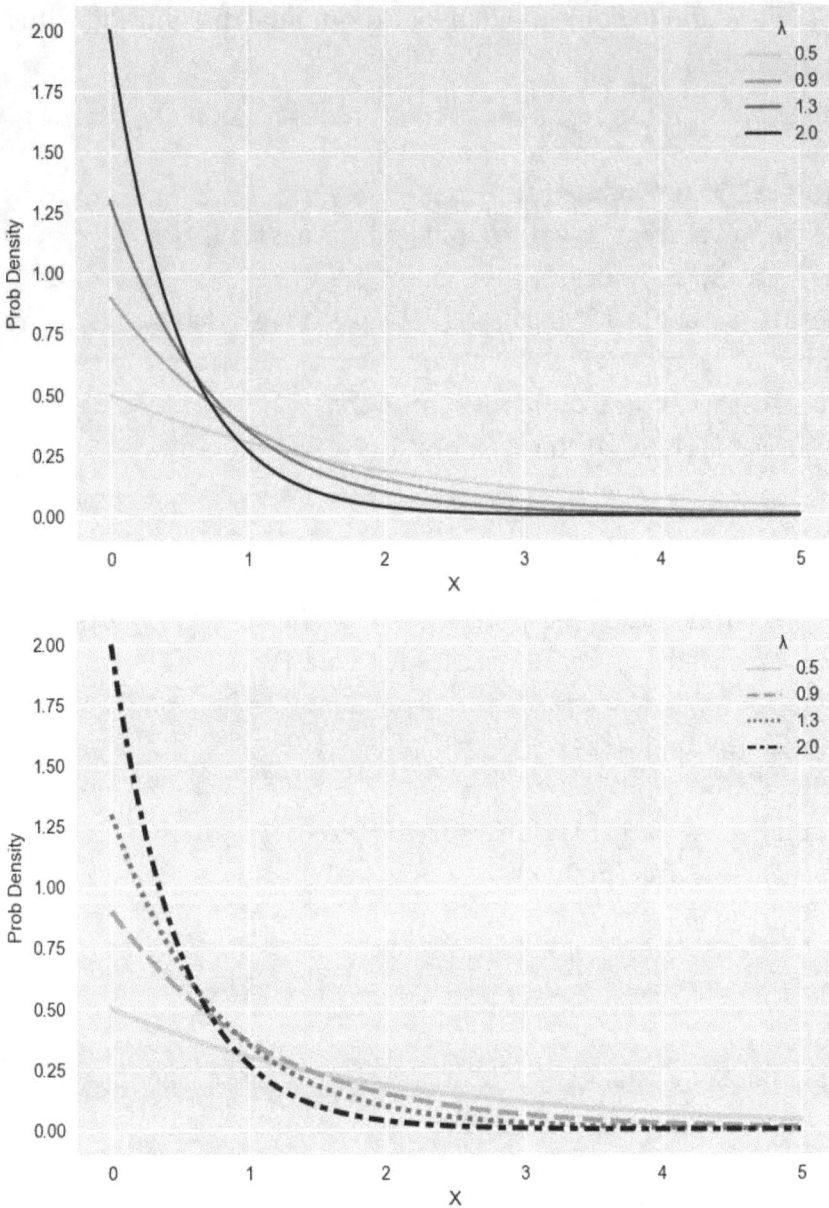

Figure 3-5. *PDF plots of exponential distribution for different λ values*

Gaussian/Normal Distribution

It is the most common and widely used distribution. It is said that almost everything around us follows Gaussian, a.k.a. normal distribution. There is a strong reason behind this. It is the distribution of real numbers, and who doesn't know that real numbers are an essential part of our life, and so is Gaussian distribution. Be it people's height and weight, numbers scored in mathematics by eighth standard students, and the topic of this book – stock values of any company – all are supposed to follow Gaussian distribution in some sense. However, in later chapters, we will evaluate the true distribution of the stock price, and you will see that it is not exactly the vanilla Gaussian distribution but a transformed version of it.

PDF of Gaussian distribution is given by

$$f_{Gaussian}(x;\mu,\sigma^2) = \frac{1}{\sigma\sqrt{2\pi}} e^{-\frac{1}{2}\left(\frac{x_i-\mu}{\sigma}\right)^2}, \qquad \sigma > 0, -\infty < \mu < \infty$$

with parameters μ and σ^2.

The *mean* and *variance* of the Gaussian distribution are directly given by the parameters as μ and σ^2, respectively. We use different values of these parameters and plot the Gaussian density function as shown in Listing 3-4.

Listing 3-4. Function to compute PDF of Gaussian distribution with a set of different parameters

```
from scipy.stats import norm

def gaussian_distribution():
    # a set of different (μ,σ) pairs
    params_mu_sigma = [(85, 90), (-6, 70), (43, 40), (-10, 19)]
    # generate a sample of input x (both positive & negative) that work as
    random variates
    x = np.linspace(start=-500, stop=500, num=100)
    # Get probabilities of input x for different (μ,σ) pairs
    prob_x = {
        "(%d,%d)" % (mu_sigma[0], mu_sigma[1]): (
            x,
            # pdf returns the probability of input x from normal PDF
            norm.pdf(x, loc=mu_sigma[0], scale=mu_sigma[1]),
        )
        for mu_sigma in params_mu_sigma
    }
    # plotting x vs probabilities for different (μ,σ) pairs
    vs3.gaussian_plot(prob_x)
```

CHAPTER 3 PROBABILITY

Figure 3-6 shows the output from Listing 3-4. Notice that a higher mean makes the densities sharper, whereas a higher variance causes a wider shape.

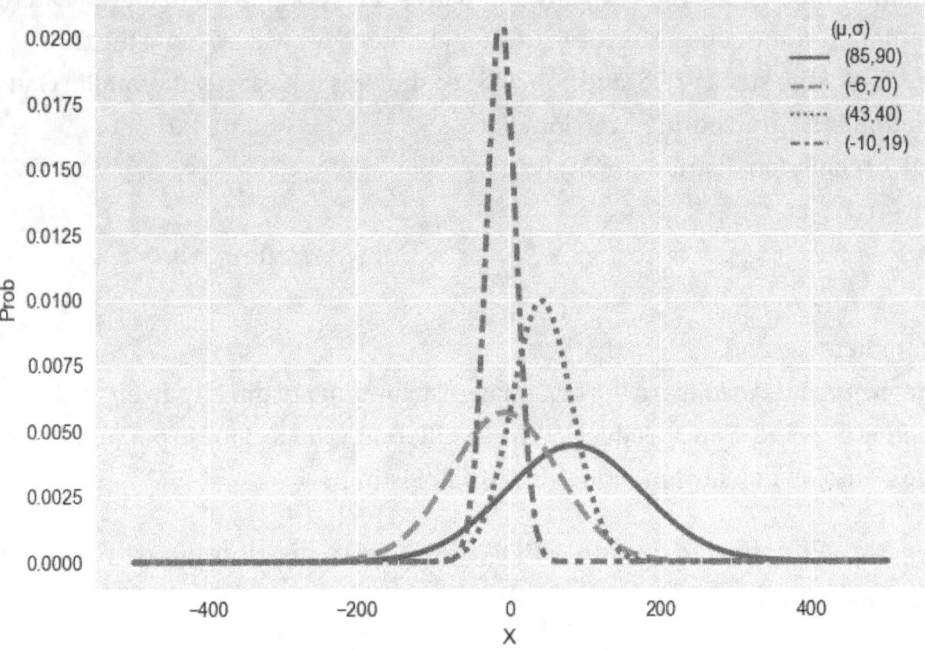

Figure 3-6. *PDF plots of Gaussian distribution for different (μ,σ) values*

Characteristic Function

The *characteristic function (CF)* is the Fourier transform of probability density. It is defined as a function of frequency ω and given by

$$\Phi(\omega;\theta) = E(e^{j\omega x}), \quad -\infty < \omega < \infty$$
$$= \int e^{j\omega x} f(x;\theta) dx, \text{ for continous random variable}$$
$$= \sum e^{j\omega x} f(x;\theta), \text{ for discrete random variable}$$

where j is the imaginary unit, $j = \sqrt{-1}$. Being a Fourier transform, the *characteristic function* carries different hidden features of the random variable as frequencies – it is a feature decomposition. Sometimes, computations in the frequency domain are far easier than the spatial domain; the same goes for characteristic functions.

Using Euler's formulae,

$$e^{j\omega x} = \cos(\omega x) + j\sin(\omega x)$$

$\Phi(\omega;\theta)$ can be decomposed into two parts as given below:

$$\Phi(\omega;\theta) = \int \cos(\omega x) f(x;\theta) dx + j \int \sin(\omega x) f(x;\theta) dx$$

Formulating $\Phi(\omega;\theta)$ like the above sometimes helps to ease off the computational complex. CF also supports reverse transformation, i.e., you can get back the original distribution from CF – apply inverse Fourier transform to it. It is given by

$$f(x;\theta) = \int e^{-j\omega x} \Phi(\omega;\theta) d\omega$$
$$= \sum e^{-j\omega x} \Phi(\omega;\theta)$$

Note that for forward and inverse transforms, operators $e^{j\omega x}$ and $e^{-j\omega x}$ can be used interchangeably as the frequency variable ω ranges from $-\infty$ to $+\infty$. CF has great significance in *Stochastic Finance* for computing complex distributions of multiple random variables in the frequency domain especially when there is difficulty in managing the distribution in closed form. One such example is estimating the distribution of financial securities like *options*. Computing the distribution of random variables, which are linear combinations of others, is another example where CF greatly helps. To elaborate, suppose this relation exists:

$$Z = \sum_I \alpha_i X_i$$

where Z and X_i are random variables. CF of Z is a product of individual CF of X_i if all X_i are independent to each other, and it is given by

$$\Phi_Z(\omega) = \prod_I \Phi_{X_i}(\omega)$$

This is useful to model the price path of securities with jumps, and the distribution can be thought of as a mixture of many components.

Let's now study the CFs of the densities we discussed earlier.

$$\Phi_{Gaussian}(\omega;\mu,\sigma^2) = e^{j\omega\mu - \frac{1}{2}\sigma^2\omega^2}$$

$$\Phi_{Uniform}(\omega;b,a) = \frac{e^{j\omega b} - e^{j\omega a}}{j\omega(b-a)}$$

$$\Phi_{Exponential}(\omega;\lambda) = \frac{e^{j\omega b} - e^{j\omega a}}{j\omega(b-a)}$$

$$\Phi_{Poisson}(\omega;\lambda) = e^{\lambda(e^{j\omega}-1)}$$

Listing 3-5 shows how to implement the abovementioned CFs.

Listing 3-5. Generation of characteristic function values for different densities

```
import numpy as np
import chapter3.visualization as vs3
import pandas as pd

def characteristic_funcs():
    # Generate frequencies. Ideally frequency can lie between -∞ to +∞.
    # We generate samples from -100 to 100.
    ω_arr = np.linspace(start=-100, stop=100, num=100)

    def _ϕ_gaussian(ω, μ, σ2): # Characteristic function for
    Gaussian density
        return np.exp((μ * ω * 1j) - (0.5 * ω * ω * σ2))

    def _ϕ_uniform(ω, b, a): # Characteristic function for Uniform density
        return (np.exp(1j * ω * b)-np.exp(1j * ω * a))/(1j * ω * (b - a))

    def _ϕ_exponential(ω, λ): # Characteristic function for
    Exponential density
        return 1.0/(1.0 - ((ω * 1j)/λ))

    def _ϕ_poisson(ω, λ): # Characteristic function for Poisson density
        return np.exp(λ * (np.exp(1j * ω)-1))
```

```python
def _generate_ϕ_ω_values(ϕ_ω, **θ):
    """
    Generate ϕ(ω) values for all given frequencies and use the
    real part only for plotting
    """
    return pd.DataFrame([{'ω':ω, 'ϕ(ω)':ϕ_ω(ω, **θ).real} for ω
    in ω_arr])

# Generate ϕ(ω) values for four different densities with fixed
parameters
μ = 200
σ2 = 10
b = 990
a = 90
λ = 10.0
poisson_λ = 100

cf_gaussian = ('Gaussian ϕ(ω; μ, σ2)', _generate_ϕ_ω_values(ϕ_ω=_ϕ_
gaussian,
                    μ=μ,
                    σ2=σ2))
cf_uniform = ('Uniform ϕ(ω; b, a)', _generate_ϕ_ω_values(ϕ_ω=_ϕ_
uniform,
                    b=b,
                    a=a))
cf_exponential = ('Exponential ϕ(ω; λ)', _generate_ϕ_ω_values(ϕ_ω=_ϕ_
exponential,
                    λ=λ))
cf_poisson = ('Poisson ϕ(ω; λ)', _generate_ϕ_ω_values(ϕ_ω=_ϕ_poisson,
            λ=poisson_λ))

vs3.plot_cf([cf_gaussian, cf_uniform, cf_exponential, cf_poisson])
```

CHAPTER 3 PROBABILITY

HANDLING COMPLEX NUMBERS IN PYTHON

Python can handle complex numbers in two ways. For example, to take complex number 5 + 4j in a variable x:

1) You can mention the complex component by multiplying it with 1j. For this case, you can use the statement: *x = 5 + 4 * 1j*

2) Use the function *complex* like this way: *x = complex(5, 4)*

To access *real* and *imaginary* components, use *real* and *imag* properties – *x.real* and *x.imag* return 5 and 4, respectively.

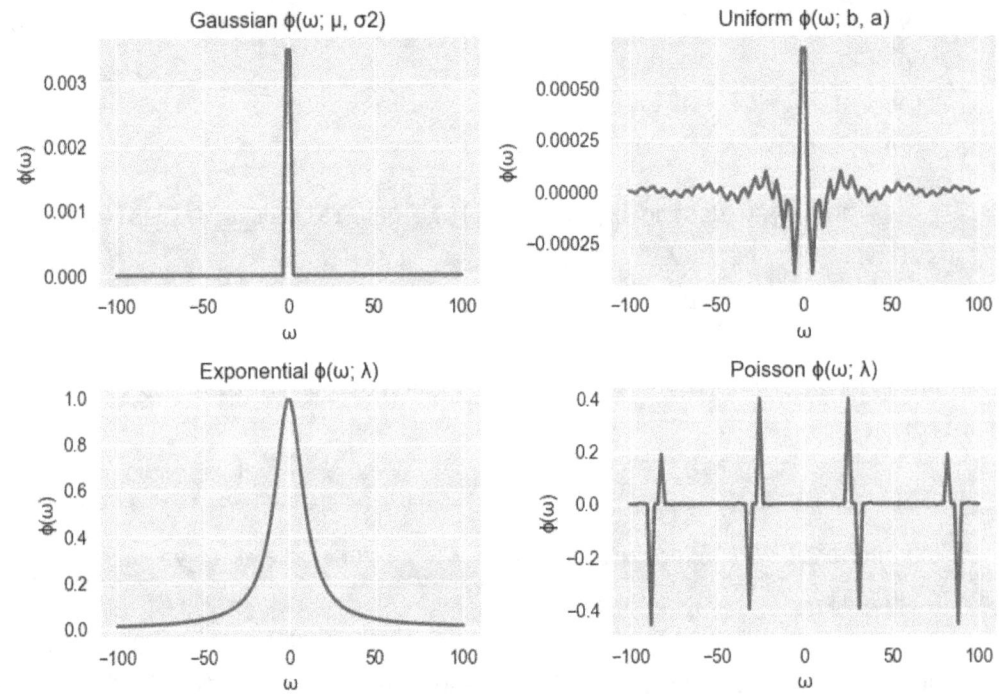

Figure 3-7. *Characteristic functions of different density functions*

Figure 3-7 shows the output generated by function *characteristic_funcs*. Note that the shape of CFs is also dependent on parameters, just like the PDFs. In Listing 3-5, we only used a set of fixed parameters; varying them will change the shapes, as we observed the same for PDFs in Figures 3-5 and 3-6. Figure 3-8 demonstrates this phenomenon (code for this can be found in *chapter3/dist_shapes.py*). Knowledge of computing CFs will come in handy when we face the challenge of estimating the distribution of *options* in Chapter 8.

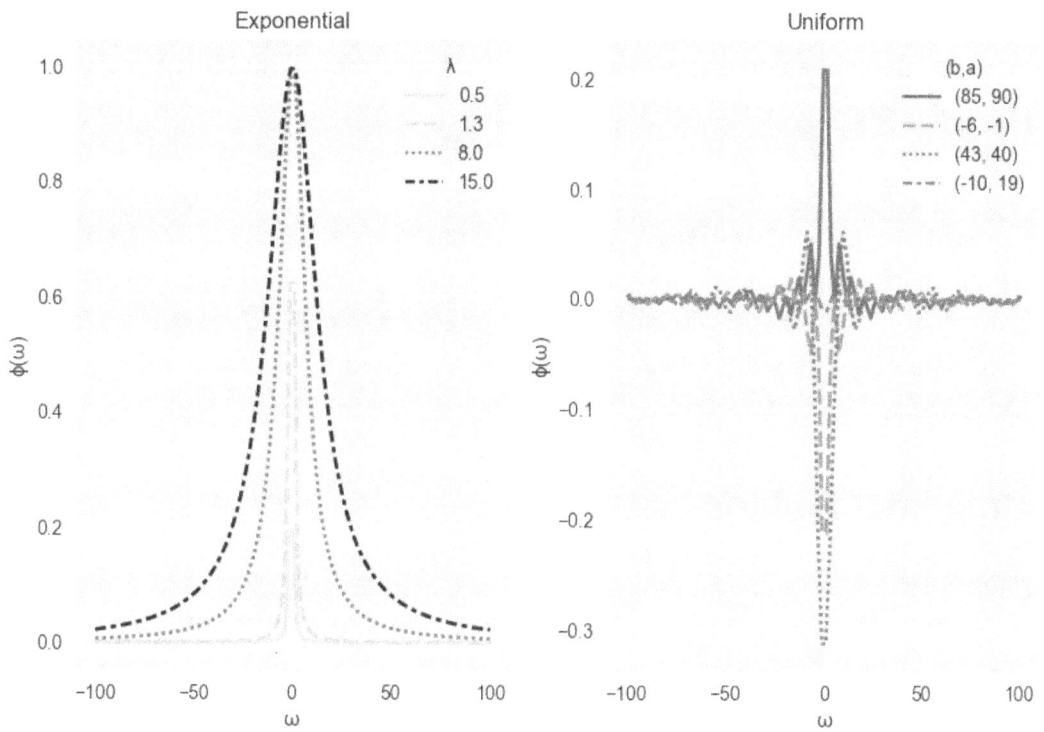

Figure 3-8. *Characteristic function shapes for different parameters*

Parameter Estimation

We often assume that a particular distribution has generated the data and is left to estimate the parameter values. *Data generation* may sound alien to you at this moment, but once you finish Chapter 4, you will know the reverse process of computing probability, i.e., generating data from the distribution. On a simpler note, a correct estimation of the parameters makes the probability distribution a perfect fit for the data. As said earlier, the choice of the distribution comes from our assumption, and again, this assumption often comes from domain knowledge. For example, you may choose a Gaussian distribution to model the stock market data, as Gaussian is the best choice for this use case. But what exactly do we mean by fitting stock market data into Gaussian or any other distribution? Well, *fitting* says that the distribution with a correct parameter set can generate the data with the best quality. Here, *quality* refers to the *best probable* data, as *probability* means the chance of the existence of that data in the real world. *Data with a low probability are less likely to be real* – this statement is almost treated like an axiom

CHAPTER 3   PROBABILITY

while modeling. So, intuitively, we should seek for the distribution that can maximize the chance, i.e., the probability of the data. Figure 3-6 shows a set of Gaussian distributions with various parameter sets. Given an input *x*, which one would you choose? Obviously, the one that gives the maximum probability would be the perfect choice. But, in this case, you know the parameters, enabling you to compute likelihood and choose the right distribution. But what if you don't know the parameters? Then it would be best if you think of it like an optimization (maximization rather) problem, and mathematically, this should be done w.r.t the parameters given the dataset, i.e., all of *x* as vectors. There are two schools of methods to do this parameter estimation – *frequentist and Bayesian* – discussed next.

Frequentist Method

In *frequentist* methods, we have a few assumptions: data sufficiency to give us almost correct estimates of the parameters; samples result from a random experiment performed in ideal conditions, i.e., they are independent and identically distributed (i.i.d.). Based on these, we try formulating some criteria, a.k.a. risk function. One example is $E(\hat{\theta} - \theta)^2$, where $\hat{\theta}$ is the estimator and function is known as *MSE (mean squared error)*. This MSE is computed in many trials of random experiments, and the number of trials should be infinite under pure theoretical settings. The frequentist assumption is that we build our knowledge about the parameters from the ground stage, and the experiment results are considered as truth values, i.e., the realizations of the random variables. There is no scope for incorporating your idea or knowledge in determining the parameter values. Observations should be sufficient to guide us there. For example, if we want to model *Pfizer* stocks based on the observations from 2020 to 2021, as shown in Figure 2-2, you must assume that this should be enough to capture the *whole world* of *Pfizer* stocks. As said earlier, the frequentist idea follows the classical definition of probability, i.e., the frequency ratio is computed as a limiting value resulting from many trials. It is also known as the *objective view of probability,* where the definition strictly follows some conditions. In the next section, we discuss two methods that adhere to frequentism philosophy.

Maximum Likelihood Estimation (MLE)

Suppose X is the random variable, and we have realized many values of X as a dataset x_1, $x_2, \ldots, x_n$ with PDF $f(x;\theta)$ in multiple trials. With this setting, the likelihood of observing x_i in the ith trial is given by $f(x_i;\theta)$. This is a theoretical understanding without knowing the correct value for θ. To proceed further, we define the *likelihood function* as the compound likelihoods of all realizations like below:

$$L(\theta;\boldsymbol{x}) = \prod_{i=1}^{n} p(x_i|\theta)$$
$$= \prod_{i=1}^{n} f(x_i;\theta)$$

There is a fundamental difference between likelihood function and density function $f(x;\theta)$ – density function is expressed as function of random variable considering parameter θ as fixed whereas likelihood function is just the opposite of it. After defining the likelihood function, we must maximize it w.r.t θ, and the resulting $\hat{\theta}$ is our target parameter value. Mathematically,

$$\hat{\theta} = armax\{L(\theta;x)\}$$

In practice, we work with the logarithm of the function, known as log-likelihood, to have better asymptotic behavior. The likelihood, being a value between 0 and 1, causes a decimal point underflow problem when multiplied, affecting the overall optimization solution. Natural logarithm helps to overcome that limitation. Logarithm version of $L(\theta;\boldsymbol{x})$ can be rewritten as

$$LL(\theta;\boldsymbol{x}) = \log L(\theta;\boldsymbol{x})$$
$$= \log \prod_{i=1}^{n} f(x_i;\theta)$$
$$= \sum_{i=1}^{n} \log f(x_i;\theta)$$

So, the expression became a summation of log values instead of the product of likelihoods, making it much easier to handle. In the same way, optimal $\hat{\theta}$ will be

$$\hat{\theta} = armax\{LL(\theta;x)\}$$

Let's study this now for two well-known densities.

Log-Likelihood Function of Exponential and Gaussian Distribution

Putting exponential density function in $L(\theta;x)$, we get

$$LL_{Exponential}(\lambda;x) = \sum_{i=1}^{n} \log(\lambda e^{-\lambda x_i})$$

$$= n\log \lambda - \lambda \sum_{i=1}^{n} x_i$$

And, similarly for Gaussian density,

$$LL_{Gaussian}(\mu, \sigma^2;x) = \sum_{i=1}^{n} \log\left[\frac{1}{\sigma\sqrt{2\pi}} e^{-\frac{1}{2}\left(\frac{x_i-\mu}{\sigma}\right)^2}\right]$$

$$= -n\log(\sigma\sqrt{2\pi}) - \frac{1}{2}\sum_{i=1}^{n}\left(\frac{x_i-\mu}{\sigma}\right)^2$$

To study the behavior of the log-likelihood function, we should simulate a series of parameter values with a fixed set of observations and feed that into the $LL(\theta;x)$. For now, we don't explicitly seek for optimization of the $LL(\theta;x)$, rather we want to explore its pattern and, in the process, would like to observe optimal θ visually. I propose a template in Python to do log-likelihood function analysis with the support of parameter simulation. This template can also be used later to optimize the $LL(\theta;x)$ for any special density function.

Let's begin with an abstract class *LogLikelihoodFunctionAnalysis* as given in Listing 3-6. This class expects you to provide arrays of sample parameters as needed for the specific density function.

Listing 3-6. Template base class for log-likelihood analysis

```python
from abc import ABC, abstractmethod
from typing import TypedDict, List, Dict

class LogLikelihoodFunctionAnalysis(ABC):
    """
    Base class for Loglikelihood function for any continuous probability
    distribution. This should be extended, and _compute_likelihood function
    should be overridden to have any density-specific behaviour.

    This class provides a study of the log-likelihood function with
    appropriate visualization.
    """
    __instance_key = object()

    class Dataset(TypedDict):
        """
        This specially typed dictionary works as a key-valued dataset.
        'source' is the name of the data source, and 'x' is the
        data array.
        """
        source: str
        x: List

    def __init__(self, instance_key,
                 θ_sets: Dict[str, List],
                 datasets: List[Dataset]):
        assert (
            instance_key == LogLikelihoodFunctionAnalysis.__instance_key
        ), "LogLikelihoodFunctionAnalysis cannot be instantiated explicitly from outside. Always use the instantiate function"

        self._θ_sets = θ_sets
        self._datasets = datasets
```

CHAPTER 3 PROBABILITY

```python
        self._total_loglikelihood = self._compute_total_loglikelihood()
        self._max_loglikelihood_details = self._get_max_loglikelihoods()

    @abstractmethod
    def _compute_likelihood(self, x, **θ):
        """
        The sub-class should override this function. It should return the
        likelihood of x. You may use the readily available likelihood
        function or implement any custom one.
        """

    ...

    @classmethod
    def for_parameters_and_datasets(
        cls, θ_sets: Dict[str, List], datasets: List[Dataset]
    ):
        """
        Factory function to create a new instance of
        LogLikelihoodFunctionAnalysis
        """
        return cls(LogLikelihoodFunctionAnalysis.__instance_key, θ_sets,
        datasets)
```

Now, let's see how to generate parameter combinations. Suppose you have two parameters α and β for a distribution with their domains defined as $-\infty < \alpha < \infty$ and $\beta > 0$. Their sample values are given as two arrays: [-4, 100, 8, -45,70] and [9, 5, 14, 2]. There should be 16 (4 × 4) possible combinations of values as given by (-4,9), (-4, 5), (100,9), (100,14), (-45, 2), (70, 14), and so on. For each of these tuples, corresponding likelihoods can be computed easily. Note that none of the tuples should permute values within itself as that will cause a violation of domain restrictions for some parameters. This algorithm is implemented in *_prepare_combibnations_for_θ* function under the class *LogLikelihoodFunctionAnalysis* as shown in Listing 3-7.

Listing 3-7. Function to prepare combinations of parameters for the specific density

```python
import numpy as np

def _prepare_combibnations_for_θ(self) -> Dict[str, List]:
    """
    Prepare combinations of parameters from the list of supplied
    simulated values.
    For example, in a two-parameter setting, if the supplied values are
    [3,5,10] and
    [-6,8,190] respectively, then the few combinations are (3,-6),
    (3,190),(5,8),
    (5,-6) and so on.

    The function returns combinations as a dictionary of values, keeping
    the positional indices intact.
    """
    θ_grid = None
    θ_name_grid_index = {}
    for i, (θ_name, θ_val) in enumerate(self._θ_sets.items()):
        if i == 0:
            θ_grid = np.meshgrid(θ_val)
        else:
            θ_grid = np.meshgrid(θ_grid, θ_val)

        θ_name_grid_index[θ_name] = i

    return {
        θ_name: θ_grid[θ_index].flatten()
        for θ_name, θ_index in θ_name_grid_index.items()
    }
```

The actual work of computing the likelihoods for all data sources is done in Listing 3-8. It leverages parameter combinations generated by Listing 3-7.

CHAPTER 3 PROBABILITY

Listing 3-8. Function to compute total log-likelihood for each of the data sources

```python
def _compute_total_loglikelihood(self):
    """
    Computes total log-likelihood for each of the data sources in
    self._datasets.
    It uses combinations of parameters as returned by _prepare_
    combibnations_for_θ and feeds each of those into the likelihood
    function to create parameter likelihood tuples.
    """
    total_llh = {}

    def _get_single_name_value_for_θ(index, θ_combs):
        return {
            θ_combs_k: θ_combs_v[index] for θ_combs_k, θ_combs_v in
            θ_combs.items()
        }

    θ_combs = self._prepare_combibnations_for_θ()
    num_θ_values = len(list(θ_combs.values())[0])

    # Create dictionaries of tuples of format (θ, likelihood) for
    each dataset
    for ds in self._datasets:
        llh = [
            (
                _get_single_name_value_for_θ(i, θ_combs),
                self.get_loglikelihood_for_observations(
                    ds["x"], **_get_single_name_value_for_θ(i, θ_combs)
                ),
            )
            for i in range(num_θ_values)
        ]
        total_llh[ds["source"]] = llh

    return total_llh
```

We talked about the optimization of the log-likelihood function. Listing 3-9 shows the function that should be the target of the optimization algorithm.

Listing 3-9. Function to compute log-likelihood for parameters and observations

```
def get_loglikelihood_for_observations(self, x, **θ):
    """
    Gets total log-likelihood for a given observation.
    This function can be used for parameter optimization by external
    components.
    """
    return np.sum(np.log(self._compute_likelihood(x, **θ)))
```

While designing diffusion models for the *stock price* in Chapter 6, we will see how to optimize this function. However, for now, we have a function (as shown in Listing 3-10) that finds the maximum by iterating over the list of computed log-likelihood values for the given set of parameters, and this is the *maximum likelihood estimate (MLE)* found by exploration. Doing it this way helps to understand the log-likelihood curve and its asymptotic properties through visual inspection.

Listing 3-10. Function to compute maximum of the log-likelihood

```
def _get_max_loglikelihoods(self):
    """
    It iterates over all log-likelihoods and returns the maximum for
    each data source.
    """

    return {
        k: max(v, key=lambda t: t[1]) for k, v in self._total_
        loglikelihood.items()
    }
```

After all this heavy lifting by the base components, Listing 3-11 shows how to use that for exponential distribution. Notice the use of the *scipy* module of Python. You could have also implemented exponential distribution by directly using the formula. It is one of the advantages of this design template – it allows you to onboard your custom-made density function.

Listing 3-11. Class for log-likelihood analysis of exponential distribution

```python
from scipy.stats import expon

class ExponentialLogLikelihoodFunctionAnalysis(LogLikelihoodFunction
Analysis):
    """
    Class for studying the likelihood function of Exponential
    distribution with parameter λ.
    """

    def _compute_likelihood(self, x, λ):
        return expon.pdf(x, loc=0, scale=1 / λ)
```

Now, let's see how it works.

Listing 3-12. Testing exponential likelihood analysis

```python
def test_exponential_likelihood_func_analysis():
    datasets = [
        {
            "source": "Dataset 1",
            "x": np.linspace(start=200, stop=300, num=1000),
        },
        {
            "source": "Dataset 2",
            "x": np.linspace(start=2, stop=8, num=1000),
        },
    ]
    θ_sets = {"λ": np.linspace(start=0, stop=3, num=500)}

    ExponentialLogLikelihoodFunctionAnalysis.for_parameters_and_datasets(
        θ_sets=θ_sets, datasets=datasets).plot()
```

The function *plot* is defined under *LogLikelihoodFunctionAnalysis* only (you will find it in *chapter3/estimation.py*), which has the nitty-gritty details of generating the visualization for the log-likelihood function. Anyway, Listing 3-12 (you will find it in *chapter3/test/test_estimation.py*) produces the output shown in Figure 3-9.

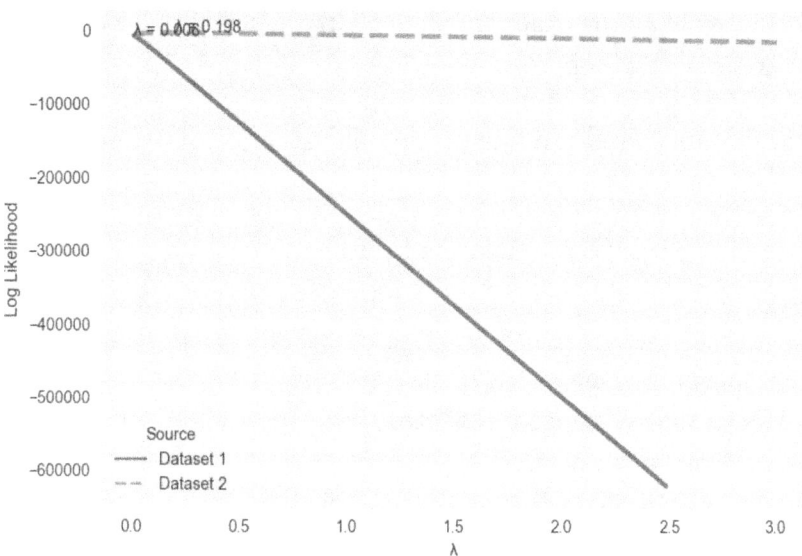

Figure 3-9. *Log-likelihood function of exponential distribution for two sets of observations*

Observe the two data points with maximum log-likelihood values at λ=0.006 and λ = 0.198, respectively. Are they the real MLE estimates? Well, they may not be, as the likelihoods are computed only with a limited set of provided parameter values. Those points did not exactly come from the output of any optimization algorithm, but still, they provide some idea about the function and its asymptotic behavior.

Let's now turn to the Gaussian log-likelihood function. It is a function of two parameters: μ and σ^2. Listing 3-13 shows the class that extends from *LogLikelihoodFunctionAnalysis* like in Listing 3-11. Notice the usage of the multiparameter function *_compute_likelihood*.

Listing 3-13. Class for log-likelihood analysis of Gaussian distribution

```
from scipy.stats import norm

class GaussianLogLikelihoodFunctionAnalysis(LogLikelihoodFunctionAnalysis):
    """
    Class for studying the likelihood function of Gaussian distribution
    with parameters μ & σ2.
    """

    def _compute_likelihood(self, x, μ, σ2):
        return norm.pdf(x, loc=μ, scale=np.sqrt(σ2))
```

Unlike what we did for the exponential function, we now test this component with the ADP and Apple stock's data.

Listing 3-14. Testing Gaussian likelihood analysis with ADP and Apple stock's data

```
def test_gaussian_likelihood_func_analysis():
    datasets = [
        {
            "source": "Apple Inc",
            "x": YahooFinancialsAdapter(
                ticker="AAPL",
                training_set_date_range=("2021-02-01", "2021-04-30"),
            ).training_set["stock price"],
        },
        {
            "source": "ADP",
            "x": YahooFinancialsAdapter(
                ticker="ADP",
                training_set_date_range=("2021-02-01", "2021-04-30"),
            ).training_set["stock price"],
        },
    ]
    θ_sets = {
        "μ": np.linspace(start=100.0, stop=200, num=10),
        "σ2": np.linspace(start=100.0, stop=400, num=10),
    }
    GaussianLogLikelihoodFunctionAnalysis.for_parameters_and_datasets(
        θ_sets=θ_sets, datasets=datasets
    ).plot(θ_names=["μ", "σ2"])
```

Note that the *plot* function takes parameter names as input for plotting the graph, which is optional if the distribution is of a single parameter. We pass all parameter names for Gaussian distribution as shown in Listing 3-14. Currently, the function only supports 2D and 3D plots, as visualizing likelihood relationships with more than two parameters is difficult. It will show the behavior of the likelihood function w.r.t the only supplied parameters in case there are more than two. Listing 3-14 produces log-likelihood function surfaces, as shown in Figure 3-10 for two datasets.

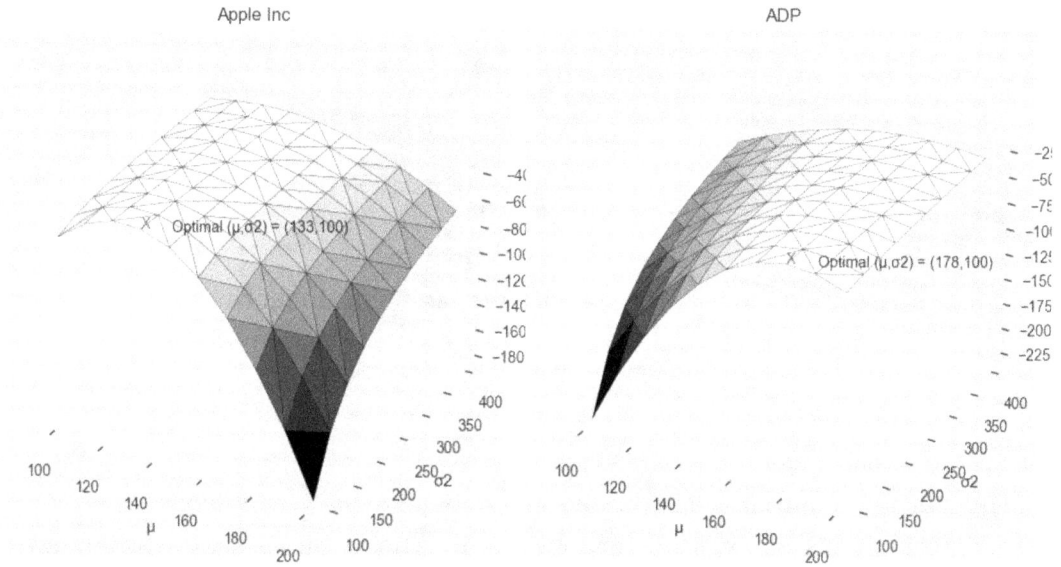

Figure 3-10. *Log-likelihood function surfaces of Gaussian distribution for Apple and ADP stock's data*

Method of Moments

Maximum likelihood estimation requires full distribution knowledge and is a greedy parameter estimation approach. When the underlying data only partially follow the assumed distribution, computing likelihoods on the total dataset often lead to erroneous results. As an alternative, the *method of moments* takes a much softer approach where we don't try matching the entire dataset with the distribution. As moments exhibit certain distribution characteristics and show where the *mass* is concentrated, just like a set of junction points, this property is leveraged in this method, i.e., we match moments instead of the total likelihoods. As we know, moments are expressed as functions of distribution parameters; much like the Likelihood function, population moments can be computed in closed form, and these can be used to construct a special set of equations known as *moment conditions*. These equations match population moment expressions with the numerically computed sample moments, and their solution is our desired result, i.e., estimated values of the distribution parameters.

CHAPTER 3 PROBABILITY

To be more precise, consider a distribution f with p parameters defined by parameter vector θ, which must be estimated from n observations of random variable X given by $x_1, x_2, ..., x_n$. If expressions of k population moments $\mu_1(\theta), \mu_2(\theta), ..., \mu_k(\theta)$ are approximated by numerically computed sample moments $m_1, m_2, ..., m_k$, then we get k equations:

$$\mu_1(\theta) = m_1$$
$$\mu_2(\theta) = m_2$$
$$...$$
$$\mu_k(\theta) = m_k$$

Or these can be written in more compact form as direct functions:

$$M_i(\theta) = 0, \quad 1 \leq i \leq k$$

where $M_i(\theta) = \mu_i(\theta) - m_i$.

Functions $M_i(\theta)$ are known as the abovementioned *moment conditions*. While computing moments, *raw moments* are obvious first choice, but for some distributions, if convenient expressions are found for other moments, then we consider that as alternatives.

Let's discuss an example from the gamma distribution whose density is given by

$$f_{Gamma}(x; \alpha, \beta) = \frac{x^{\alpha-1} e^{-\beta x} \beta^{\alpha}}{\Gamma(\alpha)}$$

Observe that $\theta = \{\alpha, \beta\}$. It can be shown that this distribution, any kth-order population moment is given by

$$\mu_k(\alpha, \beta) = E(X^k)$$
$$= \frac{1}{\beta^k} \prod_i^n (\alpha + i - 1)$$

From there, first two moments can be easily obtained as

$$\mu_1(\alpha, \beta) = \frac{\alpha}{\beta}$$
$$\mu_2(\alpha, \beta) = \frac{\alpha(\alpha+1)}{\beta^2}$$

As discussed earlier, first two raw sample moments can be computed numerically from the observations $(x_1, x_2, ..., x_n)$:

$$m_1 = E(X)$$

$$= \sum_{i=1}^{n} x_i$$

$$m_2 = E(X^2)$$

$$= \sum_{i=1}^{n} x_i^2$$

Equating raw sample moments with population moments, we get following system of equations:

$$\frac{\alpha}{\beta} - m_1 = 0$$

$$\frac{\alpha(\alpha+1)}{\beta^2} - m_2 = 0$$

Observe that there are two unknowns α and β and two equations. So, by linear algebra, we can have one unique solution for α and β that defines the gamma density function for the observations $(x_1, x_2, ..., x_n)$. Similar to MLE, solutions from *method of moments* are specific to the observations, i.e., the dataset. Changing $(x_1, x_2, ..., x_n)$ will also change the estimates.

Naturally, there will be a question on the number of moment conditions. How many of them are sufficient? We have to decide it intuitively. From linear algebra, we know that to solve for p unknowns, we need at least p equations, and the same goes for moment conditions, i.e., at least p moment conditions are required to estimate the parameter vector of size p for any distribution. When we say we have expressions for kth-order moment, then k should be the same as p, and the parameter vector $\boldsymbol{\theta}$ is *exactly identified*. But what happens if $k > p$ or $k < p$? First case occurs when we consider more than sufficient moment conditions. For example, to estimate four parameters, if we take seven moment conditions, then the parameter vector $\boldsymbol{\theta}$ is *overidentified*, and we get multiple solutions for the system of equations. There is no solution for $k < p$, which is out of scope of discussion. *Overidentification* is a common problem as almost all probability densities have generic moment expressions that are valid for any order k. Restricting k to be equal

CHAPTER 3 PROBABILITY

to *p* leads to loss of potential information about the distribution. Also, basic assumptions about equating sample and population moments may not be fully valid causing wrong estimation. As a workaround, a more generic approach known as the *generalized method of moments (GMM)* is proposed, where a weighted linear combination of moment conditions is taken, and the sum of those is minimized to find a good estimate for θ. Discussing GMM is out of the scope of this book, and interested readers can refer to [2].

As moments indicate the concentration of probability mass/densities, this phenomenon can be leveraged to model financial instruments. In Chapter 7, we will study how moments can help detect jumps in financial asset prices. Basically, moments of different orders reveal different statistical properties of the asset price over time, especially if that has high or low values. Once the parameters are computed through moment matching, these can be leveraged to generate asset paths, thus helping to forecast.

Bayesian Method

Before discussing the Bayesian approach, we need to know some details of different types of uncertainties tackled by the probability distribution or even by a model based on some distribution. The uncertainty handled by the frequentist method is known as **aleatoric uncertainty**, which is inherent in the data. As we know, the purpose of modeling any financial asset price is to capture the influence of unknown factors that can help forecast its future behavior, so we try reducing aleatoric uncertainty originating from the realizations of random variables, i.e., the observations. In short, it happens due to the random nature of the system under study, and that's why probability theory is introduced. Basically, that system's behavior is captured via a probability distribution as we cannot decide its state in a full deterministic mechanism. The frequentist view of probability gives us the relative frequency of events in long-run repeated trials of some random experiment. For example, after observing a handful of Apple stock price records, we can conclude something about it. You may consider that these observations result from repeated trials of a random experiment named "Capture Apple Stock prices." As said in the "Frequentist Method" section, we start computing probabilities from ground zero without any initial knowledge of the system, and for that, we need enough observations, i.e., the dataset for modeling. But what if we encounter three situations like below:

a) We don't have enough observations.

b) The observations do not reflect the true system, i.e., frequencies computed are not fully correct as they do not capture the full behavior of the system.

c) We have initial ideas about the system and want to incorporate our knowledge while computing the distribution.

Situations (a) and (b) are somewhat closely related, with a small difference. Situation (a) occurs due to a lack of data which can be explained from the definition of probability. Recall that the probability is expressed as the limiting ratio of two, and the denominator should have a limiting value to infinity, i.e., theoretically, the random experiment should be repeated an infinite number of times, resulting large number of observations. One reason for occurring situation (b) is the situation (a) itself. Due to situation (a), computed frequencies are not fully error free. So, in short, for both situations (a) and (b), we cannot quantify some uncertainties that are not in our hands. This is known as ***epistemic uncertainty***, representing a lack of knowledge about the system. Situation (b) is also caused by a wrong choice of distribution while modeling the data, which is the difference with situation (a).

Let's take a small example – you have stock price observations for some fictitious company A, and with that, you are trying to fit Gaussian distribution. But you are not fully satisfied with the readings as you know that this company's stocks should be valued, on average, close to $50. This comes from your experience of dealing with that company's stocks. How do you augment the to-be-fitted Gaussian distribution with your knowledge? That's what situation (c) says. Financial analysts and data scientists sometimes enrich the model with their domain knowledge to fill the gap when they face data shortage, and that's how situations (a), (b), and (c) are related. An alternative definition of probability is needed to incorporate this domain knowledge, and here comes the Bayesian view of probability and Bayes theorem. This idea is based on any individual's initial belief about any system, which is nothing but the earlier-mentioned *domain knowledge*. This belief is fully subjective in nature and will be different from another individual's assessment of the system, and it impacts the computation of the likelihood of events. For example, if you and your friends' beliefs about company A's average stock price are $50 and $75, then the corresponding computed likelihoods of tomorrow's stock price reaching $70 will be different. This is the principle of the Bayesian definition of probability.

CHAPTER 3   PROBABILITY

Bayes' Theorem

Bayes' theorem, named after the eighteenth-century English mathematician *Thomas Bayes (1702-1761)*, talks about creating an alternative definition of probability by linking a distribution of a random variable with its conditional distribution. We denote our belief before observing the data as event A and the observing data as event B. With this setting, The Bayes' theorem updates the belief with this:

$$P(A|B) = \frac{P(B|A)P(A)}{P(B)}$$
$$= \frac{P(B|A)P(A)}{\sum_A P(B|A)P(A)}$$

There is a particular nomenclature for all the probabilities you can see in the above expression as described next:

    $P(A)$: Prior probability or the initial belief

    $P(A)$: Conditional probability, a.k.a. likelihood

    $P(B)$: Marginal probability of B over A

    $P(B)$: Posterior probability or the updated belief

In practice, all these probabilities are considered distributions, and we can use appropriate density functions to compute. With that in place, B represents the parameter of the distribution. So, a better representation of Bayes' theorem is

$$g(\theta|x) = \frac{f(\theta|x)\pi(\theta)}{f(x)}$$
$$= \frac{f(\theta|x)\pi(\theta)}{\int f(x|\theta)\pi(\theta)d\theta}$$

where $\pi(\theta)$ is the prior distribution of parameter θ; $f(\theta)$ is the likelihood of observed x given θ, a.k.a. conditional distribution of x; and $g(x)$ is the posterior distribution of parameter θ.

Denominator $f(x)$ is the total likelihood and a constant. It is known as a *normalizing constant*. We can ignore $f(x)$ while comparing posterior probability distribution by leveraging the following property:

$$g(\theta|x) \propto f(x|\theta)\pi(\theta)$$

We will see this later while determining the posterior of Gaussian distribution parameters with the Gaussian prior.

Note that the biggest difference between Bayesian and frequentist methods is how the parameters are treated – *for the frequentist method, parameter is a constant, but for Bayesian, it is a distribution, i.e., the parameter itself is a random variable*. The likelihood is written as $f(x|\theta)$ for the Bayesian method, which is a conditional distribution, whereas for frequentist, we wrote it as complete function $f(x;\theta)$ because of θ being constant. This sounds interesting because you are estimating the parameter of a probability distribution, which in turn follows another probability distribution. That's how the Bayesian method can quantify the epistemic uncertainty. In any case, the parameter is the captured knowledge about the observations, so adding an initial belief is possible through parameters, and this validates having the prior distribution.

For frequentist methods (*MLE* or *methods of moments*), parameter optimization happens either through a separate algorithm that optimizes a target function or solving a system of equations, and in both, we need a complete view of the observations that make the solution eager in nature. But for Bayesian, this happens through mutual handshaking between prior and posterior distribution and is sequential in nature. This is helpful for situations where we don't get the observations at a time, i.e., the full view isn't available. For example, suppose you want to model the *Apple* stock prices with some distribution, and the observations are coming as streaming data. So, you are getting everything together; hence, the Bayesian approach can help you. You should start off with a prior and keep updating beliefs with posteriors as and when new data comes through the stream. Note that you keep computing the likelihood of newly available data through, as shown in the expression of $g(\theta|x)$. So, the entire method can be summarized as an algorithm, like below:

> **BAYESIAN BELIEF UPDATE ALGORITHM**
>
> 1. Initialize belief with a prior distribution having a set of parameters.
> 2. Compute likelihood and posterior distribution.
> 3. Set posterior distribution as the prior distribution.
> 4. Go to Step 1 when no more observation is available or prior and posterior distribution converges; otherwise, end.

Once the algorithm ends, we are left with a final posterior distribution of parameters. Now, the question is how to leverage it. We haven't covered it yet; we need to know how to draw samples from a probability distribution to do that. You will learn this in the next chapter. But, for now, assume that if, somehow, we can draw samples from a posterior distribution (it's nothing but a set of different values of the random variable), we get a set of possible parameter values, and with that, the likelihood from the target probability distribution can be computed, just like we do same with MLE or method of moments after getting the estimates.

Parameter Estimation of Gaussian Distribution with Gaussian Prior

In Bayesian view, we start our analysis of Gaussian distribution parameters – μ and σ. As both parameters are continuous in nature, choice of prior distribution should be from the family of density functions and not from mass functions. This is true not only for Gaussian but for choosing prior for any distribution parameters. So, we can choose from any of the exponential related family – *beta, gamma, exponential,* and *Gaussian* itself. For now, we choose Gaussian to proceed further, and it forms a Gaussian-Gaussian conjugate prior.

> **CONJUGATE PRIOR AND FAMILY**
>
> If prior $\pi(\theta)$ and posterior $g(\theta|x)$ belong to the same family of distributions, then they are known as *conjugate prior. Family* refers to the collection of distributions having similar mathematical forms.

Though there are two parameters in μ and σ, for the current example, we consider σ to be 1 (or any other constant) and find the correct posterior estimate for μ. In notational form,

$$X \sim Gaussian(\mu, \sigma^2)$$

And the prior for μ,

$$\mu \sim Gaussian(\alpha, \beta^2)$$

We will use real stock price observations of *Apple Inc.* as we did for likelihood function plots. Before that, let's see how we can find a suitable expression for the posterior distribution of μ in closed form. Putting appropriate terms for $f(x|\theta)$, $\pi(\theta)$, and θ, we can compute the following for a single data observation x_1:

$$f(x_1|\theta)\pi(\theta) = \frac{1}{\sqrt{2\pi}}e^{-\frac{1}{2}\left(\frac{x_1-\mu}{\sigma}\right)^2} \times \frac{1}{\beta\sqrt{2\pi}}e^{-\frac{1}{2}\left(\frac{\mu-\alpha}{\beta}\right)^2}$$

$$= e^{-\frac{1}{2}\left[\left(\frac{x_1-\mu}{\sigma}\right)^2 + \left(\frac{\mu-\alpha}{\beta}\right)^2\right]}$$

Now, after expanding and rearranging exponent term and then completing the square, we get

$$-\frac{1}{2}\left[\left(\frac{x_1-\mu}{\sigma}\right)^2 + \left(\frac{\mu-\alpha}{\beta}\right)^2\right] = -\frac{\mu^2}{2}\left(\frac{1}{\sigma^2}+\frac{1}{\beta^2}\right) + \mu\left(\frac{x_1}{\sigma^2}+\frac{\alpha}{\beta^2}\right)$$

$$= -\frac{1}{2\frac{\beta^2\sigma^2}{\beta^2+\sigma^2}}\left[\mu - \frac{\beta^2\sigma^2}{\beta^2+\sigma^2}\left(\frac{x_1}{\sigma^2}+\frac{\alpha}{\beta^2}\right)\right]^2$$

We can rewrite the posterior distribution as

$$f(x_1|\theta)\pi(\theta) \propto e^{-\frac{1}{2\frac{\beta^2\sigma^2}{\beta^2+\sigma^2}}\left[\mu - \frac{\beta^2\sigma^2}{\beta^2+\sigma^2}\left(\frac{x_1}{\sigma^2}+\frac{\alpha}{\beta^2}\right)\right]^2}$$

Expression of the posterior distribution is proportional to the Gaussian kernel, and hence, we can conclude that it follows a Gaussian distribution like the below:

$$f(x_1|\theta)\pi(\theta) \sim Gaussian\left(\frac{\beta^2\sigma^2}{\beta^2+\sigma^2}\left(\frac{x_1}{\sigma^2}+\frac{\alpha}{\beta^2}\right), \frac{\beta^2\sigma^2}{\beta^2+\sigma^2}\right)$$

It is an example of *Gaussian-Gaussian conjugate prior,* which says that prior and posterior both follow Gaussian distribution with different parameters. The above expression results from observing the first data point x_1, and as per the *Bayesian belief update algorithm,* this posterior will become prior when we observe x_2, i.e., the second data point, and the process continues until we exhaust all data points. Basically, this idea of prior and posterior distribution of the Bayesian framework is fully relative in nature as they keep changing positions – what is prior now will be posterior in the next iteration.

After all these theories, it's time to do some hands-on. Let's have a look at the stock prices of Apple Inc. from *January 1, 2021, to June 30, 2022* (Figure 3-11).

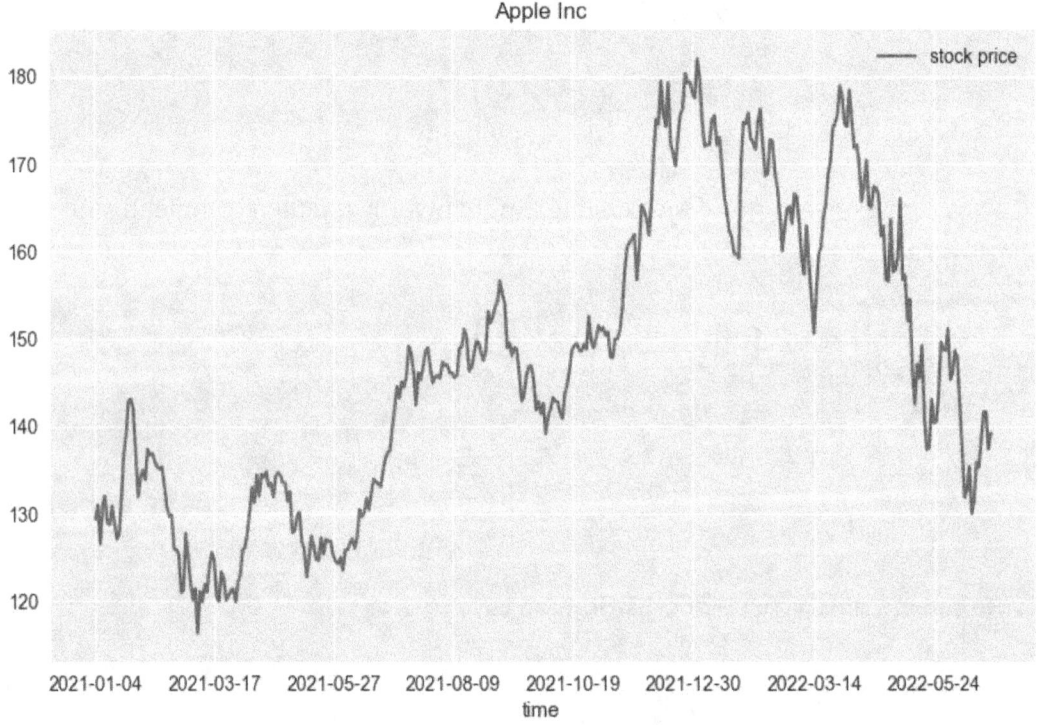

Figure 3-11. *Apple Inc. stock prices for the period January 1, 2021, to June 30, 2022*

Assume these data aren't available to us at a time and come as a stream. We will have different prior views of the Apple stock price and use them for modeling the distribution. Set these views at 110, 146, 150, and 160, respectively. These are the prior means of the distributions. As explained earlier, these priors are our beliefs about the Apple stock price. Though we haven't seen the whole dataset, we keep the idea that the average *Apple* stock price could be from any of the four values. Going through the belief update algorithm, we validate this and develop posterior distributions. In the entire process, we assume the following:

i) The variance of the price distribution is known to us, and we set this as 100.

ii) We are only interested in estimating the mean μ of the stock price distribution; hence, priors are only set on this parameter.

Listing 3-15 shows the Python function to do all of these.

Listing 3-15. Iterative Bayesian belief update algorithm on Apple stocks data

```
from scipy.stats import norm, expon
import numpy as np

def iterative_gaussian_gaussian_bayesian_estimation_with_prior(x,
                                                                prior_α=None,
                                                                prior_β_2=None,
                                                                σ2=None):
    '''
        Bayesian belief update algorithm for Gaussian-Gaussian settings.
    '''
    posterior_α = 0.0
    posterior_β_2 = 0.0

    temp_prior_α = prior_α
    temp_prior_β_2 = prior_β_2

    # Iteratively compute posteriors in closed form for the
    Gaussian-Gaussian
    # settings assuming x is a streaming dataset.
```

```python
    for x_i in x:
        posterior_β_2 = (temp_prior_β_2 * σ2) / (
            temp_prior_β_2 + σ2
        )

        posterior_α = posterior_β_2 * (
            (x_i / σ2) + (temp_prior_α / temp_prior_β_2)
        )

        # Update priors with computed posteriors for the next iteration
        temp_prior_β_2 = posterior_β_2
        temp_prior_α = posterior_α

    # Draw samples from prior & posteror distrubutions
    prior_μ_rvs = norm.rvs(loc=prior_α, scale=np.sqrt(prior_β_2),
    size=1000)
    posterior_μ_rvs = norm.rvs(
        loc=posterior_α, scale=np.sqrt(posterior_β_2), size=1000
    )

    # Compute all sample likelihoods from prior & posterior distributions
    # for visualization
    prob_x = {
        "Prior μ": (
            prior_μ_rvs,
            norm.pdf(prior_μ_rvs, loc=prior_α, scale=np.sqrt(prior_β_2)),
        ),
        "Posterior μ": (
            posterior_μ_rvs,
            norm.pdf(
                posterior_μ_rvs,
                loc=posterior_α,
                scale=np.sqrt(posterior_β_2),
            ),
        ),
    }

    return prob_x, prior_α, posterior_α
```

CHAPTER 3 PROBABILITY

Listing 3-15 is the core algorithm for the *Gaussian-Gaussian* conjugate prior settings and is very specific to Gaussian distribution. For any other prior distribution, analytical expressions will change for obvious reasons. That's why I didn't propose any generic design template here, unlike other topics. The function in Listing 3-15 is tested with the Apple stocks data in Listing 3-16.

Listing 3-16. Testing Bayesian estimation with four different parameter settings

```python
import chapter3.visualization as vs3

def test_iterative_bayesian_estimation():
    # Observations for Bayesian parameter estimation
    yf_adapter = YahooFinancialsAdapter(
        ticker="AAPL",
        training_set_date_range=("2021-01-01", "2022-06-30"),
    )
    x = yf_adapter.training_set['stock price']

    σ2 = 100 # Asssume σ2 is constant and known to us, so no prior distribution is set on this

    # Compute posterior distributions for a collection of four prior parameter settings (for μ)
    prob_x_arr = [
        iterative_gaussian_gaussian_bayesian_estimation_with_prior(x=x,
                                                prior_α=110,
                                                prior_β_2=5,
                                                σ2=σ2),
        iterative_gaussian_gaussian_bayesian_estimation_with_prior(x=x,
                                                prior_α=146,
                                                prior_β_2=2,
                                                σ2=σ2),
        iterative_gaussian_gaussian_bayesian_estimation_with_prior(x=x,
                                                prior_α=150,
                                                prior_β_2=20,
                                                σ2=σ2),
        iterative_gaussian_gaussian_bayesian_estimation_with_prior(x=x,
                                                prior_α=160,
```

CHAPTER 3 PROBABILITY

```
                                                    prior_β_2=0.5,
                                                    σ2=σ2),
    ]
    vs3.bayesian_estimation_plot(prob_x_arr)
```

Figure 3-12 shows the output obtained after executing Listing 3-16.

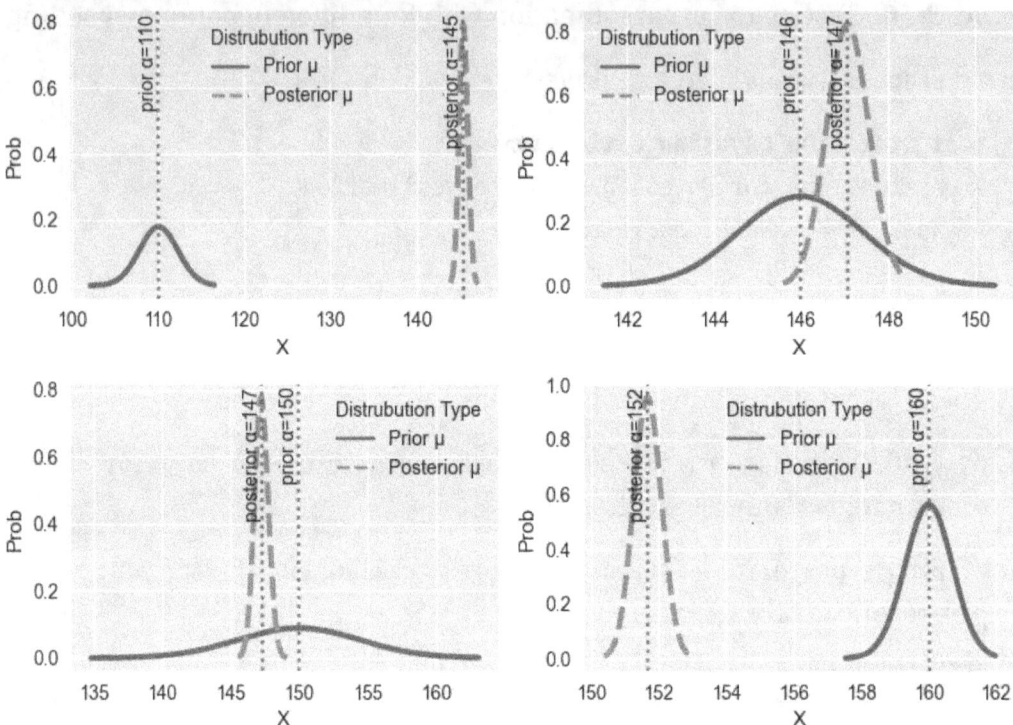

Figure 3-12. *Prior and posterior distributions for four different prior mean as set for Apple stocks data*

I hope you have noticed the behavior of posterior variance – it is always less than the prior variance. We may consider variance as the accuracy of our knowledge. Once we finish each iteration of the Bayesian belief update algorithm, our understanding becomes more accurate, which results in a reduced variance each time and makes the posterior Gaussian distribution narrower and sharper in shape (distributions are plotted by drawing samples from there). No matter how large our prior variance is, posterior estimates automatically adjust the error in the belief and give a better result. The third plot in Figure 3-12 is such an example.

Summary

This chapter reviews the most critical prerequisite to *Stochastic Finance* – the probability theory. Nobody can grasp the tools and ideas needed to model financial securities without a strong foundation in this. It covers mainly the distribution-specific views of probability theory with a hands-on introduction to a few standard distributions needed for this book. Estimating distribution parameters is essential to building any financial instruments – a comparative study of two methods, frequentist and Bayesian, is discussed with examples written in Python. You can use the Python design template explained there to study any likelihood function.

The next chapter discusses the tool to create paths of financial instruments – Monte Carlo simulation and random variate generation.

CHAPTER 4

Simulation

A collection of entities, components, or elements forms a complex, which we like to term as a *system*. These elements contain specific attributes that are often time dependent and can take numerical or logical values. In fact, for our area of interest, i.e., financial securities are examples of time-dependent nondeterministic systems whose state values are nothing, but the security values themselves. Once a nondeterministic system's probability model is in place, the next obvious stage is to generate outputs from there and explore the full state space if possible. Doing so helps to determine the average response and its variance from the system. This mechanized and virtual exploration of the system without physical involvement is known as *simulation*.

In this chapter, we explore prerequisites and methods to perform simulation while modeling the securities as required later in Part 2 of the book. We mainly touch base on Monte Carlo methods of simulation which is essential for generating paths of stochastic process.

Random Variable Generation

In a typical stochastic simulation, random numbers are induced to bring the desired randomness to the system. From a financial system standpoint, generated random numbers help explore different paths of financial securities over time. You will get more information about path generation in the next chapter while discussing the stochastic process. But for now, let's focus on the theory of random number generation.

Bringing true randomness into any system is a difficult task. Frankly speaking, there is no such universally foolproof way of generating random numbers by some algorithm that almost works like an Oracle. Enforcing artificial randomness is quite an impossible task. Yes, we are talking about probability densities and stochastic processes, and the subject itself is known as Stochastic Finance. However, stochastic behavior is still a natural phenomenon mainly due to a lack of knowledge about any system. Then, how can we create a perfect environment with some amount of knowledge deficiency? Yes, it is difficult, and that's the purpose of stochastic simulation. In practice, we try generating a pseudorandom number that appears random in human eyes and use that to simulate further random numbers. The latter is better known as random variates (random variates are states/instances of random variables). These random variates should be generated from suitable probability distributions. This process is also known as *sampling from the distribution*, and we will be frequently referring to this term in the book.

This is exactly opposite to what we discussed in Chapter 2 while fitting a probability distribution over a dataset. There, we took a *bottom-up* approach to build a model going from the realized values of random variables to finding the best parameter, whereas now, we go toward *top-down*, starting from the model and parameters to full explorations of realized random variables. The first one is the *model (fitting the distribution)*, and the second one is the *inference (sampling from the distribution)*.

Inverse Transform Method

It is based on the principle that generating random variables from any distribution is possible, given that we know how to generate samples from a uniform distribution U[0, 1]. The range between 0 and 1 says that the generated value would be a probability, and with that, we use the inverse of the distribution function (CDF) to get the original samples. We know the relationship:

$$p = F(x)$$

So,

$$x = F^{-1}(p)$$

We can say that F^{-1}, which is just the opposite of a distribution function, treats probability p as a variable and returns a random state. Unlike $F(x)$, we don't feed any explicit value for p in $F^{-1}(p)$. Had it been the other way, the process wouldn't be random. So, we let the *uniform distribution* do that for us. This is interesting as it is sampling p from the uniform distribution *U[0, 1]*, i.e., sampling a probability value from another probability distribution and feeding that into F^{-1}. Doesn't it sound like recursive? How do we sample from uniform distribution? Well, that's what pseudorandom number generators do. Observe that *U[0, 1]* always produces equal probability for the specified range, and those generators leverage this property, i.e., generating uniform and i.i.d. numbers. We cannot directly use them because of equally probable property, which is not useful in modeling financial data. As we will see in the latter chapters, financial securities follow nonuniform distributions, and we need some nonuniform generators to simulate their behaviors. As said earlier, the generation of true random numbers is extremely difficult as we need real physical phenomena to occur. For example, to generate a random number that resembles coin tossing, somebody should perform that act as flawlessly as possible, making the entire process time-consuming and costly. And that's true for any actual physical events to be simulated. Coin tossing is still a very simple example. What about the stock market? Can anybody simulate it physically? Never. Pseudorandom number generators at least try to rescue us from this complexity. They give us a base ground for further simulation. Many algorithms are there to do this – one of them is a *linear congruential generator* (LCG) that uses the following recurrence relation:

$$X_n = (aX_{n-1} + c) \bmod d.$$

Discussing details about these generators is out of the scope of this book. You may refer to *Sheldon Ross [10]* for further study.

Let's pick up the *exponential distribution* function (CDF of exponential distribution) and see its inverse:

$$p = F(x)$$
$$= 1 - e^{-\lambda x}.$$

We can rearrange the same and express *x* as a function of *p*:

$$x = -\frac{\log(1-p)}{\lambda}$$

The right-hand side is the $F^{-1}(p)$ and $p \sim Uniform(0, 1)$. You might have a question in mind about why we use CDF instead of PDF. To explain this in a more formal way, we need to know the *change of measure* or *transformations* discussed next.

CHAPTER 4 SIMULATION

Change of Measure

This is a good place to introduce this widely used method in finance. It is the effect of variable transformations on the probability density function. Suppose X and Y are two random variables related as $y = G(x)$, and then their PDFs are related as

$$p_Y(y) = p_X(x)\left|\frac{dx}{dy}\right|.$$

If $x \sim Uniform(0, 1)$, then $p_X(x) = 1$ making $p_Y(y) = \left|\frac{dx}{dy}\right|$.

Expressing $\left|\frac{dx}{dy}\right|$ in closed form is only possible if, somehow, we can find a function, inverse of G making the derivative evaluation feasible. If such function G^{-1} exists, then

$$x = \int p(y)dy = G^{-1}(y).$$

The integral over the random variable y is nothing but the CDF making G^{-1} the CDF of y. As x follows the uniform distribution over the range 0 to 1, it represents probability returned from CDF, so to get back the original y, we must again perform the inverse of G^{-1}, i.e., the inverse of the CDF. This explains the reason of using CDF instead of PDF for generating the random variable in the inverse method.

Let's implement this in Python as shown in Listing 4-1.

Listing 4-1. Generic function to generate random variable for any CDF

```
from scipy.stats import uniform

def inverse_transform_method_rvs(F_inverse, n_rv=1000):
    """
    Function to generate random variables from any inversely
    transformed density

    F_inverse:  Inverse function of the probability distribution function.
    """
    # Generate random variables from Uniform distribution.
    probs = uniform(0, 1).rvs(size=n_rv)

    return [F_inverse(p) for p in probs]
```

The above function can be leveraged for exponential distribution in the following way:

```
from scipy.stats import expon
from numpy import log

def test_inverse_transform_method_exponen():
    lamda = 2.0

    # Random variables from the original Exponential distribution
    xs = expon.rvs(scale=1 / lamda, size=1000)

    # Inverse of the Exponential distribution function
    F_inverse_exponen = lambda p: -(log(1 - p)) / lamda

    # Generated random variables from the inverse method
    xinvs = inverse_transform_method_rvs(F_inverse=F_inverse_exponen)

    # Compare and plot the densities from two generated random
      variable sets
    vs.plot_density_comparison_for_rvs(
        x_1=xs, x_2=xinvs, density_name="Exponential Density"
    )
```

What we did above is compare the random variates generated by the *scipy.stats* library and the expression for exponential distribution discussed earlier and the outputs produced by the two appear similar, as shown in Figure 4-1.

CHAPTER 4 SIMULATION

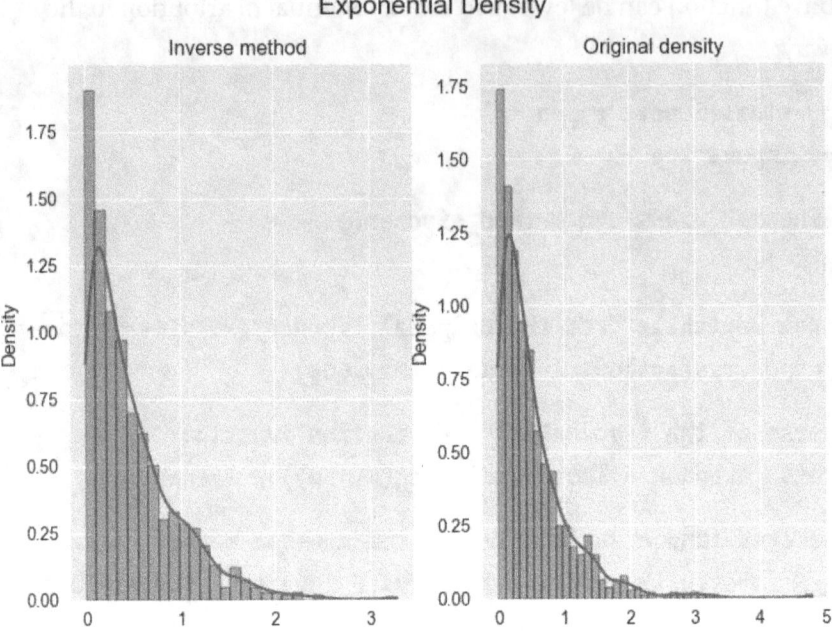

Figure 4-1. *Comparison of distributions by two generated sets of random variates*

Fortunately, we don't have to find the inverse of the CDF in every case, as Python *scipy.stats* module already provides us with those for a collection of distributions as handy. In this book, we will be using those mainly wherever required.

Inverse Method for PMF

Many schemes exist for generating random variates from a PMF. Here we discuss the one suggested by *Devroye [9]* – generation by sequential search. For PMF, giving a recursive shape to the function may be possible as the discrete random variables mostly increment by a unit. Consider rewriting the PMF for Poisson distribution in a recursive form,

$$p_{x+1} = \frac{\lambda^{x+1}}{(x+1)!}e^{-\lambda}$$
$$= \frac{\lambda}{x+1}\left(\frac{\lambda^x}{x!}e^{-\lambda}\right)$$
$$= \frac{\lambda}{x+1}p_x.$$

where $p_0 = e^{-\lambda}$.

With this in place, cumulative probabilities are computed for incremental X's and the last variate is kept if that is greater than a uniform random variate. In fact, being black box, this approach is generic enough to support any PMF (just decompose the PMF into a recurrence relation as we did above). Listing 4-2 shows a simple implementation.

Listing 4-2. Generating Poisson random variates with sequential search

```
def generate_poisson_rv(λ, n_rv):
    # inspired by [9]Devroy
    u = uniform.rvs(0, 1, n_rv)

    def _get_single_x(u_i):
        x = 0
        p = exp(-λ)
        s = p
        while u_i > s:
            x = x + 1
            p = (p * λ)/x
            s = s + p
        return x

    return [_get_single_x(u_i) for u_i in u]
```

This function generates a given number of Poisson variates with a given λ:

```
def test_generate_poisson_rv():
    print(generate_poisson_rv(5, 10))
```

Output is produced as

[6, 5, 5, 7, 7, 8, 5, 5, 8, 8].

The approach of the sequential search discussed is the simplest one; there are many more rich improvements on top of this. Discussing all of these is out of the scope of this book. I covered this one just to give you an idea of PMF random variate generation, as Poisson distribution is crucial for modeling sudden jumps in financial asset price. Fortunately, Python already provides handy APIs to do all of this (both *scipy* and *numpy*), and we will be using those while designing the actual components later.

CHAPTER 4 SIMULATION

Acceptance/Rejection Method

Everything looks fine for the inverse transform method unless you have an intractable cumulative density function (CDF). It's a common situation, especially in finance, when you deal with the density function of complex securities, or the random variable of the density itself is a linear combination of other random variables. Finding out CDFs in closed form is a real challenge there. As an alternative, an indirect method of drawing samples from a distribution is a viable option.

To introduce the idea, suppose $f(x)$ is the target PDF we are interested in drawing samples from, and there is another PDF $g(x)$ which is related as

$$f(x) \leq Cg(x),$$

with a constant $1 < C < \infty$. $g(x)$ shouldn't be just any arbitrary PDF, but the one from which sampling can be done by the inversion method more easily than $f(x)$ and preferably from the same family of distributions (i.e., the basic mathematical form of the PDFs should match). Once C and $g(x)$ are decided, sampling can proceed in accept/reject combination, i.e., sample from x' from $g(x)$, check if $f(x') \leq Cg(x')$, and then keep it; otherwise, reject it. Computing $f(x)$ for a given x is not difficult, but the reverse is not true. In fact, $f(x)$ itself need not be available in a closed form, but from an implementation standpoint, its existence as a component should suffice, which can at least provide the probability for a given x. The algorithm can be formally described as below:

ACCEPTANCE/REJECTION ALGORITHM

---

1. Determine best values for C and θ.

2. Generate a uniformly distributed array of random variates u on [0,1].

3. Draw samples from g(x; θ).

4. Iterate over samples of g(x) and check if u < f(x) / g(x; θ), and then accept the sample; otherwise, reject it.

5. Go to Step 2 if the desired number of samples are not generated; otherwise, stop.

Steps 2 to 5 should be easy to understand, but Step 1 still needs to be discussed in detail.

In this context, let's introduce the *hat function* – it is an upper bound on the target density to sample from. g(x) is known as a *proposal density*; hence, hat function is given by

$$H(x) = Cg(x; \hat{\theta}),$$

with a given C and $\hat{\theta}$. The situation is shown in Figure 4-2.

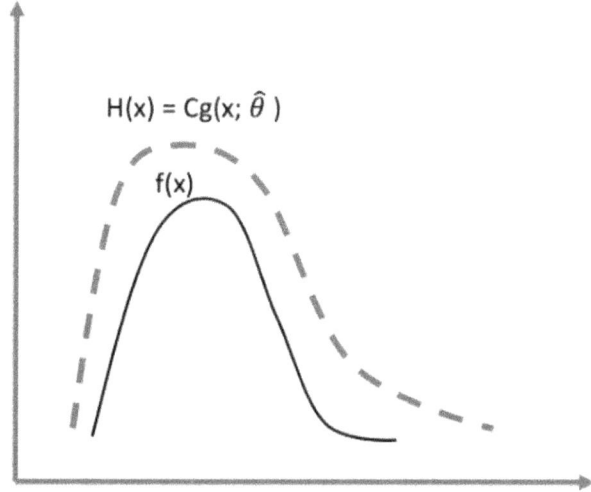

Figure 4-2. *Hat function H(x) over density f(x)*

Certainly, it looks like a hat; hence, the name has been given accordingly. The algorithm described earlier establishes the fact that a good choice of g(x) and a good design of H(x) will reduce sample rejections; otherwise, many iterations would be needed to produce the desired number of samples due to high rejections. It can be proved that 1/C is the acceptance probability of samples, so having a value of C as close as possible to 1 is always desirable. It appears that optimizing f(x)/g(x) would give C, but the case is not so straightforward. We will know the parameters of f(x) while designing the algorithm, but the parameter θ for g(x) is still unknown, which influences C. There are many schemes to design a good hat function h(x); one involves breaking it into steps and giving a complete numerical shape. According to *Devroye [9]*, a good rejection scheme would be finding a supremum of f(x)/g(x) that works as C, i.e.,

$$C = \sup_x \frac{f(x)}{g(x;\theta)}.$$

CHAPTER 4 SIMULATION

With this, we get C, but that also depends on θ as it drives the g(x). This is a bit tricky as the C should be the value which is the minimum of all possible maximum values of f(x)/g(x). Anyway, we are doing maximization w.r.t x but as that's also a function of θ, so minimization should be done on top of it. The whole technique can be written as

$$C = \min_{\theta} \left\{ \max_{x} \left\{ \frac{f(x)}{g(x;\theta)} \right\} \right\}$$

and

$$\hat{\theta} = \arg\min_{\theta} \left\{ \max_{x} \left\{ \frac{f(x)}{g(x;\theta)} \right\} \right\}.$$

This is logical, as C should be a value that can work as a factor to construct a hat as well as shouldn't be too far from f(x). If f(x) has a closed form, then the ratio f(x)/g(x) can be determined analytically, and maximization should be done accordingly. But as the whole process involves ratio computation, maximization, and minimization at the same time, in some other way, finding closed-form solutions at each step is a bit infeasible.

To keep everything generic, I propose a full numerical solution to determine C and $\hat{\theta}$ with a Python-based template. We are still in Step 1 of the algorithm; once we design this, we will go to the next stage to implement the whole algorithm leveraging this template. Note that there are many schemes to design the hat function. We are following a method suggested by *Devroye [9]*, but to keep things open for extension, we start with an interface for estimating the hat function as shown in Listing 4-3.

Listing 4-3. Interface for hat function estimator

```
class HatFunctionEstimator(ABC):
    """
    Abstract template for estimating Hat function H(x).
    It should be implemented to feed a strategy of constructing H(x)
    in the acceptance/rejection method.
    """

    @abstractmethod
    def estimate_parameters(self, f: callable, g: callable): ...
```

```
    '''
        Function to construct H(x) and estimate
        any parameters inside it.
    '''

    @abstractmethod
    def H_x(self, x): ...
    '''
     Return H(x) for a given x.
    '''
```

This is extended to implement the supremum finding method as shown in Listing 4-4.

Listing 4-4. Template for hat function estimator that finds the supremum of f/g

```
class SupremumEstimatorTemplate(HatFunctionEstimator, ABC):
    '''
    Template implementation of HatFunctionOptimizer
    which is of the form H(x) = Cg(x,θ).
    It uses the supremum of f(x)/g(x,θ) to find out C & θ.
    However, it does not provide maxima & minima functions.

    This can be extended with a suitable choice of
    function optimization algorithm.
    '''

    def __init__(self):
        self._f: callable = None
        self._g: callable = None
        self._C: float = None
        self._θ: float = None

    @abstractmethod
    def _maximize_wrt_x(self, ratio_f: callable) -> tuple: ...

    @abstractmethod
    def _minimize_wrt_θ(self, ratio_f: callable) -> tuple: ...
```

```python
    def _max_f_g_ratio(self, θ: tuple):
        '''
        Objective function to maximize f(x)/g(x, θ) w.r.t x
        '''
        def _c(x):
            c = 1.0
            proposal_prob = self._g(x, θ)
            if proposal_prob > 0:
                c = self._f(x) / proposal_prob

            return -c

        # Maximize f/g w.r.t x
        return self._maximize_wrt_x(_c)[0]

    def estimate_parameters(self, f: callable, g: callable):
        self._f = f
        self._g = g

        # Minimize maximum of f/g w.r.t θ
        result = self._minimize_wrt_θ(self._max_f_g_ratio)

        self._C = result[0]
        self._θ = result[1]
        print("Computed C", self._C, " θ = ", self._θ)

    def H_x(self, x):
        '''
        Hat function H(x) = C * g(x)
        '''
        return self._C * self._g(x, self._θ)

    @property
    def θ_optimal_for_g(self): return self._θ
```

This is still a template as it doesn't have the maxima and minima finding function schemes. Python has *scipy.optimize* module for all that work, but you are free to implement your own. However, I provide a default one leveraging the *scipy.optimize* as shown in Listing 4-5.

CHAPTER 4 SIMULATION

Listing 4-5. Default supremum implementation with optimization functions

```python
from scipy.optimize import minimize

class DefaultSupremumEstimator(SupremumEstimatorTemplate):
    '''
    Default implementation of SupremumEstimatorTemplate.
    It leverages scipy.optimize module to find the maxima & minima of
    f/g ratio.
    '''
    def __init__(self,
                 x0: List,  # Initial value of RV X of proposal density
                 # Sequence of (min, max) pairs of RV X
                 x0_bounds: List[tuple],
                 θ0: List,  # Initial value of parameter of θ
                 proposal density

                 # Sequence of (min, max) pairs of parameter of θ
                 θ0_bounds: List[tuple]
                 ):
        self._x0 = x0
        self._x0_bounds = x0_bounds
        self._θ0 = θ0
        self._θ0_bounds = θ0_bounds
        super().__init__()

    def _maximize_wrt_x(self, ratio_f: callable) -> tuple:
        res = minimize(ratio_f,
                       x0=self._x0,    # Range & initial values of x
                       bounds=self._x0_bounds)
        return -res.fun, res.x

    def _minimize_wrt_θ(self, ratio_f: callable) -> tuple:
        res = minimize(ratio_f,  # Minimize maximum f/g w.r.t θ
                       x0=self._θ0,   # Range & initial values of θ
                       bounds=self._θ0_bounds)
        return res.fun, res.x
```

CHAPTER 4 SIMULATION

Observe the *__init__* function; it takes all necessary values as directed by the *scipy.optimize.minimize* function. This class is tightly bound to *scipy*; you are free to use any optimization of your choice and extend *SupremumEstimatorTemplate* accordingly.

Let's now proceed to Step 2; we create another class, *AcceptanceRejectionMethod*, that works as a base template. Listing 4-6 shows its partial view.

Listing 4-6. Partial view of the class AcceptanceRejectionMethod that works as a base template

```
class AcceptanceRejectionMethod(ABC):
    """
    Base template for acceptance-rejection method. This should be
    extended to three functions should be overridden to implement
    drawing of samples from a target distribution
    """

    def __init__(self, hat_func_estimator: HatFunctionEstimator):
        self._hat_func_estimator = hat_func_estimator

    @abstractmethod
    def _target_pdf_f(self, x):
        '''
        Function to provide PDF of target density. This
        should be overridden by the concrete class extending
        AcceptanceRejectionMethod
        '''
        ...

    @abstractmethod
    def _proposal_pdf_g(self, x, θ: tuple):
        '''
        Function to provide PDF of proposal density. This
        should be overridden by the concrete class extending
        AcceptanceRejectionMethod
        '''
        ...
```

CHAPTER 4 SIMULATION

```
@abstractmethod
def _sample_from_proposal_g_with_θ_optimal(self, n_rv):
    '''
    Function to samples from the proposal density. This
    should be overridden by the concrete class extending
    AcceptanceRejectionMethod
    '''
    ...
```

The concrete class extending *AcceptanceRejectionMethod* should provide details of the target and proposal densities, and also, it should be able to sample from the proposal density with the optimal $\hat{\theta}$ provided by the supplied *HatFunctionEstimator*. Now, the main task of sampling from f(x) is done in the *sample* function as shown in Listing 4-7.

Listing 4-7. Function to sample from f(x) leveraging the HatFunctionEsstimator

```
def sample(self, n_rv):
    """
    Function to sample n_rv number of RV from target density f
    """
    self._hat_func_estimator.estimate_parameters(f=self._target_pdf_f,
                                                 g=self._
                                                 proposal_pdf_g)
    count_accepted = 0
    rv_f_accepted = []
    rv_f_rejected = []

    def _filter_sample(x_u):
        x, u = x_u
        return u <= self._target_pdf_f(x)/self._hat_func_estimator.H_x(x)

    while count_accepted < n_rv:
        remaining_count = n_rv - count_accepted
        rv_g = self._sample_from_proposal_g_with_θ_
        optimal(remaining_count)
        u = uniform.rvs(0, 1, remaining_count)
```

```
...
Reject samples based on criteria:
uniform random variate < f(x)/H(x)
...
accepted_samples = map(lambda x: x[0],
                       filter(_filter_sample, zip(rv_g, u)))

rv_f_accepted.extend(accepted_samples)

# Collect rejected samples
rv_f_rejected.extend(set(rv_g).difference(rv_f_accepted))

count_accepted = len(rv_f_accepted)
    samples_trace = SamplesTraceDisplay(
        rv_f_accepted, rv_f_rejected,
        self._target_pdf_f(rv_f_accepted),
        self._hat_func_estimator.H_x(rv_f_rejected))

    return rv_f_accepted, samples_trace
```

The function keeps track of the rejected samples for visualization and understanding of the algorithm (code can be found in *chapter4/random_number_gen_accept_reject.py*). Figure 4-3 shows the class diagram of the components discussed so far.

CHAPTER 4 SIMULATION

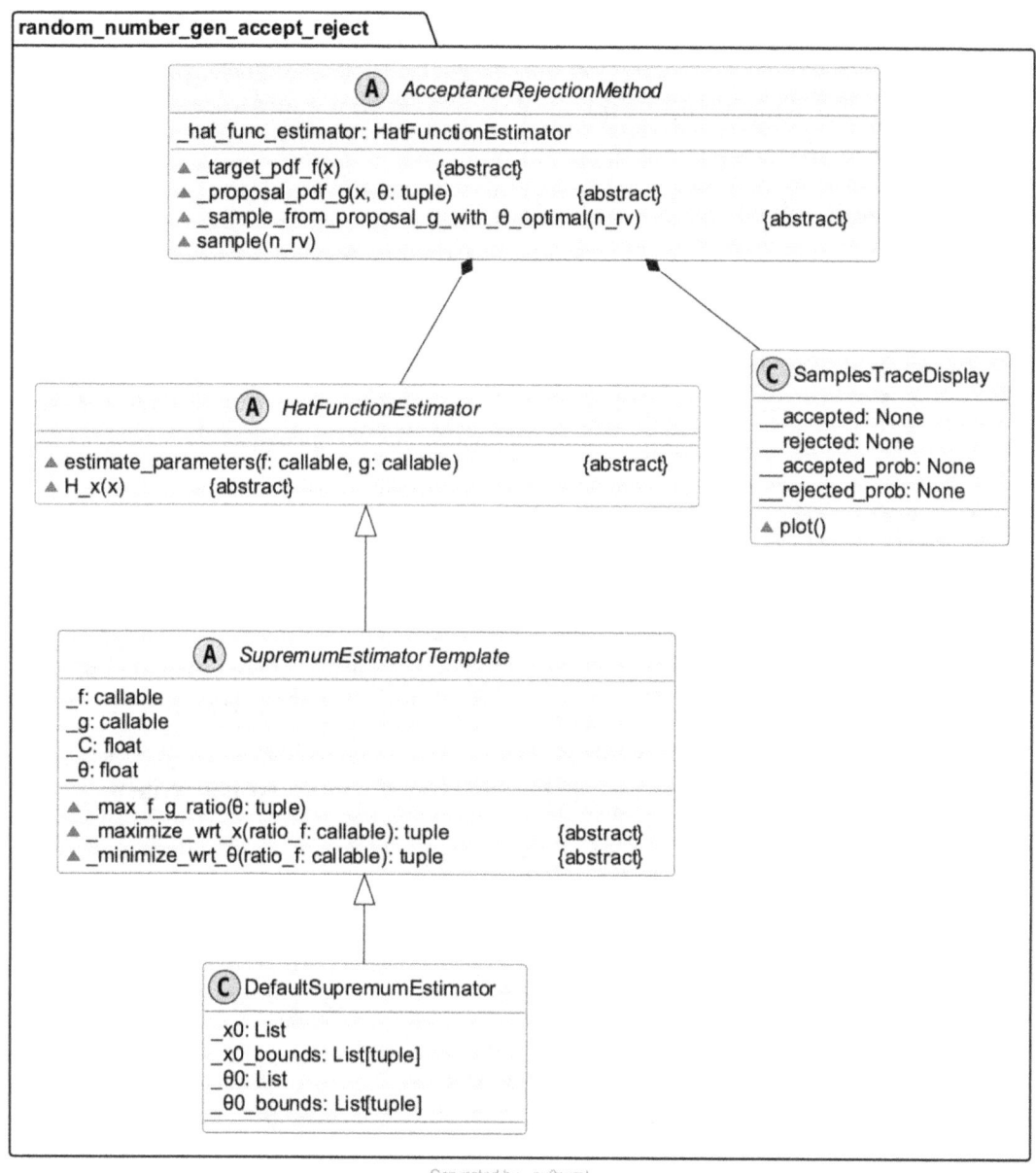

Figure 4-3. *Class diagram of HatFunctionEstimator and AccetanceRejectionMethod*

CHAPTER 4 SIMULATION

Let's now create concrete classes extending *AcceptanceRejectionMethod* with specific target and proposal densities. We plan to sample from *Gaussian* density with *exponential* as proposal density. While choosing proposal density, keep in mind a few things as described next:

a) The proposal density should have fatter tails than the target.

b) The domain of the random variables for both should match to some extent.

c) The proposal density is always better to be from the same family of distributions as the target belongs to. It somehow ensures the similarity between the geometric shapes and mathematical form of the two, which in turn helps in reducing the number of rejections.

Choosing *exponential* as a proposal for Gaussian may violate condition (b) as exponential distribution has strictly positive-valued random variates, whereas Gaussian is real valued. Therefore, generating half of the standard normal distribution and replicating the other half with the negative sign added is loosely recommended. However, the components we are going to discuss next consider the full Gaussian distribution instead of the standard normal as the target PDF. So, we can write the ratio f(x)/g(x) as

$$\frac{f_{Gaussian}(x)}{g_{Exponential}(x,\lambda)} = \frac{\frac{1}{\sigma\sqrt{2\pi}}e^{-\frac{1}{2}\left(\frac{x-\mu}{\sigma}\right)^2}}{\lambda e^{-\lambda x}}$$

$$= \frac{1}{\sigma\lambda\sqrt{2\pi}}e^{-\frac{1}{2}\left(\frac{x-\mu}{\sigma}\right)^2 + \lambda x},$$

and the hat function as

$$H(x) = C\hat{\lambda}e^{-\hat{\lambda}x}.$$

Maximizing f(x)/g(x) w.r.t. x is possible in closed form, which returns a function of λ (*_max_f_g_ratio* in Listing 4-4), and that should be again minimized in closed form w.r.t. λ to produce a final estimate for C and λ. Closed-form expressions may not be available for all distributions at all stages of this process, so the whole framework shown in Figure 4-3 solves this problem numerically, as explained earlier. To implement this, we create a class *GaussianVariateGeneratorWithExponential* as shown in Listing 4-8 (code is in *chapter4/accept_reject_method_densities.py*).

Listing 4-8. Class to sample from Gaussian density with an exponential proposal

```
from scipy.stats import expon, norm, beta, uniform, cosine

class GaussianVariateGeneratorWithExponential(AcceptanceRejectionMethod):
    """
    Class to sample from Gaussian density using an Exponential
    proposal density
    """

    def __init__(self, μ, σ, hat_func_optimizer: HatFunctionEstimator):
        self._μ = μ
        self._σ = σ
        super().__init__(hat_func_optimizer)

    def _target_pdf_f(self, x):
        return norm.pdf(x, loc=self._μ, scale=self._σ)

    def _proposal_pdf_g(self, x, θ: tuple):
        return expon.pdf(x, scale=1 / θ[0])

    def _sample_from_proposal_g_with_θ_optimal(self, n_rv):
        return expon.rvs(scale=1 / self._hat_func_estimator.θ_optimal_
        for_g[0], size=n_rv)
```

Though we used *norm.pdf* function from *scipy.stats*, in some situations, there may not be any such libraries to compute the PDF of target density. There we may have to rely on any hosted service or leverage the closed-form expression of the PDF. Also, observe the usage of *θ_optimal_for_g* and *θ* – these are generic tuples to hold parameters of any dimension. Let's test this as shown next (*chapter4/test/test_rvs_gen.py*):

```
def test_acceptance_rejection_gaussian_gen_with_exponential():
    # Estimator designed for Exponential density used as proposal density g
    exponential_supremum_estimator = DefaultSupremumEstimator(
        x0=[0.01], x0_bounds=[(0.01, None)], θ0=[0.01], θ0_
        bounds=[(0.001, None)])
```

CHAPTER 4   SIMULATION

```
_, sample_trace = GaussianVariateGeneratorWithExponential(μ=10, σ=4,
                                                          hat_func_
optimizer=exponential_supremum_estimator).sample(n_rv=1000)
    sample_trace.plot()
```

We plan to draw samples from a Gaussian distribution with a mean of 10 and standard deviation of 4. The samples are plotted, as shown in Figure 4-4.

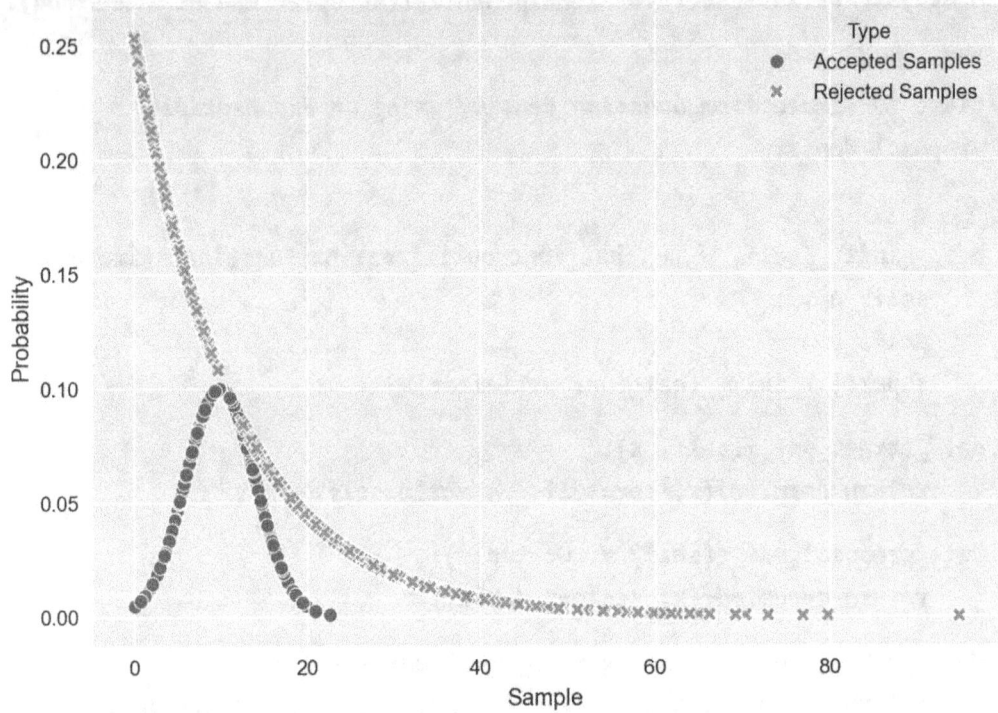

Figure 4-4. *Plotted accepted and rejected samples from a Gaussian density with exponentials as the proposal*

The output printed in the console shows estimated values of C and θ (here, θ=λ):

Estimated C 2.907026692376759 θ = [0.08769527].

Theoretically, there are chances of having negative samples for Gaussian distribution as it is real valued, but we kept the initializations passed in *DefaultSupremumEstimator* as strictly positive to stop this since the proposal density is undefined for negative samples. This way, you can somehow try to control the generation of samples to mitigate the effect of domain mismatch, as mentioned in condition (b). You can check *chapter4/ accept_reject_method_densities.py* for other implementations. Figure 4-5 shows the class diagram of the components leveraging the framework.

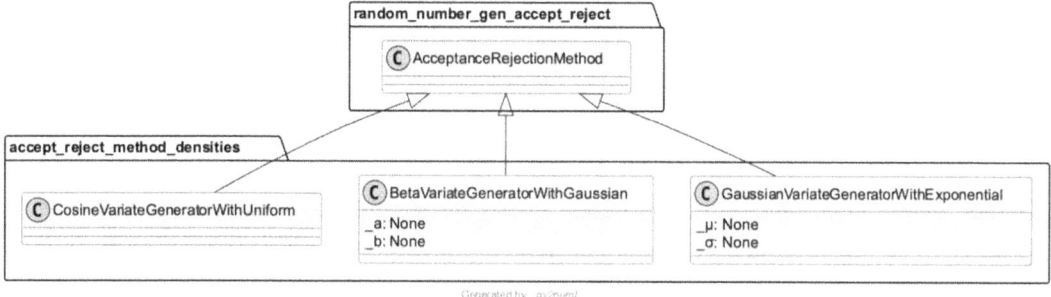

Figure 4-5. *Class diagram of components extending AcceptanceRejectionMethod*

Python's *scipy.stats* module already contains components for sampling from most of the common distributions, and we use those only primarily for doing the sampling work required for this book. But the components discussed earlier provide a benchmark of how to design sampling if the corresponding CDFs are intractable. These should help you in situations when you might have to encounter some complex mixture distributions while modeling some uncommon financial securities.

Monte Carlo Simulation

The basic idea behind the *Monte Carlo* method is about modeling and simulating a system depicting random behavior. Several random scenarios are generated to perform this, and relevant statistics are computed from the collected output of the experiments. For example, we can get the average value from the paths of a stock price. Path simulation is the random experiment here. *Simulation* is generally known as the virtual realization of some physical phenomenon without the need for a physical setup. With simulation, we somewhat get an idea about the overall nature of any system. The *Monte Carlo* method has been a popular stochastic simulation technique since the 1930s. With the advent of modern computing technology, the practicality of this method became more and more dominant. The formal name was given by the famous scientist *Metropolis* while cracking jokes with his colleague *Ulam* (both were scientists in the project ENIAC, the first electronic computer in 1946) about his uncle who used to

CHAPTER 4 SIMULATION

frequently travel to *Monte Carlo* (an administrative area under *Monaco*), the famous (or infamous!!) place for gambling. It's very relevant, as gambling is all about chance and probability, and so is the stochastic modeling of financial assets.

According to the definition, probability is a measure that gives the frequency of events, i.e., a relative measure of the volume of events compared to the universe. On the other side, the Monte Carlo method uses the reverse process of probability measure, i.e., using the frequency of events, it computes the volume. To elaborate more, it samples from the distribution, explores the sample space, and estimates the volume using the collected samples. If the probability distribution of the physical system is known, then we can compute any relevant statistics in this way – basically, we will see later that it is nothing but the stochastic method of performing area integration. The conventional trapezoidal method uses incremental deterministic samples of differential (dx) to compute the sum, whereas in the Monte Carlo method, the differential is random in nature (to know more about the trapezoidal method, refer to Mark Newman [8]) as said earlier, those are obtained by random sampling from the probability distribution. Suppose you have to find the mean value of random variable X with the probability distribution of X. As discussed in Chapter 3, the mean is given by

$$E(X) = \int_x x f(x) dx.$$

But the challenge is that you don't know anything about X's sample space and are not given any dataset. This is estimated by the Monte Carlo method as

$$\hat{E}(X) \approx \frac{1}{n} \sum_{i=1}^{n} x_i.$$

You might be confused now with this one and first-order raw moment (m_1'). Yes, that's a valid point. The expressions look similar, but conceptually, the Monte Carlo method is different from moment computation. In the second case, you don't know the parameters of the probability distribution; in fact, you do compute the moments to find out the parameters, and the most vital point is that you are given a collection of realizations of the underlying random variable as training dataset – each x_i refers to the individual realizations. On the other hand, while computing E(X) via Monte Carlo, either you will be given full knowledge of $f(x)$ with its parameters or else at least you will be able to compute $f(x)$ even if it is not available in closed form so that you can draw n number of samples from there and take the arithmetic average to estimate the expectation of X. No dataset or realizations are available in this case. Basically, the Monte Carlo method gives the inference or data from the distribution, and the traditional moment estimation gives you the opposite, i.e., distribution from the data.

In practice, we are interested in computing the mean of any function $h(x)$ w.r.t the probability measure $f(x)$ in the following way:

$$\hat{\mu}_n = E_f[h(x)] = \int_x h(x)f(x)dx$$
$$\approx \frac{1}{n}\sum_{i=1}^{n} h(x_i)$$
$$= \frac{1}{n}\sum_{i=1}^{n} H_i$$

where $H_i = h(x_i)$.

The mean $\hat{\mu}_n$ computed above is an estimate of the actual mean of $h(x)$. Its accuracy depends on the quality and size of the sample drawn from the distribution $f(x)$. (Because of the sampling process, the terms *Monte Carlo simulation* and *Monte Carlo sampling* are often used interchangeably.)

In theory, the Monte Carlo method is backed by two theorems in statistics – *the law of large numbers* and *central limit theorem*. The law of large numbers (more specifically, the strong law of large numbers) states that

$$\hat{\mu}_n \to \mu \text{ with probability 1 as } n \to \infty$$

where μ is the actual mean of $h(x)$. It means increasing the sample size will give a better estimate of the actual mean, i.e., the sample mean ($\hat{\mu}_n$) will converge toward the actual mean (μ). By the central limit theorem, the occurred error $\hat{\mu}_n - \mu$ follows the normal distribution with mean 0 and variance σ_H^2/n. To know σ_H, we need to know μ beforehand, which is impossible; that's why σ_H^2 is estimated by sample variance s_H^2 which is given by

$$s_H^2 = \frac{1}{n-1}\left(\sum_{i=1}^{n} H_i^2 - n\hat{\mu}_n^2\right).$$

With this in place, we get confidence intervals for μ as

$$\hat{\mu}_n \pm z_{\delta/2}\frac{s_H}{\sqrt{n}},$$

CHAPTER 4 SIMULATION

where z_δ is the $1 - \delta$ quantile of standard normal distribution (i.e., $\Phi(z_\delta) = 1 - \delta$). This has an asymptotic behavior when $n \to \infty$ making $s_H \to \sigma_H$ and $\hat{\mu}_n \to \mu$. The term $s_H / \sqrt{n}$ is known as *standard error (S.E.)* of $\hat{\mu}_n$, and its final expression is given by

$$S.E.(\hat{\mu}_n) = \sqrt{\frac{1}{n(n-1)}\left(\sum_{i=1}^{n} H_i^2 - n\hat{\mu}_n^2\right)}.$$

The standard error is the metric of uncertainty around the estimate $\hat{\mu}_n$ and has a great significance in risk assessment.

Now, what all of these do have to do with stochastic finance? Recall what we discussed in Chapter 1. To forecast a financial asset's behavior and capture the risk associated, we need to perform some sort of simulation of the system. You will see later that $h(x)$ is the solution of a stochastic differential equation that represents the physics of a stock price or option value, and the f(x), of course, is the probability distribution of financial asset state ($h(x)$ is the function of asset state). Being generative in nature, we can create simulated paths of financial assets, their mean value, and the risk (i.e., the standard error in this case) from the method discussed above.

With all those in place, we now create Python-based generic templates for Monte Carlo simulation that can be leveraged irrespective of the nature of $h(x)$. Listing 4-9 shows a partial view of the class *MonteCarloSimulation*.

Listing 4-9. Partial view of the class MonteCarloSimulation

```python
from dataclasses import dataclass
from numpy import average, sqrt, sum, power, vectorize

class MonteCarloSimulation:
    '''
    Class to perform Monte Carlo simulation over a function h_x_fun
    with a given
    sampling density for x and an optional variance reduction scheme
    '''
    @dataclass
    class MCEstimate:
        '''
        Dataclass returned as the output of the simulation
        '''
```

```python
        samples: List = None   # values of H(x)
        mean: float = 0.0
        standard_error: float = 0.0

    def __init__(self, h_x_fun: callable,
                 target_sampling_density: TargetSamplingDensity,
                 n_vars,
                 n_sample_paths=1,
                 var_reduction: VarReduction = NoVarReduction()):
        if not callable(h_x_fun):
            raise TypeError(
                "h_x_fun should be callable: function or class with __
                call__()")
        self._h_x_fun = h_x_fun
        self._n_vars = n_vars
        self._n_sample_paths = n_sample_paths
        self._axis, self._n = (0, self._n_sample_paths) if self._n_sample_
        paths > 1 else (
            1, self._n_vars)

        self._target_sampling_desnity = target_sampling_density

        self._var_reduction = var_reduction
        if hasattr(self._var_reduction, '_target_sampling_density'):
            setattr(self._var_reduction, '_target_sampling_density',
                    target_sampling_density)
        self._var_reduction._target_sampling_density = target_
        sampling_density
        self._var_reduction._n_sample_paths = n_sample_paths
        self._var_reduction._n_vars = n_vars
        self._var_reduction._h_x_fun = h_x_fun
        self._var_reduction._axis = self._axis
        self._var_reduction._n = self._n
```

You might be surprised looking at the *var_reduction* parameter as we haven't discussed it yet. Yes, from the name, you can guess that there must be some schemes to reduce the simulation result's variance (a.k.a. standard error). We will discuss two

CHAPTER 4　SIMULATION

of such schemes (*antithetic sampling* and *importance sampling*) in a short while. But for now, assume that there are no such variance reduction schemes by default, and for that, *NoVarReduction* is passed there. Listing 4-10 shows the structure of var reduction templates.

Listing 4-10. Abstract base class VarReduction for different schemes and NoVarReduction is used by default

```
class VarReduction(ABC):
    '''
    Template class for various reduction schemes. Underlying scheme should
    extend this class and override sample_H_x function.
    '''

    def __init__(self):
        self._axis = 0
        self._n = 0
        self._h_x_fun: callable = None
        self._n_vars = 0
        self._n_sample_paths = 1

    @abstractmethod
    def sample_H_x(self, x=None): ...
    '''
    Function to provide samples to measure H(x) from the
    provided samples of x
    '''

class NoVarReduction(VarReduction):
    '''
    Class for vanilla sampling with no variance reduction schemes.
    It is used when there is no need to adjust H(x).
    '''

    def sample_H_x(self, x=None):
        print('No Var Reduction')
        H_x = vectorize(lambda y: self._h_x_fun(y))
        return H_x(x)
```

CHAPTER 4 SIMULATION

Now let's look at the work performed in the *new_estimate* function defined in the class *MonteCarloSimulation* (Listing 4-11). This is the heart of the simulation work; calling it each time will result in a new simulation work.

Listing 4-11. Function new_estimate defined in MonteCarloSimulation

```
def new_estimate(self) -> MCEstimate:
    '''
    Function to return a new estimated result of H(x). Calling it
    each time may return different result because of the
    random simulation.
    '''
    x = self._target_sampling_desnity.sample(
        n_vars=self._n_vars, n_sample_paths=self._n_sample_paths)
    if not (len(x) == self._n_sample_paths and len(x[0]) ==
    self._n_vars):
        raise ValueError('Random variable should be in shape (' +
                         str(self._n_sample_paths) + ',' + str(self._n_
                         vars) + ')')
    estimate = MonteCarloSimulation.MCEstimate()
    estimate.samples = self._var_reduction.sample_H_x(x)
    estimate.mean = average(estimate.samples, axis=self._axis)
    estimate.standard_error =
    sqrt(_compute_standard_error(H_x=estimate.samples,
                                            mean=estimate.
mean, axis=self._axis, n=self._n))
    return estimate
```

The function *_compute_standard_error* is defined as a module function in *chapter4/monte_carlo_simulation.py* like below:

```
def _compute_standard_error(H_x, mean, axis, n):
    H_x_2 = power(H_x, 2)
    return (sum(
        H_x_2, axis=axis) - (n * (mean ** 2))) / (n*(n-1))
```

It computes the sample variance (s_H^2). We also need a template for the sampling density $f(x)$ as shown in Listing 4-12.

Chapter 4 Simulation

Listing 4-12. Base class for target sampling density

```python
class TargetSamplingDensity(ABC):
    '''
    Abstract template for implementing probabilty density to sample from.
    Monte carlo methods leverage this density to simulate random behaviour.
    '''

    @abstractmethod
    def pdf(self, x): ...

    @abstractmethod
    def sample(self, n_vars, n_sample_paths=1): ...
```

We keep a standard normal density as our target sampling density as defined in *chapter4/gaussian_mc_simulation.py* like below:

```python
from scipy.stats import norm
from chapter4.monte_carlo_simulation import TargetSamplingDensity

class StandardNormalTargetSamplingDensity(TargetSamplingDensity):
    '''
    StanddardNormalTargetSamplingDensity
    '''

    def pdf(self, x):
        return norm.pdf(x)

    def sample(self, n_vars, n_sample_paths=1):
        return norm().rvs(size=(n_sample_paths, n_vars))
```

Let's now test all these with $h(x) = e^{-x}$ and print the results like below:

```python
def test_gaussian_mc_simulation_no_var_reduction():
    mcs = MonteCarloSimulation(h_x_fun=lambda x: exp(-x),
                               n_vars=10,
                               target_sampling_density=StandardNormalTargetSam
                               plingDensity())
```

```
e = mcs.new_estimate()
print(e.mean)
print(e.standard_error)
print(e.samples)
```

We got the mean, standard error, and the samples as

[1.33135549]
[0.40075737]
[[0.31027751 3.27755228 0.95682152 0.94334838 2.070487   0.19226676
  0.67028058 0.86193798 0.29821153 3.73237132]]

Figure 4-6 shows the class diagram of the Monte Carlo simulation module.

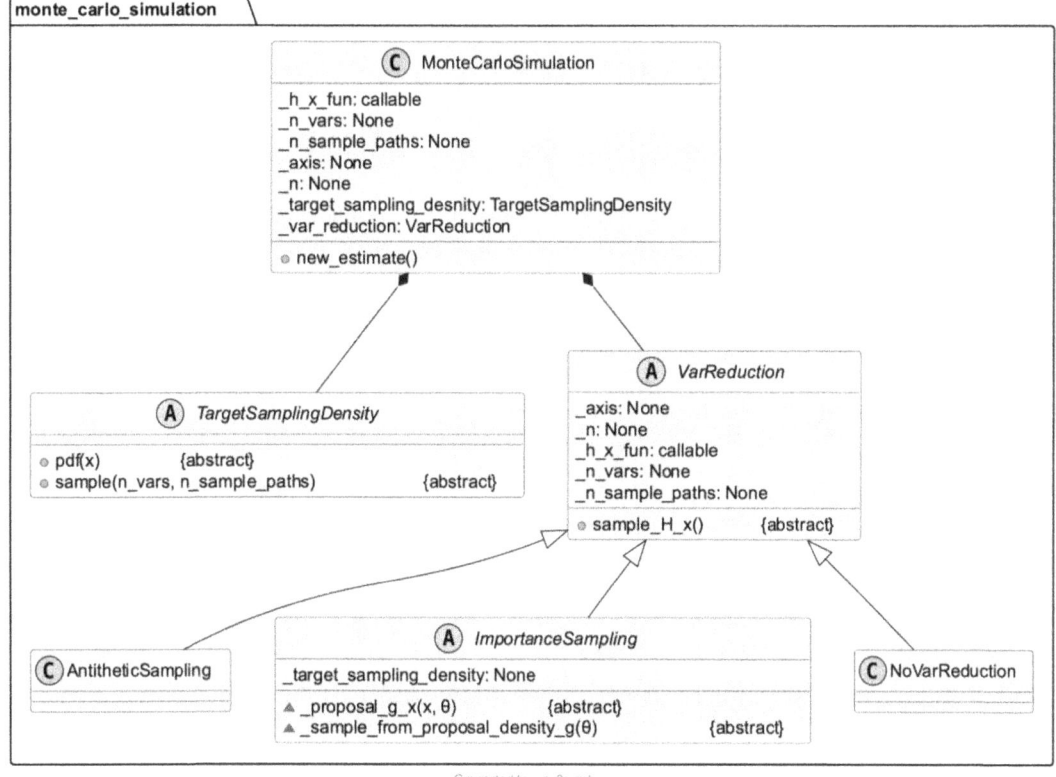

Figure 4-6. *Class diagram of Monte Carlo simulation module*

CHAPTER 4   SIMULATION

Variance Reduction

As discussed earlier by the theories of the law of large numbers and the central limit theorem, the accuracy of the Monte Carlo simulation can be improved with a large number of samples ($n \to \infty$), but with a penalty of slow convergence. Though, with today's computational power, speed is not a major concern, still more sophisticated methods backed by some statistical theory are always better options that give the desired accuracy with fewer simulation runs. One way to achieve this is by modifying the method, resulting in a faster decrease in variance, and any such things are known as *variance reduction schemes*. We discuss two such methods next.

Antithetic Sampling

It is the simplest approach to variance reduction schemes. It uses the concept of variance of the sum of the two random variables X and Y:

$$Var(X+Y) = Var(X) + Var(Y) + 2cov(X,Y).$$

Notice that if X and Y are negatively correlated (i.e., covariance is less than zero), then

$$Var(X+Y) < Var(X) + Var(Y).$$

The same idea applies to $h(x)$:

$$Var[h(x) + h(y)] < Var[h(x)] + Var[h(y)].$$

Introducing $y = -x$ will satisfy the above condition, and this doesn't change the distribution of x, giving us the scope of leveraging the same samples just by adding a negative sign, hence saving the cost of sampling from another distribution. To keep the mean unchanged, we use $[h(x) + h(-x)]/2$, which makes the H_i as

$$H_i = \frac{1}{2}\left[h(x_i) + h(-x_i)\right].$$

And, of course,

$$Var\left[\frac{1}{2}\{h(x_i) + h(-x_i)\}\right] < Var[h(x)],$$

CHAPTER 4 SIMULATION

which is also applicable to the standard error. We don't need any separate formulae for mean and standard error; just setting the H_i and leveraging the old expression for them will do the job.

It's time to leverage the *VarReduction* template in the true sense and implement the *AntitheticSampling* class (Listing 4-13).

Listing 4-13. Class for antithetic sampling

```
class AntitheticSampling(VarReduction):
    '''
    Class for Antithetic sampling as variance reduction scheme.
    It uses average of negatively correlated variables to adjust H(x)
    '''

    def sample_H_x(self, x=None):
        print('Antithetic Sampling')
        H_x = vectorize(lambda y: (self._h_x_fun(y) + self._h_x_fun(-y))/2)
        return H_x(x)
```

We are done, as the rest of the work should be performed by the framework of Monte Carlo simulation. We can test this in a similar fashion:

```
def test_gaussian_mc_simulation_antithetic_sampling():
    mcs = MonteCarloSimulation(h_x_fun=lambda x: exp(-x),
                               n_vars=10,
                               var_reduction=AntitheticSampling(),
                               target_sampling_density=StandardNormalTarget
                               SamplingDensity())
    e = mcs.new_estimate()
    print(e.mean)
    print(e.standard_error)
    print(e.samples)
```

As said earlier, doing so doesn't alter the mean; it only reduces the variance and standard error.

125

Importance Sampling

One of the reasons for the high variance in Monte Carlo simulation is the existence of rare events causing $h(x)$ to have high or low values. One way to tackle this problem is by modifying the sampling distribution to produce more relevant data points, reducing the impact of rare events. This is achieved by the change of measure technique discussed earlier in this chapter – like the acceptance-rejection method of generating random variables. For the *importance sampling*, we use $g(x)$ as proposal distribution to sample from and compute the ratio of likelihoods $f(x)/g(x)$ as weights for adjusting $h(x)$. The *mean*, as usual, is unchanged in the overall process, but a good choice of $g(x)$ helps in reducing the variance. To do this, $E_f[h(x)]$ can be written as

$$E_f\big[h(x)\big] = \int h(x)f(x)dx$$
$$= \int h(x)\frac{f(x)}{g(x;\theta)}g(x;\theta)dx$$
$$= E_g\left[h(x)\frac{f(x)}{g(x;\theta)}\right]$$
$$\approx \frac{1}{n}\sum_{i=1}^{n} h(x_i)\frac{f(x_i)}{g(x_i;\theta)}.$$

So, the expectation is taken w.r.t $g(x)$ instead of $f(x)$ to support the change of measure, and we also see that

$$H_i = h(x_i)\frac{f(x_i)}{g(x_i;\theta)}.$$

Now, let's analyze how does it affect the variance:

$$Var_g\left[h(x)\frac{f(x)}{g(x;\theta)}\right] = E_g\left[h^2(x)\left(\frac{f(x)}{g(x;\theta)}\right)^2\right] - \left(E_g\left[h(x)\frac{f(x)}{g(x;\theta)}\right]\right)^2$$
$$= E_f\left[h^2(x)\frac{f(x)}{g(x;\theta)}\right] - \left(E_f\big[h(x)\big]\right)^2.$$

And let's write down Var_f and compare the two:

$$Var_f\left[h(x)\right] = E_f\left[h^2(x)\right] - \left(E_f\left[h(x)\right]\right)^2.$$

To keep $Var_g < Var_f$, we need a good choice of $g(x;\theta)$; otherwise, there is no guarantee that the variance would be reduced; in fact, with a wrong $g(x;\theta)$, it can even reach infinity. Ignoring the square terms of $E_f[h(x)]$ on both sides, we have a condition where $Var_g < Var_f$:

$$E_f\left[h^2(x)\right] > E_f\left[h^2(x)\frac{f(x)}{g(x;\theta)}\right].$$

The factor $f(x)/g(x;\theta)$ is known as the *likelihood ratio*, and it helps to trim down extreme values of $h^2(x)$ – reason of high variance. But to do that also, $g(x;\theta)$ should be such that $f(x) < cg(x;\theta)$ for some constant c. It sounds similar to what we did for the acceptance-rejection method discussed earlier. That's why $g(x;\theta)$ should be picked up from the same family of distributions as $f(x)$, but still, we are left with determining the correct value of θ. For this, we can solve any one of the optimization problems listed below:

$$\min_{\theta}\left\{Var_g\left[h(x)\frac{f(x)}{g(x;\theta)}\right]\right\},$$

$$\min_{\theta}\left\{E_g\left[h^2(x)\left(\frac{f(x)}{g(x;\theta)}\right)^2\right]\right\},$$

$$\min_{\theta}\left\{E_f\left[h^2(x)\frac{f(x)}{g(x;\theta)}\right]\right\}.$$

For the first two, we should sample from $g(x)$, and for the third one, $f(x)$ should be used for the sampling. Once we get the optimal θ, we are bound to sample from $g(x)$; hence, we choose the first problem to solve to keep a single distribution for sampling. The final solution looks like this:

CHAPTER 4 SIMULATION

$$\hat{\theta} = \min_{\theta} \left\{ Var_g \left[h(x) \frac{f(x)}{g(x;\theta)} \right] \right\},$$

$$E_f[h(x)] \approx \frac{1}{n} \sum_{i=1}^{n} h(x_i) \frac{f(x_i)}{g(x_i;\hat{\theta})},$$

$$Var[h(x)] = Var_g \left[h(x) \frac{f(x)}{g(x;\hat{\theta})} \right].$$

As $g(x)$ is our choice, we define an abstract template for importance sampling, which should be extended, and a few functions should be overridden as shown in Listing 4-14.

Listing 4-14. Class for importance sampling

```
class ImportanceSampling(VarReduction, ABC):

    '''
    Class for Importance sampling as variance reduction scheme.
    It samples from an alternative proposal distribution g(x,θ)
    and adjusts H(x) with the likelihood ratio defined as f(x)/g(x,θ)
    '''

    def __init__(self):
        self._target_sampling_density = None
        super().__init__()

    @abstractmethod
    def _proposal_g_x(self, x, θ: tuple): ...

    @abstractmethod
    def _sample_from_proposal_density_g(self, θ: tuple): ...

    def sample_H_x(self, x=None):
        print('Importance Sampling')

        def _likelihood_ratio(x, θ):
            return self._target_sampling_density.pdf(x)/self._
            proposal_g_x(x, θ)
```

```python
def _H_x_with_θ(θ):
    x = self._sample_from_proposal_density_g(θ)
    H_x = vectorize(lambda y: self._h_x_fun(y)
                    * _likelihood_ratio(y, θ))
    return H_x(x)

def _compute_total_variance(θ: tuple):
    H_x = _H_x_with_θ(θ)
    mean = average(H_x, axis=self._axis)

    # Sum of variances of all sample paths
    return sum(_compute_standard_error(H_x=H_x, mean=mean,
    axis=self._axis, n=self._n))

# Finds the optimal θ in g(x,θ) for which the total variance of H(x) would
# be minimum
optimal_θ = minimize(_compute_total_variance, bounds=[
                    (0.001, None), ((0.001, None))], x0=[0.01,
                    0.01]).x

print('Optimal θ' + str(optimal_θ))

return _H_x_with_θ(optimal_θ)
```

Testing this component is no different than the one discussed for antithetic method only with an improvement in the output. Figure 4-7 shows the class diagram of the sampling methods.

CHAPTER 4 SIMULATION

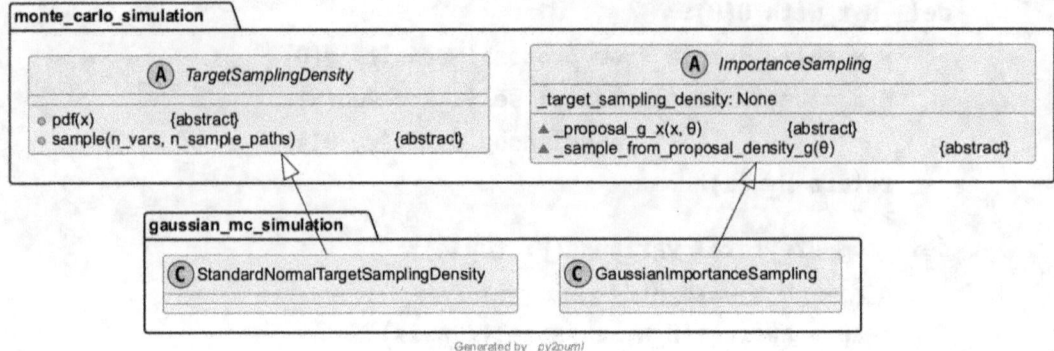

Figure 4-7. Class diagram for Gaussian MC simulation with importance sampling

While modeling the financial securities in Part 2 onwards in this book, we try leveraging the importance sampling method as much as possible. These components will come as handy and easy to integrate then.

Summary

In this chapter, we discussed essential tools and methods to provide inference from a probability model using simulation. While we keep progressing, these methods are supposed to help us in forecasting different financial securities behavior – be it stocks, options, or portfolios. As the models we discuss in this book are based on stochastic differential equations, no matter what we choose there, basic forecasting techniques always remain model agnostic. That's the purpose of making the components reusable as much as possible to enhance the ease of integration later.

Monte Carlo simulation plays a big role in finance as a forecasting method. We discussed the statistical model behind it and built components that are pluggable with variance reduction techniques to improve the forecasting accuracy. Not only that but also the component designed for the acceptance-rejection method of random variate generation has the capability to generate samples from any arbitrary and complex probability distribution. These should work as a solid base to build financial components on top.

In the next chapter, we discuss another perquisite of modeling, the stochastic process, its sample path generation, and the framework to build components as usual.

CHAPTER 5

Stochastic Process

This is the last chapter of Part 1 of the book, where we discuss the component we directly deal with while modeling asset prices – the stochastic process. So far, probability, simulations, etc., were just building blocks of this one. In this chapter, we will learn how the stochastic process behaves with time and how its realizations relate to asset movements. The key focus of the learning would be how to apply Monte Carlo simulation in realizing any stochastic process; however, parameter estimation of the same will be covered in Part 2 while discussing the asset price models.

Inception of Stochastic Process

The basic idea of the stochastic process can be drawn directly from the asset price. We learned how returns are computed in Chapter 2 along with time. Figures 2-3 and 2-5 show how *Pfizer* stock prices and returns computed from there form a stream-like view; well, that's a realization of the stochastic process. But we only learned the realization of a single random variable (RV); here, in this case, it is for a collection or stream of RVs. Let's deep dive a bit into the theoretical nitty gritty.

Given a probability space (Ω, F, P), a *stochastic process* is defined as a collection (or array) of random variables $X = \{X_t(\omega) : t \geq 0, \ \omega \in \Omega\}$. t is a scalar variable indicating the index of the collection, and it is often considered as time. The variable t may also be a vector, for example, a two-dimensional one indicating a spatial coordinate system. Observe that if you keep ω as fixed and vary t, then you will get a distribution of random variables over index t for that specific event. How does ω look like? From the definition of probability, ω is a sequence of events and more often infinite in nature. Suppose you are tossing a coin ten times. What are the possible outcomes? It is $10^2 = 100$ different possible sequences. Denoting 1 as *head* and 0 as *tail*, then the sequences look like 1011001011, 0101101100, etc. But, if it is of infinite length, i.e., if you toss an infinite number of times, then one of the possible sequences would be 1010001101100. Notice

CHAPTER 5 STOCHASTIC PROCESS

that the sequence of length 10 can be thought of as outputs from ten random variables, i.e., it is a collection of ten events. These random variables can be denoted as $X_1, X_2, ..., X_{10}$; and consequently, X_1 (head) = 1 and X_1 (tail) = 0. The same rule also goes for other variables. As a result, $X_1, X_2, ..., X_{10}$ constitute a stochastic process and are written as $X_t(\omega)$ where t is the index. If t is time, then $X_t(\omega)$ is the timely behavior of a random variable, which is analogous to a time series. For the use cases discussed in this book, t is always considered as time. Figure 5-1 shows the structure of a theoretical stochastic process X_t where an RV at time t_i is denoted as X_{t_i} and can have values $\{v^k_{t_i}\}$.

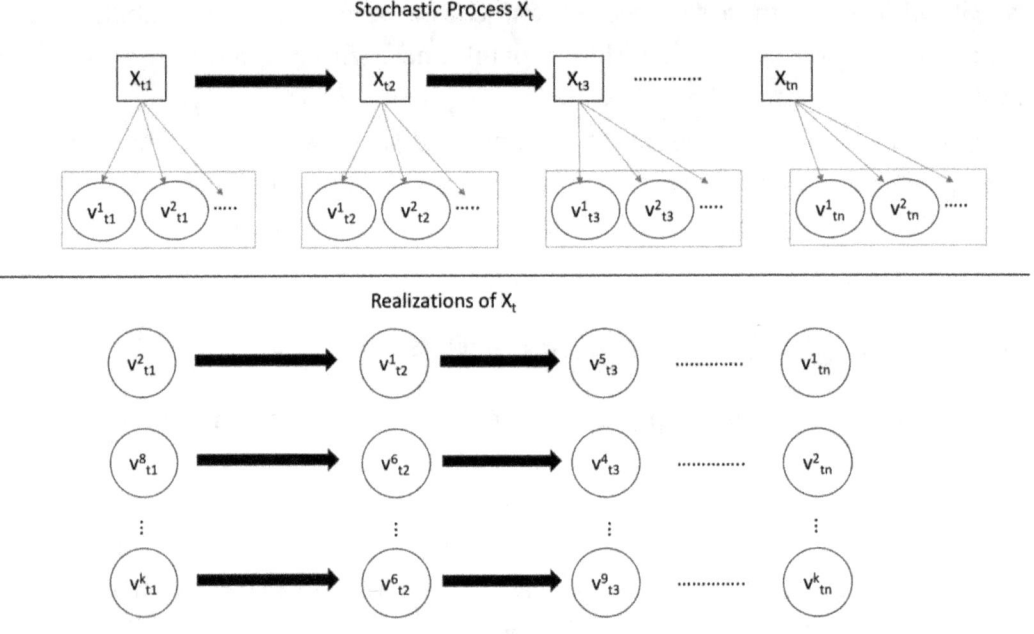

Figure 5-1. *Theoretical structure and realizations, a.k.a. sample paths of stochastic process X_t*

Multiple realizations of X_t are possible with all permutations and combinations, for example, $\{v^2_{t_1}, v^1_{t_2}, v^5_{t_3} ... v^1_{t_n}\}$, $\{v^8_{t_1}, v^6_{t_2}, v^4_{t_3} ... v^2_{t_n}\}$, and so on. Each set is known as the *sample path* of the stochastic process.

The joint density function view of any stochastic process looks like

$$f(x_1, x_2, ..., x_n, t_1, t_2, ..., t_n) = P(X(t_1) = x_1, X(t_2) = x_2, ... X(t_n) = x_n)$$

x_1, x_2, etc., are different values of random variable $X(t_k)$. Basically, these joint density functions are finite dimensional in nature (time instances or indices range from 1 to n) and snapshots of the stochastic process within a range of indices (or time). Note that t can be both discrete and continuous. Stochastic processes can also be *discrete time* and *continuous time* accordingly depending on t. In this book, we assume that the data coming from the data adapters are of discrete time in nature.

Random Walk Model

A random walk is a primitive discrete time stochastic process that forms the basis of the modeling asset paths. A very naïve way of creating the simplest random walk model could be through the same coin tossing experiment. Let X_i be the random variable representing the output of a toss – *head (+1)* or *tail (-1)*. Each experiment trial is conducted at every Δt time gap (could be seconds), and it follows the *Bernoulli distribution*. As usual, there are two probabilities involved, p = probability of head coming as output of a trial and q = same for tail. Eventually, $q = 1 - p$. Trials can be thought of as a sequence of events (just like a stochastic process) and are represented by $\omega = \omega_1 \omega_2 \omega_3 \ldots$ and so on. Let's write down the RV X_i more formally as

$$X_i = \begin{cases} 1 \text{ if } \omega_i = H \\ -1 \text{ if } \omega_i = T \end{cases}$$

We also define another RV as S_k, which is the sum of all X_i's up to kth one. Formally,

$$S_0 = 0, \quad S_k = \sum_{i=1}^{k} X_i$$

The same is expressed as a recurrence relation like below:

$$S_0 = 0, \quad S_k = S_{k-1} + X_k$$

The process S_k is known as the *symmetric random walk model*. It is called "symmetric" as the probabilities of going up and down are the same, i.e., $P(\omega_i = H) = P(\omega_i = T)$. It can be simulated graphically with steps moving upwards or downwards. Its sample path would look like that of Figure 5-2.

CHAPTER 5   STOCHASTIC PROCESS

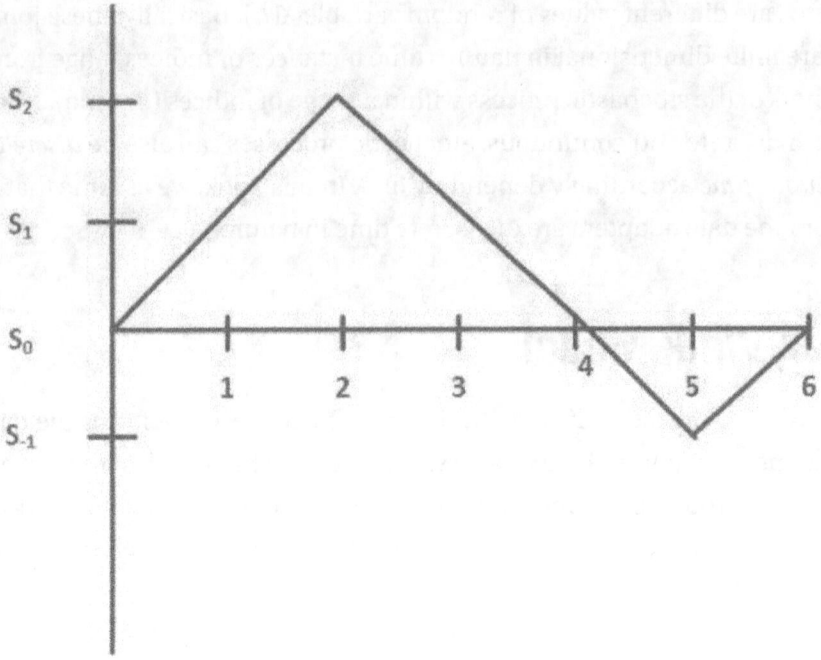

Figure 5-2. A sample path of the random walk model

Statistical Metrics of Symmetric Random Walk Model

The *mean* and *variance* of the random variable X_i of the random walk model can easily be computed like below:

$$E(X_i) = \sum_i X_i P(X_i) = (1)\frac{1}{2} + (-1)\frac{1}{2} = 0$$

$$Var(X_i) = E(X_i^2) - [E(X_i)]^2 = 1$$

Symmetric random walk has independent increments. This means that differences between any two values of the walk, i.e.,

$$S_t, (S_{t_1} - S_t), (S_{t_2} - S_{t_1}), (S_{t_3} - S_{t_2})\ldots,$$

are independent to each other (t, t_1, t_2, t_3 ... are not necessarily consecutive). Note that these intervals should be nonoverlapping in nature. If not, then independence property may not hold true. These differences indicate the change in direction of the walk. Now, let's compute the mean and variance of a generic difference $S_h - S_l$, where $h > l$.

We use the same recurrence relation of the random walk model as follows:

$$S_h - S_l = \sum_{i=l}^{h} X_i$$

Expectation and variance can now be computed as

$$E(S_h - S_l) = E\left(\sum X_i\right) = 0$$

$$Var(S_h - S_l) = Var\left(\sum_{i=l}^{h} X_i\right) = \sum_{i=l}^{h} Var(X_i) = \sum_{i=l}^{h} 1 = h - l$$

This is an interesting property of the random walk model: the variance between any two states is equal to the time difference.

Quadratic Variation of Symmetric Random Walk Model

Quadratic variation is the sum of the square of differences of two consecutive values of S_i till a time k starting from 1 which is given by the expression

$$[S,S]_k = \sum_{i=1}^{k} (S_i - S_{i-1})^2 = \sum_{i=1}^{k} 1 = k$$

Observe that, as X_i can only take two values (1 and −1), the difference between two S_i will be either 1 or −1. Thus, summing up altogether till k produces the value k for the quadratic variation. You might be wondering why we would need this expression when we already have variance in place. There is a difference. *Variance* is an expected measure, whereas *quadratic variation* is a realized one specific to one sample path. *Variance* considers all possible probabilities of movements from all possible sample paths, thus giving an expected value. That's why changing the probabilities of movements (in this case, $P(\omega_i = H)$ and $P(\omega_i = T)$, respectively) will change *variance* and that may or may not affect *quadratic variation* in turn. This measure has significance in computing the realized volatility of the asset path. For example, if you are given stock prices of *Pfizer* within a time range and you don't have any knowledge about the stochastic process, then still you can get some idea about the variance by computing the quadratic variation.

Scaled Random Walk Model

In the scaled version of the random walk model, we speed up time and scale down the time difference, a.k.a. *step size*. The random walk discussed earlier had some discontinuity in the path; scaling helps to smooth it down. *Brownian motion* – the key stochastic process for modeling asset prices – is a scaled version of the random walk only. In limited form, it can be shown that scaling leads to Brownian motion as follows:

$$W_t^f = \frac{1}{\sqrt{f}} S_{ft}$$

where f is the scaling factor of time and ft is an integer. If T is the total time of a walk, then by the same logic, time increments should be

$$\Delta t = \sqrt{\frac{T}{f}}.$$

To check it in practice, let's define a Python class as follows:

```
class ScaledSymmetricRandomWalkModel:

    UP_MOVE = 1
    DOWN_MOVE = -1

    def __init__(self, scale_factor: int, total_time):
        self.scale_factor = scale_factor
        self.T = total_time
        self.scaled_delta_t = math.sqrt(float(self.T / self.scale_factor))

    def __compute_initial_walk__(self):
        s = numpy.zeros(self.T + 1)
        for t in range(1, self.T + 1):
```

CHAPTER 5   STOCHASTIC PROCESS

```
        s[t] = s[t-1] + ScaledSymmetricRandomWalkModel.next_
        random_move()
    return s

@classmethod
def next_random_move(cls):
    prob = random.random()
    if prob >= 0.5:
        return ScaledSymmetricRandomWalkModel.UP_MOVE
    return ScaledSymmetricRandomWalkModel.DOWN_MOVE
```

Observe that the function __compute_initial_walk__ implements the same recurrence relation as discussed earlier. It simulates a vanilla symmetric random walk and stores values in array s. For the simple symmetric random walks, as the movements are fixed, we gave a random flavor, thereby drawing a random number and then deciding the states accordingly. Basically, we sampled the direction, not the movement itself. But ideally, for any other stochastic process, the movements themselves should be directly sampled from the appropriate probability distribution.

Next, let's deep dive into scaling a bit. It is a method through which we can estimate the samples of the stochastic process at any new time index between two other given time indices. In the original random walk, the new time index may not be there, i.e., it might not have been sampled while generating the path. Basically, the method is meant to decompose the RVs of the original stochastic process into a bigger set of RVs, forming a new stochastic process. With this, the new process looks more granular, taking smaller steps. For example, the daily prices of any stock will be more granular than the weekly prices. But, if daily samples are not available, the same can be estimated from the weekly ones through the scaling process. We revisit this in the next chapter while modeling.

To implement scaling, linear interpolation is recommended to handle the situation when ft is not an integer, given that a scaling factor with floating point number was used. W_t^f can be interpolated by

$$W_t^f = \frac{1}{\sqrt{f}} S_{ft_{lower}} + \frac{t - t_{lower}}{\sqrt{f}\left(t_{upper} - t_{lower}\right)} \left(S_{ft_{upper}} - S_{ft_{lower}}\right)$$

CHAPTER 5   STOCHASTIC PROCESS

where t is the target time index, t_{upper} and t_{upper} are the time indices sampled from the original random walk with the condition $t_{lower} < t < t_{upper}$, and ft_{lower} and ft_{upper} are both integers.

The whole method is captured in functions _interpolate_step_ and _compute_scaled_walk_ as follows:

```
def __interpolate_step__(self, walk, n_t, sq_root_scale_factor):
    t = float(n_t / self.scale_factor)
    t_upper = int(math.ceil(t))
    t_lower = int(math.floor(t))
    s_t_upper = walk[t_upper] / sq_root_scale_factor
    s_t_lower = walk[t_lower] / sq_root_scale_factor
    return float(s_t_lower + float((((t - t_lower) /
    (t_upper - t_lower))
        * (s_t_upper - s_t_lower))))

def __compute_scaled_walk__(self, initial_walk):
    scaled_walk = pd.DataFrame(columns=['t', 'S'])
    n_t = 0.0
    sq_root_scale_factor = math.sqrt(self.scale_factor)
    while n_t <= (self.T * self.scale_factor):
        if n_t.is_integer():
            scaled_s = float(
                initial_walk[int(math.floor(n_t))] / sq_root_
                scale_factor)
        else:
            scaled_s = self.__interpolate_step__(
                initial_walk, n_t, sq_root_scale_factor)
        scaled_walk = pd.concat(
            [scaled_walk, pd.DataFrame([{'t': n_t, 'S': scaled_s}])],
            ignore_index=True)

        n_t += self.scaled_delta_t

    return scaled_walk
```

And finally, all are put in the function *plot_scaled_walk* which is the entry point of everything as follows:

```
def plot_scaled_walk(self):
    initial_walk = self.__compute_initial_walk__()
    scaled_walk = self.__compute_scaled_walk__(initial_walk)
    self.__plot__(initial_walk, scaled_walk)
```

We can test it as follows:

```
def test_scaled_random_walk():
    m = ScaledSymmetricRandomWalkModel(scale_factor=2, total_time=20)
    m.plot_scaled_walk()
```

which produces output as shown in Figure 5-3.

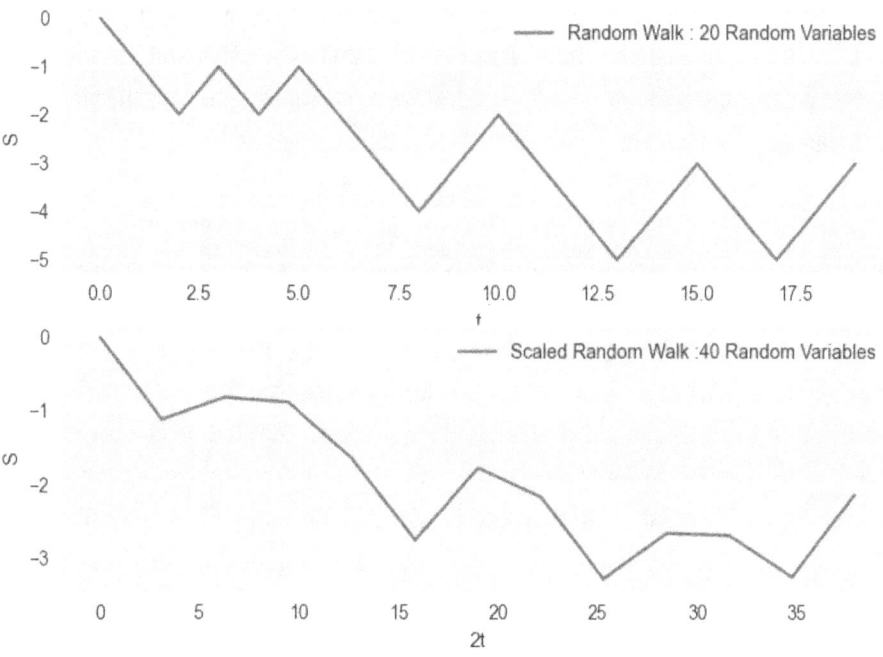

Figure 5-3. *Plot of random walk vs. scaled random walk for scale factor 2*

Observe the broken nature of the graph in the scaled version. Reason can be explained easily. Just think about it – earlier, we were taking a total of 10 steps (as 10 random variables), and in the scaled one, we took 40 steps. Obviously, our steps would be smaller in size, and directions would be a little more haphazard than the previous one.

CHAPTER 5 STOCHASTIC PROCESS

Scaled walk with a higher scale factor almost mimics the original walk. What it means that scaled walk asymptotically converges to original walk with an $f \to \infty$. This is the foundation of *Brownian motion* discussed next.

Brownian Motion

Scaled random walk asymptotically converges to a walk which is almost continuous in nature, i.e., Δt will be close to zero. With this continuous setting, a special stochastic process named *Brownian motion* (denoted as B_t) is defined as follows:

---

i) B_t has initial condition $B_0 = 0$.

ii) B_t is stationary for any values t.

iii) For all $0 = t_1 < t_2 < \ldots < t_m$, the increments of the process $B_1 - B_0, B_1 - B_0, \ldots, B_m - B_{m-1}$ are independent and follow normal distribution. In general, for any two times t and s where $t > s$, $B_t - B_s$ follows a normal distribution with zero mean and variance t-s. Mathematically, it can be written as

$$E[B_t - B_s] = 0$$

$$Var[B_t - B_s] = t - s$$

Basically, it is a customized Gaussian process. Its original idea came from the British botanist *Robert Brown*, who observed the motion of particles immersed in a liquid or gas. This motion follows a zigzag direction, which simulates the movement of many physical and virtual entities in the world. The stock price is just one of them. *Brownian motion* is an asymptotic behavior of the scaled random walk model. Observe the computed variable *scaled_delta_t* in the __init__ function of the class *ScaledSymmetricRandomWalkModel*. It is of type float that makes the time increments continuous in nature. Original random walk is a discrete time stochastic process, but the scaled one is not. There may exist an infinite number of random variables between any two-time instances depending on the value of the time increment. The same goes for the Brownian motion. It is a more refined view of the scaled random walk where movements are not fixed but rather sampled from Gaussian distribution.

From the definition, the recurrence can be formed as follows:

$$B_{t_i} = B_{t_{i-1}} + X_i \text{ where } X_i \sim N(0, \ t_i - t_{i-1}).$$

The relation looks like the one for the random walk model with the only difference in the random increments X_i. We can always generate paths from this relation itself, but we want to discuss this stochastic process from a stochastic differential equation's (SDE) perspective, as that would be a more formal and generic approach. SDE is the basis of many complex financial models. We cover more SDE-related advanced topics like *Ito lemma* in the next chapter, but before that, here we briefly introduce stochastic calculus and integrals necessary to understand SDE.

Stochastic Calculus and Integrals – A Brief Introduction

At a high level, *integral calculus* is the study of computing area under a curve. Anyone with a course in high school mathematics shouldn't have any challenges with it. But, still, for convenience, we will revisit it to better understand its stochastic variant.

The common integral forms we are familiar with are known as *Riemann integral* and *Riemann–Stieltjes integral*. Suppose f is a function of time t; then *Riemann integral* S is defined as

$$S = \int_{t_p}^{t_q} f(t) dt.$$

It is the value of the area under the curve $f(t)$ within a specified range of t. Though the expression is in analytical form, we can still evaluate it numerically as follows:

$$S = \lim_{n \to \infty} S_n = \lim_{n \to \infty} \sum_{i=1}^{n} f(t_i)(t_i - t_{i-1}) = \lim_{n \to \infty} \sum_{i=1}^{n} f(t_i) \Delta t_i,$$

which is an asymptotic version of the integral. It is obtained by dividing the difference $t_q - t_p$ into n equal parts or steps and then taking the sum of the products. The precision of S depends on how much smaller steps can be considered for computation. A higher value of n for a heavily nonlinear $f(t)$ will produce a more precise estimate. Throughout this, we keep Δt_i as constant, whereas with a varying Δt_i, i.e., Δt_i being another function of t, we have *Riemann–Stieltjes integral* as follows:

$$S = \int_{t_p}^{t_q} f(t) dg(t),$$

with the numerical form

$$S = \lim_{n\to\infty} S_n = \lim_{n\to\infty} \sum_{i=1}^{n} f(t_i)\left[g(t_i) - g(t_{i-1})\right] = \lim_{n\to\infty} \sum_{i=1}^{n} f(t_i)\Delta_i g.$$

Both differentials, be it constant (dt) or variable ($dg(t)$), are deterministic in nature, but what if they are not and are rather stochastic? A stochastic differential also makes output S as stochastic. Doesn't it sound like a Brownian motion where the increments are drawn from a Gaussian distribution? Formally, these types of integrals are known as *stochastic integrals*. Here, we study one class of stochastic integrals known as *Ito integrals*, named after the Japanese mathematician *Kiyoshi Ito*. It is defined as

$$dI(t) = f(t)dW(t),$$

which produces the integral

$$I(T) = \int_0^T f(t)dW(t).$$

$W(t)$, a.k.a. W_t, is known as the *Wiener process*. It is generally considered a Brownian motion with time step size 1, i.e., t-s is 1. Note that there is no restriction on the integrand $f(t)$, i.e., it may be either a stochastic or deterministic function. Integral $I(T)$ obtained as output is a stochastic process known as the *Ito process*. We can numerically evaluate the Ito integral in the same method of discretization as done earlier:

$$I(T) = \lim_{n\to\infty} \sum_{i=1}^{n} f(t_i)\left[W(t_i) - W(t_{i-1})\right] = \lim_{n\to\infty} \sum_{i=1}^{n} f(t_i)\Delta_i W,$$

where $W(t_i)$ is the Wiener process state at time t_i.

Stochastic Differential Equation – Financial Asset Dynamics

With the brief overview of stochastic integral, we can now introduce *stochastic differential equations (SDE),* the class of ordinary differential equations perturbed by random noise. Generally, the structure looks as follows:

$$dX(t) = b(t,X(t))dt + \sigma(t,X(t))dW(t).$$

The noise part is represented by the $W(t)$, which is a stochastic process, and the Wiener process is a good choice for this. $b(t, X(t))$ is known as the *drift term* and $\sigma(t, X(t))$ the *diffusion term*. The drift part represents the overall motion or direction of any system, in this case, the direction of the asset price. The diffusion part contains the external dynamic noise coming from the environment, i.e., the financial market dynamics. The solution of the above SDE is given by the integral form

$$X_t = X_0 + \int_0^t b(t, X_t) dt + \int_0^t \sigma(t, X_t) dW_t.$$

In this book, we are interested in the SDEs having a constant drift (μ) and diffusion (σ), and that can be written as

$$dX_t = \mu dt + \sigma dW_t,$$

with the following solution:

$$X_t = X_0 + \int_0^t \mu dt + \int_0^t \sigma dW_t.$$

The second term is a Riemann integral, and the third term is an Ito integral; both can be numerically approximated. Note that the solution of an ordinary differential equation is a deterministic function, whereas the same for an SDE is a stochastic process.

After all these discussions, we formally got an SDE that drives a Brownian motion with drift and diffusion. The Brownian motion mentioned at the beginning of the section and represented by $B_{t_i} = B_{t_{i-1}} + X_i$ doesn't have a drift component or it is zero. In this book, we always represent the asset price lifecycle by the aforementioned basic SDE or any extensions of it.

Euler's Method for Approximating SDE

I hope you understand that a closed-form solution of the SDE is difficult to obtain due to the presence of a stochastic term. The Euler method can approximate the integrals involved in the solution numerically, thus providing an estimated solution. Being a stochastic process, the solution is represented as a collection of sample paths from which further insights can be drawn. With the incremental approach for the time interval $[t_{i+1}, t_i]$, we have

$$\begin{cases} X_0 = 0, \\ X_{t_{i+1}} = X_{t_i} + \mu \Delta_i t + \sigma \Delta_i W. \end{cases}$$

CHAPTER 5 STOCHASTIC PROCESS

From the Brownian motion, we know, $\Delta_i W \sim N(0, t_{i+1} - t_i)$. For the use cases described in the book, we always take unit time intervals, i.e., $t_{i+1} - t_i = 1$. By drawing samples from the Gaussian distribution and then using the solution above, we can generate sample paths for the Brownian motion. How to do that is explained next.

Basic Forecasting Theory and Monte Carlo Simulation

By literal meaning, forecasting is knowing about the future as any stochastic process generally involves time. We are doing that already in Brownian motion's solution – $X_{t_{i+1}}$ is the future value of X_{t_i}. The relation between X_{t_i} and $X_{t_{i+1}}$ can be formally expressed in functional form as

$$X_{t_{i+1}} = h^B\left(X_{t_i}, \Delta_i W\right),$$

as $X_{t_{i+1}}$ is a function of $\Delta_i W$ and X_{t_i}. We don't know the distribution of X_{t_i}, but know that $\Delta_i W \sim N(0, 1)$. This is sufficient as each X_{t_i} can be obtained from its previous time's value. Now, we are left with a simulation problem. To explore the full distribution $X_{t_{i+1}}$, we must perform a Monte Carlo simulation, where the function h^B works like the target function $h(x)$ as explained in Chapter 4. Recall the components described there for Monte Carlo simulation – it took *n_vars* and *n_sample_paths* variables where the first one is the number of variables in a single sample path, i.e., representing a total number of time increments. These two form a grid of RVs as shown in Figure 5-4 where there is $t \times n$ number of RVs generated by the framework. These RVs should be generated at a single shot to reduce the sampling cost and feed into the paths accordingly. The simulation framework we developed in Chapter 4 takes care of it.

CHAPTER 5   STOCHASTIC PROCESS

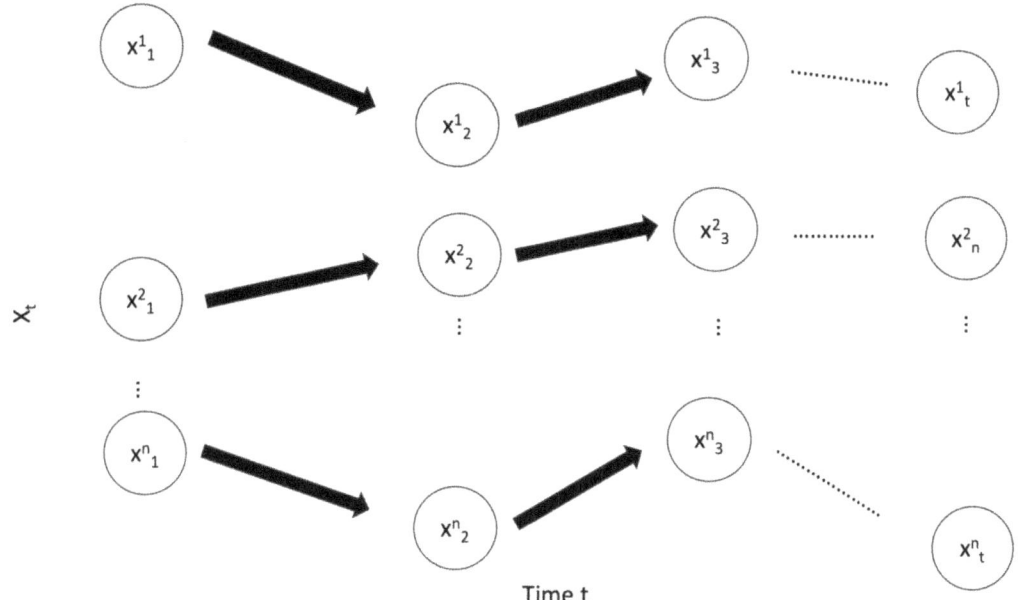

Figure 5-4. *Grid of random variable in sample paths*

To implement all these in Python, we introduce a forecasting framework that will be leveraged throughout this book for any asset price forecasting – stocks, options, and even portfolios. We create a base class *ForecastingProcess* with public function *forecast* as shown partially as follows (*/chapter5/base_forecasting.py*):

```
class ForecastingProcess(ABC):
    def __init__(self, n_sample_paths, initial_state, sampling_density:
            TargetSamplingDensity):
        self._n_sample_paths = n_sample_paths
        self._t = 0
        self._T = 0
        self._state_t = initial_state
        self._initial_state = initial_state
        self._sampling_density = sampling_density

    def forecast(self, T, var_reduction: VarReduction = NoVarReduction(),
            time_unit_transformer: TimeUnitTransformer = None) ->
            ForecastResult:
```

145

```python
        return ForecastResult(
                mcs=self._forecast_internal(T, var_reduction),
                time_unit_transformer=time_unit_transformer)

    def _forecast_internal(self, T, var_reduction):
        self._T = T
        self._t = 0
        mcs = MonteCarloSimulation(h_x_fun=self._update_current_state,
                                   n_vars=T, n_sample_paths=self._n_
                                   sample_paths,
                                   var_reduction=var_reduction,
                                   target_sampling_density=self._sampling_
                                   density)
        e = mcs.new_estimate()
        self._state_t = self._initial_state
        return e
```

The function *forecast_internal* is responsible for leveraging the *MonteCarloSimulation* and generating a total of *n_vars* ×*n_sample_paths* number of RVs to find an estimate. The significance of the other parameters – *var reduction* and *time unit transformer* – will be discussed in the next chapter while using this component to forecast the stock price with the real dataset. Two other functions are also needed to leverage this class fully as follows:

```python
@ abstractmethod
def _update_current_state(self, z): ...

def _reset_new_sample_path_state(self):
    if self._t >= self._T:
        self._state_t = self._initial_state
        self._t = 0
    self._t = self._t + 1
```

Note that one should properly override the function *_update_current_state* to keep updating future states from current states. Basically, the stochastic process is like a continuously rolling dice, where states are updated in each step. All of the stochastic processes discussed in this book extend from this base class *ForecastingProcess*.

The other class, *ForecastResult*, is responsible for crafting the sample paths, mean path, and uncertainty bounds – the last two are explicitly needed in asset price analysis. We only explore the sample paths in this chapter. The *ForecastResult* is partially shown below:

```
class ForecastResult:
    '''
    ForecastResult
    '''

    def __init__(self, mcs: MonteCarloSimulation.MCEstimate,
                 time_unit_transformer: TimeUnitTransformer = None):

        self._time_unit_transformer = time_unit_transformer
        self._sample_paths: pd.DataFrame = self._extract_sample_paths(mcs)
        self._mean_path: pd.DataFrame = self._extract_mean_path(mcs)
        self._uncertainty_bounds: tuple = self._extract_uncertainty_bounds(
            mcs)
        self._prob_dist_from_path = None
        self._prob_dist_from_sample_paths = None
        self._times_prob_dist_of_path = None
        self._log_scale_display = False

    def _extract_sample_paths(self, mcs: MonteCarloSimulation.
    MCEstimate) ->
pd.DataFrame:

        ts = self._transform_time(path=mcs.samples[0])
        return pd.DataFrame(mcs.samples, columns=ts).transpose()
```

There is a visualization component *ForecastResultDisplay* that should be used along with *ForecastResult* as shown partially:

```
class ForecastResultDisplay:

    def __init__(self, result: ForecastResult, xlabel='t', ylabel='X(t)'):
        self._result: ForecastResult = result
        self._xlabel = xlabel
```

CHAPTER 5   STOCHASTIC PROCESS

```python
        self._ylabel = ylabel
        plt.style.use("seaborn-v0_8")

    def plot_sample_paths(self, ax=None):
        ax1 = plt.gca() if ax is None else ax
        self._result.sample_paths.plot(ax=ax1,
                                        xlabel=self._xlabel,
                                        ylabel=self._ylabel)
        ax1.legend([])
        if ax is None:
            plt.show()
```

To consume the components effectively, we need to create a concrete stochastic process, and we start off with the Brownian motion (BM) as follows:

```python
class BrownianMotionProcess(ForecastingProcess):
    '''
    Class for Brownian motion process
    '''
    def __init__(self, μ, σ,
                 initial_state=0,
                 n_sample_paths=5):
        super().__init__(initial_state=initial_state,
                         n_sample_paths=n_sample_paths,
            sampling_density=StandardNormalTargetSamplingDensity())
        self._μ = μ
        self._σ = σ

    def _update_current_state(self, z):
        self._reset_new_sample_path_state()
        self._state_t = self._state_t + self._μ + (self._σ * z)
        return self._state_t
```

This is a BM process with drift and diffusion parameters (μ and σ, respectively). We now create a test suite of several BM processes with different parameter combinations and plot sample paths. One such combination is created producing 10 sample paths for each, as follows *(/chapter5/test_base_forecasting)*:

CHAPTER 5 STOCHASTIC PROCESS

```
μ_1 = 10
σ_1 = 300
n_sample_paths = 10
bmp_1 = BrownianMotionProcess(μ=μ_1, σ=σ_1,
        n_sample_paths=n_sample_paths)
result_display_1 = ForecastResultDisplay(bmp_1.forecast(T=500)),
```

and produces output, as shown in Figure 5-5.

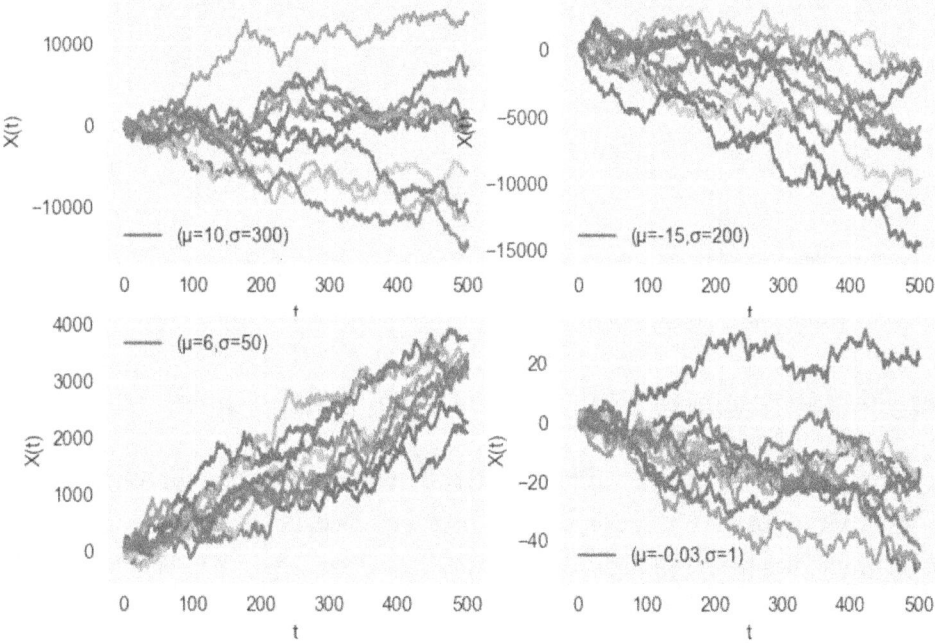

Figure 5-5. *Sample paths of the BM process for different parameters*

CHAPTER 5 STOCHASTIC PROCESS

Additionally, we can also plot the mean path as shown in Figure 5-6.

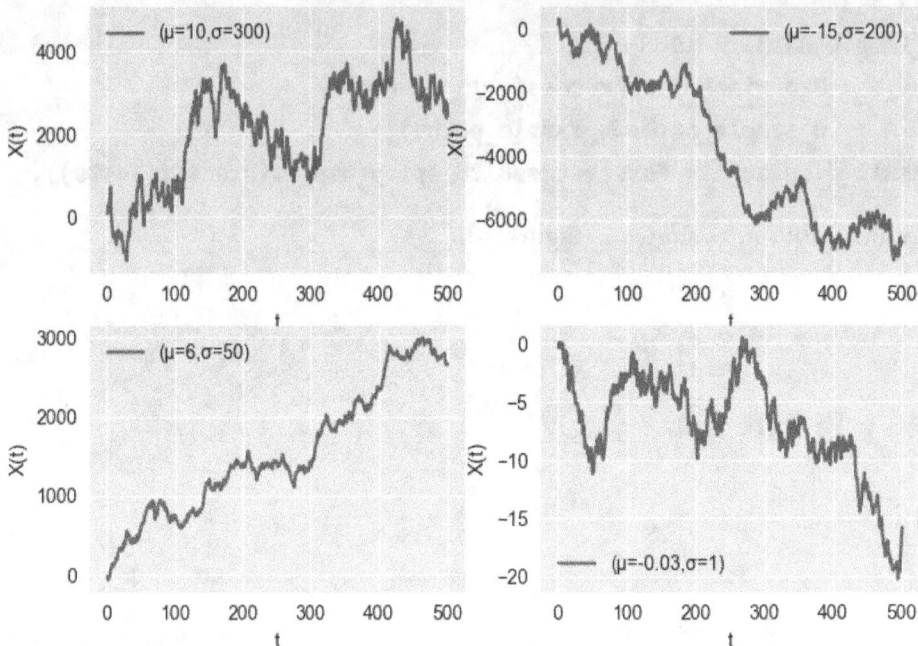

Figure 5-6. *Mean paths of the BM process for different parameters*

Both figures show how drift and diffusion change the course of directions of the paths. A higher diffusion induces more jumps, whereas drift controls the trend. Did you find any similarities between Figures 5-6 and 2-3 or even Figure 2-5. Figure 5-6 almost looks like it was plotted from some real stock price data, whereas it is not in reality. This is because of the statistical model we choose to generate paths there. Figure 5-6 drives the similar underlying physics of some real stock price data. It also shows that we are going in the right direction in our learning process.

Poisson Process

Like Poisson distribution, the stochastic process formed by the taking differences of Poisson RVs is known as the Poisson process. As discussed in Chapter 3, Poisson distribution is used to model events, and so is the Poisson process for a chain of events. A few examples would be the arrival process of customers at a store, the arrival of text messages on your cell phone, babies born in the maternity ward, and, the last and most important for this book, jumps in asset prices. It expects events to arrive in continuous intervals of time, making it a *counting process* estimating the probability of occurrence of several events by some time *t*. There exist multiple mathematical definitions of Poisson process (denoted by X_t^P). But for our interest, the one that best fits with the financial asset price movement is given below:

A Poisson process X_t^P with parameter λ is defined by
$$X_0^P = 0$$

For all 0 = t1 < t2 <... < tm, the increments of the process $X_{t_1}^P - X_{t_0}^P$, $X_{t_2}^P - X_{t_1}^P$, ..., $X_{t_m}^P - X_{t_{m-1}}^P$ are independent random variables.

The above increments follow a Poisson distribution with parameter λt for $s \geq 0$, t > 0. Formally,

$$P\left[\left(X_{t+s}^P - X_s^P\right) = k\right] = \frac{(\lambda t)^k e^{-\lambda t}}{k!}$$

Observe that the distribution of the increments only depends on the length of the interval *t* and not on the initial time *s*. As we always take $\Delta t = 1$, we can write the recurrent relation as

$$X_{t+1}^P = X_t^P + E, \quad E \sim Poisson(\lambda)$$

To implement the Poisson process, we need a sample density as required by the Monte Carlo simulation component, and this would be the Poisson density as follows:

class PoissonTargetSamplingDensity(TargetSamplingDensity):

'''

PoissonTargetSamplingDensity

'''

```
def __init__(self, λ):
    self._λ = λ

def pdf(self, x):
    return poisson(self._λ).pmf(x)

def sample(self, n_vars, n_sample_paths=1):
    return poisson.rvs(self._λ, size=(n_sample_paths, n_vars))
```

CHAPTER 5 STOCHASTIC PROCESS

This sampling density is leveraged in the same way as we did earlier for the BM process as follows:

```python
class PoissonProcess(ForecastingProcess):
    '''
    Poisson process
    '''
    def __init__(self, λ,
                 initial_state=0,
                 n_sample_paths=5):
        super().__init__(initial_state=initial_state,
                         n_sample_paths=n_sample_paths,
                         sampling_density=PoissonTargetSamplingDen
                         sity(λ=λ))
        self._λ = λ

    def _update_current_state(self, z):
        self._reset_new_sample_path_state()
        self._state_t = self._state_t + z
        return self._state_t
```

It is a simple implementation; running a similar test suite for different λ values, we get sample paths as shown in Figure 5-7.

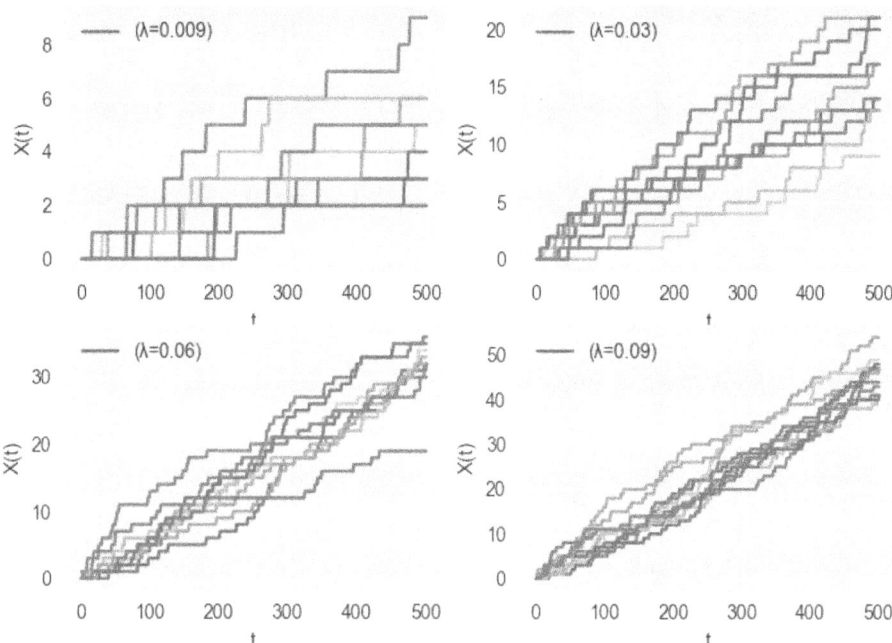

Figure 5-7. *Sample of Poisson process for different values of* λ

Notice the stepwise look of the Poisson process paths. The RV is discrete, and a higher λ produces more steps or jumps, making it look almost continuous. This path generation is for experimental purposes, as we don't use the Poisson process directly but rather embed it inside the BM process. You will learn more about this while discussing jump models in Chapter 7.

Summary

Knowing the simulation methods of the stochastic process is essential before studying SDE-based financial modeling. A stochastic process is a stream or collection of random variables that are either correlated or independent of each other. This chapter explains the life cycle of two major stochastic processes, which are needed directly or indirectly for further discussion in this book – the Brownian motion process and the Poisson process. Through numerical approximation of the Ito integral and Euler's method, an SDE can be solved and generate paths of solution stochastic process. This is the basis of financial modeling discussed in this book. We also introduced a forecasting framework to be leveraged throughout this book for implementing required stochastic processes. In Part 2 of the book, we directly start modeling financial assets with real datasets available from Yahoo Financials.

PART II

Basic Asset Price Modeling

CHAPTER 6

Diffusion Model

This chapter begins Part 2 of the book and introduces actual asset price modeling using a real dataset. As you know, Stochastic Finance requires a hefty amount of knowledge in probability and simulation, so we spent five chapters in Part 1 solidifying our grasp of these fundamentals. Don't think that we have read five chapters, but we are still about to start the crux of the subject – Stochastic Finance is never taught like that. Concepts for this subject highly overlap between the prerequisites and core topics. In some books, it is discussed completely from an applied probability perspective, and to maintain the consistency, we didn't want to deviate ourselves from there. This chapter takes the reader from the basic theory of stochastic process learned earlier to specialization with financial concepts, estimation of diffusion model parameters, computing the forecasted path distribution, capturing uncertainties in asset price, risk-neutral pricing, etc. At the end of the chapter, you should be able to do a basic asset price modeling with SDE and Monte Carlo simulation and start forecasting the future quotes.

Modeling Financial Asset Price with SDE

Financial asset price modeling has been a hot topic for many decades and will remain so in the future. It is a difficult job as we are uncertain about what drives the market. Of course, there are many floating lists, but nothing is exhaustive. From there, cherry picking the correct exogenous factors and then creating a time series model would be good for forecasting price movements. In fact, in recent years, with advancements made in machine learning (ML) and deep learning (DL) methods, a lot of significant work has been done on financial asset price modeling. These methods are data driven and sometimes explicit factor driven, whereas SDE-based methods are more traditional and physics driven. The latter captures market uncertainty explicitly inside models, unlike the ML- or DL-based approach, and both have their pros and cons. We will discuss those at the end of the chapter. First, let's explore what are the necessary steps for SDE-based models.

CHAPTER 6   DIFFUSION MODEL

SDE-Based Model-Building Steps

We can break down the overall procedure of model building into the following steps; some substeps should be familiar to you as learned from Part 1:

a) **Formation of SDE and stochastic process:** This is usually needed as the first step. The models discussed in this book are all based on one base BM process, so the SDE of the BM process is always included. On top of that, other components have been added accordingly. Here, by components, we don't really mean exogenous factors, unlike ML- or DL-based models. Factors there are more domain specific, but for SDEs, they capture much broader aspects. For example, jump components may be included in the SDE, but the reason for jumps is never explicitly specified. Once it is done, we approximate the SDE through Euler's method and then express the solution numerically as a stochastic process. Note that, along with SDE, formation of the stochastic process is also essential at this step.

b) **Estimation of PDF and its parameters:** PDF of the stochastic process must be estimated either in closed form or numerically. In both cases, the parameters of PDFs can then be estimated by MLE, GMM, or Bayesian method. But, for nonparametric models, PDF can be estimated by Kernel methods. We discuss three such flavors in this Part 2 of the book – closed form, numerically estimated PDF for the parametric approach, and Kernel method for the nonparametric approach.

c) **Inference (simulation, forecasting, and uncertainty quantification):** Once the model is built, inference can be drawn using Monte Carlo simulation and the forecasting method discussed in Chapter 5. However, one significant goal of this exercise is to capture the uncertainty of asset price paths, as that will drive investors to make informed decisions. I would say *uncertainty quantification* is the most important part of stochastic finance, and SDE methods are great with it. This step also provides the average asset price forecast that indicates the overall trend – again an important insight for investors.

With all those steps explained above, we delve into each one of those next.

CHAPTER 6 DIFFUSION MODEL

Formation of SDE – Log-Asset Price and Ito Lemma

We start off with the SDE of the diffusion model discussed in Chapter 5:

$$dX_t = \mu dt + \sigma dW_t,$$

and this is fine if the stochastic process allows all real numbers and extreme values. But, for modeling financial assets, we need some additional flavors. We need to cater to two requirements as follows:

a) Restricting to only positive real numbers as asset price will never be negative.

b) Handling extreme values to some extent, i.e., providing some cushion to the model if asset price shows a small number of high values in the paths due to unknown market shocks. (a) A log transformation can help to reduce the effects of these extremes. It's also a common practice in statistics and data analysis to apply log transformation before proceeding just to minimize the dispersion in the distribution.

As $\Delta W_t \sim N(0, 1)$, theoretically X_t can have negative values, so to stop that, log transformation is done, which also takes care of the requirement (b). Recall that we discussed log returns in Chapter 2, so something similar goes here also. With that, X_t becomes the log-transformed process of the original asset process S_t and is represented as $X_t = \log S_t$.

S_t REPRESENTS ALL TYPES OF ASSETS

By S_t, we mean all type of assets – stocks, options, and portfolios. For *stocks*, S_t holds direct values; for *options*, S_t is the value of options related to pay off, and for *portfolio*, it is the composite asset value. For convenience, we take one portfolio *S&P 500 index* as example asset to demonstrate modeling methods. Instead of asset value S_t, you may choose returns R_t as RV for modeling when you want to emphasize on returns for comparing with other assets.

We have the stochastic process for X_t, but we don't know the same for S_t. To derive it, we need *Ito lemma* as discussed next.

Ito Lemma

Ito lemma does a second-order approximation of a function of another diffusion process. To elaborate, if X_t is a diffusion process, then $g(X_t)$ can be approximated by

$$dg(X_t) = g'(X_t)dX_t + \frac{1}{2}g''(X_t)(dX_t)^2.$$

Proof of Ito lemma is outside the scope of this book; interested readers can refer to Shreve [24]. Stochastic calculus is itself a big area; it is neither possible nor does this book wish to go very in-depth there. However, nothing works better than grasping a full course on stochastic calculus before beginning financial asset price modeling.

Geometric Brownian Motion (GBM) Process and Euler Approximation

We begin with the function $g(S_t) = \log S_t$ representing the log-asset price, and to apply the Ito lemma there, we find these derivatives:

$$g'(S_t) = \frac{1}{S_t}, \quad g''(S_t) = -\frac{1}{S_t^2}.$$

Again, SDE for the log-asset BM process can be written as

$$d(\log S_t) = \mu dt + \sigma dW_t,$$

or

$$dS_t = S_t(\mu dt + \sigma dW_t).$$

We know that $\Delta W_t \sim N(0, \Delta t)$, and that leads to $E\left[\left(W_{t_{i+1}} - W_{t_i}\right)^2\right] = t_{i+1} - t_i$; as mean is zero and asymptotically when $\Delta t \to 0$, then it can be written in differential form as

$$(dW_t)^2 \approx dt.$$

We should remember this important rule in stochastic calculus.

Then to find the second-order approximation of the abovementioned SDE by applying the Ito lemma, we proceed as

$$d(\log S_t) = \frac{1}{S_t} dS_t + \frac{1}{2}\left(-\frac{1}{S_t^2}\right)(dS_t)^2$$

$$= \frac{1}{S_t} S_t(\mu dt + \sigma dW_t) - \frac{1}{2S_t^2}(S_t \mu dt + \sigma S_t dW_t)^2$$

$$= \mu dt + \sigma dW_t - \frac{1}{2S_t^2}\left(S_t^2 \mu^2 dt^2 + 2S_t^2 \mu \sigma dt dW_t + \sigma^2 S_t^2 dW_t^2\right)$$

$$= \left(\mu - \frac{1}{2}\sigma^2\right) dt + \sigma dW_t.$$

CHOICE OF TIME SCALE AND Δt

We always consider $\Delta t = 1$ in this book, but ideally, it should be your choice depending on how time scale is considered. We have taken index time, i.e., t=0,1, 2 ..., as time scale, but you may take physical timestamp (in *ms*, μs) also. This choice impacts the parameters, and reestimation is needed thereafter.

Observe that terms dt^2 and $dt dW_t$ were ignored as those are very small whereas dW_t^2 was replaced by dt as per the stochastic calculus rule. Now integrating both sides, we get

$$\int_0^t d(\log S_t) = \int_0^t \left[\left(\mu - \frac{1}{2}\sigma^2\right) dt + \sigma dW_t\right],$$

or

$$\log \frac{S_t}{S_0} = \left(\mu - \frac{1}{2}\sigma^2\right) t + \int \sigma dW_t$$

or

$$S_t = S_0 e^{\left(\mu - \frac{1}{2}\sigma^2\right) t + \int \sigma dW_t}$$

This is the expression of the geometric Brownian motion process, a.k.a. log-asset price process. With the Euler discretization scheme, this can recursively be written as

$$S_{t_{i+1}} = S_{t_i} e^{\left(\mu - \frac{1}{2}\sigma^2\right)\left(t_{(i+1)} - t_i\right) + \sigma \left(W_{t_{i+1}} - W_{t_i}\right)}.$$

CHAPTER 6 DIFFUSION MODEL

As in this book, we always take unit time interval, so $t_{(i+1)} - t_i = 1$, and with that,

$$S_{t_{i+1}} = S_{t_i} e^{\left(\mu - \frac{1}{2}\sigma^2\right) + \sigma \Delta_t W}$$

Removing the time indices would simplify the expression more:

$$S_{t+1} = S_t e^{\left(\mu - \frac{1}{2}\sigma^2\right) + \sigma \Delta_t W}$$

The above one is the very commonly used formula of the stochastic process of asset dynamics. Note that we consider drift and diffusion (μ and σ) as constant in this model, but they can be deterministic or even stochastic functions of time and expressed as $\mu(t)$ and $\sigma(t)$, respectively. In fact, $\mu(t)$ and $\sigma(t)$ can be taken as two separate individual stochastic processes. However, in this book, as of now, we don't consider such modeling approaches.

To implement this in Python, we may choose any one of the solutions for asset price dynamics – starting with S_0 or recursively computing S_{t+1} with S_t. Here, we prefer the second one to keep sampling from a single distribution. For the first one, $\Delta_t W \sim N(0, t)$ where t will be continuously incremental, thus forcing us to sample from a series of Gaussian distributions, whereas for the second one – $\Delta_t W \sim N(0, 1)$ – a single distribution suffices for the whole sampling procedure.

We now create a class *GeometricBrownianMotionProcess* and leverage the same *BrownianMotionProcess* class created in Chapter 5 as follows:

```
class GeometricBrownianMotionProcess(BrownianMotionProcess):
    '''
    GeometricBrownianMotionProcess
    '''
    def __init__(self, r, σ,
                 initial_state=1.0,
                 n_sample_paths=5):
        self._r = r
        self._σ = σ
        super().__init__(μ=self._r - (self._σ ** 2 / 2.0),
                         σ=self._σ,
```

CHAPTER 6 DIFFUSION MODEL

```
            initial_state=initial_state,
            n_sample_paths=n_sample_paths)

def _update_current_state(self, z):
    self._reset_new_sample_path_state()
    self._state_t = self._state_t * np.exp(self._σ + (self._σ * z))
    return self._state_t
```

We test this in the same way we did for the BM process, but now with different parameter scales, and one of such tests is given below (*chapter6/test/test_gbm_process.py*):

```
r_1 = -0.003
σ_1 = 0.04
bmp_1 = GeometricBrownianMotionProcess(r=r_1, σ=σ_1, n_sample_paths=5)
result_display_1 = ForecastResultDisplay(
    result=bmp_1.forecast(T=500), ylabel='S(t)')
```

Figure 6-1 shows the output obtained from a test suite done with different parameter combinations.

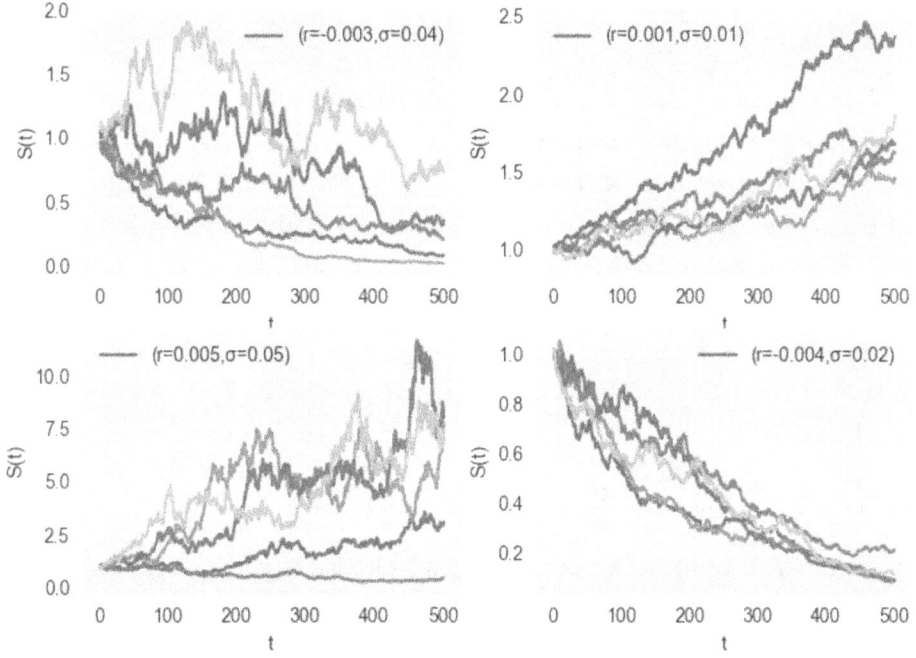

Figure 6-1. *Sample paths of the GBM process for different parameters*

163

CHAPTER 6 DIFFUSION MODEL

GBM process parameters are expressed in log scale, so it is easy to compare two GBM processes even though their magnitude of S_t doesn't match. Notice that in the code, we introduced the parameter r representing the growth rate instead of μ – why that's explained next.

Risk-Neutral Settings

Before proceeding to the estimation of PDF, it is important to discuss one financial setting that will not only change the calibration of the model but also impact all the models we discuss in this book. This introduces risk-free interest rate r (recall Chapter 2) as the drift parameter. This will be satisfied if

$$E[S_{t+\Delta t}] = S_t e^{r\Delta t}.$$

The GBM asset price process discussed earlier satisfied this condition only if the drift parameter μ is set to r, i.e., we take $\mu = r$, and then the asset price process takes the form as given by

$$S_{t+1} = S_t e^{\left(r - \frac{1}{2}\sigma^2\right) + \sigma \Delta_t W},$$

and we follow the same throughout the book for parameter estimation and forecasting.

Risk-neutral settings are introduced to reduce market risks and stabilize the system. This can be explained as follows: if there was a savings account interest r that could give the same expected return on the money, then that should theoretically be taken into computation. This savings account is hypothetical and may not exist; in fact, it doesn't. Stochastic processes for financial assets should comply with this if the risk-neutral policy is to be enforced while modeling. Generally, all the standard models we discuss follow this strictly.

Estimation of PDF and Its Parameters

To estimate the PDF, we must rearrange it to make it look like a density function. Let's start with taking the logarithms of both sides of the asset dynamics recurrence relation:

$$\log S_{t+1} = \log S_t + \left(r - \frac{1}{2}\sigma^2\right) + \sigma \Delta_t W$$

The expression above can be thought of as $\log S_{t+1}$ follows a normal distribution with mean

$$\log S_t + \left(r - \frac{1}{2}\sigma^2\right)$$

and variance $\sigma^2(\Delta_t W)^2$, i.e., σ^2 only (as $(\Delta_t W)^2 = \Delta t = 1$).

Assuming $X_{t+1} = \log S_{t+1}$,

$$X_{t+1} \sim N\left(\log S_t + \left(r - \frac{1}{2}\sigma^2\right), \sigma^2\right)$$

So the log-asset PDF is given by

$$f(X_{t+1}) = \frac{1}{\sigma\sqrt{2\pi}} e^{-\frac{1}{2}\left(\frac{X_{t+1} - \log S_t - \left(r - \frac{1}{2}\sigma^2\right)}{\sigma}\right)^2}$$

Recall the change of measure rule from Chapter 4, and by that, any two density functions f_Y and $f_{Z=e^Y}$ can be written as

$$f_{Z=e^Y}(z) = \left|\frac{dy}{dz}\right| f_Y(z) = \frac{1}{z} f_Y(z)$$

In this case, $S_t = e^{X_t}$. So $f^{Diffusion\_Model}(S_{t+1})$ and $f_{X_{t+1}}(x)$ are related as

$$f^{Diffusion\_Model}(S_{t+1}) = \frac{1}{S_{t+1}} f(X_{t+1})$$

Expanding to its full form,

$$f^{Diffusion\_Model}(S_{t+1}) = \frac{1}{\sigma S_{t+1}\sqrt{2\pi}} e^{-\frac{1}{2}\left(\frac{\log \frac{S_{t+1}}{S_t} - \left(r - \frac{1}{2}\sigma^2\right)}{\sigma}\right)^2}$$

CHAPTER 6 DIFFUSION MODEL

Estimation of Parameters – Likelihood Function and MLE

There are two paradigms for parameter estimation – *risk-neutral measure* and *real-world measure*. This bifurcation happens due to implications of the financial concept of risk neutrality discussed earlier rather than something coming from a purely probabilistic perspective.

Numerical Estimation Under the Risk-Neutral Measure

We take the discussion of PDF estimation using the risk-neutral measures as the opportunity to demonstrate a method where we have the PDF in closed form, but its parameter estimation is done numerically. We also develop components in Python that can be used as templates for parameter estimation for any PDF for asset price modeling.

To proceed, we have the risk-neutral density $f^{Diffusion\_Model}(S_{t+1})$ in closed form; from there, we write the log-likelihood function as

$$LL^{Diffusion\_Model}(r, \sigma) = \sum_{t=0}^{n-1} \log f^{Diffusion\_Model}(S_{t+1}),$$

and the estimated parameters by MLE:

$$\hat{r}, \hat{\sigma} = \underset{r,\sigma}{\operatorname{argmax}} \{LL^{Diffusion\_Model}(r, \sigma)\}.$$

I would say this method is seminumerical in nature as we still have the density in closed form, but the log-likelihood optimization is done numerically.

To implement, we create a base component in Python named *BaseAssetPriceModel* as follows:

```
class BaseAssetPriceModel(ABC):

    def __init__(self, time_unit_transformer: TimeUnitTransformer,
                param_type: str = None,
                asset_price_dataset_adapter:
                StockPriceDatasetAdapter = None,
                ll_optimizer: LoglikelihoodOptimizer = diffusion_process_
                ll_optimizer,
                n_sample_paths=100,
                training_required=True):
        self._time_u_t = time_unit_transformer
```

```python
        self._ll_optimizer = ll_optimizer
        self._n_sample_paths = n_sample_paths
        self._asset_price_dataset_adapter = asset_price_dataset_adapter
        self._training_required = training_required
        self._forecasting_process = None
        self._parameters = self._create_empty_param_instance()
        self._s_t_1 = None
        self._last_s = None

        print('BaseAssetPriceModel.training_required' + str(training_
        required))
        if training_required:
            if asset_price_dataset_adapter is None:
                raise ValueError(
                    'StockPriceDatasetAdapter is required for model
                    training.')
            if ll_optimizer is None:
                raise ValueError(
                    'An optimizer is required for model training.')
            self._s_t = asset_price_dataset_adapter.training_set
            self._fit()

    def _adjust_records(self):
        self._s_t_1 = self._s_t.shift(1)
        self._last_s = self._s_t.tail(1)

        self._time_u_t._t0 = parse(
            self._last_s['time'].iat[0], date_formats=['YYYY-MM-DD'])
        self._s_t_1.iloc[0, 1] = self._s_t.iloc[0, 1]

        self._parameters['s0'] = float(self._last_s['stock price'])
        self._parameters['t0'] = self._time_u_t._t0
```

This component can be used in two modes: *training* and *forecasting*, and for that, the *training_required* parameter specifies whether we need parameter estimation. Observe that in the PDF, we need to compute the log (S_{t+1}/S_t), i.e., the log ratio of the original and unit-lagged dataset. Function *_adjust_records* prepares the dataset for this computation by applying the shifting operation provided by the Python *pandas* module.

CHAPTER 6   DIFFUSION MODEL

BASEASSETPRICEMODEL WORKS AS TEMPLATE

BaseAssetPriceModel works as template of any asset price modeling component in this book. This can be used for both parameter estimation and inference. You should extend this one and create your own model. Usage guidelines are given as follows:

a) The actual asset price model should override these functions – *_pdf*, *_tuple_to_param_orde*, *_preprocess*, and *_create_forecasting_process*. The function *_pdf* can compute the density either via closed form or numerically (FFT or cosine method discussed in the next chapter); *_preprocess* does some extra preprocessing as explained in the code, whereas *_create_forecasting_process* expects the appropriate model-specific stochastic process to be created for forecasting with the estimated parameters.

b) Class function *load* must be used when estimation is already done and only inferencing is required given a set of parameters to be passed as dictionary.

c) *BaseAssetPriceModel* expects one likelihood optimizer to be passed in the *__init__* function though it uses a default one based on *shgo* algorithm under scipy module. It is of course your choice which one you would prefer, and you can always create your own custom optimizer by extending the class *LoglikelihoodOptimizer*.

Next, we cover the crux of the processing when *training_required* is set to true as follows:

```
def _fit(self):
    self._adjust_records()
    self._preprocess()
    θ = self._ll_optimizer.optimize(self._negative_loglikelihood)
    self._tuple_to_param_order(θ)
    self._forecasting_process = self._create_forecasting_process(
        self._parameters, self._n_sample_paths)

def _negative_loglikelihood(self, θ: tuple):
    return -np.sum(np.log(self._pdf(θ)))
```

CHAPTER 6 DIFFUSION MODEL

I don't want to recommend any specific optimizer for MLE; after all, it's your choice to pick something wisely. However, we use the *shgo* algorithm from the *scipy* module.

Next, we create a concrete class *DiffusionProcessAssetPriceModel* and override necessary functions. Some of them are shown below along with the *__init__*:

```
class DiffusionProcessAssetPriceModel(BaseAssetPriceModel):

    def __init__(self, time_unit_transformer: TimeUnitTransformer,
                 asset_price_dataset_adapter: StockPriceDataset
                 Adapter = None,
                 ll_optimizer: LoglikelihoodOptimizer = diffusion_process_
                 ll_optimizer,
                 n_sample_paths=100,
                 training_required=True,
                 ):
        self._log_ratio = None
        super().__init__(time_unit_transformer, 'DiffusionProcess
        Parameters',
                         asset_price_dataset_adapter,
                         ll_optimizer, n_sample_paths, training_required)

    def _tuple_to_param_order(self, θ):
        self._parameters['r'], self._parameters['σ'] = θ

    def _create_empty_param_instance(self):
        return DiffusionProcessParameters()

    def _preprocess(self):
        self._log_ratio = np.log(
            self._s_t['stock price'] / self._s_t_1['stock price'])
        self._s_t = self._s_t.drop([self._s_t.index[0]], inplace=False)
        self._log_ratio = self._log_ratio.drop(
            [self._log_ratio.index[0]], inplace=False)

    def _pdf(self, θ: tuple):
        r, σ = θ
        ll_factor_1 = (1/(σ * self._s_t['stock price']
                       * np.sqrt(2*np.pi)))
```

169

CHAPTER 6 DIFFUSION MODEL

```
        ll_factor_2 = np.exp(
            -0.5*np.power((self._log_ratio -
                        (r-0.5*(σ**2)))/σ, 2))

        return ll_factor_1 * ll_factor_2
```

The code should be self-explanatory, but still observe the function _pdf_ - it is simply implementing the density $f^{Diffusion\_Model}$ as explained earlier.

We test *DiffusionProcessAssetPriceModel* by setting the training mode on with the *S&P 500 index* dataset for the weekly stock data for the time January 1, 2010, to January 1, 2015, as follows.

Listing 6-1. A test case for parameter estimation of the diffusion model

```
def test_asset_price_model_estimation():
    ticker = '^GSPC'  # S&P 500 Index
    time_freq = Frequency.WEEKLY
    yfa = YahooFinancialsAdapter(
        ticker=ticker,
        frequency=time_freq,
        training_set_date_range=("2010-01-01", "2015-01-01"),
        validation_set_date_range=("2015-01-01", "2019-07-01"))

    dfp_model = DiffusionProcessAssetPriceModel(
                time_unit_transformer=IndexedTimeTransformer
                (time_freq=time_freq),
                 asset_price_dataset_adapter=yfa)
    print(ticker)
    print_parameters(dfp_model.parameters_)
```

Running this test case gave us the following parameter estimation:

```
^GSPC
s0: 2058.89990234375
t0: 2014-12-26 00:00:00
r: 0.002476615753153449
σ: 0.02042995488960794
```

It is interesting to observe parameters s0 and t0, as the procedure seemingly follows an S0-based nonrecursive model instead of the recurrent relation. But it's not. A stochastic process is expected to roll over time continuously like a stream, so it should remember the last time and the realized value to restart the rolling while forecasting. The pair s0 and t0 holds the last observed state from where fresh forecasting is expected to start. Check the second value in the variable *training_set_date_range* as shown in Listing 6-1, i.e., January 1, 2015, which should have been the t0 for estimation based on daily frequency. But as we chose weekly frequency, after the estimation, we got it as December 26, 2014, showing the previous week's value, which is technically correct. Now, details about leveraging these parameters will be covered in the forecasting section.

Closed-Form Estimation Under the Real-World Measure

We said that risk neutrality is expected to be maintained by the model. But what if it is not? PDF and parameter calibration will change. To elaborate, we start off again with the plain vanilla BM process (a.k.a. Arithmatric Brownian motion process or the ABM process) and write down its Euler method approximation (considering $\Delta t = 1$):

$$X_{t+1} = X_t + \mu + \sigma \Delta_t W.$$

This process is not expressed in log scale, and we see that

$$X_{t+1} \sim N\left(X_t + \mu, \sigma^2\right).$$

The density for this is known as a real-world measure and is given as

$$f^{real-world\ measure}\left(X_{t+1}\right) = \frac{1}{\sigma\sqrt{2\pi}} e^{-\frac{1}{2}\left(\frac{X_{t+1}-X_t-\mu}{\sigma}\right)^2}.$$

Then the log-likelihood function is given as

$$LL^{real-world\ measure}\left(\mu, \sigma^2\right) = \sum_{t=0}^{n-1} \log f^{real-world\ measure}\left(X_{t+1}\right)$$

$$= -n \log\left(\sigma\sqrt{2\pi}\right) - \frac{1}{2}\sum_{t=0}^{n-1}\left(\frac{X_{t+1}-X_t-\mu}{\sigma}\right)^2$$

CHAPTER 6 DIFFUSION MODEL

The optimal parameters would be

$$\hat{\mu}, \widehat{\sigma^2} = \underset{\mu, \sigma^2}{\operatorname{argmax}} \left\{ LL^{real-world\ measure}\left(\mu, \sigma^2\right) \right\}$$

It is possible to do the optimization analytically, and for that, let's compute the first-order derivatives and build the normal equations:

$$\frac{\partial}{\partial \mu} LL^{real-world\ measure}\left(\mu, \sigma^2\right) = 0, \; \frac{\partial}{\partial \sigma^2} LL^{real-world\ measure}\left(\mu, \sigma^2\right) = 0$$

Solving those w.r.t μ and σ^2 will give the following estimates:

$$\hat{\mu} = \frac{1}{n} \sum_{t=0}^{n-1} (X_{t+1} - X_t),$$

$$\widehat{\sigma^2} = \frac{1}{n} \sum_{t=0}^{n-1} (X_{t+1} - X_t - \hat{\mu})^2$$

The above estimates are in closed form, and computing them won't be a big deal after what we learned while computing them numerically in the previous section. We won't develop any separate Python component for this. It was shown as a demonstration for situations when we may have to take the real-world measure. Note that, theoretically, X_t can be negative, so first doing a log transformation of the asset price dataset is a must; otherwise, calibration won't be accurate. Forecasting results can later be brought back to the original scale by taking exponents. Estimates from the real-world measure can be used alongside the risk-neutral ones to get deeper insights into the asset price trends, and that should be handled carefully. For BM process, risk-neutral and real-world measures are almost same as we simply replace μ by r, but it may not be for other financial stochastic processes not directly based on BM, and in fact, it is not. Generally, the average forecasted value of a risky asset by risk-neutral measures will be lower than that by real-world measures.

Inference

After estimating parameters, we are now set for drawing inference, i.e., use the model for forecasting through simulation. As you know, the stock market is full of uncertainty, and without a holistic list of market influencer factors, we rely on stochastic simulation.

Theoretically, all these factors are captured inside drift and diffusion parameters, where drift provides the overall trend and diffusion is responsible for market uncertainty caused by many unknown factors.

Monte Carlo Simulation of Diffusion Model

The target function $h(x)$ of the Monte Carlo simulation framework for the diffusion model is given by

$$h^{Diffusion\ Model}(S_t, \Delta_t W) = S_t e^{\left(r - \frac{1}{2}\sigma^2\right) + \sigma \Delta_t W},$$

with the following relation to simulate S_{t+1}:

$$S_{t+1} = h^{Diffusion\ Model}(S_t, \Delta_t W).$$

With simulation, we keep generating different sample paths for future times. Each sample path shows us one possible future behavior of the financial asset. Recall Figure 1-4 from Chapter 1, showing the output of the stochastic system relying on simulation. Right now, while doing this forecasting exercise, we witness a realization of that diagram – an exploration of a predefined number of possible outputs through sample paths. We leverage the forecasting components as discussed in Chapter 5 for this, and just for generating sample paths, we don't have to do anything extra except override the *_create_forecasting_process* in the *DiffussionProcessAssetPriceModel* as follows:

```
def _create_forecasting_process(self,
                                parameters, n_sample_paths) ->
                                ForecastingProcess:
    return GeometricBrownianMotionProcess(
        r=parameters['r'],
        σ=parameters['σ'],
        initial_state=parameters['s0'],
        n_sample_paths=n_sample_paths)
```

CHAPTER 6   DIFFUSION MODEL

The above one is leveraged accordingly in the *BaseAssetPriceModel* as follows.

Listing 6-2. The function forecast inside BaseAssetPriceModel

```
def forecast(self, T,
             var_reduction: VarReduction = NoVarReduction(),
             prob_dist_viz_required=False,
             prob_dist_viz_settings: dict = {'n_workers': 5, 'ts':
             [5, 13, 17, 20, 22, 28]}):
    forecast_result = self._forecasting_process.forecast(
        T=T, var_reduction=var_reduction, time_unit_transformer=self._
        time_u_t)

    self._compute_prob_distribution_of_mean_path(
        forecast_result, prob_dist_viz_required, prob_dist_viz_
        settings)

    return forecast_result
```

The class *ForecastResult* is responsible for providing forecast-related metrics, such as mean, uncertainty bounds, and all sample paths (check */chapter5/base_forecasting.py*). The following code snippet shows the function *__init__* and sample path generation part.

Listing 6-3. Partial view of the class ForecastResult

```
class ForecastResult:
    '''
    ForecastResult
    '''

    def __init__(self, mcs: MonteCarloSimulation.MCEstimate,
                 time_unit_transformer: TimeUnitTransformer = None):
        self._time_unit_transformer = time_unit_transformer
        self._sample_paths: pd.DataFrame = self._extract_sample_paths(mcs)
        self._mean_path: pd.DataFrame = self._extract_mean_path(mcs)
        self._uncertainty_bounds: tuple = self._extract_uncertainty_bounds(
            mcs)
        self._prob_dist_from_path = None
```

```
        self._prob_dist_from_sample_paths = None
        self._times_prob_dist_of_path = None
        self._log_scale_display = False

    def _extract_sample_paths(self, mcs: MonteCarloSimulation.
    MCEstimate) ->
                            pd.DataFrame:
        ts = self._transform_time(path=mcs.samples[0])
        return pd.DataFrame(mcs.samples, columns=ts).transpose()
```

To test the function on the validation dataset (time range: January 1, 2015, to July 1, 2019) as shown in Listing 6-2, we use the function *load* to leverage the already estimated parameters from Listing 6-1 as follows:

```
def test_saved_asset_price_model():
    time_freq = Frequency.WEEKLY
    dsa = YahooFinancialsAdapter(
        ticker='^GSPC',
        frequency=time_freq,
        training_set_date_range=("2010-01-01", "2015-01-01"),
        validation_set_date_range=("2015-01-01", "2019-07-01"))

    params = {'s0': 2058.89990234375,
              'r': 0.002476615753153449, 'σ': 0.02042995488960794,
              't0': parse('2015-01-01', date_formats=['YYYY-mm-dd'])}

    model = DiffusionProcessAssetPriceModel.load(parameters=params,
                                              time_unit_transformer=Inde
                                              xedTimeTransformer(
                                                  time_freq=time_freq),
                                              n_sample_paths=5)
    _test_forecasting(model, dsa)
```

The output is shown in Figure 6-2, and it has three plots: all sample paths, uncertainty bounds, and backtesting results. The last two are explained later.

Time Unit Transformation

You might wonder about the time unit transformation shown in Listing 6-3. With the components we have developed so far and the convention maintained for a time, there's no place for a separate transformation, as times are taken as simple indices. But, to expose the result to the outside, we need to comply with the time scales provided by *Yahoo Financials* or any other data sources used. This adaptation is done by the base components *TimeUnitTransformer* and *IndexTimeTransformer* (you can also create your own if needed) as follows:

```python
class IndexedTimeTransformer(TimeUnitTransformer):

    def __init__(self, time_freq: Frequency):
        self._time_freq = time_freq

    def inverse_transform(self, path):
        l = len(path)
        match self._time_freq:
            case Frequency.MONTHLY:
                return [
                    str(self._t0 + relativedelta(months=m)).split(' ')[0]
                    for m in range(1,
                l+1)]
            case Frequency.WEEKLY:
                return [
                    str(self._t0 + relativedelta(weeks=w)).split(' ')[0]
                    for w in range(1, l+1)]
            case Frequency.DAILY:
                return [
                    str(self._t0 + relativedelta(days=d)).split(' ')[0] for
                    d in range(1, l+1)]
```

Note that time transformation has nothing to do with the parameter estimation or altering forecasting results; it is mainly for visualization and correct consumption of the result by the calling component.

CHAPTER 6　DIFFUSION MODEL

Average Forecast – Mean Path

While discussing Monte Carlo simulation in Chapter 4, we computed the mean and standard error of the sampled data. The mean path or the average path is nothing but that computed *mean*. If the forecasting system trading software is to quote the investor some number about the future value of the asset, the mean path is the answer. In Figure 6-2, the middle plot showing uncertainty bounds has the mean path displayed in blue and captioned as *mean*.

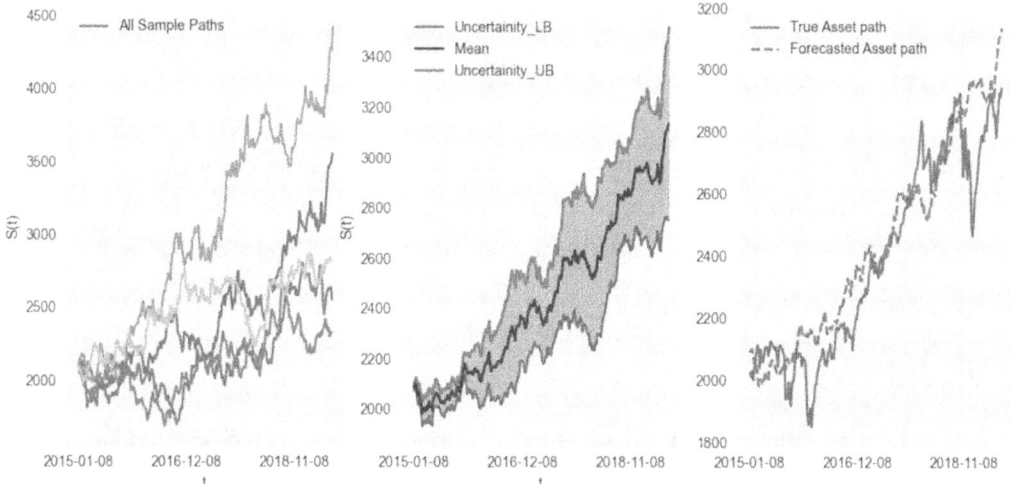

Figure 6-2. *Sample paths, uncertainty bounds, and the backtesting result of the S&P 500 index*

Function *_extract_mean_path* inside the class *ForecastResult* computes the mean as follows:

```
def _extract_mean_path(self, mcs: MonteCarloSimulation.MCEstimate) ->
            pd.DataFrame:
    ts = self._transform_time(path=mcs.mean)
    return pd.DataFrame([mcs.mean], columns=ts).transpose()
```

It simply leverages the computed mean from the Monte Carlo simulation component and just prepares a data frame with time columns out of that.

177

CHAPTER 6   DIFFUSION MODEL

Uncertainty Bounds

Uncertainty bounds come by taking a window equal to the computed standard error (S.E.) by the Monte Carlo simulation framework around the mean path, i.e., *mean ± S. E.* It is a measure of *risk* associated with the asset. Risk computation itself is a separate subject area, and there are a lot of advanced risk measures that provide far deeper insight (i.e., VaR), whereas uncertainty bounds are a very commonly used primitive risk metric. However, as a first-level guideline, it works fine. Due to unstable and unknown market conditions, mean forecasting may not be fully accurate – anyway, we are dealing with stochastic systems, so that's expected. These bounds can give investors a priori idea about what can go wrong in the future in advance. Then, it's the inventor's choice to put money into something that's very risky. Some investors prefer a high-risk, high-return strategy, whereas some are very cautious. After all, the metric should be available in advance to assess any potential loss – *uncertainty bounds* are just that metric (refer to the example explained in Chapter 1 with $100 stock value for the hypothetical company XYZ).

Function *_extract_uncertainty_bounds* inside the class *ForecastResult* computes the bounds as follows:

```
def _extract_uncertainty_bounds(self, mcs: MonteCarloSimulation.
MCEstimate) -> tuple:
    ts = self._transform_time(path=mcs.mean)
    lb = mcs.mean - mcs.standard_error
    ub = mcs.mean + mcs.standard_error

    return (pd.DataFrame([lb], columns=ts).transpose(),
    pd.DataFrame([ub],
        columns=ts).transpose())
```

In Figure 6-2, the lower and upper bounds are shown as *Uncertainty_LB* and *Uncertainty_UB* in green and red, respectively.

Backtesting and RMSE Score

In financial modeling, backtesting is an essential step no matter what model was chosen. The name itself tells the action to be performed – going ahead in time with forecasting and tallying with the past. This is only possible provided the actual asset values for the specified time range are available. We test the accuracy of the model with RMSE score as follows:

$$RMSE = \frac{1}{n-m}\sum_{t=m}^{n}\left(\widehat{S_t}^{Forecasted\ Mean} - S_t\right)^2.$$

To perform backtesting with a validation dataset, we define a class *AssetPriceBackTesing* as follows:

```
class AssetPriceBackTesting:
    def __init__(self, s_true: pd.DataFrame, s_forecast: pd.DataFrame,
    col='stock price'):
        self._s_true = s_true
        self._s_forecast = s_forecast
        self._col = col
        self._rmse_score = self._compute_rmse()
        plt.style.use("seaborn-v0_8")

    def _compute_rmse(self):
        return np.sqrt(np.average((self._s_true[self._col]
                                  - self._s_forecast.iloc[:, 0].
                                  values)**2))

    @property
    def rmse_score(self):
        return self._rmse_score
```

This is tested for *S&P 500 index* prices against the validation time period January 1, 2015, to July 1, 2019, as follows:

Listing 6-4. Backtesting and computing distributions of mean path

```
def _test_forecasting(model, dsa):
    result = model.forecast(T=len(dsa.validation_set),
                           prob_dist_viz_required=True,
                           prob_dist_viz_settings={'n_workers': 4, 'ts':
                           [50, 85, 150]})
    result_display = ForecastResultDisplay(result, ylabel='S(t)')
```

```
ap_back_testing = AssetPriceBackTesting(
    s_true=dsa.validation_set, s_forecast=result.mean_path)
print('RMSE: ' + str(ap_back_testing.rmse_score))
vz6.plot_model_forecasting_results(result_display, ap_back_testing)
result_display.plot_probability_distributions_from_path()
```

We get the RMSE score:

```
RMSE: 131.091188567087898
```

This should be good as values are in the range of 3000–4000. Note that in the function *forecast*, you need to pass value T, which is the last time unit's value, till you need forecasting.

Note that this score is not fixed but will change with the simulation. We set the number of sample paths at 5, which may influence the score. You may not get the same result when you test it on your end. To stabilize the result, an optimal number of sample paths should be set.

Change of Frequency

We estimated the parameters with the weekly data frequency. But what if we need to forecast at a biweekly or daily frequency? There are two ways to solve this problem as follows:

a) Change the Δt and reestimate the parameters. This one expects the PDFs to be changed as well. For example, for bigger leaps, we need to skip the records and pick them up at correct intervals to match Δt for parameter reestimation. But, for smaller leaps, this will only work if the records are available and that's why approach (b) is needed.

b) Suppose a financial data source provides stock quotes daily, but what if you need to forecast at 6-hour intervals? The data source may not provide data at this frequency to reestimate parameters. A workaround would be recalibration of the forecasted paths with a *scaled random walk model* as discussed in Chapter 5. Note that we don't reestimate the parameters here; rather, with the same set, we can keep recalibrating forecasted paths for different intervals and share the insights.

CHAPTER 6 DIFFUSION MODEL

Computing Distributions of the Mean Path

Check out the $f^{Diffusion\_Model}$ again, and then let's do an analysis of the forecasted mean path. For a RV S_{t+1}, the density $f^{Diffusion_{Model}}(S_{t+1})$ depends on the forecasted value of RV for the previous time index value, i.e., S_t. For example, to compute the distribution of S_{85}, the density function of the same for the *S&P 500 Index* dataset would be as follows (after putting the values of estimated r and σ):

$$f^{Diffusion\_Model}(S_{85}) = \frac{1}{0.02 * S_{85} \sqrt{2\pi}} e^{-\frac{1}{2}\left(\frac{\log \frac{S_{85}}{S_{84}} - 0.0018}{0.02}\right)^2}.$$

Sampling from $f^{Diffusion\_Model}(S_{85})$ is directly impossible as the inverse of the distribution function is difficult to deduce in closed form. Hence, we fall back to the acceptance/rejection method discussed in Chapter 4 and choose the exponential density as the proposal distribution. We can easily leverage the existing components as defined there to proceed. But note that we are sampling for computing multiple distributions as one mean path of a stochastic process will have a series of RVs. These computations are independent of each other as the values are already forecasted and not a single RV is waiting for any observation from the previous one. So, that creates a scope of using multiprocessing to speed up things. We use the Python library *loky* to implement multiprocessing – so, start by installing it as follows:

```
% pip3 install loky
```

We create a class for generating RV extending the *AcceptanceRejectionMethod* as follows:

```
class MarkovLogNormalVariateGenerator(AcceptanceRejectionMethod):
    """
    Class to sample from Markov Log Normal density using an Exponential
    proposal density
    """
    def __init__(self, r, σ, x_t_1, hat_func_optimizer:
    HatFunctionEstimator):
        self._r = r
```

```python
        self._σ = σ
        self._x_t_1 = x_t_1
        super().__init__(hat_func_optimizer)

    def target_pdf_f(self, x):
        ll_factor_1 = 1.0/(np.multiply(self._σ, x) * np.sqrt(2*np.pi))
        ll_factor_2 = np.exp(
            -0.5*np.power((np.log(np.divide(x, self._x_t_1)) - (self._r-
            0.5*self._σ*self._σ))/self._σ, 2))

        return ll_factor_1 * ll_factor_2

    def _proposal_pdf_g(self, x, θ: tuple):
        return expon.pdf(x, scale=1 / θ[0])
```

We also create a class named *CommonSupremiumEstimator* to compute the *f/g* ratio required for the acceptance/rejection method as follows:

```
class CommonSupremumEstimator(SupremumEstimatorTemplate):
    '''
    Default implementation of SupremumEstimatorTemplate.
    It leverages scipy.optimize module to find the maxima & minima of
    f/g ratio.
    '''

    def __init__(self,
                 x0_bounds: List[tuple],
                 # Sequence of (min, max) pairs of parameter of θ
                 θ0_bounds: List[tuple]
                 ):
        self._x0_bounds = x0_bounds
        self._θ0_bounds = θ0_bounds
        super().__init__()

    def _maximize_wrt_x(self, ratio_f: callable) -> tuple:
        res = shgo(ratio_f, bounds=self._x0_bounds)
        return -res.fun, res.x
```

```
def _minimize_wrt_θ(self, ratio_f: callable) -> tuple:
    res = shgo(ratio_f, bounds=self._θ0_bounds)
    return res.fun, res.x
```

It is mandatory for the subclasses extending *BaseAssetPriceModel* to declare a function named *_get_rv_generator_for_viz*. This function is solely for visualization and computing the distribution of the forecasted path and can be skipped only if visualization (when *prob_dist_viz_required* is passed as false, as shown in Listing 6-2) is not needed. The function defined in *DiffusionAssetPriceModel* is as follows:

```
def _get_rv_generator_for_viz(self, s_t_1, t):
    return MarkovLogNormalVariateGenerator(r=self._parameters['r'],
                                            σ=self._parameters['σ'],
           x_t_1=s_t_1,
hat_func_optimizer=CommonSupremumEstimator(
                    x0_bounds=[(0.001, np.inf)],
                                                    θ0_bounds=[(0.0001,
                                                    np.inf)]))
```

The function is supposed to return a RV generator object which will be consumed inside the function *_compute_prob_distribution_of_mean_path* defined in the base class *BaseAssetPriceModel* as follows:

```
def _compute_prob_distribution_of_mean_path(self, forecast_result,
        prob_dist_viz_required, prob_dist_viz_settings):
    if prob_dist_viz_required:
        if '_get_rv_generator_for_viz' not in dict(inspect.
        getmembers(type(self),
        inspect.isfunction)):
            raise NotImplementedError(
                'Subclass should define function _get_rv_generator_
                for_viz')

        forecast_result.time_indices_of_probability_distributions_
        of_path =
        prob_dist_viz_settings[ 'ts']

        def _samples_gen_task(s_t_1, t):
```

```
    '''
    Inner function to be used through a multiprocessor
    for performing a single task of generating RVs
    '''
    rv_generator = getattr(
        self, '_get_rv_generator_for_viz')(s_t_1=s_t_1, t=t)

    # generated samples & their probabilities
    samples, _ = rv_generator.sample(n_rv=500)
    probs = rv_generator.target_pdf_f(samples)

    return pd.DataFrame({"Sample": samples, "Density": probs})

def _compute_distributions_from_path(prob_dist_viz_settings,
forecast_result, _samples_gen_task):
    '''
    Inner function to compute the distributions and
    append to the forecast result
    '''

    # Task executor from loky
    viz_task_executor = get_reusable_executor(
        max_workers=prob_dist_viz_settings['n_workers'])

    mean_path = forecast_result.mean_path.values   # forecasted
    mean path

    # Sumiiting task for all of the required t's
    forecast_result.probability_distributions_from_path =
[viz_task_executor.submit(_samples_gen_task,
                                        mean_path[task_i-1][0],
                                        # for S_t_1
                                        task_i-1) for task_i in
                                                prob_
                                                dist_viz_
                                                settings
                                                ['ts']]
```

CHAPTER 6 DIFFUSION MODEL

```
viz_task_executor.shutdown(wait=False)

_compute_distributions_from_path(
    prob_dist_viz_settings, forecast_result, _samples_gen_task)
```

The function is complex, and it needs careful observation, especially since you need to pay attention to how inner functions are used to create tasks for each RV (variable *prob_dist_viz_settings['ts']* has the list of time indices for those RVs) and how that is leveraged afterward. The function has already been tested in Listing 6-4 producing output as shown in Figure 6-3 in addition to Figure 6-2.

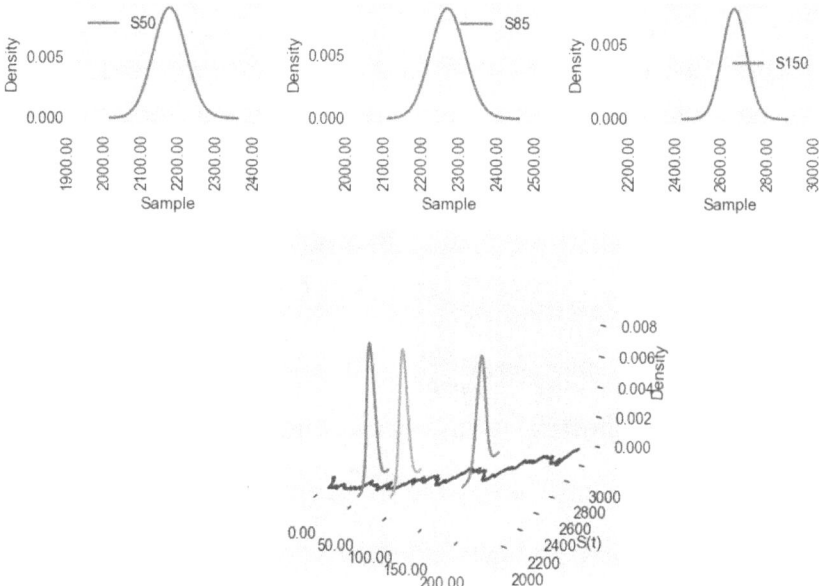

Figure 6-3. *Computing and plotting the probability distrubutions of S_{50}, S_{85}, and S_{150}*

Comparison and Improvement

SDE-based models are physics driven, unlike ML/DL-based time series models. We start off with a perception of the system's state and include all possible state variables in the SDE. These may not link to any domain-specific information but provide a handful of mechanisms to build forecasting systems. Both have their pros and cons as described below:

CHAPTER 6 DIFFUSION MODEL

a) ML/DL-based models perform better in providing pinpointed accuracy than SDE models. However, some approaches, as given below, can improve the accuracy of SDE models.

   i) **Set the correct number of sample paths while forecasting:** Hyperparameter tuning can automatically set the correct number of sample paths. Bayesian optimization is a perfect way of deciding the number of sample paths, as the simulation is a costly process, and repetition should be minimized as much as possible. Chapter 7 discusses one such approach while covering the nonparametric jump model.

   ii) **Perform var reduction while forecasting:** Var reduction methods discussed in Chapter 4 can be used at forecasting time along with simulation. Check out the function *forecast* in Listing 6-2; it takes one *VarReduction* object. You may try *antithetic sampling* or *importance sampling* with that. But be cautious while using it, as it may consume useful uncertainty information. Basically, var reduction is like a double-edged sword. Models showing too much uncertainty for noise can benefit from it.

   iii) **Choosing the right likelihood optimizer:** It is crucial and may significantly affect the result. A good model may fail due to a bad optimizer. Likelihood function analysis should be performed like what we did in Chapter 3 before setting any fixed optimizer. The likelihood function surface may have a lot of local maxima for more complex models than plain diffusion ones. Derivative-free stochastic optimizers sometimes can do better explorations to find the maximum for very rough function surfaces.

   iv) **Choosing the right model:** The diffusion model discussed in this chapter is one way of modeling financial assets. More advanced models can better handle jumps and irregularities in asset prices. Some of them are discussed in the next chapter.

b) The SDE-based approach can model the asset in far fewer parametrizations than the ML/DL ones.

c) SDE models are better interpretable while showing risks. For example, the diffusion model explicitly contains the diffusion parameter, which shows the corresponding asset's amount of diffraction, which leads to potential risk. A higher value of σ shows a higher risk. Just by looking at this model parameter, an investor can have a ballpark estimate of the asset's behaviour and hedge his risks accordingly.

d) While modeling derivatives, SDE plays a significant role – unlike its ML/DL counterparts, just by leveraging the underlying asset's parameter, the stochastic process of the derivative can be designed and numerically approximated. This means that separate parameter estimation for the derivative from a fresh dataset may not be required. You will learn more about it while we discuss the *Black-Scholes* model in Part 3.

e) Despite lacking pinpoint accuracy, in this era of the deep learning rat race, SDE models still have a dominant footprint in the quants market. Stock market assessments and billion-dollar investments still happen based on their computational insights and will definitely continue in the future. They are even great at providing baselines for more advanced DL or reinforcement learning-based models, especially for high-frequency trading.

Summary

The diffusion model is the most basic tool in modeling financial asset behavior. The vanilla diffusion model has two components: drift and diffusion. Drift gives the overall direction of the asset movement, whereas diffusion shows the diffraction or uncertainty around its path. The stochastic differential equation (SDE) is the most perfect way of expressing the diffusion model. With Ito lemma, a second-order approximation of the SDE for the diffusion model can be deduced. From there, the final solution is given with the Euler approximation of the SDE. The solution is basically a stochastic process expressed numerically to generate sample paths.

CHAPTER 6　DIFFUSION MODEL

This chapter discusses the three steps for building any financial asset model, regardless of the choice of SDE: formation of the SDE and stochastic process, parameter estimation, and inference with simulation. Derivation of the diffusion model with the Ito lemma provides a theoretical foundation for the concepts later implemented in Python. Moreover, in the parameter estimation section, two different estimation paradigms are covered: *risk-neutral measure* and *real-world measure*. The first one is more practical and helps to bring the market at low risk, whereas the second one has a more theoretical setting. As a result, PDFs of them are also different. However, being preferable settings, risk neutrality is followed in this book, and the components implemented in Python also support this.

Over the process, we set up some base components: *BaseAssetPriceModel*, *ForecastResult*, *ForecastDisplay*, *AssetPriceBackTesting*, etc. They provide a foundation for developing future models on top of them. In the subsequent chapters, all components will leverage these to build more complex models. In the next chapter, we discuss one such approach – handling sudden jumps in asset price and inclusion of them in the SDE.

CHAPTER 7

Jump Models

As we delve into the structures of the asset price model, it's crucial to grasp the significance of understanding the separate handling of jumps. This understanding is not just important; it's significant. The diffusion coefficient introduces uncertainties to mimic the dynamics of the stock market, and while the log transformation can be a preliminary defense against sudden market movements, it's never enough and statistically a not so correct method to handle jumps. In this chapter, we explore three such jump handling models – two of them are parametric and the third one is nonparametric. The urgency of understanding jumps in asset price models cannot be overstated, as it forms the basis of our financial modeling work and can significantly impact our forecasting accuracy.

General Formation of Jump Model

Jumps, sudden changes in the asset price stochastic process values, are better modeled as discrete events rather than continuous ones. As we always emphasize in this book, we are not concerned with the reasons for jumps, which could be numerous – political and economic turmoil, war, pandemic, and more. With SDE-based models, such uncertainties are included as jump components, providing a practical and comprehensive view of market movements. Let's now examine the SDE structure of a typical jump model, which is

$$dX_t = \mu dt + \sigma dW_t + J dX_t^P.$$

X_t^P is the Poisson process and J is the jump magnitude. Distribution of J would be of interest as it controls the variation in the paths produced by the solution of this SDE. The Poisson process should be familiar, as that's already covered in Chapter 5, and it controls the number of jumps within a time interval, i.e., the number of events in the Poisson distribution analogy.

CHAPTER 7   JUMP MODELS

Ito Lemma for Jump Model

We use the Ito lemma to find a closed-form solution of the jump model SDE, just as we did for the vanilla diffusion model. Note that the solution we discuss here doesn't depend on the choice of jump-magnitude distribution. However, entirely closed-form solutions exist for some suitable options. We choose a more generic approach to cater to this need, where multiple components are involved in modeling any financial instrument. The Ito lemma, as usual, plays a crucial role in finding the proper stochastic process that governs the asset paths modeled using the jump process. Its role is so vital that it can be considered the backbone of our modeling work, guiding us confidently in finding the right path for our asset price forecasts.

To begin with, we take the example of *ca' dla' g* process, which is a pure jump process without any diffusion component and is given by following SDE:

$$dX_t^{c\acute{a}dl\acute{a}g} = \alpha dt + J dX_t^P.$$

It means that the paths of the X_t are continuous from right to left with left limits, like the vanilla Poisson process, but in addition to a linear trend component α (α and J can also be a function of time, $\alpha(t)$ and $J(t)$). The Ito lemma gives the differential of any function of the process g:

$$dg\left(X_t^{c\acute{a}dl\acute{a}g}\right) = \left[\frac{\partial g}{\partial t} + \alpha \frac{\partial g}{\partial X}\right] dt + \left[g\left(X_{t-}^{c\acute{a}dl\acute{a}g} + J\right) - g\left(X_{t-}^{c\acute{a}dl\acute{a}g}\right)\right] dX_t^P.$$

Whenever a jump occurs, i.e., $dX_t^P = 1$, the process state changes from X_{t-} to X_t with the added effect of the jump size J. In practical settings, especially with our requirements, the Poisson process is duly accompanied by another Brownian motion process or vice versa, resulting in a mixed jump process, and after applying Ito Lemma for a function g, we get

$$dg(X_t) = \left[\frac{\partial g}{\partial t} + \mu \frac{\partial g}{\partial X} + \frac{1}{2}\sigma^2 \frac{\partial^2 g}{\partial X^2}\right] dt + \left[g(X_{t-} + J) - g(X_{t-})\right] dX_t^P + \sigma \frac{\partial g}{\partial X} dW_t.$$

This is a foundation for finding the stochastic process for asset price S_t that is exponential of X_t; in other words, $S_t = e^{X_t}$, in turn, makes $g(X_t) = e^{X_t}$. Applying Ito lemma for this function, we get

$$de^{X_t} = \left(\mu e^{X_t} + \frac{1}{2}\sigma^2 e^{X_t}\right)dt + \sigma e^{X_t}dW_t + \left(e^{X_{t-}+J} - e^{X_{t-}}\right)dX_t^P,$$

which can also be written as

$$\frac{dS_t}{S_t} = \left(\mu + \frac{1}{2}\sigma^2\right)dt + \sigma dW_t + \left(e^J - 1\right)dX_t^P.$$

Now, under risk-neutral settings, condition $E[dS_t] = E[rS_t dt]$ must be satisfied (recall contents from Chapter 5) where r is the risk-free interest rate. So, rewriting the condition, we get

$$E\left[S_t\left(\mu + \frac{1}{2}\sigma^2\right)dt + \sigma S_t dW_t + S_t\left(e^J - 1\right)\lambda dt\right] = E[rS_t dt],$$

and recall from Chapter 4 that $dX_t^P = \lambda dt$.

To satisfy risk neutrality, balancing two sides of the equation, it can be shown that

$$\mu = r - \frac{1}{2}\sigma^2 - \lambda E\left[e^J - 1\right].$$

It says that the resultant drift of the overall jump-diffusion process should be an adjusted diffusion drift with a correction term $\lambda E[e^J - 1]$. i.e, the drift is impacted by the abrupt jumps in the asset price.

Finally, we got the expression of the jump model SDE in terms of asset price S_t as given by

$$dS_t = S_t\left(r - \frac{1}{2}\sigma^2 - \lambda E\left[e^J - 1\right]\right)dt + \sigma S_t dW_t + S_t\left(e^J - 1\right)dX_t^P,$$

or in terms of log scale:

$$dX_t = \left(r - \frac{1}{2}\sigma^2 - \lambda E\left[e^J - 1\right]\right)dt + \sigma dW_t + J dX_t^P.$$

CHAPTER 7 JUMP MODELS

Both are independent of the nature of J, i.e., the distribution of the jumps. With this SDE, we can now find the solution by integrating both sides:

$$X_t = X_0 + \int_0^t \left(r - \frac{1}{2}\sigma^2 - \lambda E\left[e^J - 1\right] \right) dt + \int_0^t \sigma dW_t + \int_0^t J dX_t^P.$$

With the Euler methods of numerical solution for SDE, we get

$$X_{t+1} = X_t + \left(r - \frac{1}{2}\sigma^2 - \lambda E\left[e^J - 1\right] \right) + \sigma(W_{t+1} - W_t) + \sum_{k=1}^{X_t^P} J_k.$$

Expressing it in terms of S_t,

$$S_{t+1} = S_t e^{\left(r - \frac{1}{2}\sigma^2 - \lambda E\left[e^J - 1\right] \right) + \sigma(W_{t+1} - W_t) + \sum_{k=1}^{X_t^P} J_k}$$

Above is one of the generic expressions of the stochastic process for the parametric jump-diffusion model independent of the choices J and will help generate paths of the asset price.

Templates in Python for Parametric Jump-Diffusion Process

The templates should provide extension points to integrate J and increment in the process states in a generic way. The term $\int_0^t J dX_t^P$ is evaluated numerically as $J\Delta X_P$ where $\Delta X_P \sim Poisson(\lambda)$ when $\Delta t = 1$. Alternatively, we can also compute $\sum_{k=1}^{X_t^P} J_k$ from a collection of J_k and then summing them up. Both J and J_k are sampled from the jump density with the only difference being J is a single sample. We implement this in the abstract class *ParametricJumpProcess* as follows:

```
class ParametricJumpProcess(ForecastingProcess, ABC):
    '''
    Base class for jump stochastic process. Function _compute_jump_drift
    should be overridden by the child class (Merton or Kou models)
    '''
```

```python
def __init__(self, r, σ, λ, sampling_density: TargetSampling
Density = None,
        initial_state=1.0, n_sample_paths=5):
    self._r = r
    self._σ = σ
    self._λ = λ
    self._state_t = initial_state
    self._μ = self._compute_jump_drift()

    super().__init__(n_sample_paths, initial_state=initial_state,
                    sampling_density=sampling_density)

@abstractmethod
def _compute_jump_drift(self): ...

def _update_current_state(self, z):
    self._reset_new_sample_path_state()

    dW = z['dW']
    dJ = z['dJ']
    dJ_p = z['dJ_p']

    self._state_t = self._state_t * \
        np.exp(self._μ + (self._σ * dW) + (dJ*dJ_p))
    return self._state_t
```

We follow the same Euler method of path generation. For that, we must sample from the composite density of the jump-diffusion process with a choice of J, which is set as an extension point as follows (function *_sample_jumps*):

```
class ParametricJumpProcessSamplingDensity(TargetSamplingDensity, ABC):
    '''
    Base class for Sampling density of jump process
    '''

    def __init__(self, r, σ, λ):
        self._r = r
        self._σ = σ
        self._λ = λ
```

CHAPTER 7   JUMP MODELS

```
def pdf(self, x):
    return None

def sample(self, n_vars, n_sample_paths=1):
    dWs = norm.rvs(size=(n_sample_paths, n_vars))
    dJ_p = poisson.rvs(mu=self._λ, size=(n_sample_paths, n_vars))
    dJ = self._sample_jumps(n_sample_paths, n_vars)

    return np.array([[{'dW': w, 'dJ_p': j_p, 'dJ': j
                    } for w, j, j_p in zip(dw, dj, dj_p)] for dw,
                    dj, dj_p in zip(dWs, dJ, dJ_p)])

@abstractmethod
def _sample_jumps(self, n_sample_paths, n_jumps): ...
'''
    Function to sample jumps from the specific jump size distributions
'''
```

The trickiest part is where the diffusion and jump components are both staffed inside a dictionary variable z, which is again passed in method _*update_current_state*_ of the *ParametricJumpProcess*. We will leverage the above templates in implementing the individual jump models.

Characteristic Function of Jump-Diffusion Model

Let's begin with the definition of CF and putting there the expression of X_{t+1} accordingly:

$$\phi_{t+1}(\omega) = E\left[e^{j\omega X_{t+1}}\right] = E\left[e^{j\omega X_t}\right] e^{r - \frac{1}{2}\sigma^2 - \lambda E\left[e^J - 1\right]} E\left[e^{j\omega\sigma(W_{t+1} - W_t)}\right] E\left[e^{j\omega \sum_{k=1}^{x_t^P} J_k}\right]$$

It can be shown that the last term can be computed as

$$E\left[e^{j\omega \sum_{k=1}^{x_t^P} J_k}\right] = e^{\lambda t E\left[e^{j\omega J} - 1\right]},$$

and from the Wiener process, we get

$$E\left[e^{j\omega\sigma(W_{t+1} - W_t)}\right] = e^{-\frac{1}{2}\sigma^2 \omega^2}.$$

Finally, the expression comes down to

$$\phi_{t+1}^{Jump-Diffusion}(\omega) = E\left[e^{j\omega X_t}\right] e^{r - \frac{1}{2}\sigma^2 - \lambda E\left[e^J - 1\right]} e^{-\frac{1}{2}\sigma^2 \omega^2} e^{\lambda t E\left[e^{j\omega J} - 1\right]}.$$

This is a general template of the characteristic function for the jump-diffusion model, regardless of the choice of J. We will see in a while why this CF is needed while we discuss such jump-diffusion models for different choices of J.

Merton Model

We get the Merton model S_{t+1}^{Merton} when J follows a normal distribution with mean μ_J and variance σ^2_J. With this,

$$E\left[e^J - 1\right] = e^{\mu_J + \frac{1}{2}\sigma_J^2} - 1,$$

and that gives the Merton model of the jump-diffusion process:

$$S_{t+1}^{Merton} = S_t^{Merton} e^{\left(r - \frac{1}{2}\sigma^2 - \lambda\left(e^{\mu_J + \frac{1}{2}\sigma_J^2} - 1\right)\right) + \sigma(W_{t+1} - W_t) + \sum_{k=1}^{X_t^P} J_k},$$

where the μ^{Merton} is given by

$$\mu^{Merton} = r - \frac{1}{2}\sigma^2 - \lambda\left(e^{\mu_J + \frac{1}{2}\sigma_J^2} - 1\right).$$

Above one is the drift of the Merton model. The expression of S_{t+1}^{Merton} will be needed to generate paths of the Merton process with a given set of parameters. *Robert C. Merton* first proposed this model for estimating option prices where the underlying asset has jumps in the path. Numerous researchers around the world have discussed and optimized this model. However, in this chapter, we are interested in discussing how to estimate any asset price paths with jumps regardless of the derivatives involved.

CHAPTER 7   JUMP MODELS

Path Generation for Merton Model

We simply leverage the ParametricJumpProcess and override the _compute_jump_drift (/chapter7/merton_model.py) as follows:

```
class MertonProcess(ParametricJumpProcess):
    '''
    Stochastic process for Merton model
    '''

    def __init__(self, r, σ, λ, μ_j, σ_j, initial_state=1.0, n_sample_paths=5):
        self._μ_j = μ_j
        self._σ_j = σ_j

        super().__init__(r=r, σ=σ, λ=λ, n_sample_paths=n_sample_paths,
                    initial_state=initial_state,
                                    sampling_density=MertonProcessSampl
                                    ingDensity(
              r=r, σ=σ, λ=λ, μ_j=μ_j, σ_j=σ_j))

    def _compute_jump_drift(self):
        return self._r - (0.5*(self._σ**2)) - (self._λ *
                                    (np.exp(self._μ_j +
                                    0.5*(self._σ_j**2)-1)))
```

As for the Merton model, J is normally distributed; we create the *MertonProcessSamplingDensity* as follows:

```
class MertonProcessSamplingDensity(ParametricJumpProcessSamplingDensity):
    '''
    Sampling density for generating RVs for Merton model
    '''

    def __init__(self, r, σ, λ, μ_j, σ_j):
        self._μ_j = μ_j
        self._σ_j = σ_j

        super().__init__(r=r, σ=σ, λ=λ)
```

CHAPTER 7 JUMP MODELS

```
def _sample_jumps(self, n_sample_paths, n_jumps):
    return norm.rvs(size=(n_sample_paths, n_jumps),
                    loc=self._μ_j, scale=self._σ_j)
```

We test with a given set of parameters as follows:

```
def test_merton_process_paths():
    mp = MertonProcess(
        r=0.003,
        σ=0.004,
        λ=0.009,
        μ_j=0.0001,
        σ_j=0.093,
        n_sample_paths=20,
        initial_state=1000)

    result = mp.forecast(T=250)
    result_display = ForecastResultDisplay(result, ylabel='S(t)')
    vz7.plot_merton_process_paths_for_single_set_params(result_display)
```

We get output as shown in Figure 7-1.

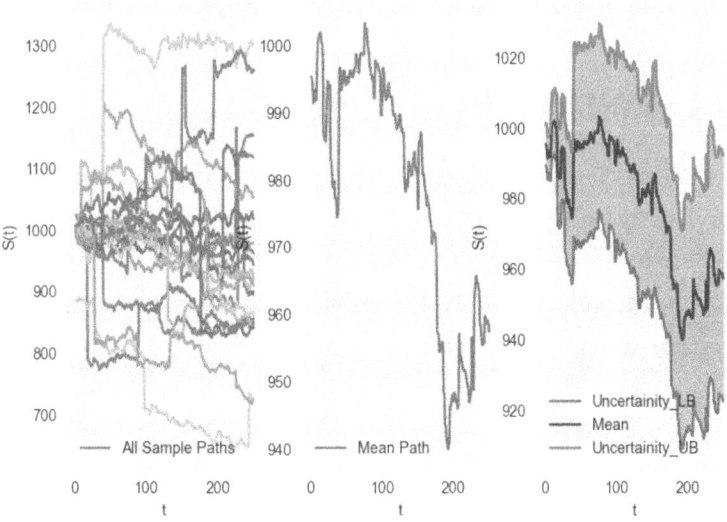

Figure 7-1. *Merton process paths and uncertainty bounds*

CHAPTER 7 JUMP MODELS

Notice the sudden stepwise jumps in the paths – this is typical behavior of any jump process. On the other hand, Figure 7-2 shows the effects on a mean path for selecting a wide range of parameters.

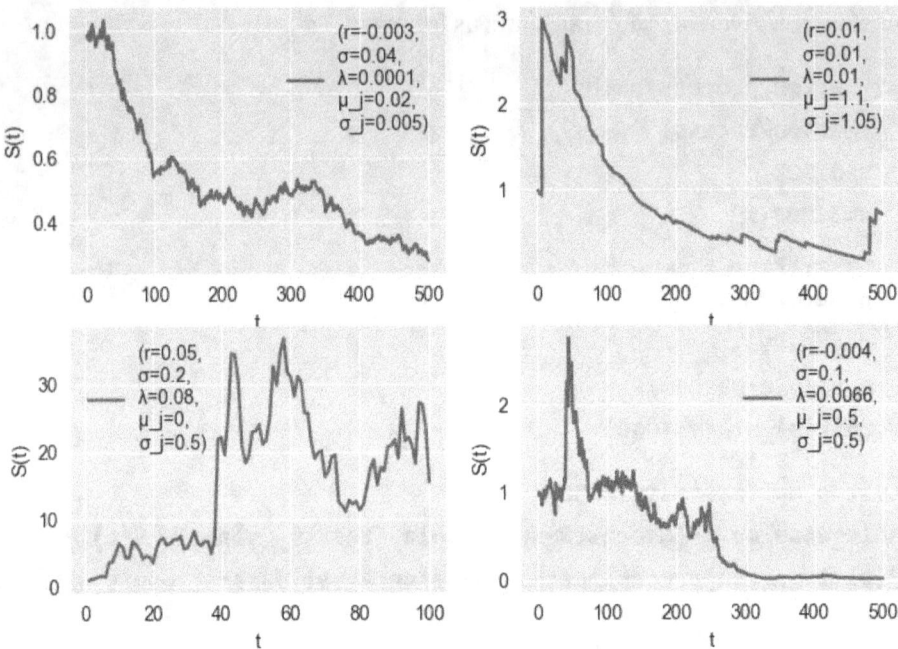

Figure 7-2. *Mean paths of Merton process for different parameters*

Parameter Estimation of Merton Model

The Merton model has five parameters: r, σ, λ, μ_J, and σ_J. As you know from earlier chapters, we can use the MLE method to estimate those, but for that, we must first understand the density of the Merton model, and that's an interesting challenge. Closely observe the random variable S_{t+1}^{Merton} – how many other random variables (RV) does it consist of? Let's note down the following:

- One normal RV N(0,1) that governs $W_{t+1} - W_t$
- One Poisson RV that decides the number of jumps X_t^P
- X_t^P number of normal RVs, each of them having mean μ_J and variance σ_J^2

CHAPTER 7 JUMP MODELS

That makes the total number of RVs within a unit time difference as $X_t^P + 2$, which is dynamic and a random variable. This is a situation where you need to find the density of an RV, which is the sum of other RVs whose individual densities are already known. Let's take a simpler example:

$$Z = X + Y,$$

where Z, X, and Y are all random variables and respective densities of X and Y are $f_X(x)$ and $f_Y(y)$. As we deal with all independent RVs, $f_Z(z)$ is obtained as

$$f_Z(z) = (f_X * f_Y)(z) = \int_{-\infty}^{\infty} f_X(z-y) f_Y(y) dy.$$

Above one is a convolution operation between the densities of two RVs. For simple use cases, computing this convolution integral in closed form isn't that challenging, but it is for a complex and deterministically unspecified number of RVs. For Merton model, closed-form solutions of the density exist. Still, I think it is an excellent platform to discuss a modern and numerical approach (based on the Fourier transform), which is very generic and applicable to situations in financial asset modeling, where the stochastic process is much more complex and composed of many other RVs. But for this, we must know the characteristic function (CF) of the Merton stochastic process, as given by

$$\phi_{t+1}^{Merton}(\omega) = E\left[e^{j\omega X_t}\right] e^{\left(r - \frac{1}{2}\sigma^2 - \lambda\left(e^{\mu_J + \frac{1}{2}\sigma_J^2} - 1\right)\right)} e^{-\frac{1}{2}\sigma^2 \omega^2} e^{\lambda e^{j\omega \mu_J - \frac{1}{2}\omega^2 \sigma_J^2} - 1}.$$

We got the expression by substituting the respective terms $E[e^J - 1]$ and $E[e^{j\omega J} - 1]$ with appropriate expressions evaluated for the Merton model. *C.W. Oosterlee* has suggested a model by augmenting the ϕ_{t+1}^{Merton} by constant $\left[e^{j\omega X_0}\right]$, which comes down to $e^{j\omega X_0}$, and incrementing time by t instead of unit time. So, finally we get

$$\phi_{t+1}^{Merton}(\omega) = e^{j\omega X_0} e^{\left(r - \frac{1}{2}\sigma^2 - \lambda\left(e^{\mu_J + \frac{1}{2}\sigma_J^2} - 1\right)\right)t} e^{-\frac{1}{2}\sigma^2 \omega^2 t} e^{\lambda t e^{j\omega \mu_J - \frac{1}{2}\omega^2 \sigma_J^2} - 1}.$$

Basically, it is the CF of the Merton model, where the time step is taken as t (recall that the same was discussed for the simple log-asset price model). Note that this model will be used while estimating the parameters for convenience, as we don't have to keep on multiplying reclusively by $e^{j\omega X_t}$.

CHAPTER 7   JUMP MODELS

The CF can be rearranged to have a more compact form which will be used in our implementation as follows:

$$\phi_{t+1}^{Merton}(\omega) = e^{j\omega X_0} e^{j\omega \mu^{Merton} t - \frac{1}{2}\sigma^2 \omega^2 t} \psi^{Merton}(\omega, t),$$

$$\psi^{Merton}(\omega, t) = e^{\lambda t e^{j\omega \mu_J - \frac{1}{2}\omega^2 \sigma_J^2} - 1},$$

$$\mu^{Merton} = r - \frac{1}{2}\sigma^2 - \lambda \left(e^{\mu_J + \frac{1}{2}\sigma_J^2} - 1 \right)$$

Density Recovery with Fourier Transform

From Chapter 3, we know that the characteristic function (CF), the Fourier transform of the PDF, is a frequency domain representation of the probability densities. The PDF lies in some different form, and yes, we can recover the underlying PDF by inverting the CF. This is useful when we know the CF in closed form but not the PDF, precisely depicting any complex jump-diffusion model scenario. To elaborate, we can compute the CF of a composite RV consisting of several independent RVs by multiplying their respective CFs (as discussed in Chapter 3) and then finally get back the composite RV just by inverting the result and thus avoiding convolution operation. Observe that the expression of $\phi_{t+1}^{Merton}(\omega)$ has four components multiplied together as those are independent (jumps are assumed to be independent of the diffusion and trend components present in the model). So, the Fourier transform and its inversion are the basis of the recovery method. Next, we discuss two such approaches, which are closely related.

To proceed, we first define a template for density recovery in Python as follows (Listing 7-1).

Listing 7-1. Base template for density recovery methods

```
class DensityRecoveryMethod(ABC):
    '''
    Base class for recovering density from characteristic function
    '''
```

```python
def __init__(self, N_freq, ϕ_φ: callable):
    self._N_freq = N_freq
    self._ϕ_φ = ϕ_φ

def _get_integration_range(self, x_i, cumulants: Cumulants):
    intg_range = 8.0
    if (cumulants['κ2'] > 0 and cumulants['κ4'] > 0):
        intg_range = 8 * \
            np.sqrt(cumulants['κ2'] + np.sqrt(cumulants['κ4']))
        if isclose(intg_range, 0.00):
            intg_range = 8.0

    a = x_i + cumulants['κ1'] - intg_range
    b = x_i + cumulants['κ1'] + intg_range
    return b, a

@abstractmethod
def recover(self, x_i, t, cumulants: Cumulants, θ): ...
'''
    The method returns density commputed at point x_i
'''
```

We will discuss in a while about the cumulants and the integration range while covering two methods next.

Recovery by FFT Method

Concerning the work done by *Werner Hürlimann [21]*, we plan to use the fast Fourier transform (FFT) to approximate the Fourier inversion process. It is also based on approximating an integral over a defined range using quadrature rules. We use the one known as the left point rule (LPR) for any function *f(x)* within a defined interval *a* and *b* as given by

$$\int_a^b f(x)dx \approx f(a).(b-a).$$

Fourier inversion of any characteristic function can be approximated as follows:

$$f_X(x) = \frac{1}{2\pi}\int_{-\infty}^{\infty} e^{-j\omega x}\phi_X(\omega)d\omega \approx \frac{1}{2\pi}\int_a^b e^{-j\omega x}\phi_X(\omega)d\omega.$$

CHAPTER 7   JUMP MODELS

The interval (b, a) should be sufficiently large, and the distribution $f_X(x)$ should be mostly concentrated there. This range should further be divided into N subintervals producing frequencies needed for the Fourier operator to perform the discrete approximation. Here comes the application of *discrete Fourier transform (DFT)*, which is, in theory, a numerical approximation of the Fourier integral used for converting a sequence of N complex numbers into another sequence of the N complex numbers and vice versa. To elaborate, suppose $x_0, x_1, \ldots, x_{N-1}$ and $\omega_0, \omega_1, \ldots, \omega_{N-1}$ are the two sets of numbers to be converted to and fro; then,

$$\omega_i = \sum_{k=0}^{N-1} x_k e^{-j2\pi k \frac{i}{N}}, \quad x_i = \frac{1}{N} \sum_{k=0}^{N-1} \omega_k e^{j2\pi k \frac{i}{N}}.$$

The operators $e^{-j2\pi k \frac{i}{N}}$ and $e^{j2\pi k \frac{i}{N}}$ are interchangeable rather than fixed. In practice, ω_i and x_i are samples of some functions, i.e., in our case, these will be samples of the PDF and CF. Now, going back to the old problem, to approximate $f_X(x)$, applying LPR, for each subinterval N, then using DFT, we get

$$f_X(x) \approx \frac{1}{b-a} \sum_{k=0}^{N-1} e^{-j2\pi x u_k} \phi_X(2\pi u_k), \quad u_k = \frac{k - \frac{N}{2}}{b-a}, \quad k = 0, 1, \ldots, N-1.$$

u_j's expression is recommended by *Werner Hürlimann [21]*. This represents the ordinary frequencies corresponding to spatial variable x_k while the term $2\pi u_j$ is the angular frequency which can also be represented as ω_j. Of course, it is meaningless to use x directly there, as we are dealing with a range and therefore should be decomposed into a range of values like $x_k = a + kd$, $d = b - a$, $k = 0, 1, \ldots, N - 1$. Since $e^{-j\pi} = 1$, rearranging $f_X(x)$, we get

$$f_X(x) = C \odot DFT(\phi_X),$$

where C and $DFT(\phi_X)$ are both vectors with

$$C_k = (-1)^{\left(\frac{a}{b-a} + \frac{k}{N}\right)N}, \quad k = 0, 1, \ldots, N-1,$$

$$\phi_X^j = (-1)^{\left(\frac{2a}{b-a}\right)j} \phi_X(2\pi u_j), \quad u_j = \frac{j - \frac{N}{2}}{b-a}, \quad j = 0, 1, \ldots, N-1$$

CHAPTER 7 JUMP MODELS

In practice, we use *fast Fourier transform (FFT)* instead of DFT as that's faster in execution comparatively. In a nutshell, to find density for a data point x, we need to choose a range around it (a and b), then generate a set of frequencies with u_j, and at last sum up the values obtained from CF multiplied by $e^{-j2\pi x u_k}$ for inversion.

Different recommendations exist for choosing N, a, and b. The author has mentioned setting N as 2^p, p = 10, 11, 12, etc., but for a and b, we follow *Oosterlee's* recommended bounds based on cumulants:

$$[a,b] = \left[x + \kappa_1 - L\sqrt{\kappa_2 + \sqrt{\kappa_4}}, x + \kappa_1 + L\sqrt{\kappa_2 + \sqrt{\kappa_4}} \right],$$

with $L \in [6, 12]$ whereas κ_1, κ_2, and κ_4 are specific cumulants. Match this with code shared in Listing 7-1.

CUMULANTS

Cumulants are obtained from cumulant generating function (CGF) which is the log of the characteristic function. CGF is defined as

$$\psi(\omega) = \log[\phi(\omega)] = \sum_{i=1}^{n} \kappa_i \frac{(j\omega)^i}{i!}.$$

Cumulants are the value at zero frequency $\omega = 0$ of derivatives of $\psi(\omega)$ w.r.t. $j\omega$:

$$\kappa_1 = \psi'(\omega)\big|_{\omega=0}, \kappa_2 = \psi''(\omega)\big|_{\omega=0} \ldots$$

and so on.

First-, second-, and fourth-order cumulants of the Merton model are given by

$$\kappa_1 = t\left(r - \frac{1}{2}\sigma^2 - \lambda\left(e^{\mu_J + \frac{1}{2}\sigma_J^2} - 1 \right) \right)$$

$$\kappa_2 = t\left(\sigma^2 + \lambda\left(\mu_J^2 + \sigma_J^2 \right) \right)$$

$$\kappa_4 = t\lambda\left(\mu_J^4 + 6\mu_J^2 \sigma_J^2 + 3\lambda\sigma_J^4 \right)$$

CHAPTER 7 JUMP MODELS

Next, we dine the class for FFT method as follows:

```
class FFTBasedDensityRecovery(DensityRecoveryMethod):
    '''
    Class to recover density by FFT. This class should be used with
    caution as it involves hefty amount of computation.
    '''
    def __init__(self, N_freq, ϕ_φ: callable):
        self._k = np.array([i for i in range(N_freq)])
        self._j = np.array([i for i in range(N_freq)])
        super().__init__(N_freq, ϕ_φ)

    def _complex_terms(self, factors):
        return [np.ones(self._N_freq)*(-1) ** float(factor)
                for factor in factors]

    def recover(self, x_i, t, cumulants: Cumulants, θ):
        b, a = self._get_integration_range(x_i, cumulants)
        d = b - a
        u = (self._j - self._N_freq/2)/d
        φ = 2*π*u
        factors_1 = ((a/d) + (self._k/self._N_freq)) * self._N_freq
        C_k = np.divide(self._complex_terms(factors_1), d)

        factors_2 = -(2*a/d)*self._j
        ϕ_j = np.dot(self._complex_terms(factors_2), self._ϕ_φ(φ, θ, t))

        return np.abs(np.sum(np.dot(C_k, fft(ϕ_j))).real)
```

It was observed that we only take the real part of the final sum of signals as the procedure involves dealing with complex numbers.

Recovery by COS Method

FFT being computationally heavy, there is an alternative and better approach suggested by Fang and Oosterlee (*Fang and Oosterlee [22], Fang [23]*) that leverages cosine series expansion of the Fourier operator $e^{j\omega x}$ (recall Chapter 3). In any complex analysis and linear algebra book, one might have read the cosine expansion of any function $g(\theta)$:

CHAPTER 7   JUMP MODELS

$$g(\theta) = \sum_{k=0}^{\infty} A_k \cos(k\theta), \quad A_k = \frac{2}{\pi} \int_0^{\pi} g(\theta) \cos(k\theta) \, d\theta.$$

The FFT model had a spatial to frequency variable transformation; likewise, this method also follows something as suggested by the authors:

$$\theta = \frac{x-a}{b-a} \pi, \quad x = \frac{b-a}{\pi} \theta + a.$$

With this, we get a transformed function:

$$g(x) = \sum_{k=0}^{\infty} A_k \cos\left(k\pi \frac{x-a}{b-a}\right), \quad A_k = \frac{2}{b-a} \int_a^b g(x) \cos\left(k\pi \frac{x-a}{b-a}\right) dx.$$

Considering the PDF $f_X(x)$ and CF $\phi_X(\omega)$, we know

$$f_X(x) = \int_{-\infty}^{\infty} \phi_X(\omega) e^{-j\omega x} d\omega.$$

Taking $g(x)$ as the PDF $f_X(x)$, we can write

$$F_k = \frac{2}{b-a} \Re\left\{ \phi_X\left(\frac{k\pi}{b-a}\right) e^{-j\frac{ka\pi}{b-a}} \right\}.$$

The above expression comes from Euler's formulae:

$$e^{j\omega} = \cos(\omega) + j\sin(\omega), \quad \cos(\omega) = \Re\{e^{j\omega}\},$$

and ordinary frequency component, $u = \frac{k\pi}{b-a}$, and of course, $F_k \approx A_k$.

Finally, we estimate $f_X(x)$ as

$$f_X(x) = \sum_{k=0}^{\infty} F_k \cos\left(k\pi \frac{x-a}{b-a}\right).$$

Again we choose a sufficiently large number N to trim it to finite series:

$$\widehat{f_X}(x) \approx \sum_{k=0}^{N} F_k \cos\left(k\pi \frac{x-a}{b-a}\right).$$

CHAPTER 7   JUMP MODELS

It is a good practice to multiply the first term by one-half. We follow the same conventions of choosing N, a, and b as we did for the FFT method. We do a small experiment to test the COS method with Gaussian density by comparing the theoretical density and reconstructed one from the CF (*/chapter7/test_merton_model.py*).

```
def _gaussian_cf(φ, θ, t):
    mu, σ = θ
    return np.exp(1j*mu*ω-0.5*(σ ** 2)*(φ ** 2))

def _κ1(θ):
    mu, _ = θ
    return mu

def _κ2(θ):
    _, σ = θ
    return (σ ** 2)

def _κ4(θ): return 0

def test_gaussian_density_recovery_cos_method():
    θ = (3.05, 1.2)
    b = 3.0
    x = np.linspace(start=b - 1.5, stop=b + 1.5, num=1000)
    _recover(COSMethodBasedDensityRecovery(
        N_freq=2000, ф_φ=_gaussian_cf), x, θ, 'COS Method')

def _recover(recovery_method: DensityRecoveryMethod, x, θ, title: str):

    true_d = pd.DataFrame(
        {'Sample': x, 'Density': norm.pdf(x, loc=θ[0],
        scale=θ[1]), 'type':
          'true'})

    recovered_d = pd.DataFrame({'Sample': x, 'Density':
         [recovery_method.recover(x_i=s_i,
                                            t=100,
```

```
                              cumulants={'κ1': _κ1(θ),
                                         'κ2': _κ2(θ),
                                         'κ4': _κ4(θ),
                                         },
                                      θ=θ,
                                      ) for s_i in
                                      x], 'type':
                 'recovered'})
plt.style.use("seaborn-v0_8")
_, ax = plt.subplots(nrows=1, ncols=2)
sns.lineplot(ax=ax[0], data=true_d, x='Sample', y='Density',
hue='type')
sns.lineplot(ax=ax[1], data=recovered_d,
             x='Sample', y='Density', hue='type')
plt.title(title)
plt.show()
```

The function *test_gaussian_density_recovery_cos_method* produces output as shown in Figure 7-3.

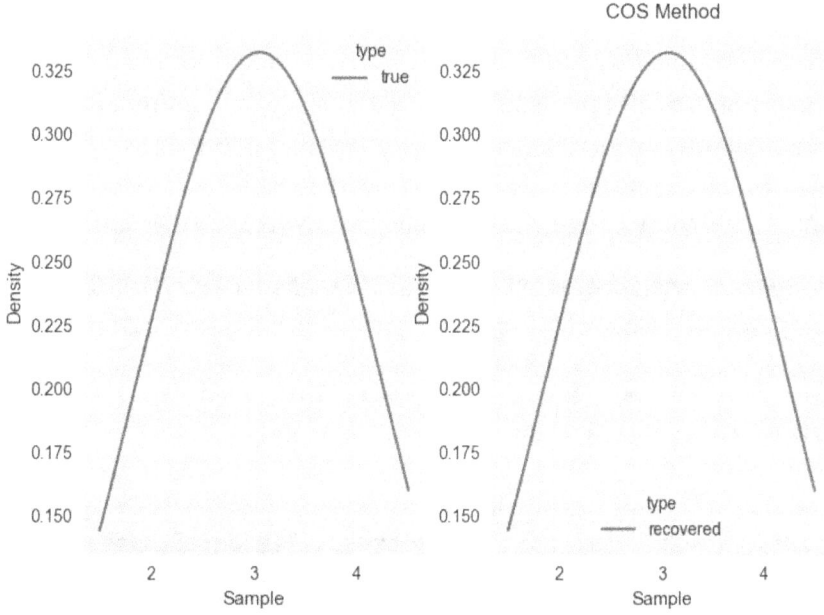

Figure 7-3. *Recovery of Gaussian density by COS method*

CHAPTER 7   JUMP MODELS

We are now at the final stage of parameter estimation. Once we recover the density, we can compute the likelihood of any data point given any parameters; and that leads to computation of the likelihood function as done for the GBM model in Chapter 6. The basic nature of the likelihood function computation remains the same, and we can leverage the same components, but with a difference in distributing the work. To elaborate, both density recovery methods, especially the FFT method, are computationally heavy, so the whole single big task can be split across multiple smaller ones. Recall the expression of the characteristic function of the jump-diffusion model; we said there that we would follow the one augmented by $e^{j\omega X_0}$, making the model free from the recursive approach and suitable for task splitting while computing the likelihood function.

So, I recommend using the distributed competing setup for three main reasons:

a) To estimate parameters with a large N which may come from hyperparameter tuning.

b) To split the dataset and distribute it across multiple tasks each computing the likelihood function for a specific range of time.

c) To know the perfect number of sample paths to generate for having the desired accuracy, and again it is also a good candidate for hyperparameter.

We leverage the same *loky* API to tackle (b), as we did for plotting the densities of forecasted paths for the GBM model. First, let's define a base component that provides some functionalities to any model using density recovery methods as follows:

Listing 7-2. Partial view of the class DensityRecoveryBasedAssetPriceModel

```
class DensityRecoveryBasedAssetPriceModel(BaseAssetPriceModel, ABC):
    '''
    Base class for any asset price model that used density recovery
    methods to estimate probability of any price.
    '''

    def __init__(self, time_unit_transformer: TimeUnitTransformer,
                 asset_price_dataset_adapter: StockPrice
                 DatasetAdapter = None,
```

CHAPTER 7 JUMP MODELS

```
             ll_optimizer: LoglikelihoodOptimizer = None,
             n_sample_paths=100,
             training_required=True,
             settings={'N_freq': 500, 'n_workers': 10}
             ):
    self._s_t_filtered = None
    self._settings = settings
    self._s_t_parts = None
    self._x0 = None

    self._recovery_method = self._create_density_recovery_method(
        self._characteristic_function_φ_φ, self._settings['N_freq'])

    super().__init__(time_unit_transformer=time_unit_transformer,
                     asset_price_dataset_adapter=asset_price_dataset_
                     adapter,
                     ll_optimizer=ll_optimizer,
                     n_sample_paths=n_sample_paths,
                     training_required=training_required)

@ abstractmethod
def _create_density_recovery_method(self, cf_φ_φ: callable,
N_Freq): ...

def _preprocess(self):
    self._x0 = np.log(float(self._s_t.head(1)['stock price']))
    self._s_t_filtered = self._s_t.drop(
        [self._s_t.index[0]], inplace=False)
    self._s_t_filtered['log_s_t'] = np.log(
        self._s_t_filtered['stock price'])

    # Capture time index
    self._s_t_filtered['t'] = self._s_t_filtered.apply(
        lambda row: row.name, axis=1)
    # Splitting the dataset into 10 parts
    self._s_t_parts = np.array_split(
        self._s_t_filtered[['log_s_t', 't']], 10)

    self._s_t = self._s_t.drop([self._s_t.index[0]], inplace=False)
```

Listing 7-2 shows that we split the dataset into ten parts, which is just a heuristic; you may choose the split numbers as per convenience according to the dataset size. Note that we plan to use the COS-based method for both parameter estimation and plotting of the densities for the forecasted path. After all, this is a choice, and feel free to use the FFT-based method to give it a try (be cautious with the FFT method as it is quite time-consuming). This class also exposes a few functions to be overridden; all related to characteristic function and cumulants as follows:

```
@abstractmethod
def _characteristic_function_ϕ_φ(self, φ, θ, t): ...

@abstractmethod
def _κ1(self, θ, t): ...

@abstractmethod
def _κ2(self, θ, t): ...

@abstractmethod
def _κ4(self, θ, t): ...
```

The next big task is to override the _pdf_ function, responsible for leveraging the recovery methods in a distributed way as follows:

```
def _pdf(self, θ: tuple):
    def _create_pdf_computation_jobs(row):
        loky_executor = get_reusable_executor(
            max_workers=self._settings.get('n_workers'))
        t = row['t']
        return loky_executor.submit(
            self._recovery_method.recover, row['log_s_t'],
            t,
            {'κ1': self._κ1(θ, t),
             'κ2': self._κ2(θ, t),
             'κ4': self._κ4(θ, t),
            },
            θ
        )
    all_jobs = [part.apply(_create_pdf_computation_jobs, axis=1)
```

```
        for part in self._s_t_parts]
    return np.concatenate(
        [job.apply(lambda row: row.result()).to_numpy() for job in
        all_jobs])
```

After the base component, we create a class specific to the Merton model, with its characteristic function and cumulants defined, as shown in Listing 7-3 *(/chapter7/merton_mode.py)*.

Listing 7-3. Partial view of the class MertonProcessAssetPriceModel

```
class MertonProcessAssetPriceModel(DensityRecoveryBasedAssetPriceModel):

    def __init__(self, time_unit_transformer: TimeUnitTransformer,
                settings={'N_freq': 200, 'n_workers': 10},
                asset_price_dataset_adapter: StockPriceDatasetAdapter = None,
                ll_optimizer: LoglikelihoodOptimizer = merton_process_ll_
                optimizer,
                n_sample_paths=100,
                training_required=True,
                ):
        super().__init__(time_unit_transformer, asset_price_dataset_adapter,
                        ll_optimizer, n_sample_paths, training_required,
                        settings=settings)

    def _create_empty_param_instance(self):
        return MertonProcessParameters()

    def _create_density_recovery_method(self, cf_φ_φ: callable, N_Freq):
        return COSMethodBasedDensityRecovery(N_Freq, cf_φ_φ)

    def _characteristic_function_φ_ω(self, ω, θ, t=None):
        r, σ, λ, μ_j, σ_j = θ
        merton_μ = r - 0.5*(σ**2) - (λ*(np.exp(μ_j+0.5*(σ_j**2))-1))
        base_term = np.exp(φ * merton_μ * 1j * t - (0.5*(σ**2)*(φ**2)*t))
        merton_model_term = np.exp(
            λ * t * (np.exp((φ * μ_j * 1j) - (0.5*(σ_j**2)*(φ**2))) - 1))

        return np.exp(1j * φ * self._x0) * base_term * merton_model_term
```

```python
    def _κ1(self, θ, t):
        r, σ, λ, μ_j, σ_j = θ
        merton_μ = r - 0.5*(σ**2) - (λ*(np.exp(μ_j+0.5*(σ_j**2))-1))
        return t * (merton_μ + (λ * μ_j))

    def _κ2(self, θ, t):
        _, σ, λ, μ_j, σ_j = θ
        return t * ((σ ** 2) + (λ * ((μ_j ** 2) + (σ_j ** 2))))

    def _κ4(self, θ, t):
        _, _, λ, μ_j, σ_j = θ
        return λ * t * ((μ_j ** 4) + (6 * (μ_j ** 2) * (σ_j ** 2)) + (3 *
    (σ_j ** 4) * λ))
```

For parameter estimation, this should suffice; the other functions present in the class will be discussed in a while, covering the forecasting part. The framework we established in Chapter 6 can be leveraged – computing likelihood function, optimizing with a chosen optimizer, and getting the parameters. We choose the *Nelder-Mead* optimizer from the Python *scipy* module and set the optimizer as follows:

```python
class NelderMeadLLOptimizer(LoglikelihoodOptimizer):

    def __init__(self, x0: List, θ0_bounds: List[tuple]):
        self._θ0_bounds = θ0_bounds
        self._x0 = x0

    def optimize(self, log_likelihood_func: callable):
        return minimize(fun=log_likelihood_func, x0=self._x0,
                        bounds=self._θ0_bounds, method='Nelder-Mead').x
```

Again, on the same line, I don't want to recommend any specific optimizer as there is a handful of them under *scipy*. You are free to implement your own using the base class *LoglikelihoodOptimizer*; as usual, it may affect the model's accuracy as well. With all that set, we test the parameter estimation process on (*/chapter7/test_merton_model.py*) S&P 500 Index data from January 1, 2011, to January 1, 2014, timeframe with daily frequency (Listing 7-4).

Listing 7-4. Estimating parameters of the Merton model

```
def test_merton_model_param_estimation():
    ticker = '^GSPC'  # S&P 500 Index
    time_freq = Frequency.DAILY
    yfa = YahooFinancialsAdapter(
        ticker=ticker,
        frequency=time_freq,
        training_set_date_range=("2011-01-01", "2014-01-01"),
        validation_set_date_range=("2014-01-01", "2015-01-01"))

    merton_asset_model = \
            MertonProcessAssetPriceModel(
        time_unit_transformer=IndexedTimeTransformer(time_freq=time_freq),
            asset_price_dataset_adapter=yfa, n_sample_paths=10)
    print(ticker)
    print(merton_asset_model.parameters_)
```

We get the estimated parameters as follows:

```
^GSPC
s0: 1848.3599853515625
t0: 2013-12-31 00:00:00
r: 0.0003015488157022716
σ: 0.004072847319647617
λ: 1.0000000000000003e-05
μ_j: 0.00010024644519917462
σ_j: 0.09300358840075287
```

Forecasting with Merton Model

With the estimated parameters, we now proceed to test the model and plot the distributions of some RVs from the forecasted path. We plan to test the forecasting from January 1, 2014, to January 1, 2015, and backtest with the original data. Therefore, we must override the function *_create_forecasting_process* coming from the base class and add one function named *_get_rv_generator_for_viz* required for plotting distributions as follows:

CHAPTER 7   JUMP MODELS

```python
def _create_forecasting_process(self,
                                parameters, n_sample_paths) ->
                                ForecastingProcess:
    return MertonProcess(
        r=parameters['r'],
        σ=parameters['σ'],
        λ=parameters['λ'],
        μ_j=parameters['μ_j'],
        σ_j=parameters['σ_j'],
        initial_state=parameters['s0'],
        n_sample_paths=n_sample_paths)

def _get_rv_generator_for_viz(self, s_t_1, t):
    θ = (self._parameters['r'], self._parameters['σ'],
         self._parameters['λ'], self._parameters['μ_j'],
         self._parameters['σ_j'])

    return RecoveredDistributionGenerator(density_recovery_method=
        COSMethodBasedDensityRecovery(
            N_freq=2000, φ_ω=self._characteristic_
            function_φ_ω),
            θ=θ,
            s_i=s_t_1,
            t=t,
            cumulants={'κ1': self._κ1(θ, t),
                       'κ2': self._κ2(θ, t),
                       'κ4': self._κ4(θ, t),
            })
```

As said earlier, we use the COS method instead of the FFT method for plotting distributions. The class *RecoveredDistributionGenerator* needs our attention, as it differs from what we saw in Chapter 6 for the diffusion model. Rather it is similar to what we did while testing the COS method earlier:

```python
class RecoveredDistributionGenerator():
    """
    Class to generate samples to display densities recovered using FFT
    or Cosine
    method
    """

    def __init__(self, density_recovery_method:
    DensityRecoveryMethod, s_i, t,
            cumulants: Cumulants, θ):
        self._θ = θ
        self._cumulants = cumulants
        self._t = t
        self._x_i = np.log(s_i)
        self._recovery_method_viz = density_recovery_method

    def sample(self, n_rv):
        return np.linspace(start=self._x_i - 1.0, stop=self._x_i + 1.0,
        num=n_rv), None

    def target_pdf_f(self, x):
        return [self._recovery_method_viz.recover(x_i=x_i,
                                                  t=self._t,
                                                  cumulants={'κ1': self._
                                                  cumulants['κ1'],
                                                            'κ2': self._
                                                            cumulants
                                                            ['κ2'],
                                                            'κ4': self._
                                                            cumulants
                                                            ['κ4'],
                                                            },
                                                  θ=self._θ
                                                  ) for x_i in x]
```

Note that the process isn't truly random while generating the samples, as we use a linearly spaced dataset around a fixed data point x_i, as shown above, but that doesn't really matter if we can comprehend distribution visually.

Next, we should set the log-scale display as true by overriding the *forecast* function as the estimation of the Merton model is done on log scale, and it is done as follows:

```python
def forecast(self, T,
             var_reduction: VarReduction = NoVarReduction(),
             prob_dist_viz_required=False,
             prob_dist_viz_settings: dict = {'n_workers': 5, 'ts':
             [5, 13, 17, 20, 22, 28]}):

    forecast_result = super().forecast(
        T, var_reduction, prob_dist_viz_required, prob_dist_viz_
        settings)

    forecast_result.log_scale_display = True
    return forecast_result
```

Finally, we execute the built model and do the backtesting (*/chapter7/test_merton_model.py*) as shown in Listing 7-5.

Listing 7-5. Backtesting the Merton model with estimated parameters and plotting the distributions

```python
def _test_forecasting_with_pdf(model, dsa):
    result = model.forecast(T=252,
                            prob_dist_viz_required=True,
                            prob_dist_viz_settings={'n_workers': 4, 'ts':
                            [20, 100, 230]})
    result_display = ForecastResultDisplay(result, ylabel='S(t)')

    ap_back_testing = AssetPriceBackTesting(
        s_true=dsa.validation_set, s_forecast=result.mean_path)

    print('RMSE: ' + str(ap_back_testing.rmse_score))
    vz7.plot_model_forecasting_results(result_display, ap_back_testing)
    result_display.plot_probability_distributions_from_path()
```

CHAPTER 7　JUMP MODELS

```python
def test_saved_asset_price_model():
    time_freq = Frequency.DAILY
    dsa = YahooFinancialsAdapter(
        ticker='^GSPC',
        frequency=time_freq,
        training_set_date_range=("2011-01-01", "2014-01-01"),
        validation_set_date_range=("2014-01-01", "2015-01-01"))

    params = {'s0': 1848.3599853515625,
              'r': 0.0003015488157022716,
              'σ': 0.004072847319647617,
              'λ': 1.0000000000000003e-05,
              'μ_j': 0.00010024644519917462,
              'σ_j': 0.09300358840075287,
              't0': parse('2013-12-01', date_formats=['YYYY-mm-dd'])}

    model = MertonProcessAssetPriceModel.load(parameters=params,
                                              time_unit_transformer=Indexed
                                              TimeTransformer(
                                                  time_freq=time_freq),
                                              n_sample_paths=5)
    _test_forecasting_with_pdf(model, dsa)
```

It uses the same parameters we obtained from Listing 7-4. We got the RMSE score as 45.85:

```
baseAssetPriceModel.train.
RMSE: 45.290264295575874
```

Figures 7-4 and 7-5 show the output that contain forecasted sample paths, backtesting results, and plotted distributions in log scale.

CHAPTER 7 JUMP MODELS

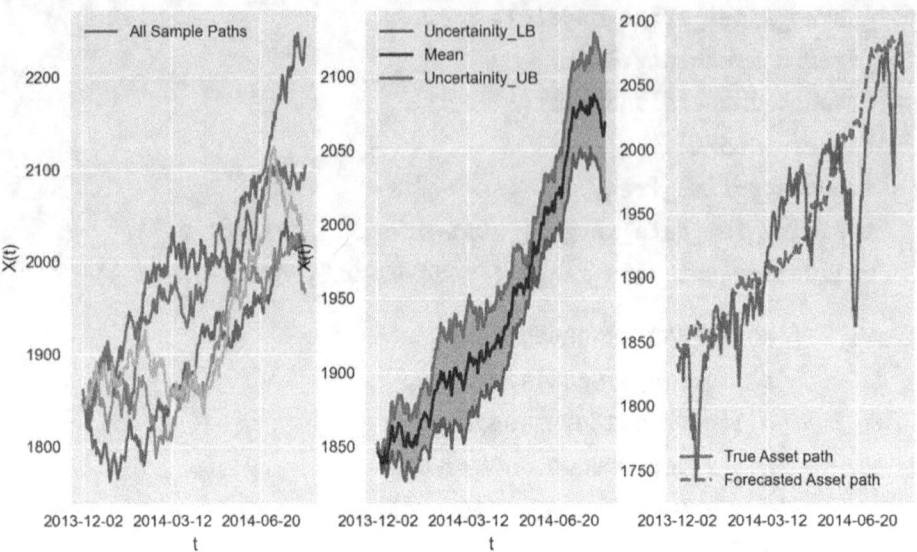

Figure 7-4. *Merton model forecasted path sand backtesting results of S&P 500 Index*

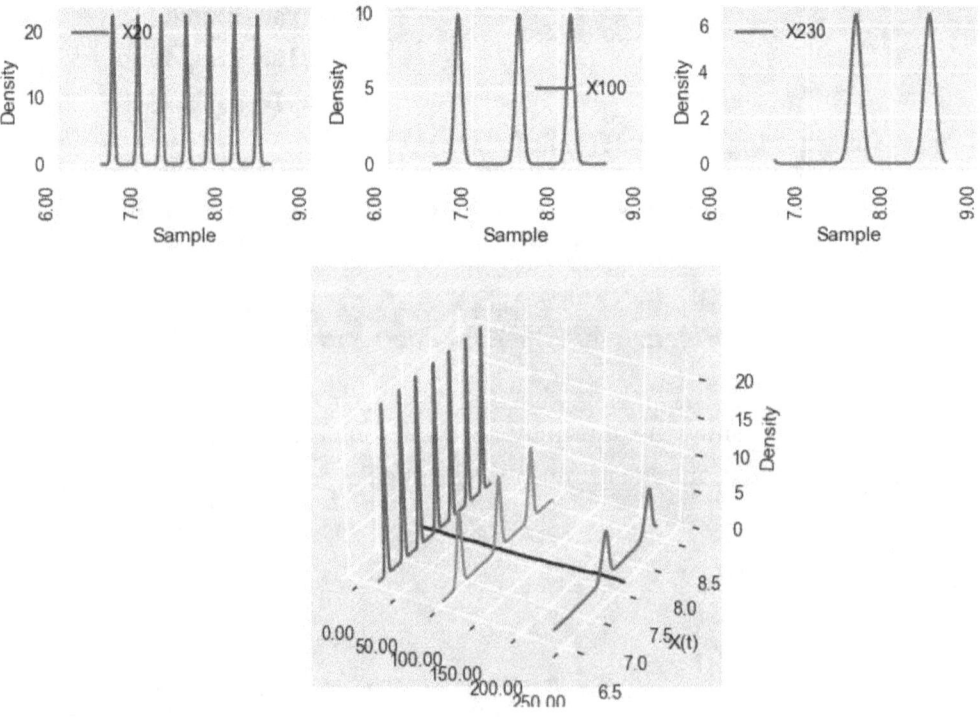

Figure 7-5. *Distribution of Merton process RVs X_{20}, X_{100}, and X_{230}*

As said earlier and in Chapter 6, this RMSE score depends on the hyperparameters N and the number of simulation paths. You may try with different settings and backtest.

Kou Model

Like the Merton model, we get the Kou model S_{t+1}^{Kou} when J follows an asymmetric double exponential distribution with parameters α_1 and α_2. The density function for the jumps is given as

$$f_J(x) = p\alpha_1 e^{-\alpha_1 x} 1_{\{x \geq 0\}} + (1-p)\alpha_2 e^{\alpha_2 x} 1_{\{x<0\}}.$$

The approach was proposed by *S.G. Kou [25]* for modeling the distribution of option prices, but we discuss the same for stocks and portfolio assets. The parameter p holds for the probability of jumps in a positive direction, which in turn makes $1 - p$ the same for the negative direction. Merton model provides a baseline solution to the sudden good or bad news in the market resulting in jumps, but it doesn't distinguish between them. Kou's model comes up with an approximation of jump distribution by explicitly including these market shocks due to good or bad news as probabilities p and $1 - p$. The final form is obtained as the weighted mixture of two exponential distributions.

Sampling Jumps from Asymmetric Double Exponential Distribution

Before going to the modeling part, we need to know how to sample from this jump distribution, and we take this opportunity to introduce a component called *AsymmetricDoubleExponentialGenerator* (/chapter7/kou_model.py) that leverages the same acceptance-rejection method for sampling. We take a Laplace distribution as a proposal density as it is a symmetric double exponential function and may work as a good hat for the target as follows:

```
from chapter4.random_number_gen_accept_reject import
AcceptanceRejectionMethod

class AsymmetricDoubleExponentialGenerator(AcceptanceRejectionMethod):

    def __init__(self, p, α_1, α_2, hat_func_optimizer:
    HatFunctionEstimator):
```

```python
        self._p = p
        self._α_1 = α_1
        self._α_2 = α_2
        super().__init__(hat_func_optimizer)

    def _proposal_pdf_g(self, x, θ: tuple):
        return laplace.pdf(x, loc=θ[0], scale=1/θ[1])

    def _sample_from_proposal_g_with_θ_optimal(self, n_rv):
        θ = self._hat_func_estimator.θ_optimal_for_g
        return laplace.rvs(loc=θ[0], scale=1/θ[1], size=n_rv)
```

Being a mixture of distribution, the computation of the pdf is bifurcated into two separate densities depending on the condition $x > 0$ as follows:

```python
def target_pdf_f(self, x):

    return np.where(np.array(x) >= 0,
                    np.dot(self._p*self._α_1,
                           np.exp(-np.dot(self._α_1, x))),
                    np.dot((1-self._p)*self._α_2,
                           np.exp(np.dot(self._α_2, x))))
```

As the technique for sampling RVs from asymmetric exponential distribution is the same as what we discussed for others in Chapter 4, we can test the component as follows (with $p = 0.7$, $\alpha_1 = 2.4$, $\alpha_2 = 0.7$):

```python
def test_sampling_of_asym_double_exponential():
    gaussian_supremum_estimator = DefaultSupremumEstimator(
        x0=[0.00001],
        x0_bounds=[(0.00001, None)],
        θ0=[0.00001, 0.00001],
        θ0_bounds=[(0.00001, None), (0.00001, None)])

    _, sample_trace = AsymmetricDoubleExponentialGenerator(
                    p=0.7,
                    α_1=2.4,
                    α_2=0.7,
hat_func_optimizer=gaussian_supremum_estimator).sample(n_rv=1000)

    sample_trace.plot()
```

We get the accepted and rejected samples as shown in Figure 7-6.

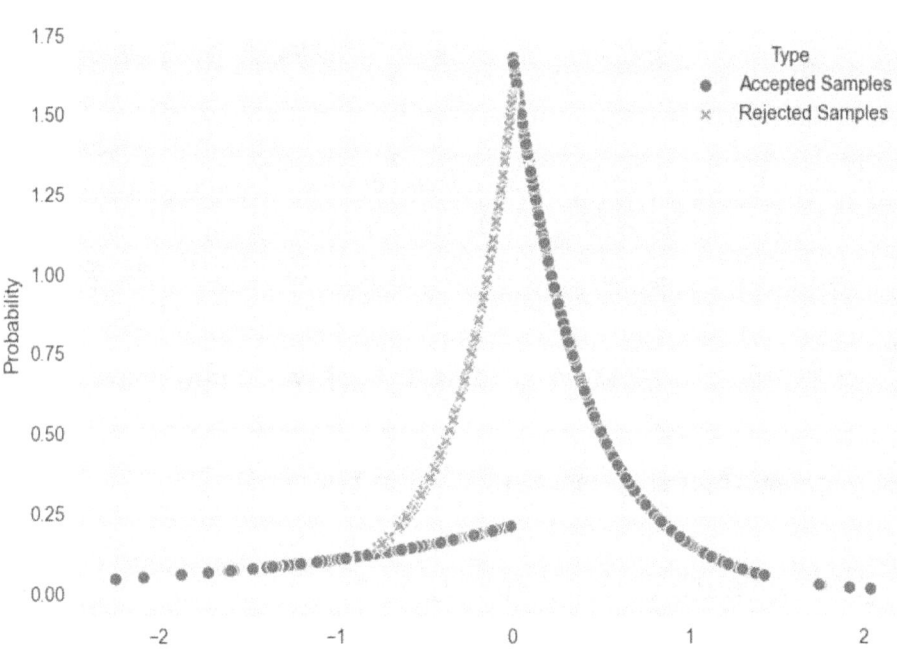

Figure 7-6. *Accepted and samples from the asymmetric double exponential and Laplace distribution*

It also shows that the Laplace is a symmetric double exponential function.

Stochastic Process for Kou Model and Path Generation

For Kou model, the expression for $E[e^J - 1]$ is given as

$$E\left[e^J - 1\right] = \frac{p\alpha_1}{\alpha_1 - 1} + \frac{(1-p)\alpha_2}{\alpha_2 + 1} - 1,$$

and from there, the stochastic process of the Kou model is given as

$$S_{t+1}^{Kou} = S_t^{Kou} e^{\left(r - \frac{1}{2}\sigma^2 - \lambda\left(\frac{p\alpha_1}{\alpha_1-1} + \frac{(1-p)\alpha_2}{\alpha_2+1} - 1\right)\right) + \sigma(W_{t+1} - W_t) + \sum_{k=1}^{x_t^p} J_k},$$

CHAPTER 7 JUMP MODELS

where the drift μ^{Kou} is given by

$$\mu^{Kou} = r - \frac{1}{2}\sigma^2 - \lambda\left(\frac{p\alpha_1}{\alpha_1 - 1} + \frac{(1-p)\alpha_2}{\alpha_2 + 1} - 1\right).$$

To implement this, we leverage the same base components for jump process just like we did in Merton model. First, the define the composite sampling density to sample from the Kou process leveraging the same *AsymmetricDoubleExponentialGenerator* as follows:

```
class KouProcessSamplingDensity(ParemetricJumpProcessSamplingDensity):
    '''
    Sampling density for generating RVs for Kou model
    '''
    def __init__(self, r, σ, λ, p, α_1, α_2):
        self._p = p
        self._α_1 = α_1
        self._α_2 = α_2

        super().__init__(r=r, σ=σ, λ=λ)

    def _sample_jumps(self, n_sample_paths, n_jumps):
        jumps, _ = AsymmetricDoubleExponentialGenerator(
                    p=self._p,
                    α_1=self._α_1,
                    α_2=self._α_2,
                                hat_func_optimizer=DefaultSupr
                                emumEstimator(
                                        x0=[0.00001],
                                        x0_bounds=[
                                        (0.00001,
                                        None)],
                                        θ0=[0.00001,
                                        0.00001],
                                        θ0_bounds=
```

```
                    [(0.00001, None), (0.00001, None)])).
                    sample(n_jumps*n_sample_paths)

    return np.array(jumps).reshape(n_sample_paths, n_jumps)
```

Next, class for the stochastic process is defined as follows:

```
class KouProcess(ParametricJumpProcess):
    '''
    Stochastic process for Kou model
    '''

    def __init__(self, r, σ, λ, p, α_1, α_2, initial_state=1.0, n_sample_
    paths=5):
        self._p = p
        self._α_1 = α_1
        self._α_2 = α_2

        super().__init__(r=r, σ=σ, λ=λ, n_sample_paths=n_sample_paths,
                    initial_state=initial_state,
                                        sampling_density=KouProcessSampli
                                        ngDensity(
                    r=r,
                    σ=σ,
                    λ=λ,
                    p=p,
                    α_1=α_1,
                    α_2=α_2))

    def _compute_jump_drift(self):
        de_term_1 = self._p*self._α_1*(1/(self._α_1-1))
        de_term_2 = (1-self._p)*self._α_2*(1/(self._α_2+1))

        return self._r - (0.5*(self._σ**2)) + (self._λ *
                                        (1-de_term_1-de_term_2))
```

CHAPTER 7 JUMP MODELS

Path generation is tested as follows for one set of parameters:

```
r_1 = 0.0003
σ_1 = 0.009
λ_1 = 0.01
p_1 = 0.1
α_1_1 = 2.5
α_2_1 = 1.5

kp_1 = KouProcess(r=r_1,
                  σ=σ_1,
                  λ=λ_1,
                  p=p_1,
                  α_1=α_1_1,
                  α_2=α_2_1,
                  n_sample_paths=5)
result_display_1 = ForecastResultDisplay(
    result=kp_1.forecast(T=500), ylabel='S(t)')
```

Figure 7-7 shows generated mean paths. The effect of positive jump probability p is visible in both cases; despite an overall negative trend, some localized spikes caused by high probability, positive jumps are observed in the second case.

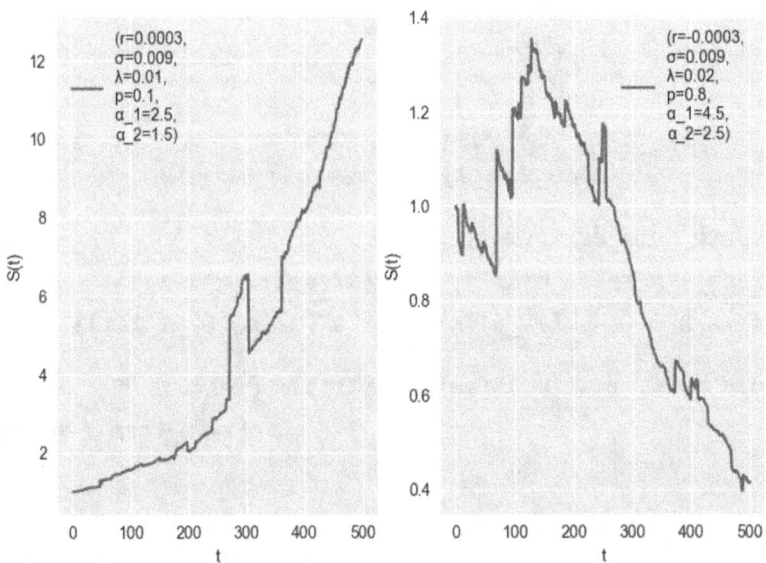

Figure 7-7. *Mean paths of the Kou process for two sets of parameters*

Parameter Estimation of Kou Model

The Kou model has six parameters: r, σ, λ, p, α_1, and α_2. The original paper gave a closed-form expression of the density, but again, like the Merton model, the stochastic process is composed of multiple RVs from different distributions, and hence, we would like to demonstrate the same numerical approach for recovering the density and then proceed for the MLE.

To proceed, first we get the CF of the Kou model by putting the expressions of $E[e^J - 1]$ and $E[e^{j\omega J} - 1]$ in CF of the generic jump-diffusion model $\phi_{t+1}^{Jump-Diffusion}(\omega)$ as follows:

$$\phi_{t+1}^{Kou}(\omega) = e^{j\omega X_0} e^{\left(r - \frac{1}{2}\sigma^2 - \lambda\left(\frac{p\alpha_1}{\alpha_1-1} + \frac{(1-p)\alpha_2}{\alpha_2+1} - 1\right)\right)t} e^{-\frac{1}{2}\sigma^2\omega^2 t} e^{\lambda t\left(\frac{p\alpha_1}{\alpha_1-j\omega} + \frac{(1-p)\alpha_2}{\alpha_2+j\omega} - 1\right)}.$$

A more compact form for implementation is written as follows:

$$\phi_{t+1}^{Kou}(\omega) = e^{j\omega X_0} e^{j\omega \mu^{Kou} t - \frac{1}{2}\sigma^2\omega^2 t} \psi^{Kou}(\omega, t),$$

$$\psi^{Kou}(\omega, t) = e^{\lambda t\left(\frac{p\alpha_1}{\alpha_1-j\omega} + \frac{(1-p)\alpha_2}{\alpha_2+j\omega} - 1\right)},$$

$$\mu^{Kou} = r - \frac{1}{2}\sigma^2 - \lambda\left(\frac{p\alpha_1}{\alpha_1-1} + \frac{(1-p)\alpha_2}{\alpha_2+1} - 1\right)$$

We need three cumulants for the Kou model as well for computing the integration range and those are given by

$$\kappa_1 = t\left(\mu^{Kou} + \lambda\left(\frac{p}{\alpha_1} + \frac{1-p}{\alpha_2}\right)\right),$$

$$\kappa_2 = t\left(\sigma^2 + 2\lambda\left(\frac{p}{\alpha_1^2} + \frac{1-p}{\alpha_2^2}\right)\right),$$

$$\kappa_4 = 24\lambda\left(\frac{p}{\alpha_1^4} + \frac{1-p}{\alpha_2^4}\right)$$

CHAPTER 7 JUMP MODELS

With all these expressions in place, we create the class *KouProcessAssetPriceModel* leveraging the *DensityRecoveryBasedAssetPriceModel*, and over the process, we plan to use the COS method for density recovery for parameter estimation and the functions are as follows:

```
def _create_empty_param_instance(self):
    return KouProcessParameters()

def _create_density_recovery_method(self, cf_φ_ω: callable, N_Freq):
    return COSMethodBasedDensityRecovery(N_Freq, cf_φ_ω)

def _tuple_to_param_order(self, θ):
    print(θ)
    self._parameters['r'], self._parameters['σ'], self._parameters[
        'λ'], self._parameters['p'], self._parameters['α_1'], self._
        parameters['α_2'] = θ

def _characteristic_function_φ_ω(self, ω, θ, t=None):
    r, σ, λ, p, α_1, α_2 = θ
    de_term_1 = p*α_1*(1/(α_1-1))
    de_term_2 = (1-p)*α_2*(1/(α_2+1))

    kou_μ = r - 0.5*(σ**2) + (λ * (1-de_term_1-de_term_2))
    base_term = np.exp(ω * kou_μ * 1j * t - (0.5*(σ**2)*(ω**2)*t))

    de_term_1_j = (p*α_1)/(α_1-1j*ω)
    de_term_2_j = ((1-p)*α_2)/(α_2+1j*ω)

    kou_model_term = np.exp(
        λ * t * (de_term_1_j + de_term_2_j - 1))

    return np.exp(1j * ω * self._x0) * base_term * kou_model_term

def _κ1(self, θ, t):
    r, σ, λ, p, α_1, α_2 = θ
    de_term_1 = p*α_1*(1/(α_1-1))
    de_term_2 = (1-p)*α_2*(1/(α_2+1))

    kou_μ = r - 0.5*(σ**2) + (λ * (1-de_term_1-de_term_2))
    return t * (kou_μ + (λ * (p/α_1 - (1-p)/α_2)))
```

CHAPTER 7 JUMP MODELS

```python
def _κ2(self, θ, t):
    _, σ, λ, p, α_1, α_2 = θ
    return t * ((σ ** 2) + (2 * λ * (p/(α_1**2)+(1-p)/(α_2**2))))

def _κ4(self, θ, t):
    _, _, λ, p, α_1, α_2 = θ
    return 24 * λ * t * (p/(α_1**4)+(1-p)/(α_2**4))
```

We test the parameter estimation process with the same dataset as done for Merton model as follows:

```python
def test_kou_model_param_estimation():
    ticker = '^GSPC'   # S&P 500 Index
    time_freq = Frequency.DAILY
    yfa = YahooFinancialsAdapter(
        ticker=ticker,
        frequency=time_freq,
        training_set_date_range=("2011-01-01", "2014-01-01"),
        validation_set_date_range=("2014-01-01", "2015-01-01"))

    kou_asset_model = KouProcessAssetPriceModel
        (time_unit_transformer=IndexedTimeTransformer(time_freq=time_freq),
                asset_price_dataset_adapter=yfa,
                n_sample_paths=10)
    print(ticker)
    print_parameters(kou_asset_model.parameters_)
```

We get the Kou model parameters as follows:

```
^GSPC
s0: 1848.3599853515625
t0: 2013-12-31 00:00:00
r: 0.00032894797531725286
σ: 0.009310530997044748
λ: 1e-05
p: 0.011733673454519264
α_1: 1.1466664732568665
α_2: 1.4526511493269534
```

CHAPTER 7 JUMP MODELS

Forecasting with Kou Model

To activate the forecasting and computation of the probability distribution of the mean path, the following two functions should be duly defined as follows (the forecasting method remains same for all):

```
def _create_forecasting_process(self,
                                parameters, n_sample_paths) ->
                                ForecastingProcess:
    return KouProcess(
        r=parameters['r'],
        σ=parameters['σ'],
        λ=parameters['λ'],
        p=parameters['p'],
        α_1=parameters['α_1'],
        α_2=parameters['α_2'],
        initial_state=parameters['s0'],
        n_sample_paths=n_sample_paths)

  def _get_rv_generator_for_viz(self, s_t_1, t):
      θ = (self._parameters['r'], self._parameters['σ'],
          self._parameters['λ'], self._parameters['p'],
          self._parameters['α_1'], self._parameters['α_2'])
      return
      RecoveredDistributionGenerator(density_recovery_method=
          COSMethodBasedDensityRecovery(
              N_freq=2000,
              φ_ω=self._characteristic_function_φ_ω),
          θ=θ,
          s_i=s_t_1,
          t=t,
          cumulants={'κ1': self._κ1(θ, t),
                     'κ2': self._κ2(θ, t),
                     'κ4': self._κ4(θ, t),
                    })
```

CHAPTER 7   JUMP MODELS

Now, we do the backtesting with same validation dataset as done for the Merton model and capture some metrics as follows (check the output as shown in Figure 7-8 & Figure 7-9):

```
def test_saved_asset_price_model():
    time_freq = Frequency.DAILY
    dsa = YahooFinancialsAdapter(
        ticker='^GSPC',
        frequency=time_freq,
        training_set_date_range=("2011-01-01", "2014-01-01"),
        validation_set_date_range=("2014-01-01", "2015-01-01"))

    params = {'s0': 1848.3599853515625,
              'r': 0.00032894797531725286,
              'σ': 0.009310530997044748,
              'λ': 1e-05,
              'p': 0.011733673454519264,
              'α_1': 1.1466664732568665,
              'α_2': 1.4526511493269534,
              't0': parse('2013-12-01', date_formats=['YYYY-mm-dd'])}

    model = KouProcessAssetPriceModel.load(parameters=params,
                                            time_unit_transformer=IndexedTim
                                            eTransformer(
                                                time_freq=time_freq),
                                            n_sample_paths=5)
    _test_forecasting_with_pdf(model, dsa)
```

RMSE: 61.83299022120203

229

CHAPTER 7   JUMP MODELS

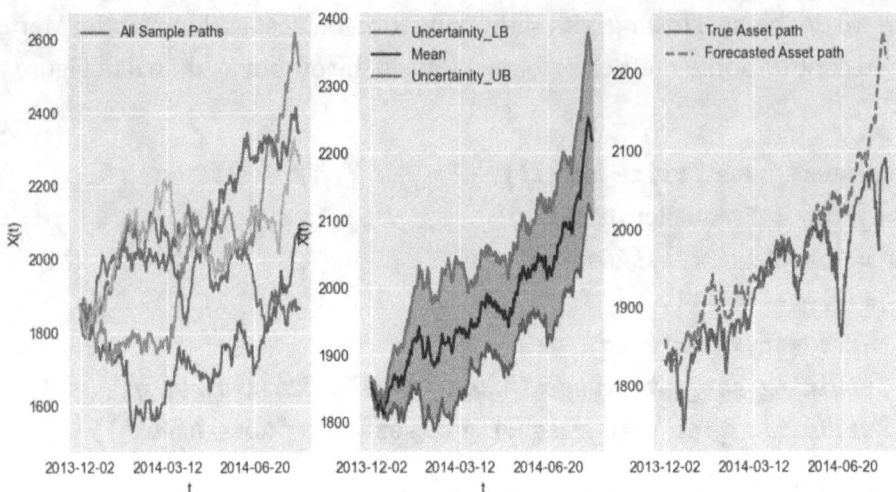

Figure 7-8. *Kou model forecasted path sand backtesting results of S&P 500 Index*

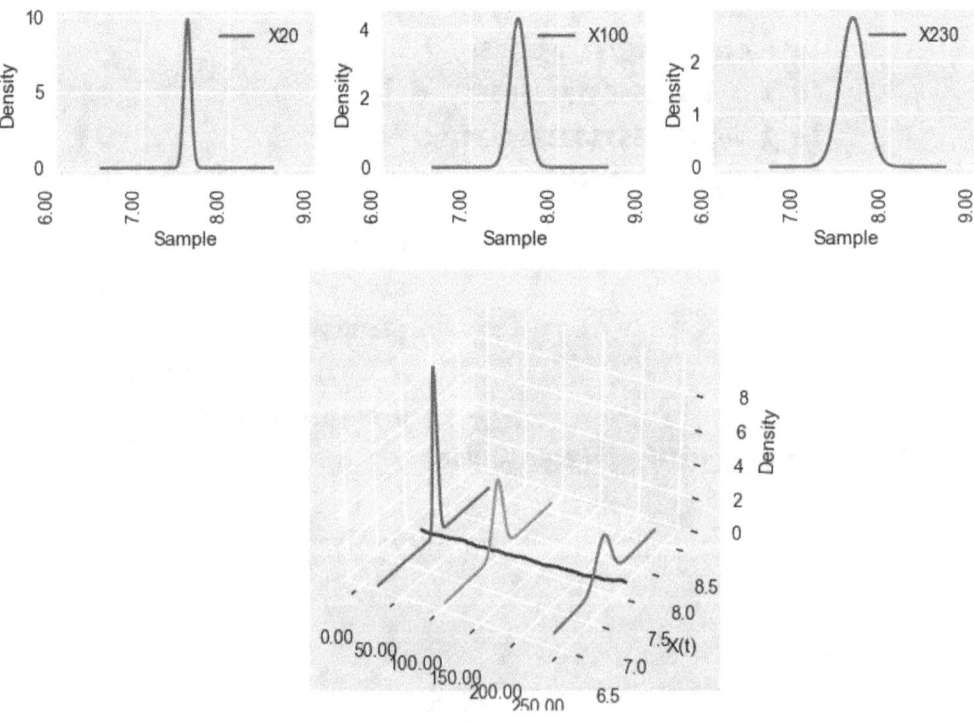

Figure 7-9. *Distributons of Kou process RVs X_{20}, X_{100}, and X_{230}*

Methods to Improve the Result

We discussed a few methods for improvement in the previous chapter, but those were very generic and still applicable to jump models. Additionally, two more can be added in the list – choice of density recovery and number of frequencies in Fourier transform. We mainly tested with COS method, but the FFT one is more generic but slower in nature; you may go ahead and try them with different frequency settings for both Merton and Kou models.

Nonparametric Models

The models discussed in this book made challenging assumptions about the asset price distributions – either log-normal, Merton process (mixed normal and Poisson), or even the Kou model. These are good if the asset follows the assumed distribution, but what if it doesn't? An ideal model for jump processes should have many hidden components responsible for simulating abnormally shaped spikes (results of sudden market crashes or surges of bulls in the market). Poisson process approximation of jumps provided a way of doing so, but that's also a hard assumption bound method. The asset price path may exhibit different behavior if the distribution deviates significantly from the assumed one. One of the apparent reasons is the incorporation of the parametric statistical methods with the limitation of forcing the modeling to certain families of distribution with a known set of parameters. We studied the geometric Brownian motion process, which was used for modeling in Chapters 5 and 6, which has a specific parametric form whose distribution is evaluated as log-normal. Even for modeling the jump process, it was mixed with a Poisson process, which has a particular form again. In every case, a known set of parameters is computed using MLE.

In contrast, nonparametric methods don't assume these specific forms; in most cases, they calculate the probabilities based on the definition, i.e., by counting events. The kernel method is one such example – though it is not entirely function free or parameter free, it is free from any known assumptions about distributions. Unlike parametric models, there are no global function approximators that will give densities for a random variable; rather, nonparametric methods rely on some other functions that help in counting events iteratively. Parameters also complement those functions to do the job accurately for a dataset, which is slightly different from what we mean by parameters for parametric models.

We will discuss that in a while, but before, let's review the stochastic differential equation of the log of the stock process again:

CHAPTER 7 JUMP MODELS

$$dX_t = \mu(X_t)dt + \sigma(X_t)dW_t.$$

Did you notice any difference? Trends and diffusions are no longer constants but rather functions of the random variables. The methods we discuss here are accessible from the constraints of specific distributions and adaptable for handling variable trends and diffusion, which is crucial to handling jumps. This adaptability is concerning papers *Bandi and Nguyen [15]* and *Bandi and Philips [16]*. Recall from Chapter 5 that trends and diffusions are the average first- and second-order instantaneous changes in the asset price process, which are given by

$$\mu(x) = E[X_{t+\Delta t} - X_t | X_t = x],$$
$$\sigma^2(x) = E\left[(X_{t+\Delta t} - X_t)^2 | X_t = x\right].$$

These are nothing but the first- and second-order raw moments of price changes, a concept we discussed in detail in Chapter 3. Estimating and understanding these moments is crucial for grasping the foundations of nonparametric methods. Theoretically, a standard asset price process with no jumps is supposed to have no higher-order moments greater than two. But with the jump's component included, the SDE looks like

$$dX_t = \mu(X_t)dt + \sigma(X_t)dW_t + dJ_t,$$

which will have moments like

$$M_k(x) = E\left[(X_{t+\Delta t} - X_t)^k | X_t = x\right] > 0 \,\&\, k > 2,$$

and

$$J_t = \sum_{i=1}^{N_t} Y_i,$$

where N_t follows some counting process and Y is the size of the jumps. We are primarily interested in computing three conditional moments given as

$$M_1(x) = E[X_{t+\Delta t} - X_t | X_t = x] = \mu(x)$$

$$M_2(x) = E\left[(X_{t+\Delta x} - X_t)^2 | X_t = x\right] = \sigma^2(x) + \lambda(x)E_Y(Y^2)$$

$$M_k(x) = E\left[(X_{t+\Delta x} - X_t)^k | X_t = x\right] = \lambda(x)E_Y(Y^k).$$

This $\lambda(x)$ is the dynamic jump intensity resulting from the counting process N_t. Just like the Merton model, jumps have some effects on the overall diffusion of the model, the factor $\lambda(x)E_Y(Y^2)$ representing that effect. So now, we are left with estimating $\mu(x)$, $\sigma^2(x)$, $\lambda(x)$, and $\sigma_Y^2(Y)$. Per the papers, we consider jumps following normal distribution with a parameter set $(0, \sigma_Y^2)$ for convenience. Recall the method of moments from Chapter 3, as we have three-moment equations here. Sample moments must be estimated from the dataset (realized sample path) to evaluate the parameters. Being nonparametric, we don't know the exact form of the density of the stochastic process. For moment computation, we fall back to the kernel density estimation method with a choice of the kernel function. With that setup, estimates of three conditional moments are given as

$$\widehat{M_1}(x) = \frac{\sum_{t=1}^n K\left(\frac{X_t - x}{h}\right)(X_{t+1} - X_t)}{\sum_{t=1}^n K\left(\frac{X_t - x}{h}\right)},$$

$$\widehat{M_2}(x) = \frac{\sum_{t=1}^n K\left(\frac{X_t - x}{h}\right)(X_{t+1} - X_t)^2}{\sum_{t=1}^n K\left(\frac{X_t - x}{h}\right)},$$

$$\widehat{M_k}(x) = \frac{\sum_{t=1}^n K\left(\frac{X_t - x}{h}\right)(X_{t+1} - X_t)^k}{\sum_{t=1}^n K\left(\frac{X_t - x}{h}\right)}, k > 2.$$

The choice of kernel function K and bandwidth h should be estimated again using a separate method. X_t function is, of course, the realization of the stochastic process obtained from the training set. Next, we briefly review the kernel density estimation method. Readers familiar with the kernel method may skip this section and go directly to *parameter estimation*.

CHAPTER 7 JUMP MODELS

Brief Review of the Kernel Method

Readers of this book must be familiar with frequency histograms taught in any introductory descriptive statistics course. These histograms give a pictorial representation of the bin-based frequency distribution. Dividing each bin's count by the total number of records would give the probability of the bin's existence. However, this is still hard counting and inappropriate for continuous data, resulting in approximation errors. It shows the same probability for all elements in a single bin, B_i, as

$$P(x \in B_i) = \frac{\sum 1_i}{N}.$$

To mitigate approximation error and provide a smoothed version of frequency counting, 1 should be replaced with some weight and that too for each $x \in B_i$. With this, the binning structure will change, and each bin should now be centralized around each x. These bins would be imaginary rather than real because of the decomposition of the original histogram. Considering $2h$ as the width of each histogram where h is infinitesimal, then by the rule of probability density (refer to Chapter 3),

$$f(x) = \lim_{h \to o} \frac{1}{2h} P(x - h < x < x + h).$$

If $I(\cdot)$ is the indicator function, then the naïve probability density estimator can be written as

$$\hat{f}(x) = \frac{1}{2nh} \sum_{i=1}^{n} I(x - h < X_i < x + h).$$

The indicator function counts all the data points around the neighborhood $2h$ of x. That's what the expression $\sum 1_i$ was doing as well for a bin belonging to the histogram. We can think of a smoothing weight assigning function K which will estimate $\hat{f}(x)$ like below:

$$\hat{f}(x) = \frac{1}{2nh} \sum_{i=1}^{n} I(x - h < X_i < x + h)$$
$$= \frac{1}{2nh} \sum_{i=1}^{n} I\left(-1 < \frac{X_i - x}{h} < 1\right)$$
$$= \frac{1}{nh} \sum_{i=1}^{n} K\left(\frac{X_i - x}{h}\right).$$

The estimator is known as the *kernel density estimator (KDE)* or the *Parzen-Rosenblatt estimator*, function K is called a *kernel*, and the parameter h is called the *bandwidth* of the estimator. The KDE is summing up all weights around point x with help of the function K instead of hard counting – that's a smoothing operation.

K cannot be any function but must satisfy the following conditions:

$$\int K(x)dx = 1,$$
$$\int xK(x)dx = 0,$$
$$\int x^2 K(x)dx < \infty,$$
$$K(x) \geq 0 \text{ for all } x,$$
$$K(x) = K(-x),$$

that is, the kernel function must be symmetric, continuous PDF with mean zero, and bounded variance. An example of such a function is the Gaussian kernel as given by

$$K(x) = \frac{1}{\sqrt{2\pi}} e^{-\frac{1}{2}x^2}.$$

So, the final form of a KDE with Gaussian kernel is given by

$$\hat{f}(x) = \frac{1}{n} \sum_{i=1}^{n} \frac{1}{h\sqrt{2\pi}} e^{-\frac{1}{2}\left(\frac{X_i - x}{h}\right)^2}.$$

Apparently, the estimator looks like a Gaussian distribution; you might be wondering what's different. The difference lies in the approach – parametric vs. nonparametric. This estimator is not a function approximator of the whole dataset but rather a distance function that computes the sum of the exponential distance of an input data point from the whole dataset. In that sense, the estimator computes localized densities rather than having a global view.

As per the paper, we use the Gaussian kernel only for modeling the stochastic process with jumps. We define the Gaussian kernel like below:

```
def gaussian_kernel(x):
    return np.exp(-(x*x/2)) / np.sqrt(2*np.pi)
```

CHAPTER 7 JUMP MODELS

With this, let's do a short experiment with a test function and see what the density looks like:

```
def test_gaussian_kernel_density_estimate():
    # Create a mixture of data points from three different distributions
    x_arr = sorted(np.concatenate((norm.rvs(loc=150, scale=100, size=100),
                                   norm.rvs(loc=15, scale=10, size=100),
                                   norm.rvs(loc=1000, scale=200, size=5))))
    n = len(x_arr)

    def f(x, h):
        return np.sum(gaussian_kernel((x_arr-x)/h))/(n*h)

    # Setup a pool of bandwidths to be tested
    h_1 = 15
    h_2 = 30
    h_3 = 100
    h_4 = 60
    vz7.plot_kde_with_hs((x_arr, [f(x, h_1) for x in x_arr], h_1),
                        (x_arr, [f(x, h_2) for x in x_arr], h_2),
                        (x_arr, [f(x, h_3) for x in x_arr], h_3),
                        (x_arr, [f(x, h_4) for x in x_arr], h_4))
```

We got the density plot for different bandwidths, as shown in Figure 7-10.

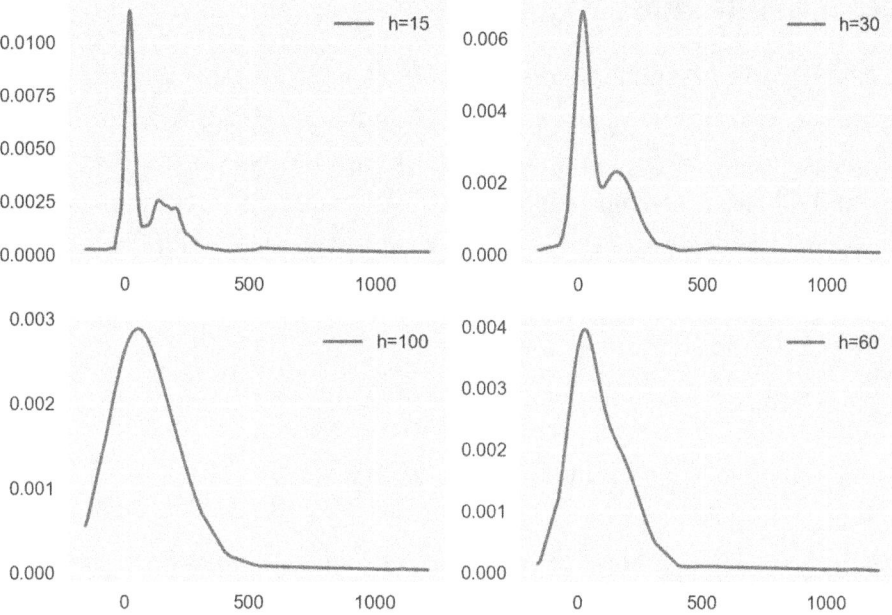

Figure 7-10. *Density plots with different bandwidths*

This experiment shows that a bigger bandwidth produces smoother densities, i.e., with fewer peaks.

Now, the question is how to estimate a good value for bandwidth for any kernel function. Let's first write the likelihood function considering h as parameter:

$$L(h) = \prod_{i=1}^{n} \hat{f}(x_i; h)$$

$$= \prod_{i=1}^{n} \frac{1}{nh} \sum_{j=1}^{n} K\left(\frac{X_j - x_i}{h}\right)$$

$$= n^{-n} h^{-n} \prod_{i=1}^{n} \sum_{j=1}^{n} K\left(\frac{X_j - x_i}{h}\right).$$

For infinitesimal value of h, i.e., $h \to 0$, $L(h) \to \infty$. So, the likelihood function is unbounded for KDE and that makes direct evaluation of MLE difficult. Putting some restrictions on the optimization problem may yield some solutions. However, cross-validation and some very domain-specific methods are other alternatives. We discuss a few such methods next.

CHAPTER 7   JUMP MODELS

Parameter Estimation

We have a total of five parameters to estimate – $\mu(x)$, $\sigma^2(x)$, $\lambda(x)$, $\sigma_Y^2(Y)$, and h. Notice that the first three are functions of x, and the last two should be statically determined. This determination is strictly under the condition that jumps follow a normal distribution with zero mean and σ_Y^2 variance. A different distribution (i.e., mixed normal jumps) will produce different parameter estimates. As per *Johannes M. [17]*, $\mu(x)$, $\sigma^2(x)$, and $\lambda(x)$ are estimated as

$$\widehat{\mu(x)} = \widehat{M_1}(x),$$

$$\widehat{\lambda(x)} = \frac{\widehat{M_4}(x)}{3\sigma_Y^4(Y)},$$

$$\widehat{\sigma^2(x)} = \widehat{M_1}(x) - \widehat{\lambda(x)}\sigma_Y^2(Y).$$

$\widehat{M_4}(x)$ is, as usual, the fourth sample raw moment of increments $X_{t+1} - X_t$. These three estimates depend on estimates $\sigma_Y^2(Y)$ and h, which we will discuss later. As these estimates are functions of x instead of being constants, they can better capture the dynamic and local effect of jumps in the asset path. Extreme values in the asset path heavily influence the traditional MLE method, and this is often known as producing incorrect estimates of the parameters. To some extent, this error is mitigated in the kernel approach. In short, jumps are handled in two ways:

a) Incorporation of the method of moments doesn't try to match the whole distribution with the dataset. This helps if the underlying asset doesn't completely follow any assumed distribution. Matching nodes like moments is a much more realistic and nongreedy approach when the presence of jumps causes some deviation from the theoretical distribution.

b) The kernel method reduces any distribution-related assumptions made while modeling with Merton or Kou's approach, as the presence of jumps can cause significant deviation from theoretical distributions like Gaussian or Poisson. However, the kernel approach is not fully assumption free; a choice for the kernel function still exists, which can impact the model's accuracy. But overall, the assumption is much softer than the hard assumption of complete data distribution.

You might still wonder about the difference between KDE and the characteristic function (CF)-based method discussed earlier – both seemingly doing the same task of density computation. That's true, but the two methods have a theoretical disparity – KDE is density "estimation," while the other is density "recovery." In the CF-based method, we at least know the closed-form density in the frequency domain, and there, the task is to do the domain mapping, bringing it back into the spatial domain numerically. However, we don't know about the closed-form density in the KDE method. Therefore, the estimation of bandwidth and then kernel function computation is necessary to get density – and it is about computing density from scratch without any scope of recovering from other domains.

With that in place, we proceed now with a choice of kernel function as Gaussian kernel, and first, we design the stochastic process for path simulation with the given $\sigma_Y^2(Y)$ and h.

Stochastic Process with Gaussian Jumps and Path Simulation

Euler approximation of SDE for kernel method can be written as

$$X_{t+1} = X_t + \widehat{\mu(X_t)} + \widehat{\sigma(X_t)}(W_{t+1} - W_t) + \widehat{\lambda(X_t)}J_t$$

Unlike the Merton model, we don't assume jumps following the Poisson process or even the X_t following a log-normal distribution like the geometric Brownian motion. Instead, the normal random variate J_t multiplied by the jump intensity $\lambda(X_t)$ produces the total jump effect in the SDE instead of separately summarizing all jumps as done in the Merton model. This SDE can simulate the jump process paths with a given $\sigma_Y^2(Y)$ and h. Later, we will see how to estimate some good values for these two parameters.

Let's first write the Python class for sampling density and override the function *sample* as shown below:

```
class CompositeJumpSamplingDensity(TargetSamplingDensity):
    '''
    Class for sampling a combination of standard normal
    variate and a normal variate with variance σ_2_J
    '''
    def __init__(self, x_arr, h, σ_2_J):
        self._x_arr = x_arr
```

CHAPTER 7 JUMP MODELS

```
        self._h = h
        self._σ_2_J = σ_2_J
        self._n = len(self._x_arr)

    def sample(self, n_vars, n_sample_paths=1):
        dJs = norm.rvs(size=(n_sample_paths, n_vars),
                      scale=np.sqrt(self._σ_2_J))
        dWs = norm.rvs(size=(n_sample_paths, n_vars))
        '''
        Return the variates as an array of dictionaries as there
        are two different random variables
        '''
        return np.array([[{'dW': w, 'dJ': j} for w, j in zip(dw, dj)]
                         for dw, dj in zip(dWs, dJs)])
```

The technique of generating two random variates for diffusion and jump and returning everything wrapped inside an array of dictionaries is similar to that used for the Merton model.

The crucial function kth_raw_moment_of_increments is defined under the module chapter7/non_parametric_jump_process_model.py for computing moments:

```
def kth_raw_moment_of_increments(x_arr, x, h, increments_k):
    '''
    kth raw moment is computed as,
```

$$\widehat{M_k}(x) = \frac{\sum_{t=1}^{n} K\left(\frac{X_t - x}{h}\right)(X_{t+1} - X_t)^k}{\sum_{t=1}^{n} K\left(\frac{X_t - x}{h}\right)}$$

```
    K is the Gaussian Kernel
    '''
    kernel_sum = np.sum(
        gaussian_kernel(
            (x_arr-x)/h))
```

```
# increments_k is computed as (X_{t + 1} − X_t)^k
  weighted_increments = np.sum(
      gaussian_kernel(
          (x_arr-x)/h) * increments_k)

  return weighted_increments / kernel_sum
```

We now define *GaussianKernelJumpProcess,* which is the class for the jump stochastic process as below *(__init__* function):

```
class GaussianKernelJumpProcess(ForecastingProcess):
    '''
    Class for simulating paths of Gaussian Kernel-based
    jump stochastic process.
    '''

    def __init__(self,
                 x_arr,
                 σ_2_J: float,
                 increments,
                 initial_state,
                 h,
                 n_sample_paths=20):
        # Variance of the jumps
        self._σ_2_J = σ_2_J

        # Tarining set X_t
        self._x_arr = x_arr

        # Kernel bandwidth h
        self._h = h

        # Pre-compute all required powers of increments (X_(t+1)-X_t )^k
        self._increments = increments
        self._increments_2 = increments ** 2
        self._increments_4 = increments ** 4

        self._state_t = initial_state
```

CHAPTER 7 JUMP MODELS

```
super().__init__(n_sample_paths, initial_state=initial_state,
                 sampling_density=CompositeJumpSamplingDensity
                 (x_arr=x_arr, h=h,
    σ_2_J=σ_2_J))
```

Notice that increments are provided in the class and then used to precompute the required factors for computing three different moments. There is a slight difference between this and the stochastic processes designed for other asset price models done so far. This one needs the dataset to generate paths due to the usage of the kernel function, whereas for others, once the parameters are computed, datasets are no longer needed. Let's now see how to compute two parameters and three moments required for path generation:

```
def _λ_x(self, x):
    return self._M_4_x(x)/(3 * (self._σ_2_J ** 2))

def _σ_2_x(self, x, λ_x):
    M_2 = self._M_2_x(x)
    return M_2 - (λ_x * self._σ_2_J)

def _M_1_x(self, x):
    return kth_raw_moment_of_increments(x_arr=self._x_arr, x=x,
    h=self._h,
  increments_k=self._increments)

def _M_2_x(self, x):
    return kth_raw_moment_of_increments(x_arr=self._x_arr, x=x,
    h=self._h,
  increments_k=self._increments_2)

def _M_4_x(self, x):
    return kth_raw_moment_of_increments(x_arr=self._x_arr, x=x,
    h=self._h,
  increments_k=self._increments_4)
```

Now, the most important function *_update_current_state* is shown below:

```python
def _update_current_state(self, z):
    self._reset_new_sample_path_state()

    dW = z['dW']
    dJ = z['dJ']

    λ_x = self._λ_x(self._state_t)
    σ_2_x = self._σ_2_x(self._state_t, λ_x)

    '''
     σ_2_x can be negative so, the sign should be handled
     separately to avoid error
    '''
    self._state_t = self._state_t + self._M_1_x(self._state_t) + (
        np.sqrt(abs(σ_2_x)) * np.sign(σ_2_x) * dW) + (λ_x * dJ)

    # Exponential conversion to bring back from log-scale
    return np.exp(self._state_t)
```

Two critical tricks to remember here are sign handling of $\widehat{\sigma^2(x)}$ and exponential conversion at the end (sign handling is required as $\widehat{\sigma^2(x)}$ is the jump-adjusted variance).

So, let's see all these in action by testing with real data. We use training and validation datasets for the *S&P 500 Index* available from Yahoo Financials with daily frequency. We must do log transformation and first-order increment computation as a prerequisite for *GaussianKernelJumpProcess* like below:

```python
ticker = '^GSPC'   # S&P 500 Index
time_freq = Frequency.DAILY
yfa = YahooFinancialsAdapter(
    ticker=ticker,
    frequency=time_freq,
    training_set_date_range=("2010-01-01", "2011-01-01"),
    validation_set_date_range=("2016-01-01", "2018-07-01"))
```

```
# Prepare dataset for kernel function
_s_t = yfa.training_set
_s_t_1 = _s_t.shift(1)
_x_t = np.log(_s_t['stock price'])
_x_t_1 = np.log(_s_t_1['stock price'])
_increments = _x_t - _x_t_1
_x_t = _x_t.drop([_x_t.index[0]], inplace=False)
_increments = _increments.drop([_increments.index[0]], inplace=False)
```

Once done, we should assign relevant values for the initial state (X_0), h, and $\sigma_Y^2(Y)$. Note that we want to simulate the sample paths and mean path with different combinations h and $\sigma_Y^2(Y)$ as we still haven't estimated these two parameters correctly. One such combination is done like below:

```
initial_state = np.log(2000.00)

h_1 = np.log(1000)
σ_2_J_1 = np.log(3000)
gjp_1 = GaussianKernelJumpProcess(
    h=h_1, x_arr=_x_t, increments=_increments, σ_2_J=σ_2_J_1,
    initial_state=initial_state)

result_display_1 = ForecastResultDisplay(
    result=gjp_1.forecast(T=100), ylabel='S(t)')
```

The function *test_non_parametric_jump_process_params_familiarization* under *chapter 7/test_non_parametric_jump_process.py* generates paths with several of these parameter combinations, and the final output is shown in Figure 7-11.

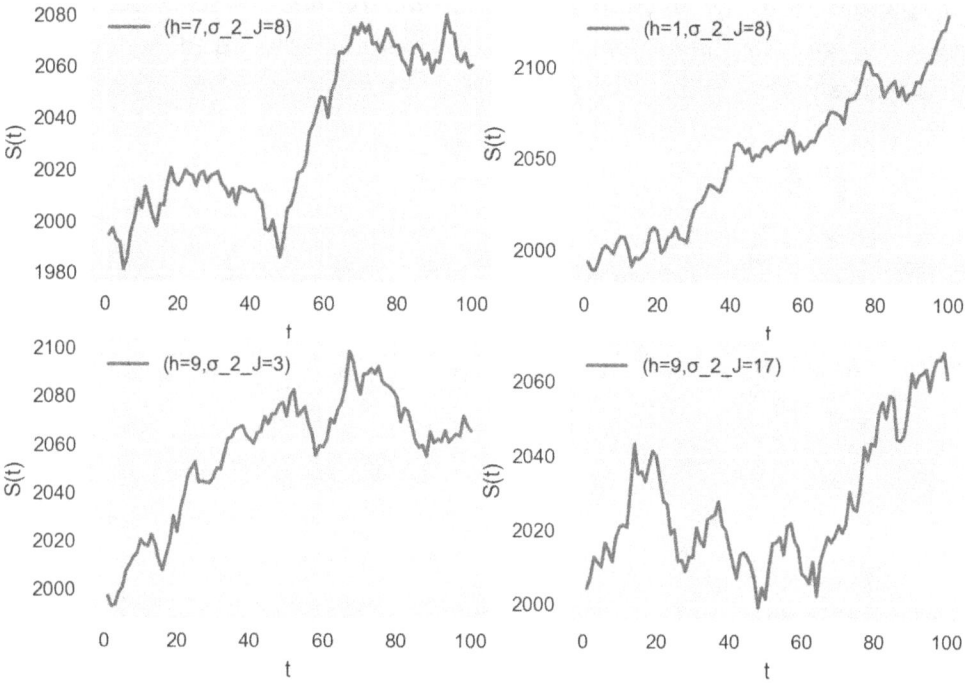

Figure 7-11. *Mean path of Gaussian kernel jump process with different bandwidth and jump variance*

Notice that using a higher jump variance produces a more turbulent path, as shown in the fourth chart in Figure 7-1. We now do a more elaborate experiment with a fixed bandwidth and jump variance, test sample paths and mean path, and do the backtesting, as given below:

```
n_sample_paths = 5
h = 5.5
σ_2_J = 0.044
gjp = GaussianKernelJumpProcess(
    h=h, x_arr=_x_t, increments=_increments, σ_2_J=σ_2_J,
    initial_state=initial_state, n_sample_paths=n_sample_paths)
forecast_result = gjp.forecast(T=250)
ap_back_testing = AssetPriceBackTesting(
    s_true=yfa.validation_set, s_forecast=forecast_result.mean_path)
print('RMSE: ' + str(ap_back_testing.rmse_score))

vz7.plot_full_testing_results(ForecastResultDisplay(
    forecast_result, ylabel='S(t)'), ap_back_testing, h=h, σ_2_J=σ_2_J)
```

CHAPTER 7   JUMP MODELS

This piece is inside the function *test_non_parametric_jump_process_full* in *chapter 7/test_non_parametric_jump_process.py*. It produces an excellent output, as shown in Figure 7-12.

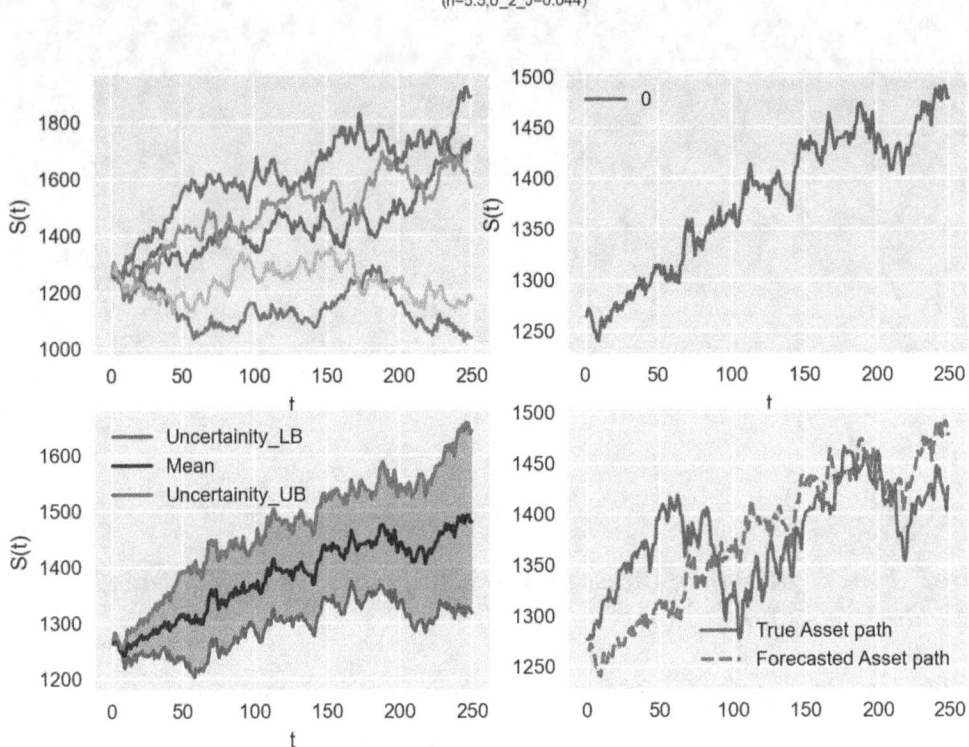

Figure 7-12. *All sample paths, mean path, uncertainty bounds, and backtesting results are shown for forecasting the S&P 500 Index*

We get the forecasting error:

RMSE: 51.88829875319624

This score is good because the range of asset prices is in thousands, so the forecasting process produced only around 3% error (dividing RMSE by average price).

This experiment shows that asset paths can be forecasted without using a separate model class by leveraging the class designed for stochastic processes with a good choice of h and $\sigma_Y^2(Y)$. However, choosing these will be cumbersome for a trader not well versed in statistics. Some high-level guidelines are explained next.

246

CHAPTER 7 JUMP MODELS

Strategy for Selecting h and $\sigma_Y^2(Y)$

a) The bandwidth h is the influencing factor while computing densities. As said in the kernel section, a higher h will produce a smoother distribution with fewer peaks and vice versa. A trader can choose h wisely depending on their market view – a turbulent market will have higher h producing more jumps and vice versa.

b) A higher $\sigma_Y^2(Y)$ level will produce bigger jumps in the asset path, allowing the trader to apply the same selection strategy h.

We ran another experiment with different combinations of h and $\sigma_Y^2(Y)$ and got the backtesting result as shown in Figure 7-13.

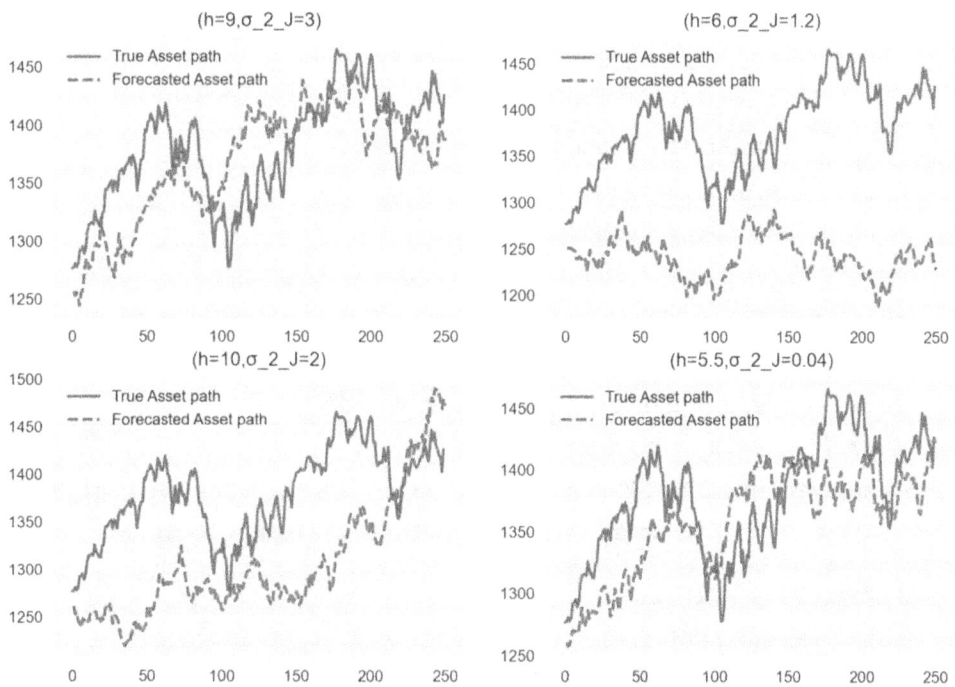

Figure 7-13. *Backtesting experiment with different h and $\sigma_Y^2(Y)$ for S&P 500 Index*

It is evident that not all combinations are doing well; that's why choice of h and $\sigma_Y^2(Y)$ is crucial.

247

CHAPTER 7   JUMP MODELS

Estimating h and $\sigma_Y^2(Y)$

Formal estimation methods exist for both h and $\sigma_Y^2(Y)$. We will do this in parallel while designing a Gaussian kernel jump process model class. We start with the *__init__* and other few required functions overridden from *BaseAssetPriceModel*:

```
class GaussianKernelJumpAssetPriceModel(BaseAssetPriceModel):
    '''
    This is a a model class for Gaussian Kernel jump process with
    estimations for h &  ⟦σ_Y⟧ ^2 (Y).
    '''

    def __init__(self, time_unit_transformer: TimeUnitTransformer,
                asset_price_dataset_adapter: StockPriceDataset
                Adapter = None,
                bandwidth='silverman',
                bandwidth_bounds: tuple = None,
                n_sample_paths=5,
                training_required=True,
                ):
        self._n = 0
        self._bandwidth = bandwidth
        self._bandwidth_bounds = bandwidth_bounds
        super().__init__(time_unit_transformer,
        'GaussianKernelJumpProcessParameters', asset_price_dataset_adapter,
                    None, n_sample_paths, training_required)

    def _preprocess(self):
        self._parameters['x_arr'] = np.log(self._s_t['stock price'])
        _x_t_1 = np.log(self._s_t_1['stock price'])
        self._parameters['increments'] = self._parameters['x_arr'] - _x_t_1
        self._parameters['x_arr'] = self._parameters['x_arr'].drop(
            [self._parameters['x_arr'].index[0]], inplace=False)
        self._parameters['increments'] = self._parameters
        ['increments'].drop(
            [self._parameters['increments'].index[0]], inplace=False)
```

```
        self._parameters['x0'] = np.log(self._parameters['s0'])
        self._n = len(self._parameters['x_arr'])
    def _fit(self):
        self._adjust_records()
        self._preprocess()

        self._estimate_bandwidth()
        self._estimate_σ_2_J()

        self._forecasting_process = self._create_forecasting_process(
            self._parameters, self._n_sample_paths)
    def _create_forecasting_process(self,
                                    parameters, n_sample_paths) -> 
                                    ForecastingProcess:
        return GaussianKernelJumpProcess(
            h=parameters['h'],
            x_arr=parameters['x_arr'],
            increments=parameters['increments'],
            σ_2_J=parameters['σ_2_J'],
            initial_state=parameters['x0'],
            n_sample_paths=n_sample_paths)
```

First, we see how to estimate $\sigma_Y^2(Y)$ as mentioned in the paper of *Johannes M. [17]* and *Bandi and Nguyen [15]*:

$$\widehat{\sigma_Y^2(Y)} = \frac{1}{n}\sum_{t=1}^{n}\frac{\hat{M}_6(X_t)}{5\hat{M}_4(X_t)}.$$

So, we need to compute the sixth and fourth raw moments of increments like below:

```
    def _M_6(self):
        return np.array([kth_raw_moment_of_increments(
            x_arr=self._parameters['x_arr'], x=x_i,
                h=self._parameters['h'], increments_k=self._
                parameters['increments'] ** 6) for x_i
            in self._parameters['x_arr']])
```

```
def _M_4(self):
    return np.array([kth_raw_moment_of_increments(
        x_arr=self._parameters['x_arr'], x=x_i,
            h=self._parameters['h'], increments_k=self._parameters
        ['increments'] ** 4) for x_i
    in self._parameters['x_arr']])
```

Finally, the estimate for $\sigma_Y^2(Y)$ is produced as follows:

```
def _estimate_σ_2_J(self):
    self._parameters['σ_2_J'] = np.sum(
        self._M_6()/(5 * self._M_4()))/self._n
```

For estimating h, we follow a few strategies that depend on the user's choice. These are implemented one by one as given below:

a) **Silverman's approach:** This is obtained by minimizing the kernel density's MSE (mean squared error) w.r.t h. MSE is the expected squared difference between the kernel estimate $\hat{f}(x)$ and true density $f(x)$:

$$MSE(\hat{f}) = E\left[\hat{f}(x) - f(x)\right]^2.$$

This can be further decomposed into bias and variance terms; then using Taylor series expansion and simple calculus, it can be shown that $\hat{h}$ is given by

$$\hat{h} = \left(\frac{R(K)}{\mu_2(K)^2 R(f'')n}\right)^{1/5},$$

where

$$R(K) = \int K(x)^2 \, dx,$$
$$\mu_2(K) = \int x^2 K(x) \, dx,$$
$$R(f'') = \int f''(x)^2 \, dx.$$

This expression is generic and independent of the choice of kernel K or true density f (for details, refer to *Silverman* [20]). With choices of K and f as the Gaussian kernel and Gaussian density, respectively, $\hat{h}$ comes down to

$$\hat{h} = 1.06\hat{\sigma}n^{-1/5},$$

where $\hat{\sigma}$ is the sample standard deviation of the dataset. Note that, to compute $\hat{\sigma}$, you don't have to consider the dataset to be the realization of the Markov stochastic process. Just do a simple standard deviation computation, as you would do for a single variable dataset, as shown below:

```
def _estimate_bandwidth(self):
    match self._bandwidth:
        # Silverman's approach
            case 'silverman': self._parameters
            ['h'] = 1.06 *
            self._parameters['x_arr'].std()
                * (self._n ** (-0.2))
```

But remember one thing: this approach will only work well if the underlying true density is Gaussian; in practice, otherwise, $\hat{h}$ would give a wrong estimate, and it is pretty unlikely that the distribution of any asset price with jumps would be Gaussian. So be cautious and properly research asset price data before using it.

b) **Interquartile range:** The presence of outliers may cause $\hat{\sigma}$ to be too high, resulting in a bandwidth that is too large. Interquartile range $IQR = Q_3 - Q_1$ is a better alternative in this case, and using this,

$$\hat{h} = 1.06 \min\left\{\hat{\sigma}, \frac{IQR}{1.34}\right\} n^{-1/5}.$$

CHAPTER 7 JUMP MODELS

This is implemented as follows:

```
# Interquartile range approach
case 'iqr':
    Q3 = self._parameters['x_arr'].quantile(0.75)
    Q1 = self._parameters['x_arr'].quantile(0.25)
    self._parameters['h'] = 1.06 * min(self._parameters
    ['x_arr'].std(),
                                    (Q3-Q1)/1.34) *
                                    (self._n ** (-0.2))
```

c) **Auto:** This is based on a hyperparameter searching approach.

```
case 'auto': self._parameters['h'] = self._bayesian_search()
```

The function *_bayesian_search()* is implemented as follows:

```
def _bayesian_search(self):
    '''
    Function to search for optimal h within a given
    bounds using Bayesian optimization.
    '''
        def _average_rmse_score(h):
        '''
            Target function to be optimized using Bayesian
            optimization.
            It is used inside the acquisition function and
            returns an average RMSE score by running the
            forecasting simulation multiple times on
            test dataset
        '''
            test_set = self._asset_price_dataset_adapter.
            validation_set
            T = len(test_set)
            self._parameters['h'] = h
                    self._estimate_σ_2_J()
                    temp_forecasting_process = self._
                    create_forecasting_process(
```

```
                self._parameters, self._n_
                sample_paths)
        def _get_rmse_score():
                return AssetPriceBackTesting(
                        s_true=test_set,
        s_forecast=temp_forecasting_process.forecast(T=T).\
        mean_path).rmse_score

    # Mutiprocessing-based backtesting to compute average
    RMSE score
    on test dataset
    back_testing_executor = get_reusable_executor(max_workers=8)

    rmse_scores = [back_testing_executor.submit(
        _get_rmse_score) for _ in range(10)]
    back_testing_executor.shutdown(wait=False)
    wait(rmse_scores)
    return np.average([rmse_score.result() for rmse_score in
    rmse_scores])

if self._bandwidth_bounds is None:
    raise ValueError(
        'Bandwidth bounds should be supplied if bandwidth is set
        as auto')

# Run Bayesian Optimization on given bounds
return gp_minimize(_average_rmse_score,
            self._bandwidth_bounds, n_calls=10).x[0]
```

Bayesian optimization is used where the target function is costly and black box. Simulation is generally considered costly if used with many sample paths, so it is a potential candidate for Bayesian optimization.

CHAPTER 7 JUMP MODELS

> **NOTE – BAYESIAN OPTIMIZATION**
>
> Bayesian optimization uses Gaussian process (GP) to proxy (surrogate model) the costly target function for avoiding multiple calls to it. The GP is a stochastic process over the target function to capture the uncertainty of outputs from multiple calls, and over the time, it tries to find the parameters for which uncertainty is less and function output is optimal (max or min).
>
> For more details, you can refer to *Peng Liu [18]*. I also wrote an article in *Towards Data Science (Avishek Nag [19])*; you can refer to that as well.

However, to reduce the cost further, we used a multiprocessing setup (recall the topic from Chapter 6 where multiprocessing was used to generate the distribution of selected random variables from the stochastic process of asset path).

d) **Default:** The user can provide any value for h, following the strategies discussed earlier.

```
case _: self._parameters['h'] = self._bandwidth
```

With all these settings in place, let's do formal testing of the component with a training set ranging from January 1, 2011, to January 1, 2014:

```
ticker = '^GSPC'  # S&P 500 Index
time_freq = Frequency.DAILY
yfa = YahooFinancialsAdapter(
    ticker=ticker,
    frequency=time_freq,
    training_set_date_range=("2011-01-01", "2014-01-01"),
    validation_set_date_range=("2014-01-01", "2015-01-01"))

    kernel_jump_model = GaussianKernelJumpAssetPriceModel(time_
    unit_transformer=IndexedTimeTransformer(time_freq=time_freq),
                                            bandwidth='auto',
                                            bandwidth_
                                            bounds=[(
                                                1.0, 10.0)],
```

```
                                    asset_price_
                                    dataset_
                                    adapter=yfa)
print(kernel_jump_model.parameters_)
result = kernel_jump_model.forecast(T=252, prob_dist_viz_
required=False)
ap_back_testing = AssetPriceBackTesting(
s_true=yfa.validation_set, s_forecast=result.mean_path)
print('RMSE: ' + str(ap_back_testing.rmse_score))
vz7.plot_full_testing_results(ForecastResultDisplay(
    result, ylabel='S(t)'), ap_back_testing, h=kernel_jump_
    model.parameters_['h'],
    σ_2_J=kernel_jump_model.parameters_['σ_2_J'])
```

We used the option "auto" for bandwidth and provided bandwidth bounds (in log scale), which triggered a Bayesian optimization-based hyperparameter search and produced the result shown in Figure 7-14.

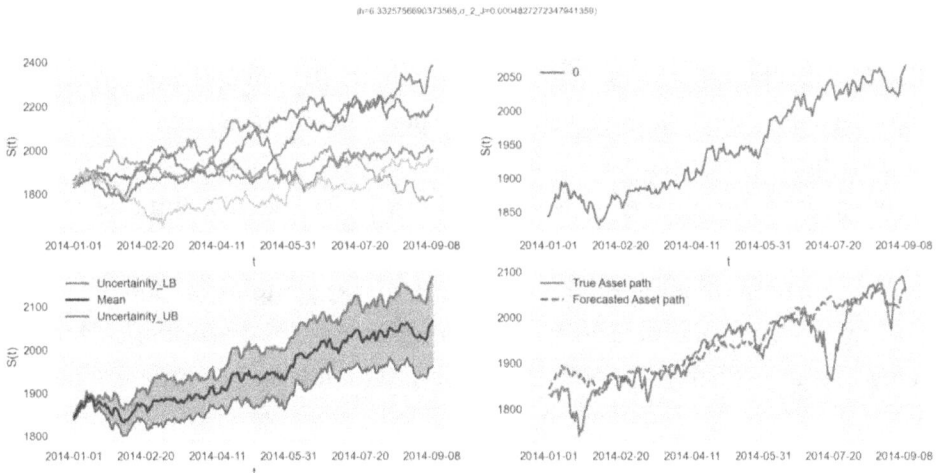

Figure 7-14. Backtesting experiment with different auto searching h

We got the RMSE as around 44.42.

CHAPTER 7   JUMP MODELS

Summary

Log transformations may provide a first cushion to handle sudden irregularities caused by market shocks to asset prices, but are never correct methods to handle jumps. Including jump components explicitly in the SDE is always recommended over anything else. Jumps can be modeled as counting processes, as initially discussed in Chapter 3 while covering the Poisson distribution. However, a separate RV is also needed to contain jump size. Including these two is the crux of the jump models discussed in this chapter.

These two models – Merton and Kou – have separate SDEs, where jump size follows a normal and asymmetric double exponential distribution, respectively, while the number of jumps, as usual, follows a Poisson process. In both cases, though closed-formed solutions of the PDFs of the corresponding stochastic processes exist, we introduced a much generic method of recovering the density from a characteristic function where independent RVs form a linear or any other combination. Again, two such methods – one fast Fourier transform based and the other one cosine series based – are discussed, but both originated from characteristic functions. Once PDFs are recovered, parametric estimation by MLE method followed by forecasting is done as usual.

The chapter also discusses a slightly different method based on a nonparametric approach. While the basic SDE formation doesn't differ much, the PDF estimation is done using the nonparametric kernel method, whereas the parameter estimation task is handled by the method of moments as the drift and diffusion can be expressed by different orders of moment. As suggested in the paper we followed, there's no such restriction on jump assumption, resulting in Gaussian jumps being assumed.

Over the process, we also set up templates in Python to provide suitable extension points for the modeling jump processes, especially for the parametric ones. You may take those templates as inspiration to implement further complex models.

We begin Part 3 with the next chapter covering derivatives like options which are built on top of some underlying assets behaving as a function of another stochastic process.

PART III

Financial Options Modeling

CHAPTER 8

Options and Black-Scholes Model

After covering stocks in the book's second part, this chapter delves into one of the key driving factors of the financial market: *options*. With the short introduction discussed in Chapter 2, as of now, you must know that options are not direct assets but derivatives on top of underlying assets. Readers of this book who do regular share market trading should be well accustomed to the useability aspects of options. But what may not be known is the underlying statistical theory, or more precisely the background of some cryptic-looking formulae they might regularly use to trade in options. As said in Chapter 2, estimating the premium paid in option trading is our fundamental problem. In this process, we will learn the *Black-Scholes* model, a powerful tool that can help you understand and predict option prices and estimate Greeks (different rates on option value), which are crucial for risk management. We will also explore the design of Python components, a practical and efficient way to perform these computations. What I said about *probability theory* in Chapter 3 also holds here, i.e., countless books have been written on option modeling and Black-Scholes theory, and many available resources are lying everywhere in the forms of books, online tutorials, videos, and whatnot. But I always felt something needed to be added; some are heavy on theory with no hands-on items, or a pile of dry Jupyter Notebooks implementing some mysterious formulae with no theoretical background explained. In this chapter, I will try to construct a bridge between these two extreme borders, providing a theoretical background as well as practical implications. Let's begin this journey!

CHAPTER 8   OPTIONS AND BLACK-SCHOLES MODEL

Options – Basics and Formulations

Derivative trading, though it may seem modern and sophisticated, has a rich and fascinating history. Its roots can be traced back to the *Code of Hammurabi*, a Babylonian legal text from 1755–1750 BC, containing the earliest known references to option trading. Even in the fifteenth century, references to the derivatives business were found, indicating its long-standing presence in human commerce. This long history is a testament to the enduring relevance and importance of option trading.

An *option* contract is a financial contract that gives the trader the right to execute the trade at a predefined price. To avoid market fluctuations, the trader can buy or sell the asset at the settled price mentioned in the contract. However, unlike futures contracts, the trader must pay a premium to the counterparty to avail of this facility. With the premium, the right to execute a trade is sold, and this is a right but not an obligation. If the underlying asset does not perform well, the holder (or buyer) of the option may choose not to exercise it, resulting in not trading in the asset. However, the counterparty, i.e., the writer (or seller) of the option, does not have this flexibility, and they have no choice but to be obliged to trade in the asset when the holder decides to exercise the option.

Option Nomenclatures

Options can be divided into two categories: *call* and *put*. A *call option* gives the option holder the right to buy an asset at a predefined *strike price* (denoted by K) on a specific date, a.k.a. *expiry time* (denoted by T). In contrast, a *put option* gives the right to sell the asset at the strike price on its expiry. In the case of *European options*, the exercise can only happen at the expiry date, not before that, whereas for *American options*, the option buyer also has the right to exercise at any date before expiry. In this book, we only discuss about European options. For both call and put options, the premium paid to the option seller will be forfeited by the buyer if the asset price does not move in the buyer's favor and they decide not to exercise the option.

To elaborate the scenario with an example, suppose you bought the call option to buy stock A at a strike price of K=$115 on expiry time t=T. You possess a bullish view of the market and anticipate that the price may go up to $130 or more than that on time T while it is running at $110 at present. So, buying a call option may save $15 per share. The premium you pay for this is $5 per share, which adjusts your minimum potential net profit to $10. If the price reaches that level, you can profit this much by buying at $115

CHAPTER 8   OPTIONS AND BLACK-SCHOLES MODEL

and immediately selling those at $130 or more at expiry. This happy scenario is shown in the graph on the right side of Figure 8-1, where the price crossed $150, thus making the net profit per share more than $30 (premium adjusted).

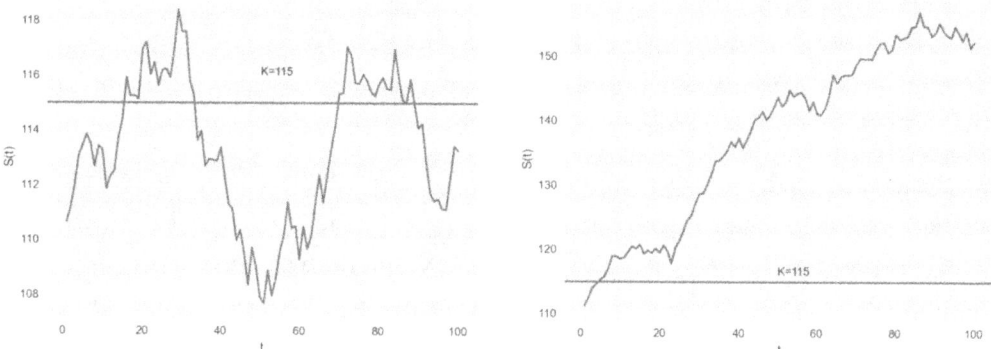

Figure 8-1. *Unhappy and happy scenario for call option with strike price K=$115*

The picture may not look this good if the asset price falls below $115, as shown on the left side of Figure 8-1. There, the option is valueless, as there is no point in buying an asset at $115 if its market value is less than that, and as a result, the premium paid to the option seller will be forfeited. These two scenarios result from the asset having two different sample paths until time T. The same analysis also applies to the put option, with the only difference being in anticipation of the market. For example, to have put options, you possess a bearish view of the market and expect the asset price to fall below $110 while the current running price is the same. So, you went and bought a put option with a strike price of $115. At expiry, the market price can decrease and settle at $100, which benefits you as you can sell it at $115 and make a net profit of $10 (premium adjusted). In the unhappy scenario, the price may go up to $130, and the option becomes valueless, causing the premium to be forfeited. For option buyers, the cost is immediate, and the benefit is long term, whereas for the seller, the cost comes in the long run, and the benefit is immediate (from the premium paid to them). Both roles have pros and cons, which the traders play in an exchangeable fashion to hedge their portfolios for risk management.

As said before, knowing the premium option's good value is a critical problem. This is essential for both option buyers and sellers so they can plan their portfolios accordingly. As we never know precisely which sample path the underlying asset will take, the option's value is uncertain and cannot be computed precisely at any time. The way we generated paths for stocks in Part 2 of the book, something similar should also be done here, but before that, we must know the mathematical form of the option's value and its distribution.

261

CHAPTER 8 OPTIONS AND BLACK-SCHOLES MODEL

Payoff Function

The *payoff* is the value of the option at any time t and is represented by positive functions for call and put, respectively, as

$$V_C(S_t, t; K, T) = \max\{S_T - K, 0\}, \text{ for } call$$
$$V_P(S_t, t; K, T) = \{K - S_T, 0\}, \text{ for } put$$

At exercise time, the values become V_C and V_P, respectively. Option sellers will be interested in knowing the value at t=0, i.e., $V_C(S_0, 0; K, T)$ and $V_P(S_0, 0; K, T)$. As S_t is the stochastic process of the underlying asset, V_C and V_P are both stochastic processes which are functions of S_t. That makes $V_C(S_0, 0; K, T)$ and $V_C(S_0, 0; K, T)$ the expected values of respective stochastic processes at time t=0. Considering the time-adjusted risk-free interest rate included in the calculation, we can write

$$V_C(S_0, 0; K, T) = e^{-rT} \mathbb{E}_{f_{V_C}}\left[\max\{S_T - K, 0\}\right] = e^{-rT} \int \max\{S_T - K, 0\} f_{V_C}(y, T) dy$$

$$V_P(S_0, 0; K, T) = e^{-rT} \mathbb{E}_{f_{V_P}}\left[\max\{K - S_T, 0\}\right] = e^{-rT} \int \max\{K - S_T, 0\} f_{V_P}(y, T) dy$$

where $f_{V_C}(y, T)$ and $f_{V_P}(y, T)$ are the respective densities. These expressions can be written in a more generic form as

$$V_C(S_t, t; K, T) = e^{-r(T-t)} \mathbb{E}_{f_{V_C}}\left[\max\{S_T - K, 0\}\right] = e^{-r(T-t)} \int \max\{S_T - K, 0\} f_{V_C}(y, T) dy$$

$$V_P(S_t, t; K, T) = e^{-r(T-t)} \mathbb{E}_{f_{V_C}}\left[\max\{S_T - K, 0\}\right] = e^{-r(T-t)} \int \max\{S_T - K, 0\} f_{V_P}(y, T) dy$$

This is the theoretical setting of the option irrespective of call or put. As $V_C(S_t, t; K, T)$ and $V_P(S_t, t; K, T)$ are the option's values at time t, upon its evaluation, the option seller will have a complete distribution of values at different times for a given strike price. Figure 8-2 shows the nature of the payoff functions for call and put w.r.t. S, respectively.

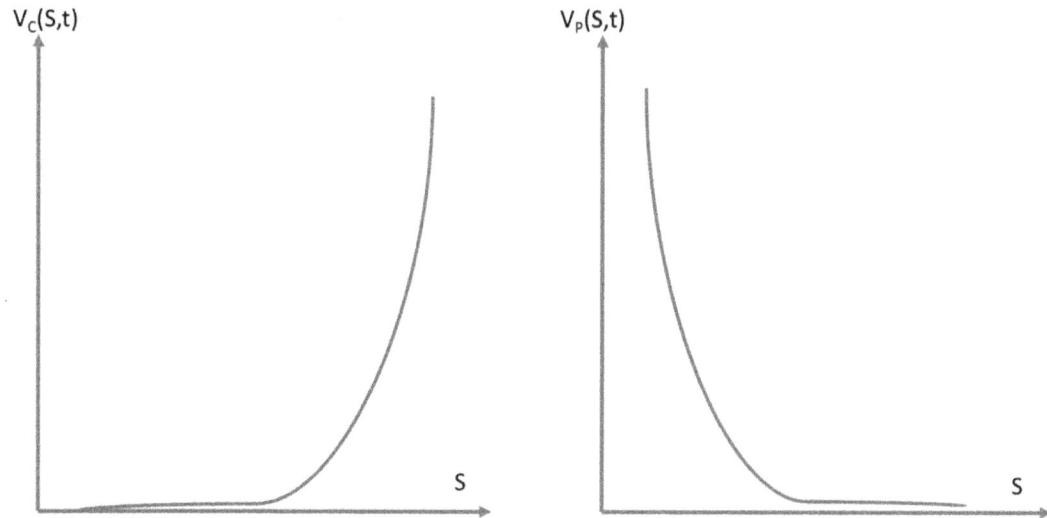

Figure 8-2. *Payoff of call and put with respect to S*

The critical problem is to estimate V(S, t) analytically or numerically; we discuss this next.

Put-Call Parity

Suppose you are playing the role of both option buyer and seller at the same time for the same underlying with the same strike price and expiry time. Creating a portfolio with these two must comply with the no-arbitrage principle, i.e., you shouldn't be able to generate cash out of nothing as there is a chance of doing so by taking a long position on call and short on put. But adding up, these two should equal the difference between asset value at time t and time-adjusted strike price with the risk-free interest, and it looks like

$$V_C(S_t, t; K, T) - V_P(S_t, t; K, T) = S_t - Ke^{-r(T-t)}$$

This relationship should hold until its expiry time, and not adhering to it will result in riskless arbitrage opportunities.

CHAPTER 8   OPTIONS AND BLACK-SCHOLES MODEL

Black-Scholes Model

Several authors published option trading documents in the nineteenth century, but a formal approach to modeling options came much later (refer to *Lintner [11]* and *Modigliani [12]*). However, the benchmark was set by Black-Scholes and Merton in their several papers *(Merton [13]* and *Black and Scholes [14]*), which became an essential tool in financial engineering practice across the world. Merton and Scholes were awarded the Nobel Memorial Prize in Economics in 1997 for their contribution.

Black-Scholes just changed the world of financial markets beyond imagination, and even after so many years, this model is still considered the baseline. However, there are some assumptions that need to be kept in mind before using the Black-Scholes model, as described below:

1) **The underlying asset follows a geometric Brownian motion:** It obviously means that the asset prices are log-normally distributed with risk-free interest rate r and volatility σ.

2) **There are no jumps in the asset price path:** If the asset prices are modeled using the jump-diffusion process, then the Black-Scholes model cannot be directly applied to estimate the option price. It adheres to the higher-level assumption that the market is efficient and frictionless.

3) **The risk-free interest rate is constant:** Not only that, r should be known beforehand. In some cases, r can also be a deterministic continuous function of time.

4) **No dividends are paid for the underlying asset during the option's lifespan:** This restriction is not very strong, as dividends can be incorporated in some alternative versions of the Black-Scholes model. But in this book, we assume that dividends are not present between counterparties.

The above list is not exclusive, but this should suffice for the scope of our work. In general, the biggest advantage of SDE-based approach for modeling derivatives is that the actual data points are not needed for parameter estimation. In fact, there's no separate parameter estimation, and the model can be built solely relying on the underlying asset's already available parameters. For example, suppose a new company just registered six months back in a stock exchange has recently released their options for

CHAPTER 8   OPTIONS AND BLACK-SCHOLES MODEL

traders. So, there's no chance of getting past the history of option values, which makes direct parameter estimation impossible for that derivative. Yes, of course, some insights can be drawn from similar derivatives released by some other companies, but that will never be sufficient. Modern ML/DL-based models tackle these types of problems with transfer learning by leveraging other models provided that's a mapping between underlying asset and derivative value. SDEs, though quite traditional, come up with a nice analytical solution by expressing the derivative as a function of the underlying, resulting in a stochastic process that can approximate the life cycle of the derivative, and that too with only leveraging the underlying's existing parameter. The Black-Scholes model is an example of that approach.

Two proven methods exist to solve the Black-Scholes model: the *PDE and risk-neutral probabilistic methods*. In Part 2 of the book, we discussed how to capture the dynamics of stock prices with SDE. Similarly, a PDE can be constructed to model option price dynamics, which contains various change rates of option price with respect to other variables. We will go through this in the next chapter, but for now, we will focus on the second one – the risk-neutral probability method.

Risk-Neutral Probability Method

The initial setting of the risk-neutral method is already discussed in the previous section. What we are left with is the evaluation of the integrals $\int \max\{S_t - K, 0\} f_{V_C}(y, T) dy$ and $\int \max\{S_t - K, 0\} f_{V_P}(y, T) dy$. Theoretically, we must find the measure for V, but a more straightforward method would be to compute the integral with the measure of S, as V depends on S and K is a constant. S_t is a stock price, following the Markov process (recall Chapter 3), so the density $f(S_T|S_t)$ we are interested in is the last value of density, i.e., at the expiry time T, and computing it back, we obtain its equivalent price at t=0, or any given t < T. With this in place, we try computing the integral for a call option as

$$\begin{aligned}
V_C(S_t, t; K, T) &= e^{-r(T-t)} \int \max\{S_T - K, 0\} f(S_T|S_t) dS_T \\
&= e^{-r(T-t)} \int_{-\infty}^{\infty} (S_T - K)^+ f(S_T|S_t) dS_T \\
&= e^{-r(T-t)} \int_{K}^{\infty} (S_T - K) f(S_T|S_t) dS_T \\
&= I_1 - I_2
\end{aligned}$$

265

CHAPTER 8 OPTIONS AND BLACK-SCHOLES MODEL

where

$$I_1 = e^{-r(T-t)} \int_K^\infty S_T f(S_T|S_t) dS_T$$

$$I_2 = e^{-r(T-t)} \int_K^\infty K f(S_T|S_t) dS_T$$

We know that

$$f(S_T|S_t) = \frac{1}{S_T \sigma \sqrt{2\pi(T-t)}} e^{-\frac{1}{2}\left(\frac{\log \frac{S_T}{S_t} - \left(r - \frac{1}{2}\sigma^2\right)}{\sigma\sqrt{T-t}}\right)^2}$$

By substitution, we let

$$u = \frac{\log \frac{S_T}{S_t} - \left(r - \frac{1}{2}\sigma^2\right)}{\sigma\sqrt{T-t}}$$

which makes

$$I_1 = e^{\log S_t} \int_{\frac{\log K - \log S_t - \left(r - \frac{1}{2}\sigma^2\right)(T-t)}{\sigma\sqrt{T-t}}}^\infty \frac{1}{\sqrt{2\pi}} e^{-\frac{1}{2}\left(u - \sigma\sqrt{T-t}\right)^2} du.$$

By further simplification, we get the final form

$$I_1 = S_t \Phi(d_1),$$

where

$$d_1 = \frac{\log \frac{S_t}{K} - \left(r + \frac{1}{2}\sigma^2\right)(T-t)}{\sigma\sqrt{T-t}},$$

and $\Phi \cong N(0,1)$.

Doing similar substitution in I_2, we get

$$I_2 = K e^{-r(T-t)} \int_{\frac{\log K - \log S_t - \left(r - \frac{1}{2}\sigma^2\right)(T-t)}{\sigma\sqrt{T-t}}}^\infty \frac{1}{\sqrt{2\pi}} e^{-\frac{1}{2}u^2} du.$$

CHAPTER 8 OPTIONS AND BLACK-SCHOLES MODEL

With the same approach as done for I_1 we get

$$I_2 = Ke^{-r(T-t)}\Phi(d_2),$$

where

$$d_2 = d_1 - \sigma\sqrt{T-t}.$$

Finally, we get the expression for call option

$$V_C(S_t, t; K, T) = S_t\Phi(d_1) - Ke^{-r(T-t)}\Phi(d_2)$$

NOTE: $\Phi'(x)$ AND $\Phi(x)$

We use CDF of standard normal distribution ($\Phi(x)$) for all computation related to options because of the integral ranging between K and infinity. For Greeks, we use PDF ($\Phi'(x)$) in some cases, but that too because of the derivatives of option values computed there.

For put option, we can evaluate the integrals in the same way or leverage the put-call parity relationship. Taking the second method, we get

$$\begin{aligned} V_P(S_t, t; K, T) &= V_C(S_t, t; K, T) - S_t + Ke^{-r(T-t)} \\ &= S_t\Phi(d_1) - Ke^{-r(T-t)}\Phi(d_2) - S_t + Ke^{-r(T-t)} \\ &= Ke^{-r(T-t)}(1-\Phi(d_2)) - S_t(1-\Phi(d_1)) \\ &= Ke^{-r(T-t)}\Phi(-d_2) - S_t\Phi(-d_1). \end{aligned}$$

So, the final expression

$$V_P(S_t, t; K, T) = Ke^{-r(T-t)}\Phi(-d_2) - S_t\Phi(-d_1)$$

CHAPTER 8   OPTIONS AND BLACK-SCHOLES MODEL

The Black-Scholes model has the advantage of tractability and easy computability. Just look at the call and put option value expressions – these can even be computed with an Excel sheet. Traders can easily leverage these formulae without the need to rely on some external heavy computing power. Putting t=0 in the expressions, anyone can get the present value of the call or put price. But as said earlier, the interesting part is that $V_P(S_t, t; K, T)$ and $V_C(S_t, t; K, T)$ are both stochastic processes, so it is possible to generate possible sample paths, estimate mean path, and uncertainty bounds as we did while forecasting stock prices.

We know that S_t is a stochastic process, but for a discrete evaluation of option value using Black-Scholes model, we may not need the full life cycle of S_t. If the trader is only interested in knowing the values at t=0 and t=T, i.e., the premium and the expiry time value, then from their trading experience, $V_P(S_t, t; K, T)$ and $V_C(S_t, t; K, T)$ can be evaluated using some realistic values for S_t. In that case, trader should have a good view of the market to guess S_t. But statistically, it is assumed that $V_P(S_t, t; K, T)$ and $V_C(S_t, t; K, T)$ should be backed by a correct estimation of S_t at any given point. Following this assumption, in this book, we create option pricing models backed by statistical estimation of S_t, and we do so by generating sample paths.

To begin with, let's do some simple computations and visually introspect $V_P(S_t, t; K, T)$ and $V_C(S_t, t; K, T)$. For that, we create a class *BlackScholesOptionsGBMProcessStatistics* (you will find it under chapter9/test/test_black_scholes_gbm_model.py) which will have a few functions to test and visualize option values for a defined set of parameters. Note that this class should only be used for experimental purposes as we will later create a formal framework for evaluating options and Greeks. Anyways, for now, let's focus on *BlackScholesOptionsGBMProcessStatistics* as shown below:

```
import numpy as np
from scipy.stats import norm as Φ

class BlackScholesOptionsGBMProcessStatistics(ABC):

    @staticmethod
    def d1(s, t, r, σ, K, T):
        return (np.log(s/K) + (r + 0.5*(σ ** 2)) * (T-t))/(σ *
        np.sqrt(T-t))

    @staticmethod
    def d2(s, t, r, σ, K, T):
```

```
    return BlackScholesOptionsGBMProcessStatistics.d1(s, t, r, σ, K, T)
- σ * np.sqrt(T - t)

class Call(ABC):

    @staticmethod
    def option_value(s, t, r, σ, K, T):
        d1_val = BlackScholesOptionsGBMProcessStatistics.d1(
            s, t, r, σ, K, T)
        d2_val = BlackScholesOptionsGBMProcessStatistics.d2(
            s, t, r, σ, K, T)

        return (s * Φ.cdf(d1_val)) - (K * np.exp(-r*(T-t)) * Φ.
        cdf(d2_val))
```

We use the S&P500 Index as the underlying asset and the same parameters discovered in Chapter 4, as shown below, to test and plot the option values:

```
def test_call_put_simulation():
    n = 50
    T = 100
    ts = [t_i for t_i in range(T)]
    # Sample asset values
    S = np.linspace(1000, 5000, n)
    time_grid, s_grid = np.meshgrid(ts, S)
    r, σ = 0.009757165676274302, 0.03720863108733509

    V_call = [BlackScholesOptionsGBMProcessStatistics.Call.option_value(
        s=s, t=t, r=r, σ=σ, T=T, K=3000) for s, t in zip(s_grid,
        time_grid)]

    test_plot_options_surface(t=np.array(time_grid), S=np.array(
        s_grid), V=np.array(V_call), label="Call")

    V_put = [BlackScholesOptionsGBMProcessStatistics.Put.option_value(
        s=s, t=t, r=r, σ=σ, T=T, K=8000) for s, t in zip(s_grid,
        time_grid)]

    test_plot_options_surface(t=np.array(time_grid), S=np.array(
        s_grid), V=np.array(V_put), label="Put", is_call=False)
```

CHAPTER 8   OPTIONS AND BLACK-SCHOLES MODEL

Note that we used stock values generated in an equally spaced linear fashion where *n* indicates the number of virtual sample paths, although those don't exist. This same set of asset values for all paths is combined with an equally spaced similar time grid of the same size, resulting in a mesh structure (recall the way we generated parameter mesh in Chapter 3 while plotting likelihood function). The reason for doing this is to study the surface of option values in a 3D view. Let's see the body of the function *test_plot_options_surface* before viewing the output:

```
def test_plot_options_surface(t, S, V, label, is_call=True):
    plt.style.use("seaborn-v0_8")
    fig = plt.figure(figsize=(10, 7))
    ax1 = fig.add_subplot(121, projection="3d")
    ax2 = fig.add_subplot(122)
    print(S.shape)
    print(V.shape)
    sns.scatterplot(ax=ax2, x=S.flatten(), y=V.flatten())

    if is_call:
        ax1.plot_surface(t, S, V, rstride=5, cstride=5,
                         cmap=plt.cm.gnuplot2, edgecolor="black")

        ax1.set_xlabel('t')
        ax1.set_ylabel('S')
    else:
        ax1.plot_surface(S, t, V, rstride=5, cstride=5,
                         cmap=plt.cm.gnuplot2, edgecolor="black")

        ax1.set_xlabel('S')
        ax1.set_ylabel('t')

    ax1.set_zlabel(label)

    ax2.set_xlabel('S')
    ax2.set_ylabel(label)

    fig.tight_layout()
    plt.show()
```

CHAPTER 8   OPTIONS AND BLACK-SCHOLES MODEL

The option surface is an array of tuple *time, asset value,* and *option value.* We also plot the *call vs. S,* and the whole story for the call option looks as shown in Figure 8-3.

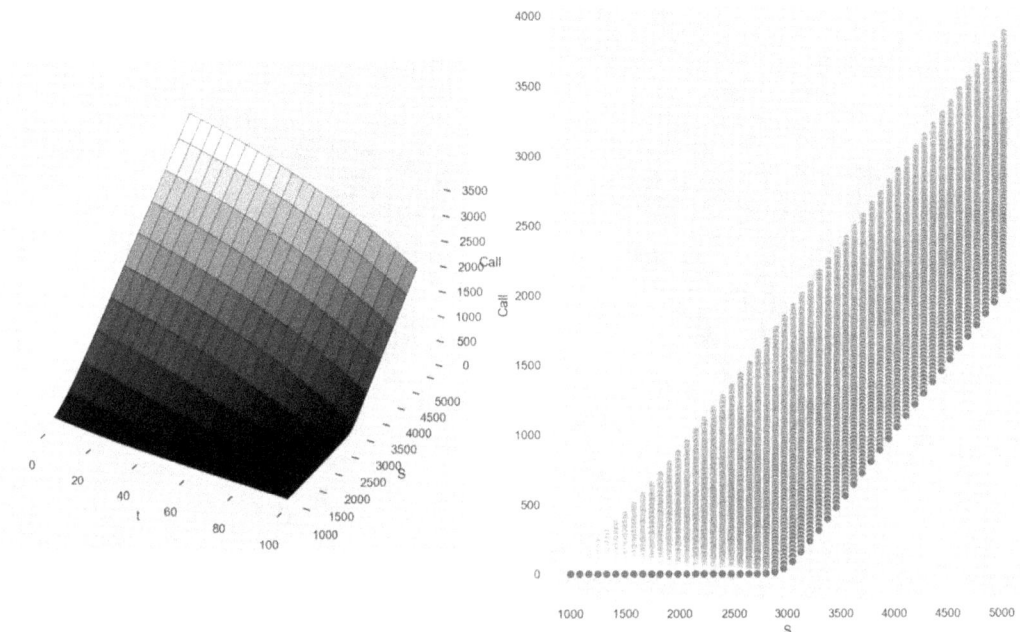

Figure 8-3. *Call option surface and call vs. S plot*

Notice the similarity with the payoff plot of the call option of Figure 8-2. Figure 8-3 represents the simulated data with real parameters. You will be a little surprised by the band-type looks of the *call vs. S plot.* It is caused by the repetitive usage of the same set of asset values for all sample paths, and for the same reason, we are able to explore the full surface of the call option on the left side. The grid is equally spaced, as we didn't use the random values of assets. Rather, a deterministic linear set of asset values is generated by the *linspace* function of *numpy.* This wouldn't be the case once we use the real data as stock or asset values will never be equally spaced for sure. There will be a complex superposition of random asset paths on this surface, so the final output may be a little difficult to comprehend. To go in that direction, it is necessary to know the full shape of the surface; that's why we did this practice with a fixed set of asset values.

Figure 8-4 shows the output for the put option.

CHAPTER 8   OPTIONS AND BLACK-SCHOLES MODEL

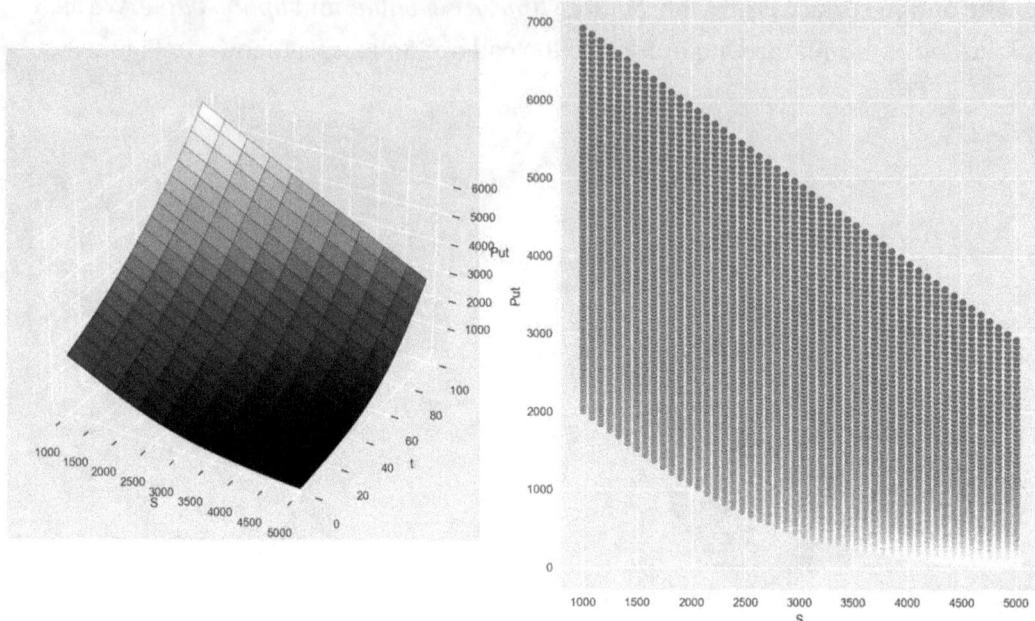

Figure 8-4. *Put option surface and put vs. S plot*

With all that in place, it is time to start formally designing the component for option and *Greeks* computation. As the option values follow a stochastic process, we begin with an abstract class to do that (go through the code documentation):

Listing 8-1. Partial view of the class for the stochastic process for option and Greeks

```
from chapter6.diffusion_model import GeometricBrownianMotionProcess

class _BlackScholesOptionsGBMProcess(GeometricBrownianMotionProcess, ABC):
    '''
    Abstract class for the stochastic process of Options & Greeks.
    This should be extended by Call, Put & corresponding 5 Greeks
    to create their respective processes.

    Options & Greeks should follow the GBM process to leverage
    this class.
    '''
```

```python
def __init__(self, r, σ,
             strike_price_K=None,
             expiry_time_T=None,
             initial_state=1.0,
             n_sample_paths=5):

    super().__init__(r=r,
                     σ=σ,
                     initial_state=initial_state,
                     n_sample_paths=n_sample_paths)

    self._underlying_s_values = np.ndarray(
        shape=(n_sample_paths, expiry_time_T+1), dtype=float)
    self._current_sample_path = 0
    self._strike_price_K = strike_price_K
    self._expiry_time_T = expiry_time_T

    # V(S,0;K,T)
    self._initial_v_state = self._pay_off_and_greek_f(
        self._initial_state, self._t)

    # V(S,t;K,T)
    self._v_state = self._pay_off_and_greek_f(
        self._initial_state, self._t)
```

The class shown partially in Listing 8-1 is responsible for generating all sample paths, uncertain bounds, and the mean path of the options and Greeks. The variable *_initial_v_state* is nothing but the $V_P(S_0, 0; K, T)$ and $V_C(S_0, 0; K, T)$ for call and put options, respectively. Let's now explore the remaining part of the class (Listing 8-2).

Listing 8-2. Remaining part of the class for the stochastic process for option and Greeks having functions for H(x), d1, d2, and others

```
def _update_current_state(self, z):
    '''
    Function H(x) of the Monte-Carlo framework for simulating
    sample paths
    of the stochastic process. It computes the current V(S,t;K,T)
    and stores underlying asset values of the current sample path.
```

CHAPTER 8 OPTIONS AND BLACK-SCHOLES MODEL

```
    '''
    super()._update_current_state(z)
    self._underlying_s_values[self._current_sample_path][self._t] =
    self._state_t
    self._v_state = self._pay_off_and_greek_f(self._state_t, self._t)
    return self._v_state

def _reset_new_sample_path_state(self):
    if self._t >= self._T:
        self._state_t = self._initial_state
        self._v_state = self._pay_off_and_greek_f(
            self._initial_state, self._t)
        self._t = 0
        self._current_sample_path = self._current_sample_path + 1
    self._t = self._t + 1

def _d1(self, s_t, t):
    '''
```

Term d1 in the expression for both call & put

$$V_C(S_t, t; K, T) = S_t \Phi(d_1) - Ke^{-r(T-t)}\Phi(d_2)$$
$$V_P(S_t, t; K, T) = Ke^{-r(T-t)}\Phi(-d_2) - S_t\Phi(-d_1)$$

It is given by

$$d_1 = \frac{\log \frac{S_t}{K} - \left(r + \frac{1}{2}\sigma^2\right)(T-t)}{\sigma\sqrt{T-t}}$$

```
    '''
    return (np.log(s_t/self._strike_price_K) +
            (self._r + 0.5*(self._σ ** 2)) *
            (self._expiry_time_T-t))/(self._σ * np.sqrt(self._expiry_
            time_T-t))

def _d2(self, s_t, t):
    '''
```

Term d2 in the expression for both call & put

$$V_C(S_t, t; K, T) = S_t \Phi(d_1) - Ke^{-r(T-t)}\Phi(d_2)$$
$$V_P(S_t, t; K, T) = Ke^{-r(T-t)}\Phi(-d_2) - S_t\Phi(-d_1)$$

```
        It is given by
            d_2 = d_1-σ√(T-t)
    '''
    return self._d1(s_t, t) - self._σ * np.sqrt(self._expiry_
    time_T - t)

@property
def value_at_0(self):
    '''
    This is the fair value of the premium paid to the
    option seller. This is a present value of the price
    at expiry time i.e., measured at t=0

    '''
    return self._initial_v_state

@property
def underlying_s_values(self):
    '''
    All values of sample paths of the underlying asset.
    '''
    return self._underlying_s_values

@abstractmethod
def _pay_off_and_greek_f(self, s_t, t): ...
    '''
    Payoff function of call, put & greeks. This should be
    overridden by the implementing class.
    '''

@property
@abstractmethod
def label(self): ...
```

This is an abstract class, so the corresponding *call*, *put*, and *Greeks* should extend it and override two functions: *_pay_off_and_greek_f* and *label*. Keep in mind that this is only for the stochastic process, not the direct model for options. Before we do that, let's see how to extend this class for call and put options as shown in Listing 8-3.

Listing 8-3. Classes for the stochastic processes of call and put options

```python
class _CallOptionsGBMProcess(_BlackScholesOptionsGBMProcess):
    '''
    Class for call options
    '''

    def _pay_off_and_greek_f(self, s_t, t):
        d1 = self._d1(s_t, t)
        d2 = self._d2(s_t, t)
        '''
        It computes the call value as given by,
                V_c(S_t, t; K, T) = S_t Φ(d_1) - Ke^{-r(T - t)}Φ(d_2)
        '''
        return (s_t * Φ.cdf(d1)) - (self._strike_price_K * np.exp(-
        self._r*(self._expiry_time_T-t)) * Φ.cdf(d2))

    @property
    def label(self):
        return "Call Option V(S,t)"

class _PutOptionsGBMProcess(_BlackScholesOptionsGBMProcess):
    '''
    Class for put options
    '''

    def _pay_off_and_greek_f(self, s_t, t):
        d1 = self._d1(s_t, t)
        d2 = self._d2(s_t, t)
        '''
        It computes the put value as given by,
                V_p(S_t, t; K, T) = Ke^{-r(T-t)}Φ(-d_2) - S_t Φ(-d_1)
        '''
        return (self._strike_price_K * np.exp(-self._r*(self._expiry_
        time_T-t)) * Φ.cdf(-d2)) - (s_t * Φ.cdf(-d1))
```

CHAPTER 8   OPTIONS AND BLACK-SCHOLES MODEL

We are still left with creating the actual model class for options within whom call and put process classes should be leveraged. For that, we first create a template for options modeling as shown in Listing 8-4.

Listing 8-4. Interface and response types for options

```
@dataclass
class OptionsResult:

    value_at_0: float = None   # premium paid for call & put options

    all_values: ForecastResult = None   # simulation result

    underlying_s_values: np.ndarray = None

    label: str = None

    for_call_option: bool = True

class OptionsTemplate(ABC):
    '''
    Interface for all type of options - Vanilla, Asian, or Barrier
    '''

    @abstractmethod
    def estimate_call(self, expiry_time_T, strike_price_K,
                    **kwargs) -> tuple: ...
    '''
    Function to compute call option. It returns tuple of
    forecast results that may contain greeks.
    '''

    @abstractmethod
    def estimate_put(self, expiry_time_T, strike_price_K,
                    **kwargs) -> tuple: ...
    '''
    Function to compute put option. It returns tuple of
    forecast results that may contain greeks.
    '''
```

CHAPTER 8   OPTIONS AND BLACK-SCHOLES MODEL

With the interface defined above, we now create a formal class for modeling options, as shown in Listing 8-5.

Listing 8-5. Partial view of class BlackScholesOptionsRiskNeutralGBMModel

```
class BlackScholesOptionsRiskNeutralGBMModel(OptionsTemplate):
    '''
    Class for computing call, put & greeks based on
    BlackScholes model.
    '''

    def __init__(self, parameters: DiffusionProcessParameters,
                 time_unit_transformer: TimeUnitTransformer,
                 n_sample_paths=5):
        self._parameters = parameters
        self._time_u = time_unit_transformer
        self._time_u._t0 = parameters['t0']

        self._n_sample_paths = n_sample_paths

    def estimate_call(self, expiry_time_T, strike_price_K, greeks:
    List[OptionGreeks]
       = None) -> tuple:

        call_process = _CallOptionsGBMProcess(
                 r=self._parameters['r'],
                 σ=self._parameters['σ'],
                 initial_state=self._parameters['s0'],
                 expiry_time_T=expiry_time_T,
                 strike_price_K=strike_price_K,
                 n_sample_paths=self._n_sample_paths)

             # Forecast call options & greeks till expiry time T
             return self._forecast_options(expiry_time_T,
                                    call_process), self._forecast_
                                    greeks(expiry_time_T,
```

CHAPTER 8   OPTIONS AND BLACK-SCHOLES MODEL

```
                                                     strike_
                                                     price_K,
                                                     greeks)

    def estimate_put(self, expiry_time_T, strike_price_K, greeks:
    List[OptionGreeks]
      = None) -> tuple:

      put_process = _PutOptionsGBMProcess(
                r=self._parameters['r'],
                σ=self._parameters['σ'],
                initial_state=self._parameters['s0'],
                expiry_time_T=expiry_time_T,
                strike_price_K=strike_price_K,
                n_sample_paths=self._n_sample_paths)

            # Forecast put options & greeks till expiry time T
            return self._forecast_options(expiry_time_T,
                                          put_process), self._forecast_
                                          greeks(expiry_time_T,
                                                     strike_price
                                                     _K, greeks,
                                                     for_call_
                                                     option=
                                                     False)

def _forecast_options(self, expiry_time_T, options_process:
    _BlackScholesOptionsGBMProcess, for_call_option=True):
            '''
            Leverage the stochastic process of options (call or put) and
            return the forecast result wrapped inside OptionsResult.
            '''
            result = options_process.forecast(
                T=expiry_time_T, time_unit_transformer=self._time_u)

    return OptionsResult(all_values=result,
                                value_at_0=options_process.value_at_0,
```

279

CHAPTER 8   OPTIONS AND BLACK-SCHOLES MODEL

```
                            underlying_s_values=options_process.
                            underlying_s_values,
                            label=options_process.label, for_call_
                            option=for_call_option)
```

Ignore the Greeks part for now, as we will cover that in a while. The forecasting part should look like what we discussed about stock forecasting in Chapter 6. Options forecasting is no different than that because both are treated as assets or derivatives on top of assets, and ultimately, these are stochastic processes.

We test this class with the underlying stock S&P500 Index and parameters, as determined in Chapter 4.

```python
from chapter2.stock_price_dataset_adapters import Frequency
from chapter9.options_common import plot_options_surface
from chapter9.black_scholes_gbm_model import
BlackScholesOptionsRiskNeutralGBMModel, OptionGreeks

from chapter5.base_forecasting import ForecastResultDisplay
from chapter6.diffusion_model import IndexedTimeTransformer

def test_BS_call_process():
    params = {'s0': 2043.93994140625,
              'r': 0.009757165676274302, 'σ': 0.03720863108733509,
              't0': parse('2015-12-01', date_formats=['YYYY-mm-dd'])}

    time_freq = Frequency.MONTHLY
    gbm_options_model = BlackScholesOptionsRiskNeutralGBMModel(
        params,
        IndexedTimeTransformer(time_freq=time_freq))

    result, _ = gbm_options_model.estimate_call(
        expiry_time_T=100,
        strike_price_K=3000.00)

    print('Call Value at 0: ' + str(result.value_at_0))

    result_display = ForecastResultDisplay(
        result.all_values, ylabel=result.label)
```

CHAPTER 8   OPTIONS AND BLACK-SCHOLES MODEL

```
result_display.plot_sample_paths()
result_display.plot_uncertainity_bounds()

plot_options_surface(result)
```

We intentionally omit the *Greeks* parameter in the function *estimate_call* to keep the results specific to call options. We want to see the option values for a strike price of $3000 at an expiry time of 100 units (this time index and not the original physical time; we used *IndexedTimeTransformer* for conversion while displaying the result). We get the estimated premium as

Call value at 0: 926.43283207135.

Figure 8-5 shows the stochastic process of the call option and its uncertainty bounds. Its interoperation would be interesting. Generally, investors will be keen to know the premium value, i.e., the value at t=0, which is already shared. But Figure 8-5 gives a complete set of recommendations for the future, i.e., forecasted derivative paths. This can come in a dashboard of the option seller's trading software – given a strike price, a distribution of option values at different time steps till expiry – a holistic view of the option trajectory.

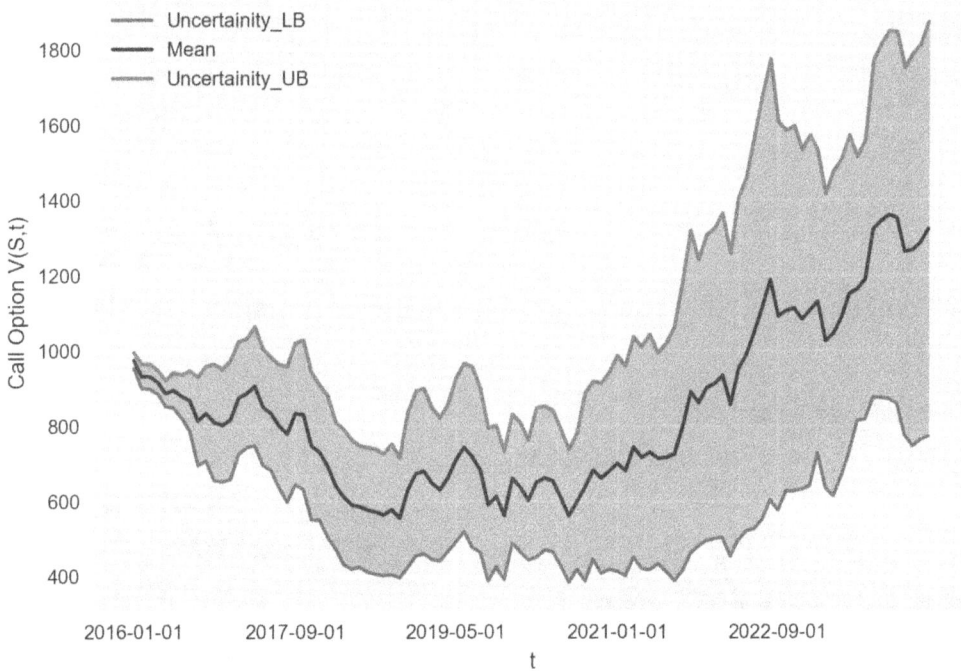

Figure 8-5. *Stochastic process of a call option with a strike price of $3000 and its uncertainty paths*

281

CHAPTER 8 OPTIONS AND BLACK-SCHOLES MODEL

Figure 8-6 shows the call option surface and $V(S,t)$ vs. S plot. It is the superposition of the surface generated by fixed-width asset values (as shown in Figure 8-3) and the forecasted random paths by the asset model. The figure may look a little cryptic, but that's what it is when you use parameters from real data. On the right side, the $V(S,t)$ vs. S plot has data points from all of the sample paths of the underlying asset. Notice asset values are separately captured in variable *_underlying_s_values* as shown in Listing 8-2 as the function *_update_current_state* is supposed to return only $V(S,t)$ and not the $S(t)$.

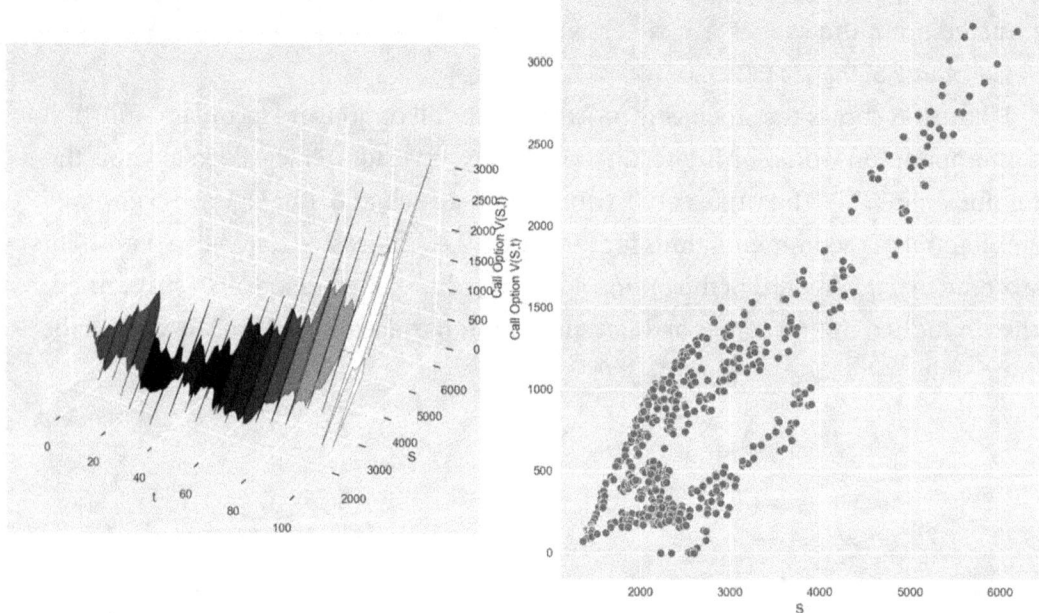

Figure 8-6. *Call option surface with forecasted asset paths and V(S,t) vs. S plot*

Let's now turn to the put option and test it with the same settings as call like the following:

```
def test_BS_put_process():
    params = {'s0': 2043.93994140625,
              'r': 0.009757165676274302, 'σ': 0.03720863108733509,
              't0': parse('2015-12-01', date_formats=['YYYY-mm-dd'])}
    time_freq = Frequency.MONTHLY
    gbm_options_model = BlackScholesOptionsRiskNeutralGBMModel
    (params, IndexedTimeTransformer(
        time_freq=time_freq))
```

```
result, _ = gbm_options_model.estimate_put(
    expiry_time_T=100, strike_price_K=3000.00)

print('Put Value at 0: ' + str(result.value_at_0))

result_display = ForecastResultDisplay(
    result.all_values, ylabel=result.label)
result_display.plot_sample_paths()
result_display.plot_uncertainity_bounds()

plot_options_surface(result)
```

We get the premium as follows:

Put value at 0: 13.259390310523571

Figure 8-7 shows the stochastic process of the put option. Due to the high strike price, option values become close to zero in the vicinity of expiry time; otherwise, using a lower strike price would have made them zero much earlier. With this setting, the option buyer will most likely lose the bet, and the premium will be forfeited. As said earlier, these recommendations are subject to the Black-Scholes model only and may produce different results if any other model is used.

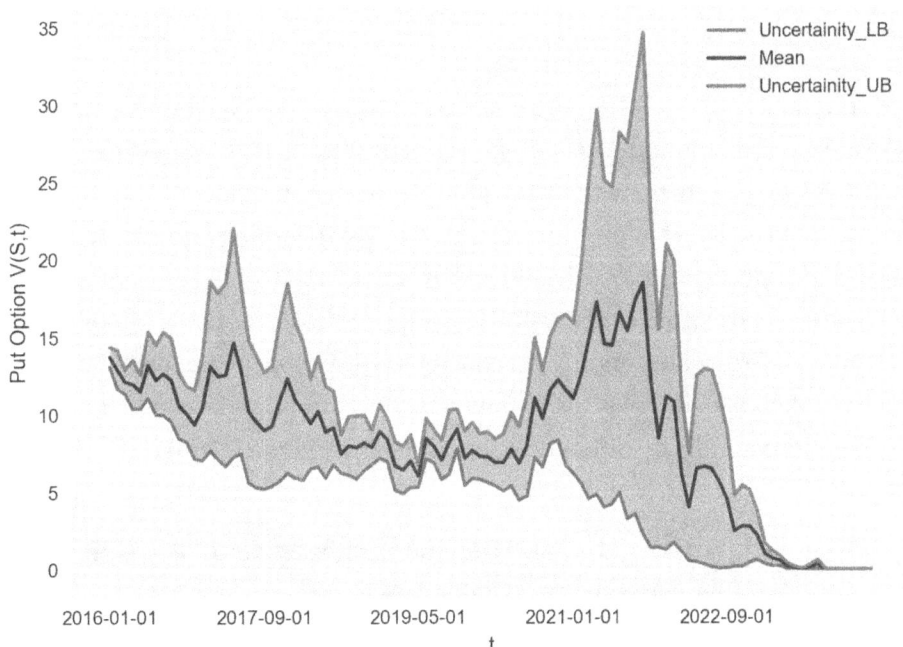

Figure 8-7. *Stochastic process of a put option with a strike price of $3000 and its uncertainty paths*

CHAPTER 8   OPTIONS AND BLACK-SCHOLES MODEL

The option surface shown in Figure 8-8 validates the fact said before.

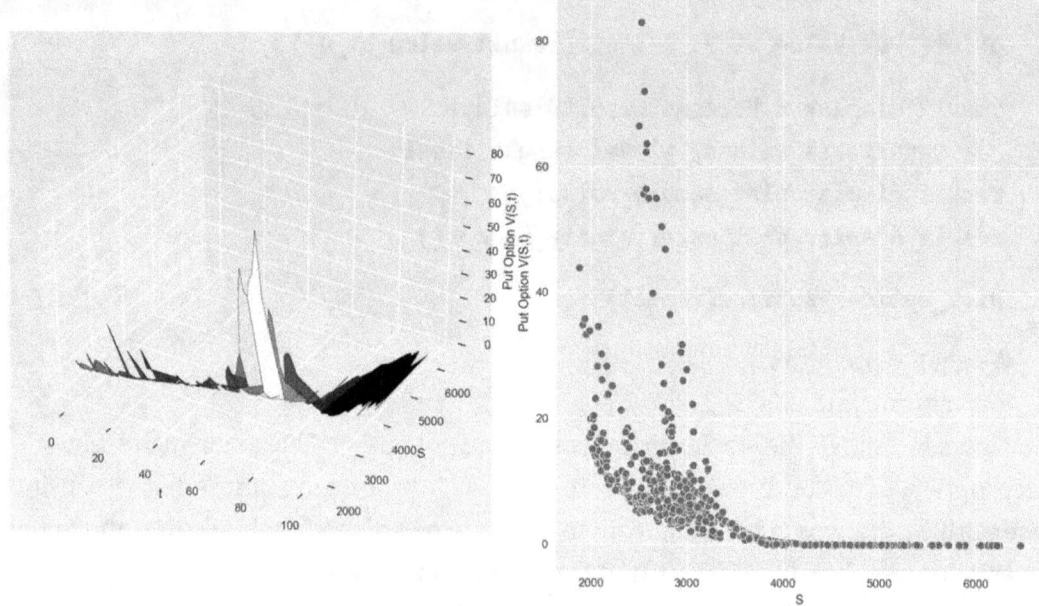

Figure 8-8. *Put option surface with forecasted asset paths and V(S,t) vs. S plot*

Greeks

Thanks for your patience!! At last, we are in the "Greeks" section! No, it is not something alien; these are rates or mathematical derivatives of the option with respect to other variables. Greeks are helpful in hedging the portfolio from potential risk. When the option seller decides not to hedge, that position is termed a *naked position* and can be risky. Sensitivities of the option price are all captured in Greeks and labeled as Greek letters (Δ, Γ, *etc.*). These can be found analytically if the Black-Scholes model of option pricing is followed. However, *Greeks* are generalized concepts not specific to the Black-Scholes model.

As the Black-Scholes model is fully analytical in nature, Greeks can be found for both call and put options simply by differentiation. Therefore, some useful differentials need to be computed first, later to be reused:

a) We know $d_1 - d_2 = \sigma\sqrt{T-t}$, and from here, differentials of this with respect to other variables are obtained as

$$\frac{\partial d_1}{\partial S_t} = \frac{1}{S_t \sigma \sqrt{T-t}}$$

$$\frac{\partial d_1}{\partial S_t} - \frac{\partial d_2}{\partial S_t} = 0$$

$$\frac{\partial d_1}{\partial r} - \frac{\partial d_2}{\partial r} = 0$$

$$\frac{\partial d_1}{\partial t} - \frac{\partial d_2}{\partial t} = -\frac{\sigma}{2\sqrt{T-t}}$$

$$\frac{\partial d_1}{\partial \sigma} - \frac{\partial d_2}{\partial \sigma} = \sqrt{T-t}$$

b) Differential of the CDF of standard normal distribution Φ is given by

$$\Phi'(z) = \frac{1}{\sqrt{2\pi}} e^{-\frac{1}{2}z^2},$$

which is the PDF of the standard normal distribution. This is leveraged in computing differential with respect other variables as

$$\frac{\partial \Phi(d_1)}{\partial S_t} = \Phi'(d_1) \cdot \frac{\partial d_1}{\partial S_t},$$

$$\frac{\partial \Phi(d_2)}{\partial S_t} = \Phi'(d_2) \cdot \frac{\partial d_2}{\partial S_t},$$

$$\frac{\partial \Phi(d_1)}{\partial r} = \Phi'(d_1) \cdot \frac{\partial d_1}{\partial r},$$

$$\frac{\partial \Phi(d_2)}{\partial r} = \Phi'(d_2) \cdot \frac{\partial d_2}{\partial r},$$

$$\frac{\partial \Phi(d_1)}{\partial t} = \Phi'(d_1) \cdot \frac{\partial d_1}{\partial t},$$

$$\frac{\partial \Phi(d_2)}{\partial t} = \Phi'(d_2) \cdot \frac{\partial d_2}{\partial t},$$

CHAPTER 8   OPTIONS AND BLACK-SCHOLES MODEL

$$\frac{\partial \Phi(d_1)}{\partial \sigma} = \Phi'(d_1) \cdot \frac{\partial d_1}{\partial \sigma},$$

$$\frac{\partial \Phi(d_2)}{\partial \sigma} = \Phi'(d_2) \cdot \frac{\partial d_2}{\partial \sigma}.$$

c) Now, compute $d_2^2 - d_1^2$ like below.

First,

$$d_2 - d_1 = -\sigma\sqrt{T-t},$$

$$d_2 + d_1 = -2\left[\frac{\log\frac{S_t}{K}}{\sigma\sqrt{T-t}} + \frac{r}{\sigma}\sqrt{T-t}\right],$$

$$d_2^2 - d_1^2 = (d_2 - d_1)(d_2 + d_1) = -2\log\frac{S_t}{K} - r(T-t).$$

Putting $d_2^2 = d_1^2 - 2\log\frac{S_t}{K} - \sigma(T-t)$, we get

$$\Phi'(d_2) = \frac{1}{\sqrt{2\pi}} e^{-\frac{1}{2}d_2^2}$$

$$= \frac{1}{\sqrt{2\pi}} e^{-\frac{1}{2}\left[d_1^2 - 2\log\frac{S_t}{K} - r(T-t)\right]}$$

$$= \Phi'(d_1) \cdot \frac{S_t}{K} \cdot e^{r(T-t)}$$

or, in short,

$$S_t\Phi'(d_1) = Ke^{-r(T-t)}\Phi'(d_2)$$

We will discuss five Greeks each for both call and put options, which make ten combinations. Go back to Listing 8-5; you will see a list of *OptionGreeks* enum objects that are passed to the functions *estimate_call* and *estimate_put*. This enum is shown now in Listing 8-6.

CHAPTER 8 OPTIONS AND BLACK-SCHOLES MODEL

Listing 8-6. Enum for Greeks

```python
class OptionGreeks(Enum):

    class _Greek:

        def __init__(self, greek_label, call_process, put_process):
            self.greek_label = greek_label
            self.call_process = call_process
            self.put_process = put_process

        def __hash__(self):
            return hash(self.greek_label)

        def __eq__(self, obj):
            return self.greek_label == obj.greek_label

    Δ = _Greek('Delta', _DeltaForCallOptionsGBMProcess.__name__,
            _DeltaForPutOptionsGBMProcess.__name__)

    Γ = _Greek('Gamma', _GammaForCallOptionsGBMProcess.__name__,
            _GammaForPutOptionsGBMProcess.__name__)

    Θ = _Greek('Theta', _ThetaForCallOptionsGBMProcess.__name__,
            _ThetaForPutOptionsGBMProcess.__name__)

    K = _Greek('Vega', _VegaForCallOptionsGBMProcess.__name__,
            _VegaForPutOptionsGBMProcess.__name__)

    P = _Greek('Rho', _RhoForCallOptionsGBMProcess.__name__,
            _RhoForPutOptionsGBMProcess.__name__)
```

Along with this, Listing 8-5 uses a function *_forecast_greeks* that evaluates Greeks' stochastic processes, whose details are given in Listing 8-7.

Listing 8-7. Function _forecast_ greeks

```python
def _forecast_greeks(self, expiry_time_T, strike_price_K, greeks:
    List[OptionGreeks] = None, for_call_option=True) ->
            _GreeksProcessOutputDict:

    greeks_process_result: _GreeksProcessOutputDict = None
```

CHAPTER 8 OPTIONS AND BLACK-SCHOLES MODEL

```
if greeks:
    glb = globals()
    greeks_process_result = {}
    option_greek_process = None
    for greek in greeks:
        if for_call_option:
            option_greek_process = greek.value.call_process
        else:
            option_greek_process = greek.value.put_process

        greeks_process_result[greek] = self._forecast_options(
            expiry_time_T, glb[option_greek_process](r=self._
    parameters['r'],
                                                    σ=self._
                                                    parameters
                                                    ['σ'],
                                                    initial_
                                                    state=self.
                                                    _parameters
                                                    ['s0'],
                                                    expiry_time_
                                                    T=expiry_
                                                    time_T,
                                                    strike_price_
                                                    K=strike_
                                                    price_K,
                                                    n_sample_
                                                    paths=self.
                                                    _n_sample
                                                    _paths),
            for_call_option=for_call_option)
    return greeks_process_result
```

Notice how it works – iterating over all Greeks and preparing the forecasting results. Everything should look fine, but did you see the *_GreeksProcessOutputDict*? It is a dictionary keyed by *OptionGreeks* enum itself and looks like

CHAPTER 8   OPTIONS AND BLACK-SCHOLES MODEL

```
class _GreeksProcessOutputDict(TypedDict):
    '''
    Dictionary holding output from Greeks processes.
    '''
    OptionGreeks.Δ: OptionGreeks
    OptionGreeks.Γ: OptionGreeks
    OptionGreeks.Θ: OptionGreeks
    OptionGreeks.K: OptionGreeks
    OptionGreeks.P: OptionGreeks
```

With all these components in place, let's explore the Greeks one by one.

Delta (Δ)

Delta is the option's sensitivity to the underlying asset's price. It is given as

$$\Delta = \frac{\partial V}{\partial S_t}.$$

To hedge against the price movement, investor must buy Δ units of the underlying and add it to the portfolio like this:

$$\Pi_{Delta-Hedged} = \Pi + \Delta S_t.$$

As the underlying moves, the investor has to keep on adjusting the hedged position by adding the underlying depending on the intensity of the moves. To do this, delta should be computed and forecasted over a period.

Delta for call option is computed as

$$\begin{aligned}\Delta_{Call} &= \frac{\partial V_C}{\partial S_t} \\ &= \Phi(d_1) + S_t \Phi'(d_1)\frac{\partial d_1}{\partial S_t} - Ke^{-r(T-t)}\Phi'(d_2)\frac{\partial d_2}{\partial S_t} \\ &= \Phi(d_1).\end{aligned}$$

CHAPTER 8   OPTIONS AND BLACK-SCHOLES MODEL

And for the put option,

$$\begin{aligned}\Delta_{Put} &= \frac{\partial V_P}{\partial S_t} \\ &= -Ke^{-r(T-t)}\Phi'(-d_2)\frac{\partial d_2}{\partial S_t} + S_t\Phi'(-d_1)\frac{\partial d_1}{\partial S_t} - \Phi(-d_1) \\ &= \Phi(d_1) - 1, \ (Using\ a), b), c), \Phi'(-z) = \Phi'(z)\ and\ \Phi(-z) = 1 - \Phi(z))\end{aligned}$$

The expressions is formally summarized as

$$\begin{aligned}\Delta_{Call} &= \Phi(d_1), \\ \Delta_{Put} &= \Phi(d_1) - 1.\end{aligned}$$

First, we do the calculation using *BlackScholesOptionsGBMProcessStatistics* with an equally spaced asset price grid for gamma put option:

```
@staticmethod
def delta(s, t, r, σ, K, T):
    d1_val = BlackScholesOptionsGBMProcessStatistics.d1(
        s, t, r, σ, K, T)
    return Φ.cdf(d1_val)
```

, and do the testing,

```
def test_greeks_simulation():
    n = 50
    T = 100
    ts = [t_i for t_i in range(T)]
    S = np.linspace(1000, 5000, n)
    time_grid, s_grid = np.meshgrid(ts, S)
    r, σ = 0.009757165676274302, 0.03720863108733509

    V_delta_call = [BlackScholesOptionsGBMProcessStatistics.Call.delta(
        s=s, t=t, r=r, σ=σ, T=T, K=3000) for s, t in zip(s_grid,
        time_grid)]

    test_plot_options_surface(t=np.array(time_grid), S=np.array(
        s_grid), V=np.array(V_delta_call), label="Delta Call")
```

The output of this is shown in Figure 8-9.

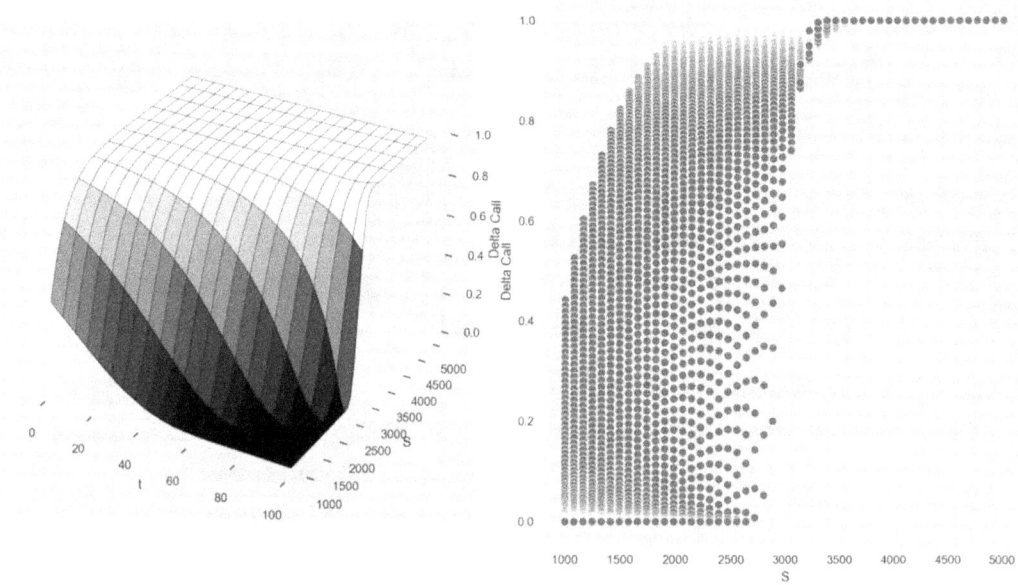

Figure 8-9. *Option surface for delta call*

To formally do the same, we create two classes for the stochastic processes of delta call and put (Listing 8-8).

Listing 8-8. Call and put processes for gamma

```
class _DeltaForCallOptionsGBMProcess(_BlackScholesOptionsGBMProcess):

    def _pay_off_and_greek_f(self, s_t, t):
        return Φ.cdf(self._d1(s_t, t))

    @property
    def label(self):
        return OptionGreeks.Δ.value.greek_label + " Call Option " +
            OptionGreeks.Δ.value.greek_label + "(S,t)"

class _DeltaForPutOptionsGBMProcess(_BlackScholesOptionsGBMProcess):

    def _pay_off_and_greek_f(self, s_t, t):
        return Φ.cdf(self._d1(s_t, t)) - 1
```

CHAPTER 8 OPTIONS AND BLACK-SCHOLES MODEL

```
    @property
    def label(self):
        return OptionGreeks.Δ.value.greek_label + " Put Option " +
            OptionGreeks.Δ.value.greek_label + "(S,t)"
```

These can be formally tested as

```
def test_BS_delta_for_call_process():
    params = {'s0': 2043.93994140625,
              'r': 0.009757165676274302, 'σ': 0.03720863108733509,
              't0': parse('2015-12-01', date_formats=['YYYY-mm-dd'])}

    time_freq = Frequency.MONTHLY
    gbm_options_model = BlackScholesOptionsRiskNeutralGBMModel(params,
                                    IndexedTimeTransformer(
                                        time_freq=time_freq))

    _, greeks_result = gbm_options_model.estimate_call(
        expiry_time_T=100, strike_price_K=3000.00, greeks=[OptionGreeks.Δ])

    delta_result = greeks_result[OptionGreeks.Δ]
    print('Delta Call Value at 0: ' +
          str(delta_result.value_at_0))

    delta_result_display = ForecastResultDisplay(
        delta_result.all_values, ylabel=delta_result.label)
    delta_result_display.plot_sample_paths()
    delta_result_display.plot_uncertainity_bounds()

    plot_options_surface(delta_result)
```

Output is shown in Figure 8-10.

CHAPTER 8   OPTIONS AND BLACK-SCHOLES MODEL

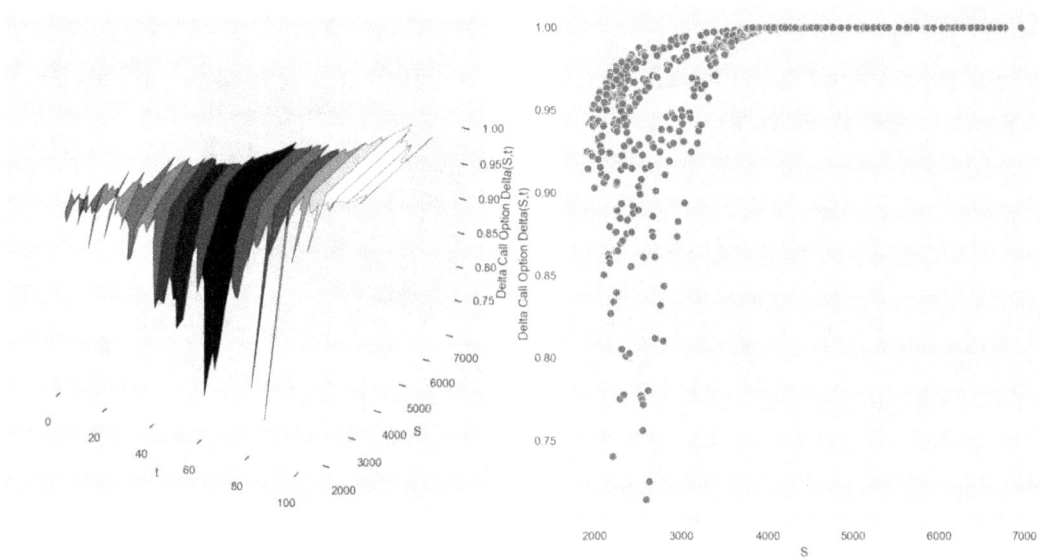

Figure 8-10. *Option surface for delta call with all real sample paths*

Before proceeding with other Greeks, let's view how the components are tied together in the class diagram, as shown in Figure 8-11. This shows the framework only with delta; other Greeks can come in between as we proceed further.

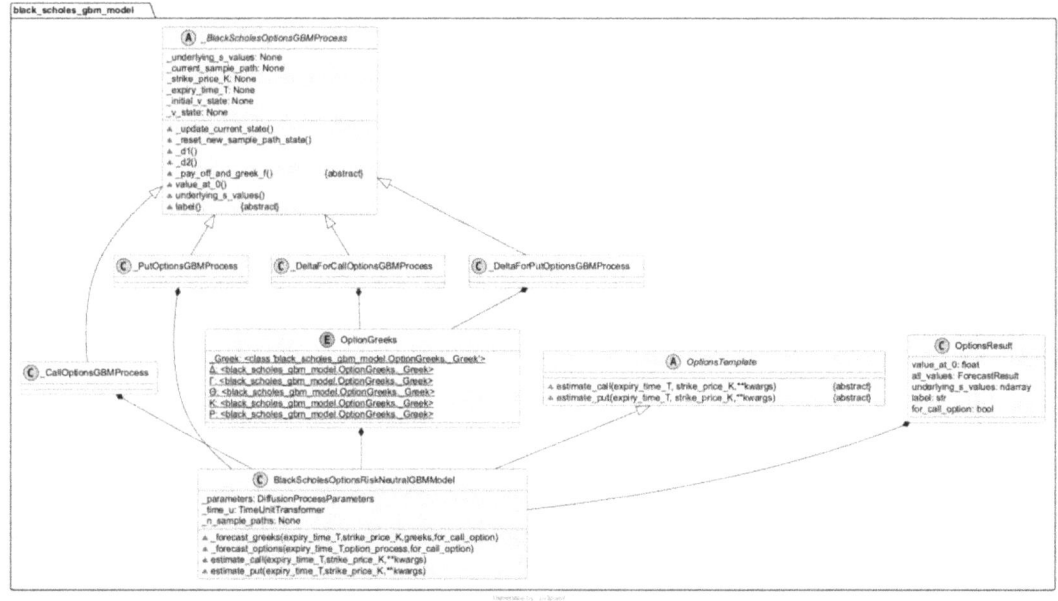

Figure 8-11. *Class diagram of the option pricing components*

CHAPTER 8 OPTIONS AND BLACK-SCHOLES MODEL

Gamma (Γ)

Gamma provides the measure of the second-order sensitivity of the option to the asset price movement. It is given as

$$\Gamma = \frac{\partial^2 V}{\partial S_t^2}.$$

It allows a second-order correction to the delta, basically that makes it the first-order sensitivity of the delta to the price movement. To gamma hedge a portfolio, square of asset price should be multiplied with gamma and added there as

$$\Pi_{Gamma-Hedged} = \Pi + \Gamma S_t^2.$$

Gamma for call option is computed with the help of a), b), and c) as

$$\begin{aligned}
\Gamma_{Call} &= \frac{\partial^2 V_C}{\partial S_t^2} \\
&= \frac{\partial}{\partial S_t}\left(\frac{\partial V_C}{\partial S_t}\right) \\
&= \Phi'(d_1)\frac{\partial d_1}{\partial S_t}, (using\ a),b),c)) \\
&= \frac{\Phi'(d_1)}{S_t \sigma \sqrt{T-t}}.
\end{aligned}$$

As $\Delta_{Put} = \Phi(d_1) - 1$, so

$$\Gamma_{Put} = \frac{\Phi'(d_1)}{S_t \sigma \sqrt{T-t}}$$

$$\Gamma_{Call} = \frac{\Phi'(d_1)}{S_t \sigma \sqrt{T-t}},$$

$$\Gamma_{Put} = \frac{\Phi'(d_1)}{S_t \sigma \sqrt{T-t}}$$

First, we do the calculation using *BlackScholesOptionsGBMProcessStatistics* with an equally spaced asset price grid for gamma put option:

```
@staticmethod
def gamma(s, t, r, σ, K, T):
    d1_val = BlackScholesOptionsGBMProcessStatistics.d1(
        s, t, r, σ, K, T)
    return Φ.pdf(d1_val)/(σ * s * np.sqrt(T-t))
```

and do the testing:

```
V_gamma_put = [BlackScholesOptionsGBMProcessStatistics.Put.gamma(
    s=s, t=t, r=r, σ=σ, T=T, K=4000) for s, t in zip(s_grid,
    time_grid)]

test_plot_options_surface(t=np.array(time_grid), S=np.array(
    s_grid), V=np.array(V_gamma_put), label="Gamma Put", is_call=False)
```

The output of this is shown in Figure 8-12.

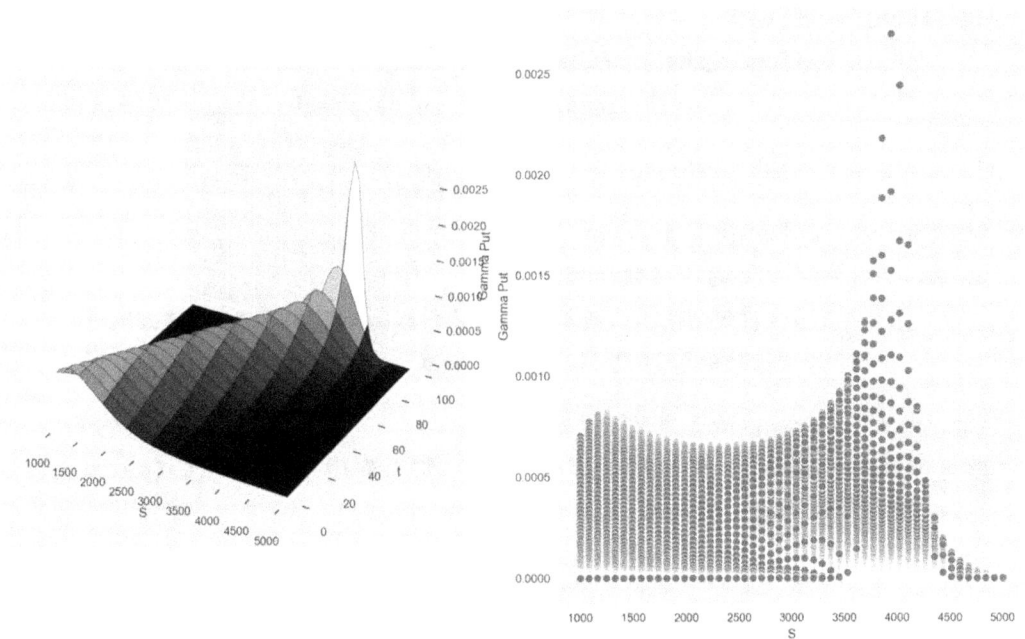

Figure 8-12. *Option surface for gamma put*

To formally do the same, we create two classes for the stochastic processes of gamma call and put (Listing 8-9).

CHAPTER 8 OPTIONS AND BLACK-SCHOLES MODEL

Listing 8-9. Call and put processes for gamma

```python
class _GammaForCallOptionsGBMProcess(_BlackScholesOptionsGBMProcess):

    def _pay_off_and_greek_f(self, s_t, t):
        return Φ.pdf(self._d1(s_t, t))/(self._σ * s_t * np.sqrt(self._expiry_time_T-t))

    @property
    def label(self):
            return OptionGreeks.Γ.value.greek_label + " Call Option " +
                            OptionGreeks.Γ.value.greek_label + "(S,t)"

class _GammaForPutOptionsGBMProcess(_BlackScholesOptionsGBMProcess):

    def _pay_off_and_greek_f(self, s_t, t):
        return Φ.pdf(self._d1(s_t, t))/(self._σ * s_t * np.sqrt(self._expiry_time_T-t))

    @property
    def label(self):
        return OptionGreeks.Γ.value.greek_label + " Put Option " +
                        OptionGreeks.Γ.value.greek_label + "(S,t)"
```

These can be formally tested as,

```python
def test_BS_gamma_for_put_process():
    params = {'s0': 2043.93994140625,
              'r': 0.009757165676274302, 'σ': 0.03720863108733509,
              't0': parse('2015-12-01', date_formats=['YYYY-mm-dd'])}

    time_freq = Frequency.MONTHLY
    gbm_options_model = BlackScholesOptionsRiskNeutralGBMModel(params,
      IndexedTimeTransformer(time_freq=time_freq))

    _, greeks_result = gbm_options_model.estimate_put(
        expiry_time_T=100, strike_price_K=4000.00, greeks=[OptionGreeks.Γ])

    gamma_result = greeks_result[OptionGreeks.Γ]
    print('Gamma Put Value at 0: ' +
        str(gamma_result.value_at_0))
```

```
gamma_result_display = ForecastResultDisplay(
    gamma_result.all_values, ylabel=gamma_result.label)

gamma_result_display.plot_sample_paths()
gamma_result_display.plot_uncertainity_bounds()
plot_options_surface(gamma_result)
```

Output is shown in Figure 8-13.

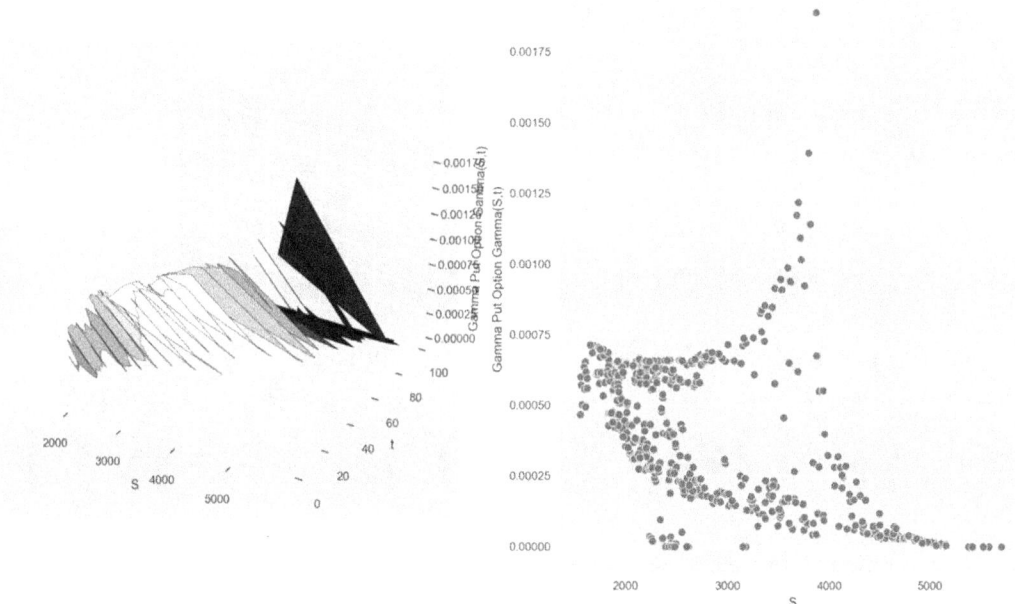

Figure 8-13. *Option surface for gamma put with all real sample paths*

Theta (Θ)

Theta of an option is the rate at which its value varies over time. It is given by

$$\Theta = \frac{\partial V}{\partial t}.$$

CHAPTER 8   OPTIONS AND BLACK-SCHOLES MODEL

Theta for call option is computed as

$$\Theta_{Call} = \frac{\partial V_C}{\partial t}$$

$$= S_t \Phi'(d_1) \frac{\partial d_1}{\partial t} - rKe^{-r(T-t)} \Phi(d_2) - rKe^{-r(T-t)} \Phi'(d_2) \frac{\partial d_2}{\partial t}$$

$$= -S_t \Phi'(d_1) \left[\frac{\partial d_2}{\partial t} - \frac{\partial d_1}{\partial t} \right] - rKe^{-r(T-t)} \Phi(d_2)$$

$$= -\frac{\sigma S_t \Phi'(d_1)}{2\sqrt{T-t}} - rKe^{-r(T-t)} \Phi(d_2).$$

and the same for put option:

$$\Theta_{Put} = \frac{\partial V_P}{\partial t}$$

$$= -Ke^{-r(T-t)} \Phi'(-d_2) \frac{\partial d_2}{\partial t} + rKe^{-r(T-t)} \Phi(-d_2) + S_t \Phi'(-d_1) \frac{\partial d_1}{\partial t}$$

$$= -S_t \Phi'(-d_1) \left[\frac{\partial d_2}{\partial t} - \frac{\partial d_1}{\partial t} \right] + rKe^{-r(T-t)} \Phi(-d_2)$$

$$= -\frac{\sigma S_t \Phi'(-d_1)}{2\sqrt{T-t}} + rKe^{-r(T-t)} \Phi(-d_2)$$

$$\Theta_{Call} = -\frac{\sigma S_t \Phi'(d_1)}{2\sqrt{T-t}} - rKe^{-r(T-t)} \Phi(d_2),$$

$$\Theta_{Put} = -\frac{\sigma S_t \Phi'(-d_1)}{2\sqrt{T-t}} + rKe^{-r(T-t)} \Phi(-d_2)$$

Theta can informally be computed with *BlackScholesOptionsGBMProcessStatistics* for call option:

```
@staticmethod
def theta(s, t, r, σ, K, T):
    d1_val = BlackScholesOptionsGBMProcessStatistics.d1(
        s, t, r, σ, K, T)
    d2_val = BlackScholesOptionsGBMProcessStatistics.d2(
        s, t, r, σ, K, T)
```

CHAPTER 8   OPTIONS AND BLACK-SCHOLES MODEL

```
    return -((σ * s * Φ.pdf(d1_val))/(2.0*np.sqrt(T-t))) \
        - (r * K * np.exp(-r*(T-t)) * Φ.cdf(d2_val))
```

and tested as

```
V_theta_call = [BlackScholesOptionsGBMProcessStatistics.Call.theta(
    s=s, t=t, r=r, σ=σ, T=T, K=4000) for s, t in zip(s_grid,
    time_grid)]

test_plot_options_surface(t=np.array(time_grid), S=np.array(
    s_grid), V=np.array(V_theta_call), label="Theta Call")
```

Output is shown in Figure 8-14.

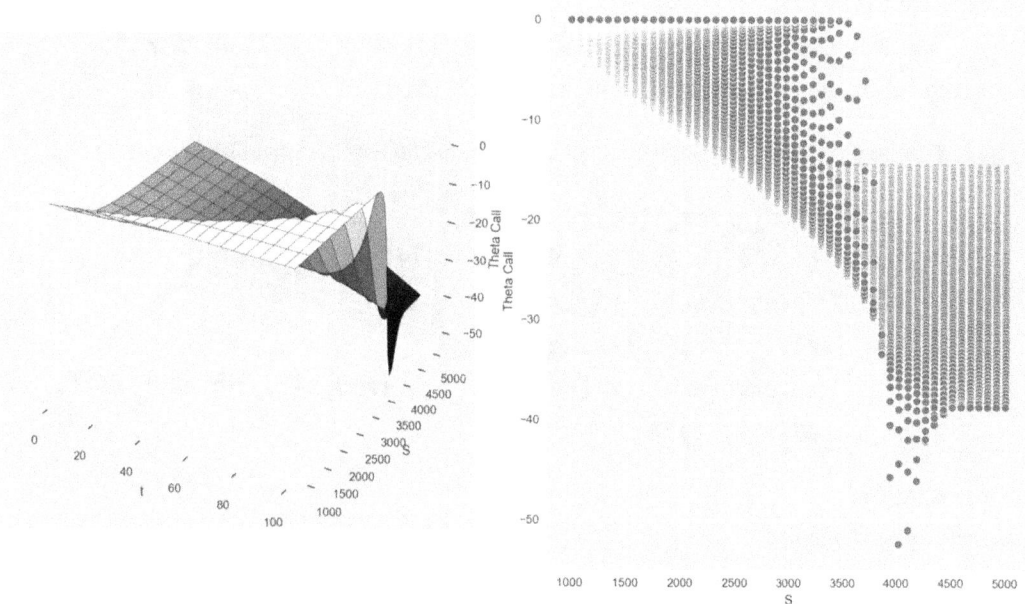

Figure 8-14. *Option surface for theta call*

Formally, two classes for theta call and theta put process is created (Listing 8-10).

Listing 8-10. Call and put processes for theta

```python
class _ThetaForCallOptionsGBMProcess(_BlackScholesOptionsGBMProcess):

    def _pay_off_and_greek_f(self, s_t, t):
        return -((self._σ * s_t * Φ.pdf(self._d1(s_t, t)))/(2.0*np.sqrt(self._expiry_time_T-t))) \
            - (self._r*self._strike_price_K *
                np.exp(-self._r*(self._expiry_time_T-t))*Φ.cdf(self._d2(s_t, t)))

    @property
    def label(self):
        return OptionGreeks.Θ.value.greek_label + " Call Option " +
        OptionGreeks.Θ.value.greek_label + "(S,t)"

class _ThetaForPutOptionsGBMProcess(_BlackScholesOptionsGBMProcess):

    def _pay_off_and_greek_f(self, s_t, t):
        return -((self._σ * s_t * Φ.pdf(-self._d1(s_t, t)))/(2.0*np.sqrt(self._expiry_time_T-t))) \
            + (self._r*self._strike_price_K *
                np.exp(-self._r*(self._expiry_time_T-t))*Φ.cdf(-self._d2(s_t, t)))

    @property
    def label(self):
        return OptionGreeks.Θ.value.greek_label + " Put Option " +
            OptionGreeks.Θ.value.greek_label + "(S,t)"
```

Testing should be the same as the previous Greeks. Figure 8-15 shows the output.

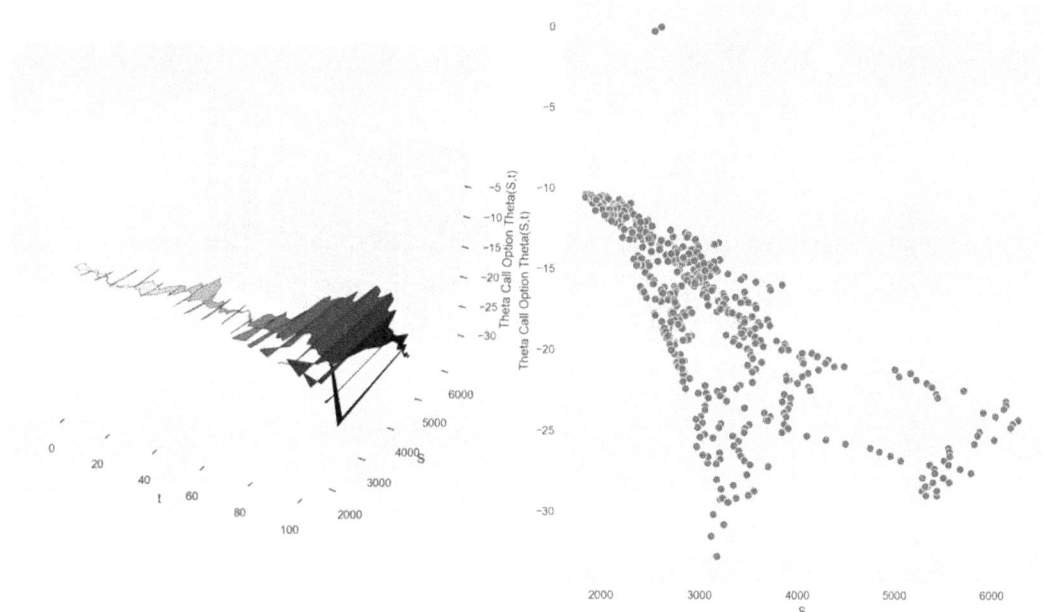

Figure 8-15. Option surface for theta call with all real sample paths

Vega (Κ)

Vega is the sensitivity of the option price with respect to volatility and is given by

$$\Kappa = \frac{\partial V}{\partial \sigma}.$$

It is little confusing as volatility is constant for Black-Scholes model but holds true if implied volatility is applied here. One can vega hedge to reduce the sensitivity to the volatility.

Vega for call option is computed as

$$\begin{aligned}
\Kappa_{Call} &= \frac{\partial V_C}{\partial \sigma} \\
&= S_t \Phi'(d_1) \frac{\partial d_1}{\partial \sigma} - K e^{-r(T-t)} \Phi'(d_2) \frac{\partial d_2}{\partial \sigma} \\
&= S_t \Phi'(d_1) \left[\frac{\partial d_1}{\partial \sigma} - \frac{\partial d_2}{\partial \sigma} \right] \\
&= S_t \Phi'(d_1) \sqrt{T-t}
\end{aligned}$$

CHAPTER 8   OPTIONS AND BLACK-SCHOLES MODEL

and the same for the put:

$$K_{Put} = \frac{\partial V_P}{\partial \sigma}$$

$$= -Ke^{-r(T-t)}\Phi'(-d_2)\frac{\partial d_2}{\partial \sigma} + S_t\Phi'(-d_1)\frac{\partial d_1}{\partial \sigma}$$

$$= S_t\Phi'(-d_1)\left[\frac{\partial d_1}{\partial \sigma} - \frac{\partial d_2}{\partial \sigma}\right]$$

$$= S_t\Phi'(d_1)\sqrt{T-t}$$

$$K_{Call} = S_t\Phi'(d_1)\sqrt{T-t}$$
$$K_{Put} = S_t\Phi'(d_1)\sqrt{T-t}$$

Vega can informally be computed with *BlackScholesOptionsGBMProcessStatistics* for call option:

```
@staticmethod
def vega(s, t, r, σ, K, T):
    d1_val = BlackScholesOptionsGBMProcessStatistics.d1(
        s, t, r, σ, K, T)
    return Φ.pdf(d1_val) * (σ * s * np.sqrt(T-t))
```

and tested as

```
V_vega_put = [BlackScholesOptionsGBMProcessStatistics.Put.vega(
    s=s, t=t, r=r, σ=σ, T=T, K=4000) for s, t in zip(s_grid,
    time_grid)]

test_plot_options_surface(t=np.array(time_grid), S=np.array(
    s_grid), V=np.array(V_vega_put), label="Vega Put")
```

,

producing output shown in Figure 8-16.

CHAPTER 8 OPTIONS AND BLACK-SCHOLES MODEL

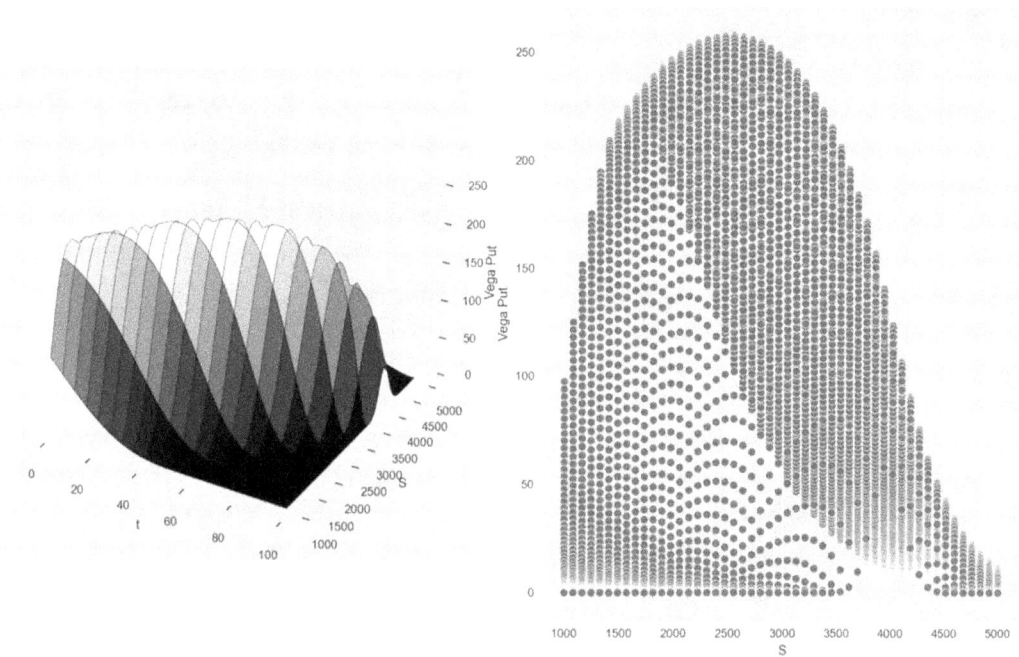

Figure 8-16. *Option surface for vega put*

Formally, two classes for vega call and vega put process are created (Listing 8-11).

Listing 8-11. Call and put processes for vega

```
class _VegaForCallOptionsGBMProcess(_BlackScholesOptionsGBMProcess):

    def _pay_off_and_greek_f(self, s_t, t):
        return Φ.pdf(self._d1(s_t, t))*(self._σ * s_t * np.sqrt(self._
        expiry_time_T-t))

    @property
    def label(self):
        return OptionGreeks.K.value.greek_label + " Call Option " +
            OptionGreeks.K.value.greek_label + "(S,t)"

class _VegaForPutOptionsGBMProcess(_BlackScholesOptionsGBMProcess):

    def _pay_off_and_greek_f(self, s_t, t):
        return Φ.pdf(self._d1(s_t, t)) * (self._σ * s_t * np.sqrt(self._
        expiry_time_T-t))
```

303

CHAPTER 8   OPTIONS AND BLACK-SCHOLES MODEL

```
@property
def label(self):
    return OptionGreeks.K.value.greek_label + " Put Option " +
        OptionGreeks.K.value.greek_label + "(S,t)"
```

Testing should be the same as the previous Greeks. Figure 8-17 shows the output.

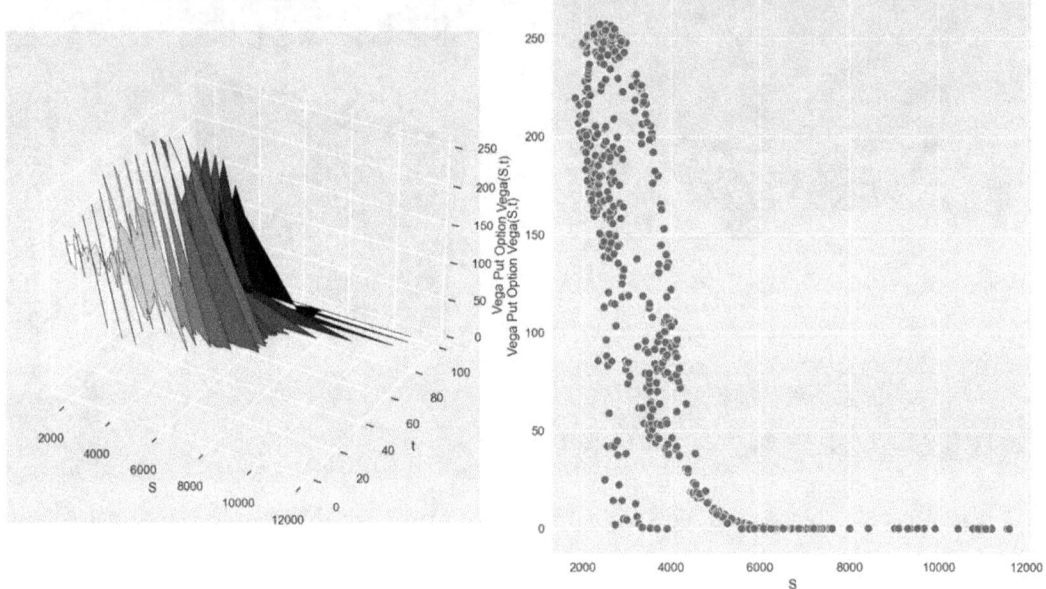

Figure 8-17. *Option surface for vega put with all real sample paths*

Rho (P)

Rho is the sensitivity of the option price to the movement of interest rates and is given by

$$P = \frac{\partial V}{\partial r}.$$

The time value of the call increases when interest rates rise, whereas the opposite is true for put value.

Rho for call and put are computed as

$$\begin{aligned}
P_{Call} &= \frac{\partial V_C}{\partial r} \\
&= S_t \Phi'(d_1)\frac{\partial d_1}{\partial r} - Ke^{-r(T-t)}\Phi'(d_2)\frac{\partial d_2}{\partial r} + K(T-t)e^{-r(T-t)}\Phi(d_2) \\
&= S_t \Phi'(d_1)\left[\frac{\partial d_1}{\partial r} - \frac{\partial d_2}{\partial r}\right] + K(T-t)e^{-r(T-t)}\Phi(d_2) \\
&= K(T-t)e^{-r(T-t)}\Phi(d_2)
\end{aligned}$$

and

$$\begin{aligned}
P_{Put} &= \frac{\partial V_P}{\partial r} \\
&= -Ke^{-r(T-t)}\Phi'(-d_2)\frac{\partial d_2}{\partial r} - K(T-t)e^{-r(T-t)}\Phi(-d_2) + S_t\Phi'(-d_1)\frac{\partial d_1}{\partial r} \\
&= S_t\Phi'(-d_1)\left[\frac{\partial d_1}{\partial r} - \frac{\partial d_2}{\partial r}\right] - K(T-t)e^{-r(T-t)}\Phi(-d_2) \\
&= -K(T-t)e^{-r(T-t)}\Phi(-d_2).
\end{aligned}$$

$$\begin{aligned}
P_{Call} &= K(T-t)e^{-r(T-t)}\Phi(d_2), \\
P_{Put} &= -K(T-t)e^{-r(T-t)}\Phi(-d_2)
\end{aligned}$$

Rho can informally be computed with *BlackScholesOptionsGBMProcessStatistics* for call option:

```
@staticmethod
def vega(s, t, r, σ, K, T):
    d1_val = BlackScholesOptionsGBMProcessStatistics.d1(
        s, t, r, σ, K, T)
    return Φ.pdf(d1_val) * (σ * s * np.sqrt(T-t))
```

CHAPTER 8   OPTIONS AND BLACK-SCHOLES MODEL

and tested as (output is shown in Figure 8-18)

```
V_rho_call = [BlackScholesOptionsGBMProcessStatistics.Call.rho(
    s=s, t=t, r=r, σ=σ, T=T, K=4000) for s, t in zip(s_grid,
    time_grid)]

test_plot_options_surface(t=np.array(time_grid), S=np.array(
    s_grid), V=np.array(V_rho_call), label="Rho Call")
```

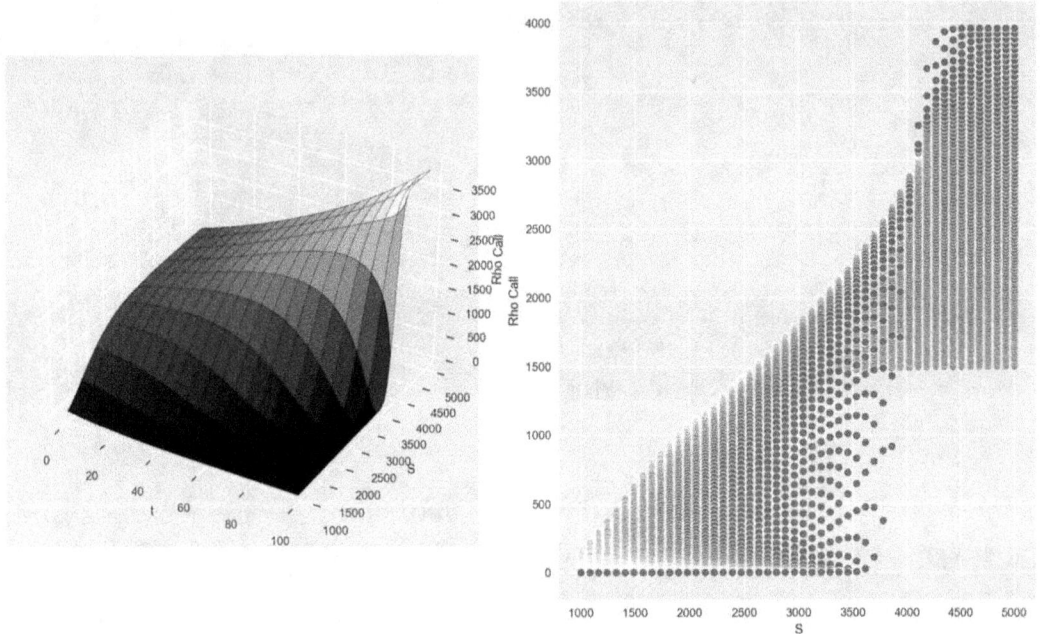

Figure 8-18. Option surface for rho call

Formally, two classes for rho call and put process is created (Listing 8-12).

Listing 8-12. Call and put processes for rho

```python
class _RhoForCallOptionsGBMProcess(_BlackScholesOptionsGBMProcess):

    def _pay_off_and_greek_f(self, s_t, t):
        return self._strike_price_K * np.exp(-self._r*(self._expiry_
        time_T-t)) *
            Φ.cdf(self._d2(s_t, t))
```

306

CHAPTER 8 OPTIONS AND BLACK-SCHOLES MODEL

```
    @property
    def label(self):
        return OptionGreeks.P.value.greek_label + " Call Option " +
            OptionGreeks.P.value.greek_label + "(S,t)"

class _RhoForPutOptionsGBMProcess(_BlackScholesOptionsGBMProcess):

    def _pay_off_and_greek_f(self, s_t, t):
        return -1.0 * self._strike_price_K * np.exp(-self._r*
        (self._expiry_time_T-t)) *
            Φ.cdf(-self._d2(s_t, t))

    @property
    def label(self):
        return OptionGreeks.P.value.greek_label + " Put Option " +
            OptionGreeks.P.value.greek_label + "(S,t)"
```

Testing should be the same as the previous Greeks. Figure 8-19 show the output.

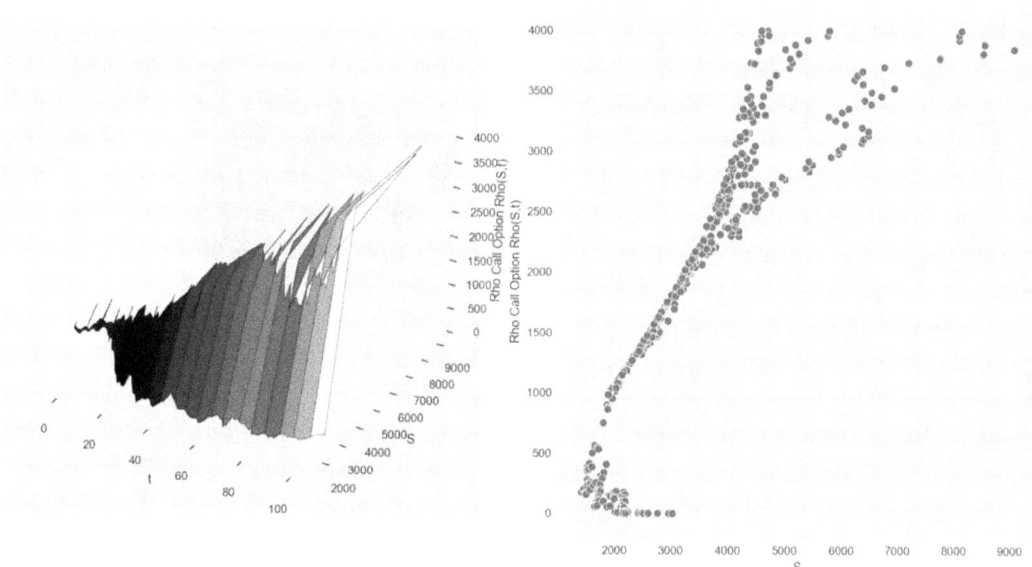

Figure 8-19. Option surface for rho call with all real sample paths

CHAPTER 8 OPTIONS AND BLACK-SCHOLES MODEL

Summary

This chapter discussed the basic concepts of financial options theory: nomenclatures, probabilistic models, and, most importantly, the Black-Scholes model of options. Options are drivers of the modern-day financial market, so estimating their right value is essential for an investor to have their portfolio looking good. Risk-neutral probabilistic method of option price evaluation is one of the ways to solve the Black-Scholes model, and we developed a template for that in this chapter. Greeks are tools to hedge against potential risks in option trading; the template has support for the analysis of Greeks, forecasting their values and plotting the surface for deeper analysis. Overall, these templates can be used if you are planning to build your personal finance portfolio or even something bigger, like a trading platform.

The next chapter discusses the PDE-based method of Black-Scholes modeling, exotic derivatives like barrier options, and the cosine method of option price evaluation.

CHAPTER 9

PDE, Finite Difference, and Black-Scholes Model

This is the book's second chapter of Part 3, and here we discuss a numerical method of solving *partial differential equations (PDE)* – the *finite difference method (FDM)* and solving the Black-Scholes PDE with it. PDEs are essential parts of financial engineering and have a significant role in determining derivatives like *options*. You may wonder why now; being a prerequisite, this should have been discussed in Part 1, but as it is very specific to *options*, I thought of doing the same here in Part 3. You may also take this chapter as a general discussion to learn methods of numerically solving PDEs, irrespective of the finance domain. We will try to keep our conversations as generic and independent as possible, though Black-Scholes PDE at the end will complete the circle of discussion being specific to financial engineering.

PDE – A Short Introduction

PDE comprises partial derivatives of the states that capture system dynamics, specifically when states are defined by multiple dimensions – physical or virtual. Like *ordinary differential equations (ODE)*, PDE utilizes fundamentals of physics-based principles to describe a system – the change of the system w.r.t its dimensions. One such example is

$$\frac{\partial^2 u}{\partial x^2} + \frac{\partial^2 u}{\partial y^2} = 0.$$

It is known as the Laplace equation – having two dimensions, x and y, and the dependent variable u. To keep things relevant, we consider a general structure of the PDE as given by

CHAPTER 9   PDE, FINITE DIFFERENCE, AND BLACK-SCHOLES MODEL

$$A\frac{\partial^2 u}{\partial x^2} + B\frac{\partial^2 u}{\partial x \partial y} + C\frac{\partial^2 u}{\partial y^2} + D\frac{\partial u}{\partial x} + E\frac{\partial u}{\partial y} + Fu + G = 0.$$

The coefficients A, B, C, etc., are either constants or real functions of x & y (as *options* are time dependent, we are only interested in PDEs with spatial variable x and time variable t as independent for this book). These subsume three categories of PDE with conditions as given by the following:

- Parabolic, when $B^2 - 4AC = 0$
- Elliptic, when $B^2 - 4AC < 0$
- Hyperbolic, when $B^2 - 4AC > 0$

Observe that we get the Laplace equation by setting A=1 and C=1 and others as zero. However, for being specific to second order (*order* is the highest degree of the partial derivatives), this is still not the most generic structure for all PDEs. But, to develop understanding, this should suffice as we deal with only second-order PDE in this book.

Elliptic PDE has applications in modeling steady-state heat conduction, harmonic functions, etc. A typical example of such is the Laplace equation itself. Parabolic PDE is the most relevant for this book because of its relationship to the *Black-Scholes* equation, which is given by

$$\frac{\partial V}{\partial t} + rS\frac{\partial V}{\partial S} + \frac{1}{2}\sigma^2 S^2 \frac{\partial^2 V}{\partial S^2} - rV = 0$$

where V is the option's price, S is the underlying security price, and V is the function of S and t and often written as $V(S, t)$ (interpretations and other details will be covered in the subsequent chapters).

To find unique solutions for these PDEs, we need to have some *initial and boundary conditions*, i.e., the value of the target function u at the spatial and time boundaries. These values can be, in turn, represented by a separate set of functions. In general, for a PDE, these can be written as

$$u\big|_{t=0} = \phi(x) \quad (\textit{Initial condition})$$
$$u\big|_{x=N} = \psi(t) \quad (\textit{Boundary condition}).$$

How many such conditions are needed depends on the degree of the PDE. For example, the Black-Scholes equation is second ordered in S and first ordered in t, which is the reason for having two spatial boundary conditions and one initial condition to get a unique solution for the option price estimation.

Solution of PDE – Finite Difference Method (FDM)

FDM is based on approximating derivatives with simple difference formulas and derivative equations with difference equations. The method was first introduced by Runge in 1908 to solve the *Poisson* equation, as given below:

$$\frac{\partial^2 u}{\partial x^2} + \frac{\partial^2 u}{\partial y^2} = \text{Constant}$$

It is almost the same as the Laplace equation, with the only difference being having a source term on the right-hand side. To proceed further, let's discuss the numerical approximation of derivatives first.

We start with the Taylor series expansion of a function $f(x + h)$:

$$f(x+h) = f(x) + hf'(x) + \frac{1}{2}h^2 f''(x) + \frac{1}{6}h^3 f'''(x) + O(h^4)$$

From there, we get

$$f'(x) = \frac{f(x+h) - f(x)}{h} + O(h)$$

So, an approximation of $f'(x)$ can be written as

$$f'(x) \approx \frac{f(x+h) - f(x)}{h}$$

The above expression is known as *forward difference* formulae for first-order derivatives.

CHAPTER 9   PDE, FINITE DIFFERENCE, AND BLACK-SCHOLES MODEL

There are a few other alternatives for computing the same – *backward difference* and *central difference*. The first one leverages the same Taylor series but with a change – using -h instead of h:

$$f(x-h) = f(x) - hf'(x) + \frac{1}{2}h^2 f''(x) - \frac{1}{6}h^3 f'''(x) + O(h^4).$$

Rearranging and neglecting higher-order terms, we get *backward difference* approximation of the first-order derivative:

$$f'(x) \approx \frac{f(x) - f(x-h)}{h}.$$

The second alternative, i.e., the *central difference* formulae, is obtained by subtracting the Taylor series of $f(x-h)$ from the same of $f(x+h)$:

$$f'(x) = \frac{f(x+h) - f(x-h)}{2h} + O(h^2).$$

Neglecting second-order terms,

$$f'(x) \approx \frac{f(x+h) - f(x-h)}{2h}.$$

The central difference formula is the best approximation among the three for having the least truncation error, which is of $O(h^2)$, since h is infinitesimal. If $f(x)$ is twice differentiable, then the second-order derivative also can be approximated in the same way; hence, we get

$$f''(x) \approx \frac{f(x+h) - 2f(x) + f(x-h)}{h^2}.$$

Since we are dealing with partial derivatives, we study functions of multiple variables, and *time* is one of them. Let's denote such functions by $u(x, t)$ and apply the same central difference formula to approximate partial derivatives w.r.t. x and t.

CHAPTER 9   PDE, FINITE DIFFERENCE, AND BLACK-SCHOLES MODEL

PARTIAL DERIVATIVE – NOTE

If $u(x, y)$ is a function of multiple variables, then while taking partial derivative w.r.t. x, the other variable y is kept constant, and derivative is written as $u_x(x, y)$.

$$u_x(x,t) \approx \frac{u(x+\Delta x, t) - u(x-\Delta x, t)}{2\Delta x}$$

$$u_{xx}(x,t) \approx \frac{u(x+\Delta x, t) - 2u(x,t) + u(x-\Delta x, t)}{(\Delta x)^2}$$

$$u_t(x,t) \approx \frac{u(x, t+\Delta t) - (x, t-\Delta t)}{2\Delta t},$$

where Δx and Δt are infinitesimal changes for variable x and t.

A PDE's solution is nothing but estimating the function in closed form or numerical form. Closed-form solutions are always best, but they involve many complex analytical steps, including suitable transformation of variables, which may be challenging depending on the differential equation's complexity, especially for PDEs. Numerical methods are better alternatives as they provide a general iterative framework irrespective of the complexity. Unlike their closed-form counterpart, we directly get the function outputs evaluated for different inputs, representing the solution as a grid or table of data points. The solution procedure can be summarized below:

FDM STEPS

1) Divide the input space into different regions, i.e., prepare a mesh of inputs.

2) Decompose the PDE into a recurrence relation type equation by replacing the partial derivatives with difference formulae discussed earlier.

3) Solve for difference equations by deducing a system of equations from the recurrence relation or by using recursion. Both approaches need to leverage the initial and boundary conditions provided by the PDE.

CHAPTER 9 PDE, FINITE DIFFERENCE, AND BLACK-SCHOLES MODEL

This chapter discusses three FDM techniques – *explicit method*, *implicit method*, and *Crank-Nicolson method*. As shown in the FDM steps above, the basic principle is the same for all three.

Explicit Method

To discuss solutions, we consider the heat equation as our target PDE, whose general form is given by

$$\frac{\partial u}{\partial t} = \alpha \frac{\partial^2 u}{\partial x^2}, \quad a < x < b, t > 0;$$

where α is a constant. Spatial variable x can be multidimensional; however, we consider it single dimensional for convenience. To establish a resemblance with finance, the function u can be thought of as providing the value of an option for some underlying asset x at time t. Let the initial condition be

$$u(x,0) = f(x), \quad a < x < b,$$

defined for t = 0, and let the boundary conditions be

$$u(a,t) = g(t), \quad u(b,t) = h(t), \quad t > 0,$$

defined for $x = a$ & $x = b$. Let's not bother about the details of functions $f(x)$, $g(t)$, & $h(t)$ as they may not be related to finance but known to us.

Let's now try applying the FDM steps discussed in the previous section. First, we need to design a mesh for x & t, which shows how the increments Δx & Δt are related.

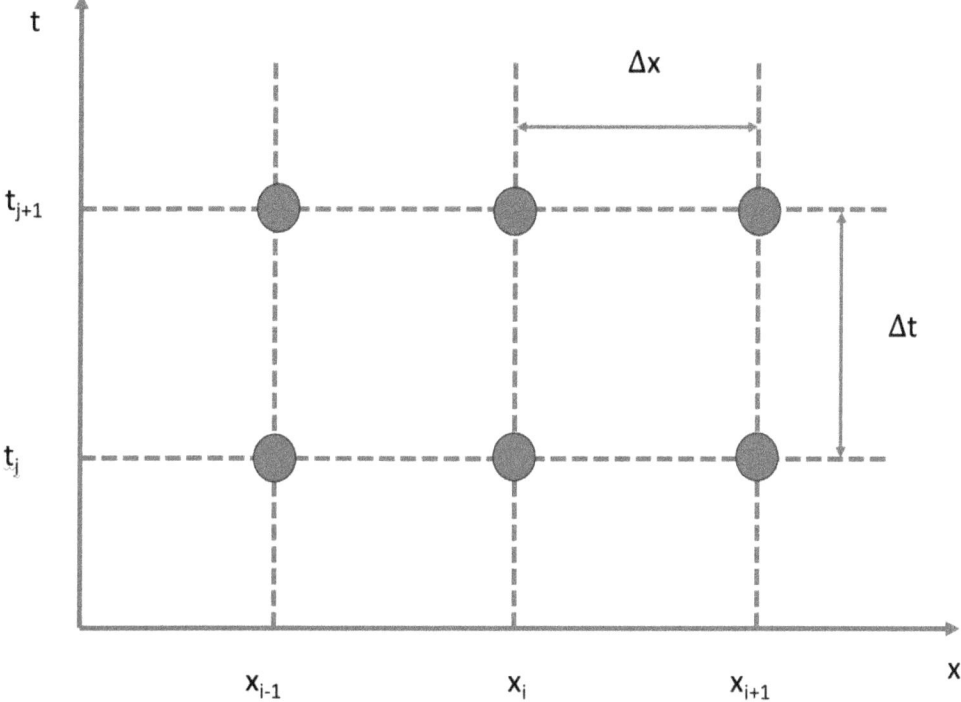

Figure 9-1. *Mesh and the grid points for FDM*

Figure 9-1 shows the grid points and the mesh structure. Note that Δx and Δt are not necessarily the same magnitude as they appear, though they have different measurement units. To apply FDM, x and t must be discretized, as shown in Figure 9-1, and for that, we assume there are N and M steps for them, respectively. With this setup in place, we get

$$\Delta x = \frac{b-a}{N},$$

and each value of x is given by

$$x_i = a + i\Delta x, \quad i = 0,\ldots,N$$

and the same approach goes for Δt

$$\Delta t = \frac{T}{M},$$

CHAPTER 9   PDE, FINITE DIFFERENCE, AND BLACK-SCHOLES MODEL

where T is the time at which we are interested in evaluating u and

$$t_j = t_0 + j\Delta t, \quad j = 0, 1, \ldots, M.$$

The grid points shown as big dots in Figure 9-1 represent value $u_{ij} = (x_i, t_j)$, though a 3D plot could have been a much better representation; however, we will see that once we implement the *explicit* method in Python.

The *explicit* method is also known as *forward Euler's method* as it uses the *forward difference* formula for approximating the first-order derivative w.r.t. time variable t and the *central difference* formula for the second-order derivate w.r.t. space variable x. So, inserting these difference formulae in the heat equation in place of the derivatives, we get

$$\frac{u_{i,j+1} - u_{ij}}{\Delta t} + O(\Delta t) = \alpha \left[\frac{u_{i+1,j} - 2u_{ij} + u_{i-1,j}}{(\Delta x)^2} \right] + O\left((\Delta x)^2\right).$$

We just used some small changes in notations above; for example, $u_{i,j+1}$ is nothing but the $u(x, t + \Delta t)$ at point (x_i, t_j). Ignoring the truncation errors, denoting the term $\frac{\alpha \Delta t}{(\Delta x)^2}$ as λ, and rearranging the whole expression, we get the recurrence relation as

$$u_{i,j+1} = \lambda u_{i-1,j} + (1 - 2\lambda) u_{ij} + \lambda u_{i+1,j}, \quad i = 1, \ldots, N \text{ and } j = 0, 1, \ldots, M.$$

More formally,

$$u_{i,j+1} = a_{Explicit} u_{i-1,j} + b_{Explicit} u_{ij} + c_{Explicit} u_{i+1,j}, \quad i = 1, \ldots, N \text{ and } j = 0, 1, \ldots, M,$$

where

$$a_{Explicit} = \lambda,$$
$$b_{Explicit} = 1 - 2\lambda,$$
$$c_{Explicit} = \lambda$$

The above one is the difference equation of the heat equation. The graphical pattern of the structure of the recurrence relation is known as a *stencil* or a *molecule* and is shown in Figure 9-2.

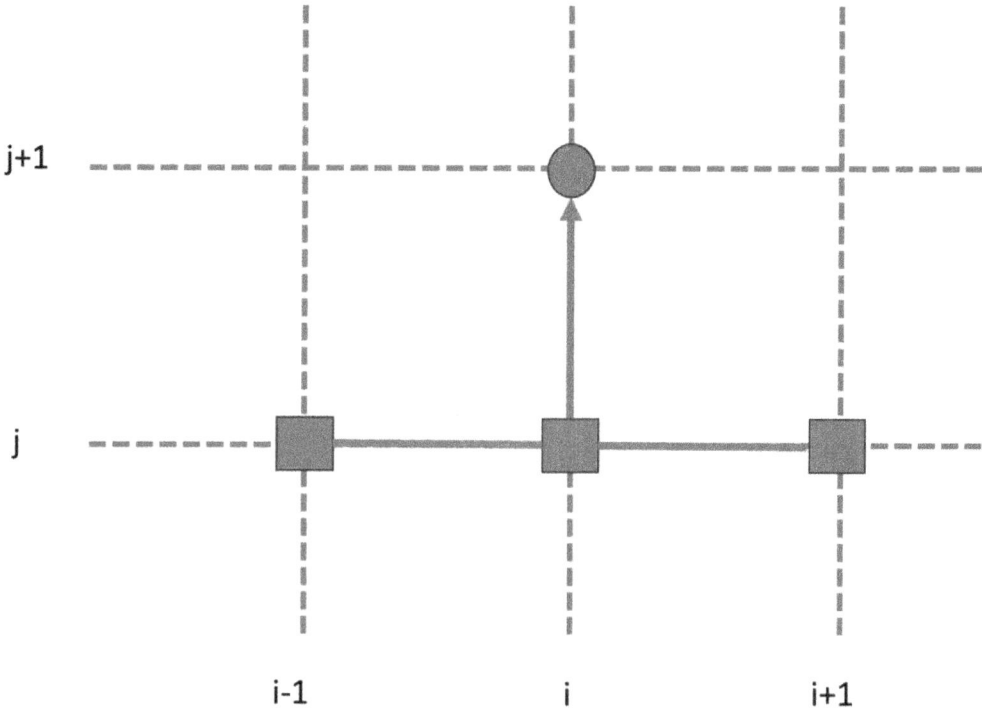

Figure 9-2. *Stencil for explicit FDM (forward Euler's method)*

Squares indicate known points, whereas the circle holds for the unknown. This appears as a recurrence relation; however, the same can be decomposed into a system of linear equations by putting successive values of *i* and *j* like below:

$$u_{11} - \lambda u_{01} - (1-2\lambda)u_{10} - \lambda u_{20} = 0$$
$$u_{22} - \lambda u_{12} - (1-2\lambda)u_{21} - \lambda u_{31} = 0$$

..., and so on.

From the initial and boundary conditions, few values are known to us; for example, all $u_{i,0}$, $u_{1,j}$, and $u_{N,j}$ values (defined for any i and j) are known and given by

$$u_{i,0} = f(x_i), u_{1,j} = g(t_j), u_{N,j} = h(t_j).$$

CHAPTER 9 PDE, FINITE DIFFERENCE, AND BLACK-SCHOLES MODEL

With this in place, $u_{10}, u_{20}, ..., u_{N-1,0}, u_{N,0}$, etc., and $u_{11}, u_{12}, ...u_{1,M-1}, ..., u_{N,1}, u_{N,2},..., u_{N,M-1}$, etc., are known. So, after rearranging, we get

$$\lambda u_{01} = g(t_0)-(1-2\lambda)f(x_1)-\lambda f(x_2)$$
$$u_{22}-(1-2\lambda)u_{21}-\lambda u_{31} = \lambda g(t_2)$$

..., and so on.

We treat u_{01}, u_{22}, u_{21}, etc., values as unknowns, and therefore, a system of linear equations can be written in matrix form

$$\begin{bmatrix} \lambda & 0 & ... & ... \\ 0 & 1 & 1-2\lambda & ... \\ \vdots & \vdots & \vdots & \vdots \end{bmatrix} \begin{bmatrix} u_{01} \\ u_{22} \\ \vdots \end{bmatrix} = \begin{bmatrix} g(t_0)-(1-2\lambda)f(x_1)-\lambda f(x_2) \\ \lambda g(t_2) \\ \vdots \end{bmatrix}.$$

In short,

$$AU = B.$$

And the solution is given by

$$U = A^{-1}B.$$

This is a general approach to solving for the grid points. But, specifically for the explicit scheme, this matrix formation is only for theoretical purposes and is practically not required as A is sparse. All spatial values at i with time $j + 1$ from the stencil can be computed from the previous j. Hence, iterative exploration of the recurrence relation is a good approach to get the output at all grid points. However, for theoretical understanding, let's see what A looks like. The matrix A for the *explicit* method is formally given by

$$A = \begin{bmatrix} 1-2\lambda & \lambda & 0 & \cdots & 0 & 0 \\ \lambda & 1-2\lambda & \lambda & \cdots & 0 & 0 \\ 0 & \lambda & 1-2\lambda & \cdots & 0 & 0 \\ \vdots & \vdots & \vdots & \ddots & \vdots & \vdots \\ 0 & 0 & 0 & \cdots & 1-2\lambda & \lambda \\ 0 & 0 & 0 & \cdots & \lambda & 1-2\lambda \end{bmatrix}$$

$$= \begin{bmatrix} b & c & 0 & \cdots & 0 & 0 \\ a & b & c & \cdots & 0 & 0 \\ 0 & a & b & \cdots & 0 & 0 \\ \vdots & \vdots & \vdots & \ddots & \vdots & \vdots \\ 0 & 0 & 0 & \cdots & b & c \\ 0 & 0 & 0 & \cdots & a & b \end{bmatrix}$$

and the unknown variable matrix as

$$u_{(j)} = \begin{bmatrix} u_{1,j} \\ u_{2,j} \\ \vdots \\ u_{N-1,j} \end{bmatrix}$$

and the boundary value matrix as

$$b_{(j)} = \begin{bmatrix} \lambda u_{0,j} \\ 0 \\ \vdots \\ 0 \\ \lambda u_{N,j} \end{bmatrix}$$

Combining everything in a vector notation, we get

$$u_{(j+1)} = A u_{(j)} + b_{(j)}$$

Again, note that we will not use the above relation to compute $u_{i,j+1}$. It is only for theoretical understanding and analysis of errors discussed later.

CHAPTER 9   PDE, FINITE DIFFERENCE, AND BLACK-SCHOLES MODEL

Python to Implement Explicit Method

In this book, we not only learn to solve second-order PDEs numerically, but the goal is to apply these methods to solve the *Black-Scholes* model for option pricing discussed in the next chapter. Therefore, I thought that building a framework for the same is essential, and hence, I propose a solution template in Python for second-order PDEs using FDM. This also comes with the necessary visualization to plot the solution in 3D. Listing 9-1 shows *SecondOrderFDMSolverTemplate,* a base class for all finite difference methods to solve second-order PDEs.

Listing 9-1. Part of base solution template for second-order PDEs using FDM

```
import numpy as np
from abc import ABC, abstractmethod
import matplotlib.pyplot as plt

class SecondOrderFDMSolverTemplate(ABC):
    """
    Base class for finding solutions of second order PDE using finite
    difference method
    """

    def __init__(self,
                 x_min,  # Max value of spatial variable
                 x_max,  # Min value of sptial variable
                 T,  # Total time
                 M,  # Number of time data points
                 N,  # Number of spatial data points
                 # variables only for plotting the solution
                 func_name="u",
                 space_var_name="x",
                 time_var_name="t",
                 terminal_condition_ind=False
                 ):
        self._u = None
        self._x = None
        self._t = None
```

CHAPTER 9 PDE, FINITE DIFFERENCE, AND BLACK-SCHOLES MODEL

```python
    self._λ = None
    self._M = M
    self._N = N
    self._δx = None
    self._δt = None
    self._terminal_condition_ind = terminal_condition_ind
    self._solution_viz: SecondOrderFDMSolverTemplate._
    Solution3DVisualizer =
        SecondOrderFDMSolverTemplate._Solution3DVisualizer(
        func_name, space_var_name, time_var_name
    )

    self._init_params(x_min, x_max, T)

def _init_params(self, x_min, x_max, T):
    self._δx = (x_max - x_min) / self._N
    self._δt = T / self._M

    # Create vectors of values of the spatial and time variables.
    # By default a uniform mesh is used for both
    self._x = np.arange(x_min, x_max, self._δx)
    self._t = np.arange(0, T, self._δt)

    self._λ = self._δt / (self._δx * self._δx)
    print("λ " + str(self._λ))

    # Filling up the solution vector with initial
    # & boundary conditions
    self._u = np.zeros((self._N, self._M), dtype="float64")
    if self._terminal_condition_ind:
        self._u[:, self._M-1] = [
            self._initial_condition(x_i) for x_i in self._x]
    else:
        self._u[:, 0] = [
            self._initial_condition(x_i) for x_i in self._x]

    self._u[0, :] = [self._first_boundary_condition(
        t_i) for t_i in self._t]
```

```
        self._u[self._N - 1, :] = [
            self._second_boundary_condition(t_i) for t_i in self._t
        ]
```

Look at the function *_init_params* – it creates N and M values for spatial and time variables, computes the value of λ, and, most importantly, fills up the solution vector *u* with the initial and boundary values. Listing 9-2 shows the remaining part of the template.

Listing 9-2. Remaining part of base solution template for second-order PDEs using FDM

```
    def solve(self):
        """
        Function to iterate over solution vector and populating
        using stencil computation logic. It may also use other matrix
        methods than dynamic programming to solve the PDE.
        """
        self._solve_internal()

        self._solution_viz.prepare_solution_for_visual_analysis(
            self._u, self._x, self._t
        )
        return self

    @abstractmethod
    def _solve_internal(self):
        """
        This function should be overridden to include actual computational
        logic - either dynamic programming or LU decomposition
        """
        ...

    @abstractmethod
    def _initial_condition(self, x):
        ...
```

CHAPTER 9 PDE, FINITE DIFFERENCE, AND BLACK-SCHOLES MODEL

```
@abstractmethod
def _first_boundary_condition(self, t):
    ...

@abstractmethod
def _second_boundary_condition(self, t):
    ...
```

Being very specific to the PDE, initial and boundary conditions are kept as abstract functions to be overridden. *HeatEquationExplicitFDMSolverTemplate* leverages the base solution and add few more things to it as shown in Listing 9-3.

Listing 9-3. Template for solving heat equation with explicit FDM

```
class HeatEquationFDMSolverTemplate(SecondOrderFDMSolverTemplate, ABC):

    @abstractmethod
    def _a(self, i=None, j=None):
        ...

    @abstractmethod
    def _b(self, i=None, j=None):
        ...

    @abstractmethod
    def _c(self, i=None, j=None):
        ...

class HeatEquationExplicitFDMSolverTemplate(HeatEquationFDMSolverTemplate, ABC):
    """
    Template Class to solve heat equation using explicit FDM. It
    doesn't contain the initial & boundary conditions
    """

    def _a(self, i=None, j=None):
        return self._λ

    def _b(self, i=None, j=None):
        return 1 - 2 * self._λ
```

CHAPTER 9 PDE, FINITE DIFFERENCE, AND BLACK-SCHOLES MODEL

```
def _c(self, i=None, j=None):
    return self._λ

def _solve_internal(self):
    for i in range(1, self._N - 1):
        for j in range(0, self._M - 1):
            self._u[i][j + 1] = (
                (self._a() * self._u[i - 1][j])
                + (self._b() * self._u[i][j])
                + (self._c() * self._u[i + 1][j])
            )
```

Let's now formally try solving the heat equation with the above templates:

$$\frac{\partial u}{\partial t} = \frac{\partial^2 u}{\partial x^2},$$

with the following initial and boundary conditions:

$$u(x,0) = \sin(2\pi x), \quad 0 < x < 1, t > 0,$$
$$u(0,t) = 0,$$
$$u(1,t) = 0.$$

We create a separate class, *HeatEquationExplicitFDMSolver*, by leveraging the same *HeatEquationExplicitFDMSolverTemplate*, and override the three functions to include the initial and boundary conditions as shown in Listing 9-4.

Listing 9-4. Solver class of the heat equation leveraging the explicit FDM templates

```
class HeatEquationExplicitFDMSolver(HeatEquationExplicitFDMSolverTemplate):
    """
    Class to solve heat equation using explicit FDM. It contains
    initial & boundary conditions
    """

    def _initial_condition(self, x):
        return np.sin(2*np.pi*x)
```

CHAPTER 9   PDE, FINITE DIFFERENCE, AND BLACK-SCHOLES MODEL

```
def _first_boundary_condition(self, t):
    return 0

def _second_boundary_condition(self, t):
    return 0
```

The class hierarchy and structure may sound a little complex as we look at them separately, but once we see the bigger picture in the class diagram, as shown in Figure 9-3, everything should be crystal clear.

Figure 9-3. Class diagram of the FDM framework and the Explicit method component for heat equation

CHAPTER 9 PDE, FINITE DIFFERENCE, AND BLACK-SCHOLES MODEL

Listing 9-5 shows how to test this:

Listing 9-5. Testing the explicit FDM solver

```
def test_heat_equation_explicit_fdm_solver():
    HeatEquationExplicitFDMSolver(x_min=0,
             x_max=1, T=0.2,
             M=1000,
             N=10).solve().plot_solution()
```

We used 1000 spatial and 10 time points to estimate the u(x, t) function. We set T=0.2, which says that we are interested in finding *u(x, t)* at time 0.2 in some sense. But, in this process, we plot the entire function behavior as shown in Figure 9-4.

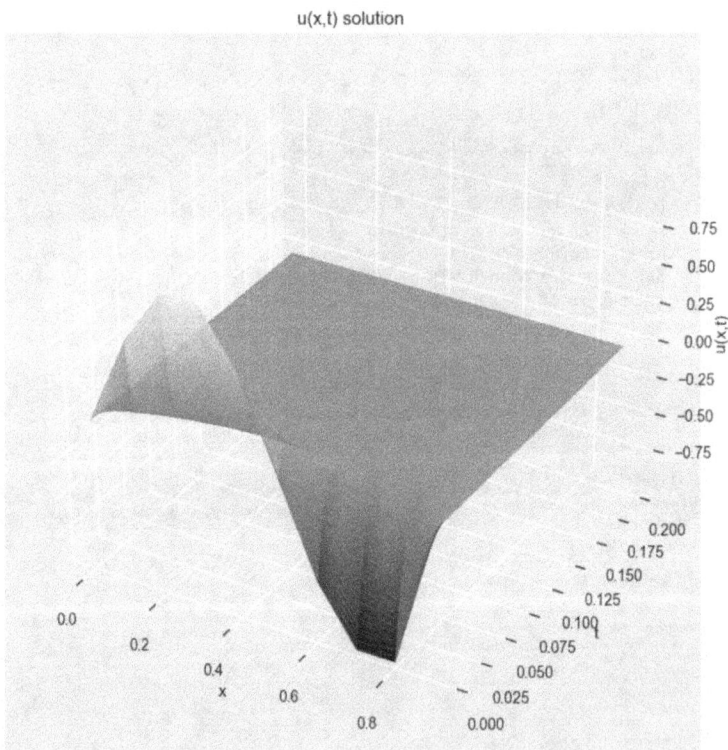

Figure 9-4. *Approximate solution of u(x, t) using explicit method*

You can try with a separate set of initial and boundary functions and plot the solution by making necessary changes in Listing 9-3. This discussion formed a base ground for solving the *Black-Scholes* equation to be discussed in the next chapter.

Stability Analysis

Stability is the impact of the error introduced while estimating $u_{i,j+1}$ in each time step. Notice that the error mainly comes from the term $u_{(j)}$ in relation to $Au_{(j+1)} = u_{(j)} + b_{(j)}$ as the boundary value $b_{(j)}$ is fixed for a specific j. Now, suppose that at jth step, if erroneous estimation is denoted by $\tilde{u}_{(j)}$, then the induced error is

$$\epsilon_{(j)} = u_{(j)} - \tilde{u}_{(j)},$$

and it holds for all time levels. From the explicit method, we can write two equations as follows:

$$u_{(j+1)} = Au_{(j)} + b_{(j)},$$
$$\tilde{u}_{(j+1)} = A\tilde{u}_{(j)} + b_{(j)}$$

Subtracting the second from the first and rearranging, we get

$$\epsilon_{(j+1)} = Au_{(j)} - A\tilde{u}_{(j)} = A\epsilon_{(j)}$$

The recurrence relation can be expanded as $\epsilon_{(j+1)} = A^{j+1}\epsilon_{(0)}$. Being a square matrix, A^{j+1} or A can be taken as linear transformations which makes multiplication of $\epsilon_{(0)}$ by A^{j+1} equivalent to multiplication by its eigenvalue, and the method can only be stable if the resulting limiting value of $\epsilon_{(j+1)}$ reaches zero, i.e., error vanishes up in the line. To make this possible, the eigenvalue of A should be less than one, and the *spectral radius* of A should also be 1 (*spectral radius* is the maxlength of eigenvalues). There are different ways to determine the conditions under which the eigenvalue of A would be less than 1. In one way, A can be expressed as $A = -\lambda T + (1-\lambda)I$ where T is again a tridiagonal matrix (with $a = -1, b = 1, c = -1$), and from there, eigenvalues of A can be expressed as

$$1 + 2\lambda\left(\cos\frac{\pi j}{M+1} - 1\right).$$

Absolute values of the above expression would be less than only if $\lambda < \frac{1}{2}$.

In another way, $\epsilon_{(j+1)}$ can be expressed as an expansion of Fourier series, and from there, conditions on λ can be deduced. Full deduction for both methods is out of the scope of this book; interested readers can refer to *Sandip Mazumder [5] and Zhilin Li [7]* for detailed proof.

CHAPTER 9 PDE, FINITE DIFFERENCE, AND BLACK-SCHOLES MODEL

In a nutshell, the *explicit* method is always conditionally stable with a setting $\lambda < \frac{1}{2}$, i.e., failing to do so will increase the error. As $\lambda = \frac{\alpha \Delta t}{(\Delta x)^2} > 0$, and from the condition $\lambda < \frac{1}{2}$, the following relation holds:

$$0 < \Delta t \leq \frac{(\Delta x)^2}{2\alpha}.$$

Δt and Δx should be carefully chosen to meet the above criteria. We always consider $\alpha = 1$ in the discussed example, as shown in Listing 9-5, which produces a value of 0.0199 for λ. The same can be tested in the printed statement of the console upon running the test case.

Implicit Method

The basic idea and mechanism are almost the same for the implicit method, similar to the explicit one discussed in the previous section, with the only difference in computing the time derivative as it is approximated by a *backward difference* formula. So, inserting the same in the heat equation, we get

$$\frac{u_{ij} - u_{i,j-1}}{\Delta t} + O(\Delta t) = \alpha \left[\frac{u_{i+1,j} - 2u_{ij} + u_{i-1,j}}{(\Delta x)^2} \right] + O\left((\Delta x)^2\right).$$

Rearranging the expression using similar techniques as done in the *explicit* method, we get

$$-\lambda u_{i-1,j} + (1 + 2\lambda) u_{ij} - \lambda u_{i+1,j} = u_{i,j-1}$$

where $i = 1, \ldots, N-1$ and $j = 1, \ldots, M$. λ is as usual considered as $\frac{\alpha \Delta t}{(\Delta x)^2}$. More formally,

$$a_{Implicit} u_{i-1,j} + b_{Implicit} u_{ij} + c_{Implicit} u_{i+1,j} = u_{i,j-1}$$

where

$$a_{Implicit} = -\lambda,$$
$$b_{Implicit} = 1+2\lambda,$$
$$c_{Implicit} = -\lambda.$$

Figure 9-5 is the stencil representation of the equation.

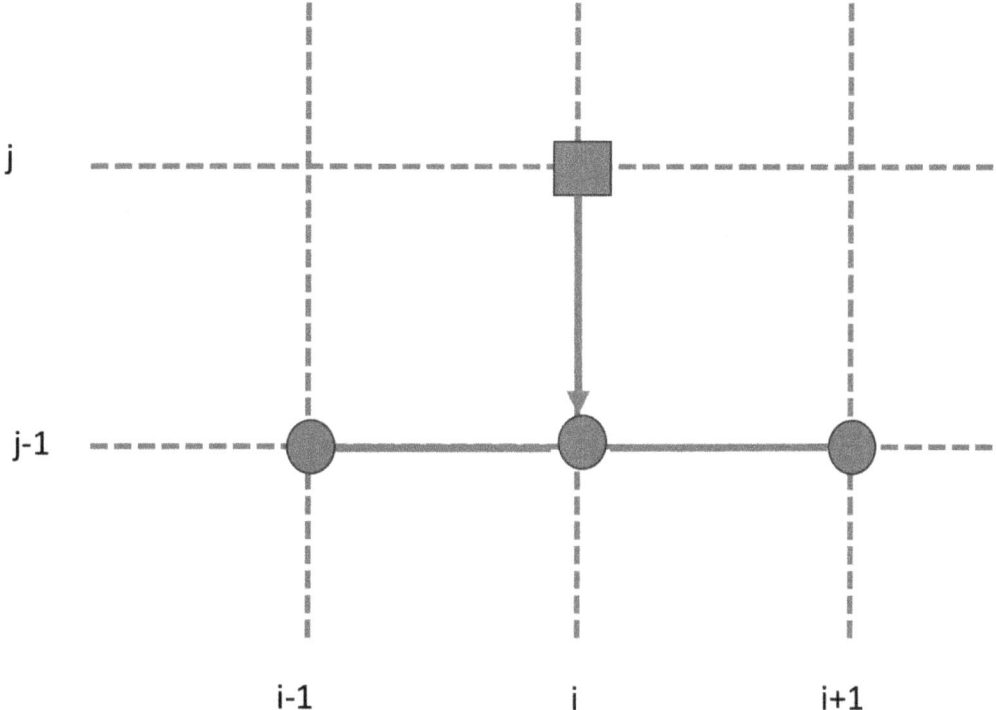

Figure 9-5. *Stencil for implicit FDM (backward Euler's method)*

Observe that there are no explicit formulae that can be iteratively and recursively applied to compute grid points, unlike the *explicit* method. To travel from time level j-1 to the next, we don't know any value at that time for any other spatial points except the ith one (stencil shows number of unknowns is three). That makes the iterative determination of unknowns difficult; if possible, they must be determined at once. To do that, we fall back to the method of forming the system of linear equations as explained earlier in short for the explicit method though we didn't use it there, now it's time to leverage it fully.

CHAPTER 9 PDE, FINITE DIFFERENCE, AND BLACK-SCHOLES MODEL

To proceed, let's write down first the decomposed system of equations:

$$-\lambda u_{0,j} + (1+2\lambda)u_{1,j} - \lambda u_{2,j} = u_{1,j-1},$$

$$-\lambda u_{1,j} + (1+2\lambda)u_{2,j} - \lambda u_{3,j} = u_{2,j-1},$$

$$\vdots$$

$$-\lambda u_{N-2,j} + (1+2\lambda)u_{N-1,j} - \lambda u_{N,j} = u_{N-1,j-1}.$$

As usual, a few of $u_{i,j}$ will be known to us - $u_{i,0}$, $u_{1,j}$, $u_{N,j}$ - from boundary and initial conditions. With this, values of $u_{1,0}$, $u_{2,0}$, etc., and u_{11}, u_{12}, ...$u_{1,M-1}$, ..., $u_{N,1}$, $u_{N,2}$,..., $u_{N,M-1}$, etc., are known, and that makes $u_{1,j}$, $u_{2,j}$,..., $u_{N-1,j}$ as unknown variables. Applying this setting, we get the coefficient matrix for the systems of equations as

$$A = \begin{bmatrix} 1+2\lambda & -\lambda & 0 & \cdots & 0 & 0 \\ -\lambda & 1+2\lambda & -\lambda & \cdots & 0 & 0 \\ 0 & -\lambda & 1+2\lambda & \cdots & 0 & 0 \\ \vdots & \vdots & \vdots & \ddots & \vdots & \vdots \\ 0 & 0 & 0 & \cdots & 1+2\lambda & -\lambda \\ 0 & 0 & 0 & \cdots & -\lambda & 1+2\lambda \end{bmatrix}$$

and the unknown variable matrix as

$$u_{(j)} = \begin{bmatrix} u_{1,j} \\ u_{2,j} \\ \vdots \\ u_{N-1,j} \end{bmatrix}$$

and the boundary value matrix as

$$b_{(j)} = \begin{bmatrix} \lambda u_{0,j} \\ 0 \\ \vdots \\ 0 \\ \lambda u_{N,j} \end{bmatrix}$$

CHAPTER 9   PDE, FINITE DIFFERENCE, AND BLACK-SCHOLES MODEL

Combining everything in a vector notation, we get

$$Au_{(j-1)} = u_{(j)} + b_{(j)}$$

This is in the same form as $AU = B$, whose solution is given by $U = A^{-1}B$. By theory, everything looks good, but in practice, it is not so easy. A is a sparse matrix, and computing its inverse is costly. Moreover, the equation $Au_{(j-1)} = u_{(j)} + b_{(j)}$ has multiple right-hand sides with the same coefficient matrix A which makes the system ideal candidate for LU decomposition.

LU stands for lower and upper triangular decomposition of a sparse matrix, i.e., coefficient matrix A can be decomposed into two matrices – lower triangular L and upper triangular U, and with this, A = LU, and the equation becomes

$$LUu_{(j-1)} = u_{(j)} + b_{(j)}.$$

Let's introduce a temporary variable $w_{(j+1)} = Uu_{(j+1)}$, and it makes the system as

$$Lw_{(j-1)} = u_{(j)} + b_{(j)}.$$

Being attached to a lower triangular matrix, $w_{(j+1)}$ can be found out with *forward substitution* and can be written as

$$w_{(j-1)} = L^{-1}\left(u_{(j)} + b_{(j)}\right).$$

In the same way, with *backward substitution*, we can solve $w_{(j+1)} = Uu_{(j+1)}$ for $u_{(j+1)}$:

$$u_{(j-1)} = U^{-1}w_{(j+1)}.$$

Putting the expression of $w_{(j+1)}$ there, we get the full solution written as

$$u_{(j-1)} = U^{-1}\left\{L^{-1}\left(u_{(j)} + b_{(j)}\right)\right\}.$$

You might be thinking, what's the point of doing so much computation to avoid an inverse where ultimately, we ended up doing two inverses L^{-1} and U^{-1}. Hold on, this pair looks like an inverse, and of course, theoretically, they are, but practically, they are computed using the forward and backward substitution as L and U are lower and upper

CHAPTER 9 PDE, FINITE DIFFERENCE, AND BLACK-SCHOLES MODEL

triangular matrices. These substitution methods are like Gaussian elimination and can be performed easily. To fully understand the topic, you need to have good knowledge of linear algebra and matrix theory, and for more details on that, refer *Dimitris Mitsotakis [6]*.

Python to Implement Implicit Method

Before discussing any design, let's focus on matrix A. It is a sparse tridiagonal matrix. Our first task would be to generate this matrix with $a_{Implicit}$, $b_{Implicit}$, and $c_{Implicit}$. The matrix looks like

$$A = \begin{bmatrix} b_{Implicit} & c_{Implicit} & 0 & \cdots & 0 & 0 \\ a_{Implicit} & b_{Implicit} & c_{Implicit} & \cdots & 0 & 0 \\ 0 & a_{Implicit} & b_{Implicit} & \cdots & 0 & 0 \\ \vdots & \vdots & \vdots & \ddots & \vdots & \vdots \\ 0 & 0 & 0 & \cdots & b_{Implicit} & c_{Implicit} \\ 0 & 0 & 0 & \cdots & a_{Implicit} & b_{Implicit} \end{bmatrix}$$

The main diagonal contains $b_{Implicit}$, $b_{Implicit}$...; upper diagonal contains $c_{Implicit}$, $c_{Implicit}$...; and the lower diagonal contains $a_{Implicit}$, $a_{Implicit}$.... To create this structure, we use *scipy* module and import required submodule:

from scipy.sparse import diags.

We create three arrays for $a_{Implicit}$, $b_{Implicit}$, and $c_{Implicit}$, respectively:

```
a = [self._a(i=i) for i in range(self._N-1)]
b = [self._b(i=i) for i in range(self._N-1)]
c = [self._c(i=i) for i in range(self._N-1)].
```

You might be thinking that weights *a*, *b*, and *c* are constants. But it is not always true. For the vanilla heat equation, they are constants, but when we touch upon the *Black-Scholes* model, we will see that these depend on x_i, i.e., the ith value of spatial variable x. And that's the purpose of creating arrays, as the templates we are building will work as a framework. Anyway, now we create the tridiagonal matrix A like below:

```
A = diags([a, b, c],
    [-1, 0, 1], shape=(self._N-1, self._N-1),
    dtype="float64").toarray().
```

To perform LU factorization, we use the *linalg* module:

```
from scipy.linalg import lu_factor, lu_solve
```

Matrix A should be factored into LU and a pivot matrix like below:

```
lu, piv = lu_factor(A)
```

Boundary condition array b should be initialized with zeros:

```
β = np.zeros(self._N-1, dtype="float64")
```

Note that the solution represented by the equation

$$u_{(j-1)} = U^{-1}\left\{L^{-1}\left(u_{(j)} + b_{(j)}\right)\right\}$$

should be performed at each time level. We solve the system at time level j for all spatial values, then proceed to the previous time level, and repeat the same process until we reach the target time. Doesn't it sound like an iterative process? Yes, it is. But in that case, isn't it contradicting what I said earlier – "That makes the iterative determination of unknowns difficult; if possible, they must be determined at once"? Well, not really. Unlike the explicit method, we don't iterate over spatial variables, we do it only for time levels. At each time level, we solve the system of equations like below and fill up all spatial variables with the solution:

```
self._u[1:, j-1] = lu_solve((lu, piv), self._u[1:, j] + β)
```

Note that we move backward in time for the implicit method. That makes sense both from applicability and theoretical perspectives. We used backward-difference formulae for time derivative estimation, which estimates $u(x, t)$ from $u(x, t - \Delta t)$ by moving backward on time. The same goes for while estimating a financial option's value, we are given the payoff value at expiry time from which premium must be computed, i.e., the value at time t =0.

After all these discussions, let's stitch together all moving parts. For that, we create a class *HeatEquationImplicitFDMSolverTemplate* in the same fashion as we did for the *explicit* method by extending from *HeatEquationFDMSolverTemplate* and overriding a few methods by putting all the code snippets discussed earlier. Listing 9-6 shows the body of the class.

333

CHAPTER 9 PDE, FINITE DIFFERENCE, AND BLACK-SCHOLES MODEL

Listing 9-6. Template for solving heat equation with implicit FDM

```
class
HeatEquationImplicitFDMSolverTemplate(HeatEquationFDMSolverTemplate, ABC):
    """
    Abstract class to solve heat equation using implicit FDM. It
    doesn't contain
    initial & boundary conditions
    """

    def _a(self, i=None, j=None):
        return -self._λ

    def _b(self, i=None, j=None):
        return 2*self._λ + 1

    def _c(self, i=None, j=None):
        return -self._λ

    def _solve_internal(self):
        a = [self._a(i=i) for i in range(self._N)]
        b = [self._b(i=i) for i in range(self._N)]
        c = [self._c(i=i) for i in range(self._N)]
        '''
        Create a tridiagonal matrix of coefficients represented
                        by A in equation
                    Au(j - 1) = u(j) + b(j)
        '''
        A = diags([a, b, c],
                  [-1, 0, 1], shape=(self._N-1, self._N-1),
                  dtype="float64").toarray()
        '''
        Decompose A into lower-triangular L & upper-triangular
        U by LU factorization
        '''
```

CHAPTER 9 PDE, FINITE DIFFERENCE, AND BLACK-SCHOLES MODEL

```
lu, piv = lu_factor(A)
'''
  Initialize an array β for boundary values represented
                    by b in equation
                  Au(j - 1) = u(j) + b(j)
'''
β = np.zeros(self._N-1, dtype="float64")
from_index, to_index = (
    self._M-2, 0) if self._terminal_condition_ind else
    (self._M-1, 1)

for j in range(from_index, to_index, -1):
    β[0] = a[1] * self._u[0][j]
    β[-1] = c[-1] * self._u[-1][j]
'''
  Directly get the solution by lu_solve and
  avoid computing
          u(j - 1) = U⁻¹{L⁻¹(u(j) + b(j))}
  which is a two step process
'''
    self._u[1:, j-1] = lu_solve((lu, piv), self._u[1:, j] + β)
```

Notice the usage of *terminal_condition_ind*, it controls the direction of movement in the timeline. To leverage this template and add necessary boundary conditions, we create a class *HeatEquationImplicitFDMSolver* exactly in the same fashion as we did for the *explicit* method, as shown earlier in Listing 9-4. The same can be tested as shown in Listing 9-7.

Listing 9-7. Testing the implicit FDM solver

```
def test_heat_equation_implicit_fdm_solver():
    HeatEquationImplicitFDMSolver(x_min=0,
            x_max=1, T=0.2,
            M=1000,
            N=10, terminal_condition_ind=True).solve().plot_solution()
```

CHAPTER 9   PDE, FINITE DIFFERENCE, AND BLACK-SCHOLES MODEL

In this context, let's discuss something about the initial conditions. In the *explicit* method, initial conditions are truly *initial* by nature, i.e., they are defined at t=0. But, for the *implicit* one, we define the same at t=T, i.e., at the final time, and from there, we move backward. Let's have a relook at some of code snippets from Listing 9-1:

```
if self._terminal_condition_ind:
    self._u[:, self._M-1] = [
        self._initial_condition(x_i) for x_i in self._x]
else:
    self._u[:, 0] = [
        self._initial_condition(x_i) for x_i in self._x]
```

It shows that the condition is set at t=T or t=0 depending on the choice of the flag *_terminal_condition_ind*. With all that in place, Listing 9-7 produces output as shown in Figure 9-6.

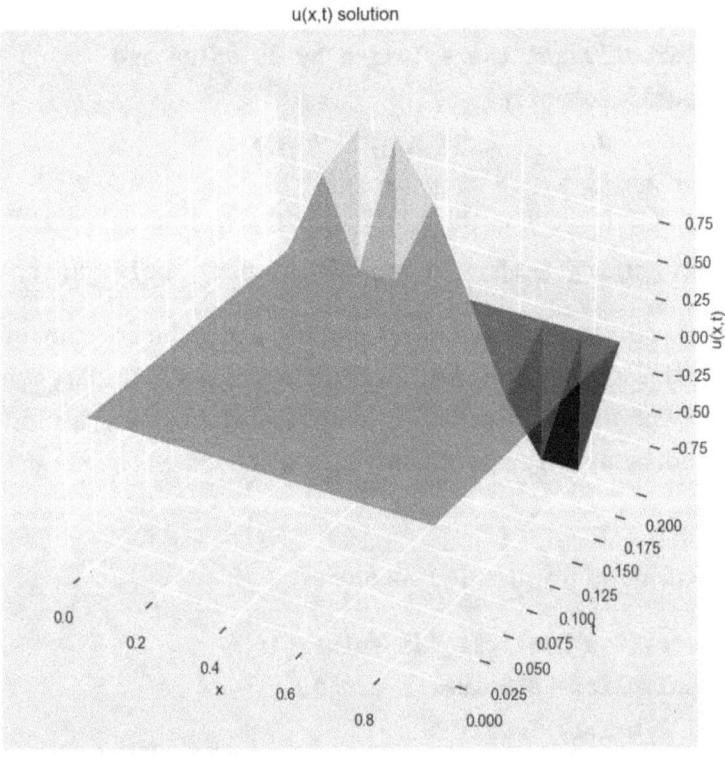

Figure 9-6. *Approximate solution of u(x, t) using implicit method*

The pattern of the solution changed due to the change in initial conditions.

CHAPTER 9　PDE, FINITE DIFFERENCE, AND BLACK-SCHOLES MODEL

Stability Analysis

Following the same line of discussion done for the *explicit* method, two equations for actual and estimated $u_{i,j-1}$ can be written as

$$Au_{(j-1)} = u_{(j)} + b_{(j)}$$
$$A\tilde{u}_{(j-1)} = \tilde{u}_{(j)} + b_{(j)}.$$

The error term can be expressed as

$$A\epsilon_{(j-1)} = u_{(j)} - \tilde{u}_{(j)} = \epsilon_{(j)}$$

or

$$\epsilon_{(j-1)} = A^{-1}\epsilon_{(j)}.$$

From the above expression, it is evident that we must find out the eigenvalues of A^{-1} unlike that of A as done in the *explicit* method. For implicit case, A can be expressed as $A = \lambda T + (1+\lambda)I$, and its eigenvalues are given by

$$1 + 2\lambda\left(1 - \cos\frac{\pi j}{M+1}\right).$$

Eigenvalues of A^{-1} are just the reciprocals of the above one. Notice that the expression of eigenvalues is always greater than 1, which makes the reciprocal always less than 1, irrespective of any value of λ. So, it is not conditional on λ; hence, the implicit method is unconditionally stable. There are no restrictions on choosing Δt and Δx (for proof using Fourier expansion, please refer to *Sandip Mazumder [5] and Zhilin Li [7]*).

Crank-Nicolson Method

To improve the stability of the implicit method, another one, named as Crank-Nicolson method (prescribed by *J. Crank and P. Nicolson, Cambridge Philosophical Society, 43*), takes the average of two central difference derivatives defined at t_j and t_{j-1} for estimating $\frac{\partial^2 u}{\partial x^2}$ and rest is kept unchanged. Following the same, the difference equation is rewritten as

CHAPTER 9   PDE, FINITE DIFFERENCE, AND BLACK-SCHOLES MODEL

$$\frac{u_{ij} - u_{i,j-1}}{\Delta t} + O(\Delta t)$$

$$= \alpha \left[\frac{1}{2} \left(\frac{u_{i+1,j} - 2u_{ij} + u_{i-1,j}}{(\Delta x)^2} \right) + \frac{1}{2} \left(\frac{u_{i+1,j-1} - 2u_{i,j-1} + u_{i-1,j-1}}{(\Delta x)^2} \right) \right]$$

$$+ O\big((\Delta x)^2\big).$$

Ignoring error terms and rearranging,

$$-\lambda u_{i-1,j} + (2+2\lambda) u_{ij} - \lambda u_{i+1,j} = \lambda u_{i-1,j-1} + (2-2\lambda) u_{i,j-1} + \lambda u_{i+1,j-1}.$$

There are four terms for the *Crank-Nicolson* method, and they are given by

$$a_{CN} = \lambda,$$
$$b_{CN} = 2 + 2\lambda,$$
$$c_{CN} = \lambda,$$
$$d_{CN} = 2 - 2\lambda.$$

The final equation looks like this:

$$-a_{CN} u_{i-1,j} + b_{CN} u_{ij} - c_{CN} u_{i+1,j} = a_{CN} u_{i-1,j-1} + d_{CN} u_{i,j-1} + c_{CN} u_{i+1,j-1}.$$

Figure 9-7 shows the stencil representation of the Crank-Nicolson method.

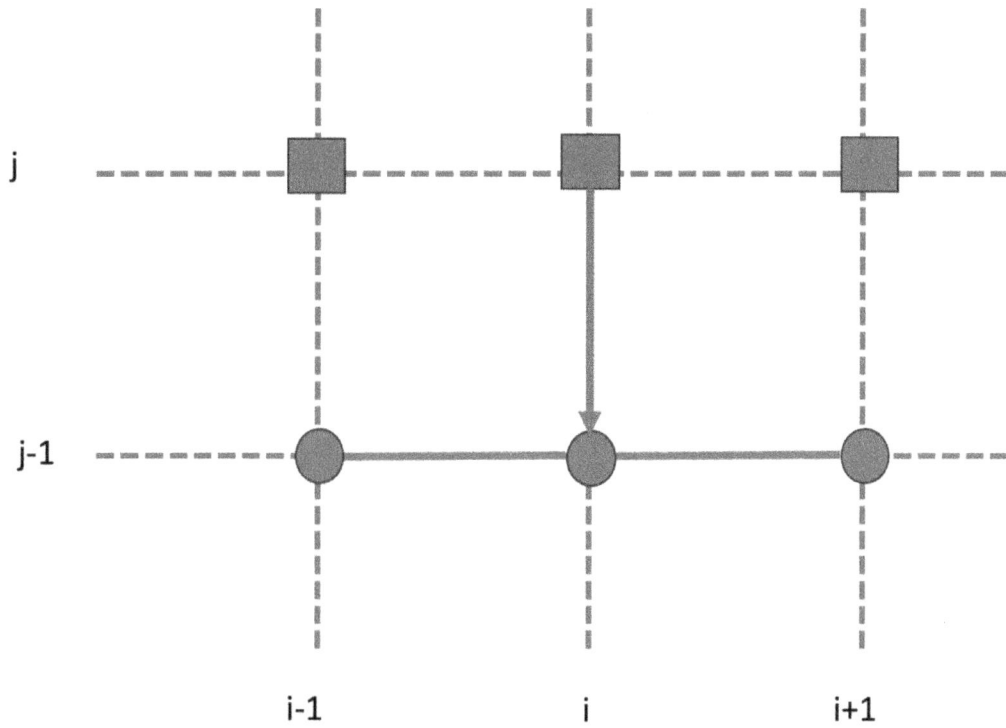

Figure 9-7. *Stencil for Crank-Nicolson FDM*

Decomposing the above equation into a system of equations, we get two coefficient matrices:

$$A = \begin{bmatrix} 2+2\lambda & -\lambda & 0 & \cdots & 0 & 0 \\ -\lambda & 2+2\lambda & -\lambda & \cdots & 0 & 0 \\ 0 & -\lambda & 2+2\lambda & \cdots & 0 & 0 \\ \vdots & \vdots & \vdots & \ddots & \vdots & \vdots \\ 0 & 0 & 0 & \cdots & 2+2\lambda & -\lambda \\ 0 & 0 & 0 & \cdots & -\lambda & 2+2\lambda \end{bmatrix}$$

$$B = \begin{bmatrix} 2-2\lambda & \lambda & 0 & \cdots & 0 & 0 \\ \lambda & 2-2\lambda & \lambda & \cdots & 0 & 0 \\ 0 & \lambda & 2-2\lambda & \cdots & 0 & 0 \\ \vdots & \vdots & \vdots & \ddots & \vdots & \vdots \\ 0 & 0 & 0 & \cdots & 2-2\lambda & \lambda \\ 0 & 0 & 0 & \cdots & \lambda & 2-2\lambda \end{bmatrix}$$

CHAPTER 9   PDE, FINITE DIFFERENCE, AND BLACK-SCHOLES MODEL

and the boundary value matrix,

$$b_{(j)} = \begin{bmatrix} \lambda u_{0,j-1} + \lambda u_{0,j} \\ 0 \\ \vdots \\ 0 \\ \lambda u_{N,j-1} + \lambda u_{N,j} \end{bmatrix}$$

Combining everything in matrix-vector notation, we get

$$Au_{(j-1)} = Bu_{(j)} + b_{(j)}$$

By following the same LU decomposition method, the solution is obtained as

$$u_{(j-1)} = U^{-1}\left\{L^{-1}\left(Bu_{(j)} + b_{(j)}\right)\right\}$$

To solve the heat equation with all these and implement everything in Python, we create two classes *BaseHeatEquationCrankNicolsonFDMSolverTemplate* and *HeatEquationCrankNicolsonFDMSolverTemplate* as shown in Listing 9-8.

Listing 9-8. Template for solving heat equation with Crank-Nicolson FDM

```
class BaseHeatEquationCrankNicolsonFDMSolverTemplate(HeatEquationFDMSolver
Template, ABC):

    @abstractmethod
    def _d(self, i=None, j=None):
        ...

class HeatEquationCrankNicolsonFDMSolverTemplate(BaseHeatEquationCrank
NicolsonFDMSolverTemplate, ABC):

    """
    Abstract class to solve heat equation using Crank-Nicolson FDM. It It
    doesn't contain
    initial & boundary conditions
    """
```

```python
def _a(self, i=None, j=None):
    return self._λ

def _b(self, i=None, j=None):
    return 2 + 2*self._λ

def _c(self, i=None, j=None):
    return self._λ

def _d(self, i=None, j=None):
    return 2 - 2*self._λ

def _solve_internal(self):
    a = np.array([self._a(i=i) for i in range(self._N-1)])
    b = np.array([self._b(i=i) for i in range(self._N-1)])
    c = np.array([self._c(i=i) for i in range(self._N-1)])
    d = np.array([self._d(i=i) for i in range(self._N-1)])

    '''
      Create a tridiagonal matrix of coefficients represented
      by A in equation
          Au_(j - 1) = Bu_(j) + b_(j)
    '''
    A = diags([-a, b, -c],
              [-1, 0, 1], shape=(self._N-1, self._N-1),
              dtype="float64").toarray()

    '''
      Create a tridiagonal matrix of coefficients represented
      by B in equation
          Au_(j - 1) = Bu_(j) + b_(j)
    '''
    B = diags([a, d, c],
              [-1, 0, 1], shape=(self._N-1, self._N-1),
              dtype="float64").toarray()

    lu, piv = lu_factor(A)
```

```
...
    Initialize an array β for boundary values represented
    by b in equation
        Au(j - 1) = Bu(j) + b(j)
...

β = np.zeros(self._N-1, dtype="float64")

from_index, to_index = (
    self._M-2, 0) if self._terminal_condition_ind else
    (self._M-1, 1)

for j in range(from_index, to_index, -1):
    β[0] = a[1] * (self._u[0][j] + self._u[0][j-1])
    β[-1] = c[-1] * (self._u[-1][j] + self._u[-1][j-1])
    
    ...
        Directly get the solution by lu_solve and
            avoid computing
                u(j - 1) = U⁻¹{L⁻¹(Bu(j) + b(j))}
        which is a two-step process
    ...
    self._u[1:, j-1] = lu_solve((lu, piv),
                            B.dot(self._u[1:, j]) + β)
```

As the *Crank-Nicolson* method is another backward-difference-based method, its initial conditions should be the same as the *implicit* method discussed earlier. With that in place, the template defined in Listing 9-8 can be tested with a solver class *HeatEquationCrankNicolsonFDMSolver*, which produces a similar output to Figure 9-6.

Stability Analysis

To investigate the stability of the *Crank-Nicolson* method, let's first write down the equations:

$$Au_{(j-1)} = Bu_{(j)} + b_{(j)},$$
$$A\tilde{u}_{(j-1)} = B\tilde{u}_{(j)} + b_{(j)}.$$

CHAPTER 9   PDE, FINITE DIFFERENCE, AND BLACK-SCHOLES MODEL

The error term can be expressed as

$$A\epsilon_{(j-1)} = Bu_{(j)} - B\tilde{u}_{(j)} = B\epsilon_{(j)}$$

or

$$\epsilon_{(j-1)} = A^{-1}B\epsilon_{(j)}.$$

So, for the *implicit* method, we must find out the eigenvalues of $A^{-1}B$. Now both A and B can be expressed as $A = \lambda T + (2 + \lambda)I$ and $B = -\lambda T + (2 - \lambda)I$. From there, the eigenvalues of $A^{-1}B$ is obtained as

$$\frac{4}{\lambda\left(1 - 2\cos\frac{\pi j}{M+1} + 1\right) + 2} - 1.$$

The above expression lies between -1 and 1, and the range is independent of λ. Therefore, the Crank-Nicolson method, just like the implicit method, is unconditionally stable (please refer to *Sandip Mazumder [5] and Zhilin Li [7]* for a detailed proof with Fourier expansion).

Black-Scholes PDE

We know the value of option V is a function of S, i.e., another diffusion process, so by 2D Ito lemma, we can write

$$\begin{aligned}
dV &= \frac{\partial V}{\partial S}dS + \frac{\partial V}{\partial t}dt + \frac{1}{2}\frac{\partial^2 V}{\partial S^2}\sigma^2 S^2 dt \\
&= \frac{\partial V}{\partial S}(\mu S dt + \sigma S dW_t) + \frac{\partial V}{\partial t}dt + \frac{1}{2}\frac{\partial^2 V}{\partial S^2}\sigma^2 S^2 dt \\
&= \left(\frac{\partial V}{\partial S}\mu S + \frac{\partial V}{\partial t} + \frac{1}{2}\frac{\partial^2 V}{\partial S^2}\sigma^2 S^2\right)dt + \frac{\partial V}{\partial S}\sigma S dW_t
\end{aligned}$$

CHAPTER 9   PDE, FINITE DIFFERENCE, AND BLACK-SCHOLES MODEL

Clearly, the differential equation is now decomposed into the drift and diffusion part. The Black-Scholes model is based on the idea of eliminating the risk-term dW_t, so for that, we create a portfolio P by borrowing m of units of money from the bank at risk-free rate r, buying α units of the same asset S, and the resultant differential is given as follows:

$$dP = \alpha dS + rmMdt.$$

Adding dP to dV creates another composite portfolio as follows (refer to basic interest theory in Chapter 2):

$$dV + dP$$
$$= \left(\frac{\partial V}{\partial S}\mu S + \frac{\partial V}{\partial t} + \frac{1}{2}\frac{\partial^2 V}{\partial S^2}\sigma^2 S^2\right)dt + \frac{\partial V}{\partial S}\sigma S dW_t + \alpha dS + rmMdt$$
$$= \left(\frac{\partial V}{\partial S}\mu S + \frac{\partial V}{\partial t} + \frac{1}{2}\frac{\partial^2 V}{\partial S^2}\sigma^2 S^2 + \alpha\mu S + rmM\right)dt + \left(\frac{\partial V}{\partial S}\sigma S + \alpha S\right)dW_t.$$

To make the composite portfolio completely risk free, we need to zero out the diffusion term dW_t and that can only be done with the coefficient being zero, i.e.,

$$\frac{\partial V}{\partial S}\sigma S + \alpha S = 0$$

or

$$\alpha = -\frac{\partial V}{\partial S}.$$

Putting this value in $dV + dP$, we get

$$dV + dP = \left(\frac{\partial V}{\partial t} + \frac{1}{2}\frac{\partial^2 V}{\partial S^2}\sigma^2 S^2 + rmM\right)dt.$$

There is no diffusion term in the above composite portfolio, which makes it give fixed returns, i.e., the portfolio asset becomes deterministic rather than stochastic. With this idea, we can also write $dV + dP$ in some other way as follows:

$$dV + dP = \left(V - \frac{\partial V}{\partial S}S + mM\right)rdt.$$

CHAPTER 9 PDE, FINITE DIFFERENCE, AND BLACK-SCHOLES MODEL

Equating both forms,

$$\left(\frac{\partial V}{\partial t}+\frac{1}{2}\frac{\partial^2 V}{\partial S^2}\sigma^2 S^2 + rmM\right)dt = \left(V - \frac{\partial V}{\partial S}S + mM\right)rdt.$$

With the cancelation of some of the terms, we get the final version of the famous *Black-Scholes PDE* as follows (irrespective of *call* or *put*):

$$\frac{\partial V}{\partial t}+\frac{1}{2}\frac{\partial^2 V}{\partial S^2}\sigma^2 S^2 + \frac{\partial V}{\partial S}rS - rV = 0.$$

The idea of creating a composite portfolio is to make the process self-financing, but this holds true only for theoretical settings. The assumption we made in Chapter 8 for Black-Scholes models also applies here, i.e., the absence of jumps in the asset price, dividends are not paid, etc. In true market conditions, most of these don't hold good, but this model still gives us a base recommendation for evaluating options.

I hope you already understood by this time that the numerical solution of the Black-Scholes PDE is the most preferred way, as the closed-form solution is difficult to derive. Risk-neutral probability approach discussed in Chapter 8 gave a complete closed-form solution of the Black-Scholes model by considering the PDF. However, PDE approach also follows the same risk neutrality but focuses mainly on the state dynamics rather taking the PDF explicitly. Not only Black-Scholes model but also the PDE approach demonstrates how to solve any derivative pricing problem by constructing the PDE first and going for numerical approximation. Next, we see how to apply the implicit method to solve Black-Scholes PDE.

Implicit FDM for the Black-Scholes Model

The Black-Scholes PDE has three derivatives – $\frac{\partial V}{\partial t}$, $\frac{\partial V}{\partial S}$, and $\frac{\partial^2 V}{\partial S^2}$.

All of these can be approximated by the forward and central difference formulae as follows:

$$\frac{\partial V}{\partial t} = \frac{V(S,t+\Delta t)-V(S,t)}{\Delta t} + O(\Delta t),$$

$$\frac{\partial^2 V}{\partial S^2} = \frac{V(S+\Delta S,t)-2V(S,t)+V(S-\Delta S,t)}{(\Delta S)^2} + O\big((\Delta S)\big)^2,$$

$$\frac{\partial V}{\partial S} = \frac{V(S+\Delta S,t)-V(S-\Delta S,t)}{2\Delta S} + O\big((\Delta S)\big)^2.$$

CHAPTER 9   PDE, FINITE DIFFERENCE, AND BLACK-SCHOLES MODEL

We denote the approximation solution vector as $u_{ij} = V(S_i, t_j)$, i.e., the value of the options as a set of grid points at different times. Putting these derivative approximations in the Black-Scholes PDE, we get

$$\frac{u_{i,j+1} - u_{ij}}{\Delta t} + \frac{1}{2}\sigma^2 S_i^2 \frac{u_{i+1,j} - 2u_{ij} + u_{i-1,j}}{(\Delta S)^2} + rS_i \frac{u_{i+1,j} - u_{i-1,j}}{2\Delta S} - ru_{ij} = 0.$$

Rearranging the above equation as per the implicit finite difference equation,

$$a_i u_{i-1,j} + b_i u_{ij} + c_i u_{i+1,j} = u_{i,j-1},$$

where

$$a_i = \frac{1}{2}\Delta t \left\{ r\frac{S_i}{\Delta S} - \sigma^2 \left(\frac{S_i}{\Delta S}\right)^2 \right\},$$

$$b_i = 1 + \Delta t \left\{ \sigma^2 \left(\frac{S_i}{\Delta S}\right)^2 + r \right\},$$

$$c_i = -\frac{1}{2}\Delta t \left\{ r\frac{S_i}{\Delta S} + \sigma^2 \left(\frac{S_i}{\Delta S}\right)^2 \right\}.$$

Step length ΔS is determined as $\Delta S = \frac{S_{max} - S_{min}}{N}$, where $S_i = S_{min} + i\Delta S$. S_{max} and S_{min} are maximum and minimum possible values of S, though sometimes $S_{min} = S_0$ is implicitly assumed.

Integration with Diffusion Model and Python Implementation

Using a guess for S_{max} and S_{min} by any investor is always possible but less likely in practice. Models should provide these necessary recommendations in an automated trade setup. Hence, we take this opportunity to integrate the Black-Scholes FDM with the components of diffusion model from Chapter 6. S_{max} and S_{min} can be approximated by the maximum and the minimum asset value either from the forecasted mean path or sample paths.

To implement this, we simply leverage the base components of implicit FDM defined earlier and thus create a class *BlackScholesPutOptionsFDMSolver* extending *HeatEquationImplicitFDMSolverTemplate*. We inspect its functions one by one; let's start with the function *__init__* and extraction of S_{max} and S_{min} as follows:

```python
class
BlackScholesPutOptionsFDMSolver(HeatEquationImplicitFDMSolverTemplate):
    """
    Class to solve Black Scholes PSDE for Put options with FDM.
    It is integrated with Diffusion Model to find the bounds on asset
    price S.
    """

    def __init__(self,
                 diffusion_asset_model: DiffusionProcessAssetPriceModel,
                 M,  # Number of time data points
                 N,  # Number of asset values data points
                 strike_price_K
                 ):
        self._strike_price_K = strike_price_K
        self._diffusion_asset_model = diffusion_asset_model
        self._σ = diffusion_asset_model.parameters_['σ']
        self._r = diffusion_asset_model.parameters_['r']
        self._M = M
        self._mean_path, self._s_min, self._s_max = self._extract_bounds()

        super().__init__(x_min=self._s_min,
                         x_max=self._s_max,
                         T=1.0,
                         M=M,
                         N=N,
                         func_name="Put V",
                         space_var_name='S',
                         time_var_name='t',
                         terminal_condition_ind=True)

    def _extract_bounds(self):
        mean_path = np.array(self._diffusion_asset_model.forecast(
            T=self._M).mean_path.values).flatten()

        return mean_path, np.min(mean_path), np.max(mean_path)
```

We choose to extract bounds from the forecasted mean path. As you know, Black-Scholes doesn't have its own parameters and only driven by the same of the underlying asset, so we leverage r and σ from the diffusion model.

Now the other the functions for computing the coefficients of the FDM equation are given as follows:

```
def _a(self, i=None, j=None):
    return 0.5 * self._δt * ((self._r*(self._x[i]/self._δx)) -
    (self._σ /
        (self._x[i]/self._δx))**2)

def _b(self, i=None, j=None):
    return 1 + self._δt * ((self._σ / (self._x[i]/self._δx))**2 +
    self._r)

def _c(self, i=None, j=None):
    return -0.5 * self._δt * ((self._r*(self._x[i]/self._δx)) +
    (self._σ / (self._x[i]/self._δx))**2)
```

Hope you remember that the crux of the option computation lies in evaluating its value at time t =0, i.e., the premium, whereas terminal value at expiry time is already known. Therefore, the terminal condition is set as true, resulting the solution vector to be filled backwards. With that idea, the payoff for the put option (this class is for estimating put options) is set as initial condition which is practically the terminal state of the options flow as follows:

```
def _initial_condition(self, x):
    return max(self._strike_price_K-x, 0)
```

For the second boundary condition, *put option* is value less when $S \to \infty$, thus

```
def _second_boundary_condition(self, t):
    return 0
```

And the first boundary condition is evaluated as $Ke^{-r(1-t)} - S_{min}$, i.e., initial payoff from the time adjusted strike price, and the same is implemented as

```
def _first_boundary_condition(self, t):
    return self._strike_price_K * np.exp(-self._r*(1.0-t)) -
    self._s_min
```

CHAPTER 9　PDE, FINITE DIFFERENCE, AND BLACK-SCHOLES MODEL

We can test the component as follows:

```
def test_BS_fdm_solver():
    params = {'s0': 2058.89990234375,
              'r': 0.002476615753153449,
              'σ': 0.02042995488960794,
              't0': parse('2015-01-01', date_formats=['YYYY-mm-dd'])}

    model = DiffusionProcessAssetPriceModel.load(parameters=params,
                                        time_unit_transformer=Inde
                                        xedTimeTransformer(
                                            time_freq=Frequency.
                                            WEEKLY),
                                        n_sample_paths=5)

    bs_put_solver =
      BlackScholesPutOptionsFDMSolver(diffusion_asset_model=model,
                                        M=250,
                                        N=10,
                                        strike_price_K=4000)
    bs_put_solver.solve()
    bs_put_solver.plot_asset_grid()
    print(bs_put_solver.premium_)
```

We take the expiry time as T=1 and strike price as 2500, and Figure 9-8 shows the asset price and time grid plotted with forecasted mean path. The grid is providing a distribution of combination (S, t), and we evaluate $V(S, t)$ at each of this pair. As a result, we get also a distribution of $V(S, t)$, and we want to see $V(S, 0)$, i.e., the premium value of the option. Displayed values of ΔS and Δt in Figure 9-8 are just for demonetarization, and actuals will be much smaller.

CHAPTER 9   PDE, FINITE DIFFERENCE, AND BLACK-SCHOLES MODEL

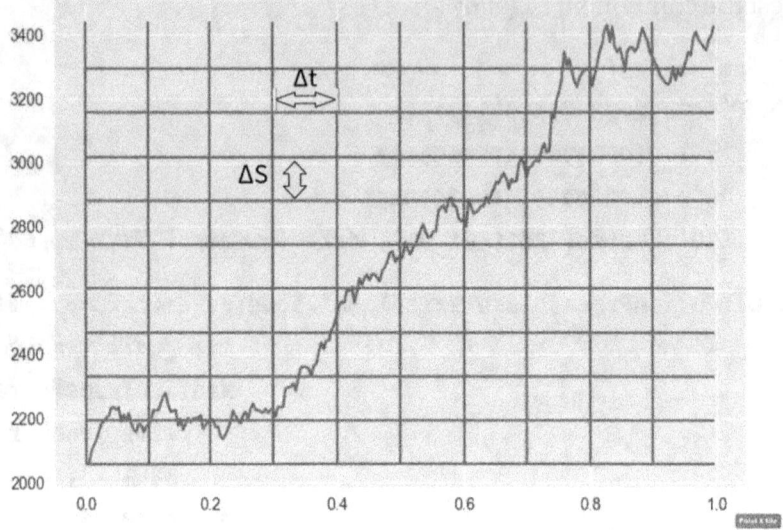

Figure 9-8. *Asset price and time grid with forecasted mean path*

The output $V(S, 0)$ is shown below which is itself a distribution:

[1.92520695e+03   2.71361444e+01 -1.75103330e-01   8.28441535e-04

It shows possible values of premium for different values of *S* which can be used as recommendation (any negative values should be considered as zero or value less options).

The technique discussed earlier can be applied for estimating *call* options; you need to override functions related to initial and boundary conditions accordingly. In fact, a total of six combinations can be constructed for both *put* and *call* using three numerical methods – implicit, explicit, and Crank-Nicolson.

Summary

In this chapter, we covered methods of numerically solving PDEs and then estimating option price with Black-Scholes PDE leveraging some of those methods. Three such methods discussed in this chapter follow one common approach of considering the input space as grid and do the function approximation of derivatives at various points with the only difference in the technique of decomposing the derivatives as difference equations. The example with the Black-Scholes PDE shows how to tackle a practical problem of derivate pricing by first constructing the PDE with some theoretical settings and solving it with FDM.

We also discussed a generic template-based design in Python to solve second-order heat equation which is leveraged later to solve Black-Scholes PDE.

The next chapter begins the Part 3 of the book and delves into the composition of derivates, asset, and other financial instruments – the portfolio construction and optimization.

PART IV

Portfolios

CHAPTER 10

Portfolio Optimization

At this point of the book, all of the focus has been on the estimating values of financial instruments and their risks individually. We never considered those as a group. In this chapter, we will study the real-world implications of instruments. In practice, most of the time, financial instruments are treated as a collection of items rather than being single. A collection may consist of different types of instruments: derivative, bond, stocks, etc. We name this collection as *portfolio*. From the discussions of Chapter 2, you should already know the concept of returns. The basis of any kind of investment is the desire to have more returns. We should, therefore, be able to quantify the returns and risks at the portfolio level and optimize the investment. Formally, the whole process of quantification is known as *portfolio optimization* which is the topic of discussion for this chapter.

Brief Idea About Portfolios

The history of portfolio management started back in 1952 when *Harry Markowitz* first published his paper which he named *portfolio selection.* In his paper, he established *modern portfolio theory (MPT)* – a framework for investment strategy. Assessment of investments is done based on the means and risks of returns from assets and the correlation between them. The result of this assessment is much more beneficial for the investors given the expectation of return they have from their investment, their personal constraints on tolerating a certain amount of risk, and the total capital they have. Ultimately, in most cases, the final goal is to get more return by reducing the risk of loss. For this reason, it is also known as *mean-variance analysis.* We will consider here *variance* as a measure of risk, though there are many other metrics (refer to Chapter 6 for computing uncertainty bounds, a.k.a. *vanilla risk*). It was also a measure of risk for single stock prices. Basically, *risk* has been characterized as the variation of the time of returns from the mean of the returns. Computing risks for a single asset like stocks is relatively simple, but doing so for a collection of assets in a portfolio involves other factors. Unlike mean return, the risk of a portfolio is not just a summation of individual risks of the assets. The correlation between the returns of different assets is also a controlling factor there. In the next section, we will formulate the portfolio theory and discuss more about the effect of risk.

The Mean-Variance Analysis

Investing in risky security always carries the burden of losses to some extent. The objective of portfolio management is to distribute the investment into multiple assets instead of a single one to mitigate risk. We cannot control the behavior of a single asset and reduce its risk, but a mixture of assets could be a useful hedge against the risks of each one.

Note that for all our computations regarding the portfolio, we will only consider stocks as assets for convenience. You can include other securities like options and futures as per your need and adjust the models accordingly. Let's now formulate a portfolio.

A portfolio of N assets $S_1, S_2, ..., S_N$ is defined by a mixture like below:

$$V^t = b_1 S_1^t + b_2 S_2^t + ... + b_N S_N^t = \sum_{i=1}^{N} b_i S_i^t$$

where V^t is the net value of the portfolio, b_i is a real number, and S_i^t denotes the *ith* asset value at time t. For our case, it represents stock value at time t. *Simple return* of a single asset i is given by

$$R_i^t(\tau) = \frac{S_i^t - S_i^{t-\tau}}{S_i^{t-\tau}}$$

As discussed in Chapter 2, return is dependent on period τ. To get an estimated value and avoid this dependency, the expected return over a distribution of periods is chosen. So,

$$R_i^t = E\left[R_i^t(\tau)\right]$$

For convenience, we will fix a certain period and compute the returns instead of taking the expectation. You may take this as an exercise.

CHAPTER 10 PORTFOLIO OPTIMIZATION

Now, to compute the return from V^t, we can write

$$R_V^t = \frac{V^t - V^{t-\tau}}{V^{t-\tau}}$$

$$= \frac{b_1\left(S_1^t - S_1^{t-\tau}\right) + \ldots + b_N\left(S_N^t - S_N^{t-\tau}\right)}{V^{t-\tau}}$$

$$= \frac{b_1 S_1^{t-\tau}}{V^{t-\tau}} \frac{S_1^t - S_1^{t-\tau}}{S_1^{t-\tau}} + \ldots + \frac{b_N S_N^{t-\tau}}{V^{t-\tau}} \frac{S_N^t - S_N^{t-\tau}}{S_N^{t-\tau}}$$

$$= w_1 R_1^t + \ldots + w_N R_N^t$$

$$= \sum_{i=1}^{N} w_i R_i^t$$

$$= D\,\mathbf{w}^T \mathbf{R}$$

where

$$w_i = \frac{b_i S_i^{t-\tau}}{V^{t-\tau}}$$

w_i is the weight assigned to the return of ith asset ($\mathbf{w}$ and $\mathbf{R}$ are the vector of weights and returns, respectively). Did you just observe that $\sum_i w_i = 1$? We will discuss how to leverage this property later.

From Chapter 2, we know how to compute a series of returns for a specified period, but these cannot be directly used in a portfolio. For that, we must take the *mean return* of the target assets. It is the average of the series for a period. A portfolio is a linear combination of stochastic processes, and each return itself is a separate stochastic process. With that idea, we define the *mean/expected return* of the portfolio as

$$\mu_V = w_1 \mu_1 + \ldots + w_N \mu_N = \mathbf{w}^T \boldsymbol{\mu}$$

where μ_i is the mean return of ith asset.

The variance of the portfolio would be a measure of risk and is defined as

$$\sigma_V^2 = \sum_{i=1}^{N} w_i w_j c_{ij} = \mathbf{w}^T \mathbf{C} \mathbf{w}$$

357

where c_{ij} is the covariance between ith and jth asset returns.

We can draw interesting insights from the expression of portfolio variance. The presence of more uncorrelated assets (i.e., $c_{ij} \to 0$) reduces the overall risk of the portfolio. In other words, when asset returns move apparently independently, there are chances of canceling out each other's induced risks. So, if you want to reduce portfolio risk, focus on adding more uncorrelated assets. On the contrary, adding more correlated assets sometimes may increase your return, but it can also increase the risk exposure.

INVESTMENT TIP

It is always advisable to break investments into parts and put them in a portfolio of moderately uncorrelated assets rather than putting everything in a single independent asset. Statistically, there is a high chance that $\sigma_V^2 < \sigma_i^2$ if assets are uncorrelated (σ_i^2 is the risk of the ith asset).

Now, let's explore the significance of *asset weights*. For that, we first take a small investment story. Suppose you have $1000, and with that, you want to invest in three companies' stocks: A, B, and C. You bought two stocks of A, three stocks of B, and one stock of C. This is at time $t = 0$, and the total value of the portfolio equals the total investment (i.e., $V^0 = \$1000$). Now, as per the weight computation formulae, we have $b_0 = 2$, $b_1 = 3$, and $b_2 = 1$. So, we can compute w_0, w_1, and w_2 from there. A *weight* physically indicates the percentage contribution of an asset in the total return of the portfolio. In reality, you may want to calculate back b_i from a given weight w_i as b_i is your *investment guideline*. Moreover, you wouldn't know each w_i initially; rather, as an investor, you are supposed to know your target, i.e., the mean return you expect from your portfolio which is nothing but $w^T \mu$. From there, through optimization techniques, the distribution of **w** and again from there **b** can be found. We will discuss all these in detail in the subsequent sections.

To proceed with implementation, we create one abstract metaclass *PortfolioAssets* with a few functions (*/chapter10/portfolio_assets.py*):

```
class PortfolioAssets(metaclass=ABCMeta):
    """
    An abstract meta-class (interface) for a portfolio
    holding a collection of assets. This should be extended
```

CHAPTER 10　PORTFOLIO OPTIMIZATION

```
    to support different dataset adapters
"""
@property
@abstractmethod
def ticker_symbols(self): ...
""" List of stock ticker symbols
    in this portfolio  """

@property
@abstractmethod
def unweighted_mean_returns(self): ...
"""Mean of returns of all assets in
    the portfolio"""

@property
@abstractmethod
def covariance_of_returns(self): ...
"""Covariance of returns of all assets in
    the portfolio"""

@property
@abstractmethod
def periodic_returns_for_different_assets(self): ...
""" Periodic returns as per the frequency set in dataset adapter """
```

We repeat the return computation method as done in Chapter 2, but now in the function *_compute_unweighted_return*, it is in the same base class *BasePortfolioAssets*:

```
def _compute_unweighted_returns(self):
    """
    Computes simple returns of all assets.
    Returns a data frame having returns in rows and
    asset names in columns.
    """
    self._returns = pd.DataFrame()
    self._periodic_returns = {}
```

```
            updated_tickers = []
            for ts in self._tickers:
                s = self._asset_adapter.get_training_set(ts)
                if s is not None:
                    # Applying R_t = (S_t-S_(t-τ))/S_(t-τ)
                    self._returns[ts] = s['stock price']/s['stock
                                                       price'].shift(1) - 1
                    self._periodic_returns[ts] = s
                    self._periodic_returns[ts]['Return'] = self._
                    returns[ts]
                    updated_tickers.append(ts)

        self._tickers = updated_tickers
```

A portfolio is a collection of assets that also needs a data source to provide quote prices for individual constituent assets. So, we need to create a component holding the composition of financial assets and to do that; we fall back on the same two data source providers introduced in Chapter 2 – *Yahoo Financials* and *Marketstack*.

First, we create *YahooFinancialsPortfolioAsssets* as follows:

```
class YahooFinancialsPortfolioAssets(BasePortfolioAssets):

    """
    Asssets are fetched from Yahoo Data source adapter with a
    provided frequency, list of ticker symbols and date range.

    Parameters
    --------
    frequency: enum,
                Frequency of stock values. Should be DAILY, WEEKLY
                or MONTHLY
    tickers: List of strings,
                Stock symbols of assets in the portfolio
    date_range: tuple of strings
                Date range for which stock values to be considered
```

CHAPTER 10   PORTFOLIO OPTIMIZATION

"""

```python
def __init__(self, frequency: Frequency, tickers: List[str],
date_range: tuple):
    super().__init__(frequency=frequency, tickers=tickers,
    date_range=date_range)

@property
def _asset_adapter(self):
    if len(self._adapter) == 0:
        for ticker in self._tickers:
            self._adapter[ticker] = YahooFinancialsAdapter(ticker=
            ticker, frequency=self._frequency, training_set_date_
            range=self._date_range)
    return self._adapter
```

It leverages the same old *YahooFinancialsAdapter* created in Chapter 2. Similarly, we have *MarketStackPortfolioAssets* that uses *MarketStackAdapter*.

A formal class diagram is shown in Figure 10-1.

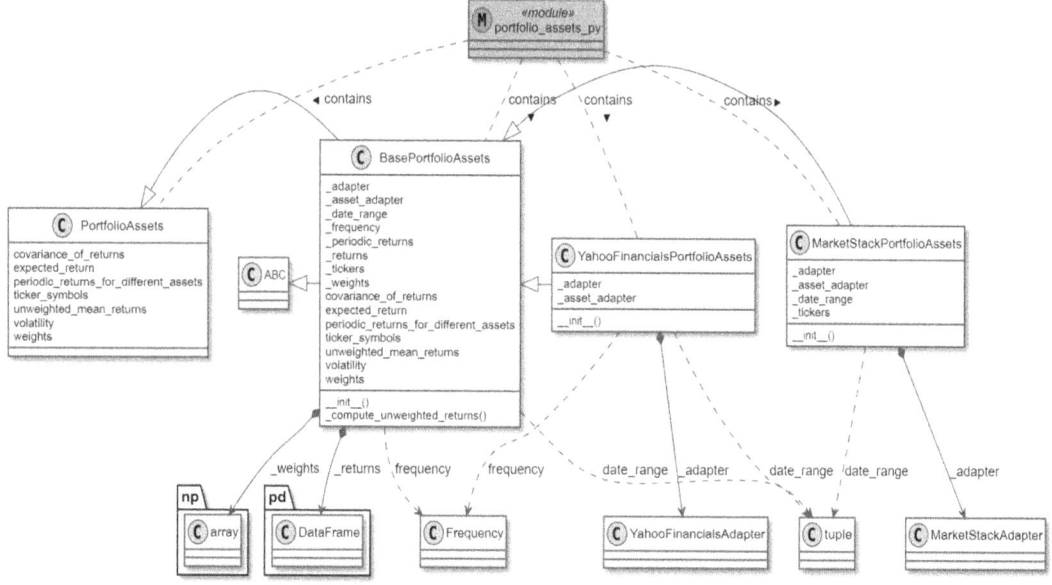

Figure 10-1. *Class diagram of ProfileAssets and its subclasses*

CHAPTER 10 PORTFOLIO OPTIMIZATION

We will now look at how to use these components to plot the daily returns of a portfolio made of three stocks: General Motors, Verizon, and Walmart as follows:

```
def test_visualize_portfolio_returns():
    training_set_date_range = ('2021-01-01','2021-12-31')
    yfp = YahooFinancialsPortfolioAssets(tickers=['GM','VZ','WMT'], \
                                        date_range=training_set_
                                        date_range,\
                                        frequency=Frequency.DAILY)

    sv.plot_returns_for_different_assets(
                yfp.periodic_returns_for_different_assets)
```

Figure 10-2 shows the output of the test.

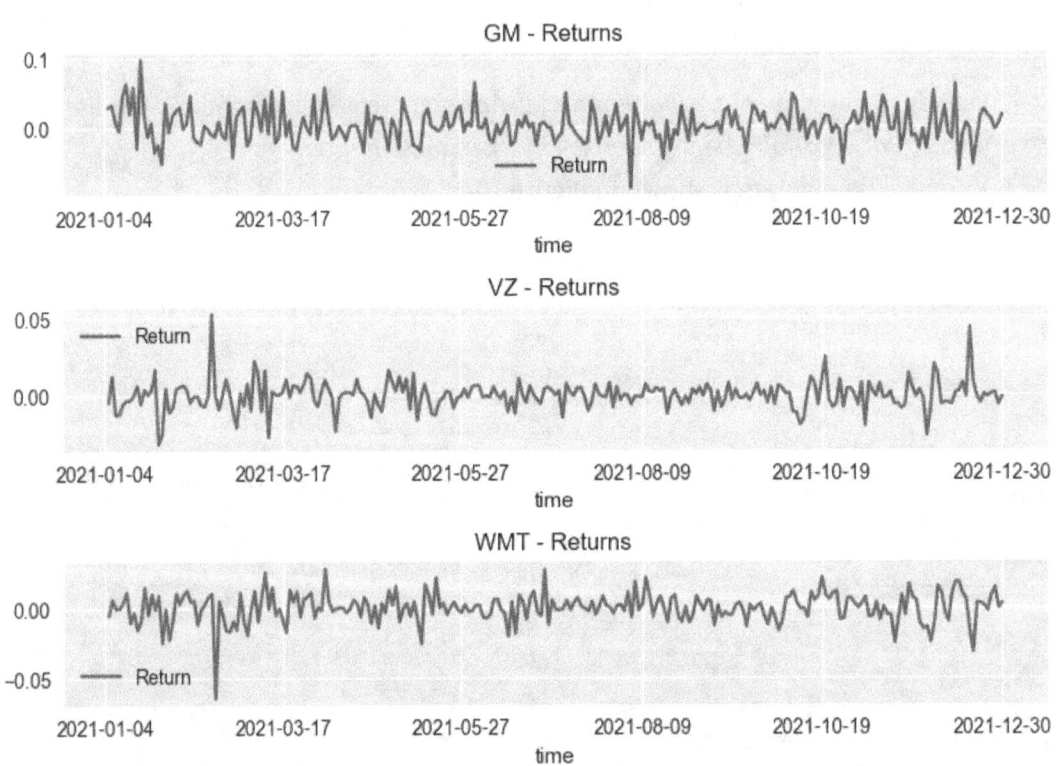

Figure 10-2. *Daily returns of General Motors, Verizon, and Walmart for year 2021*

It would also be interesting to see the covariance and mean returns of each asset from the portfolio in numerical form as follows:

```
cov = yfp.covariance_of_returns
cov['Mean Returns'] = yfp.unweighted_mean_returns
```

	GM	VZ	WMT	Mean Returns
GM	0.000592	0.000018	0.000048	0.001739
VZ	0.000018	0.000085	0.000019	-0.000434
WMT	0.000048	0.000019	0.000110	-0.000037

We don't see that much correlation between assets, which indicates this portfolio's low volatility. However, this depends on the frequency chosen (in the present case, *daily*). You may try setting it as *weekly* or *monthly*.

Portfolio Simulation

Now, we will investigate the mean vs. variance(or standard deviation) analysis of a portfolio. Figure 10-3 shows how does a *mean vs. volatility* of returns plot look like.

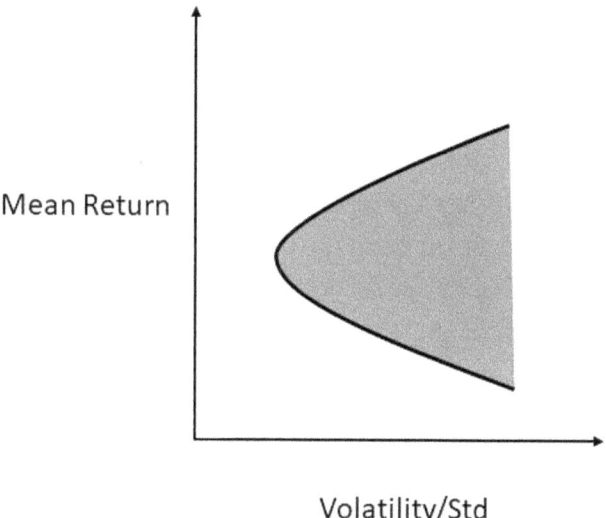

Figure 10-3. *Mean vs. standard deviation of portfolio*

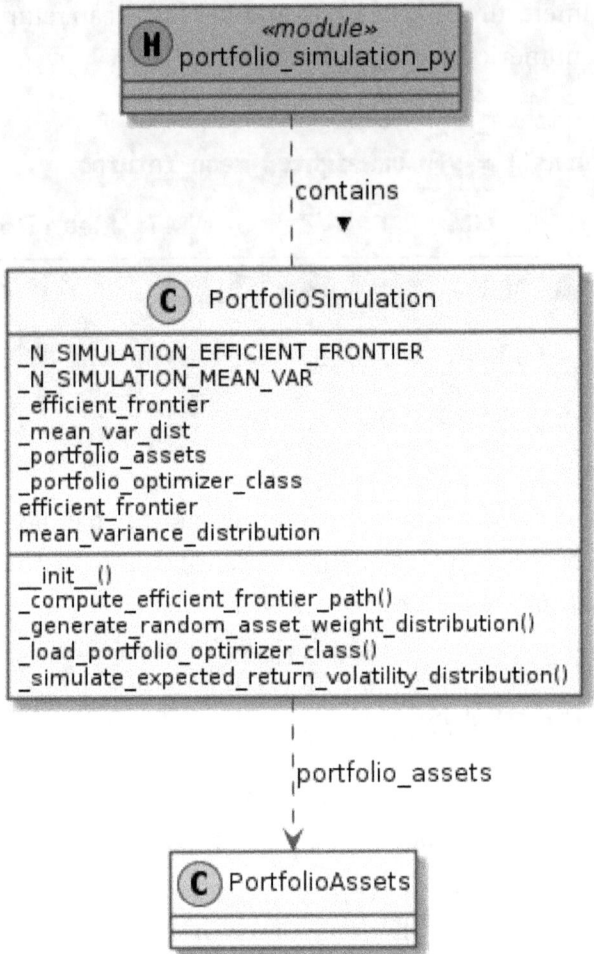

Figure 10-4. *Class diagram of PortfolioSimulation*

It looks like a horizontally lying parabola. The shaded region shows the distribution of the mean and volatility of returns, and the dark line indicates the boundary. Mean and volatility are computed from a collection of portfolios generated with different combinations of asset weights. Note that a portfolio can be generated either by putting different assets or the same assets with different weights or a combination of both. In our case, we follow the second approach. In other words, the parabola in Figure 10-3 results from portfolio simulation.

Now, let's look at the other functions of *PortfolioAssets* overridden in *BasePortfolioAssets* – these are for computing portfolio mean and volatility, as explained earlier.

CHAPTER 10 PORTFOLIO OPTIMIZATION

```python
@property
def expected_return(self):
    """
    The expected return of portfolio with adjusted weights
    """
    # Applies formulae wTμ and returns a float
    return np.dot(self._weights.T, self._returns.mean())

@property
def volatility(self):
    """Volatility of returns of the portfolio with adjusted
    weights"""
    # Applies formulae wTCw and returns a float
    return np.dot(self._weights.T,
                  np.dot(self._returns.cov(), self._weights))
```

These functions are leveraged in our mean-variance analysis of the portfolio. Now, we create a component *PortfolioSimulation (/chapter10/portfolio_simulation.py)* that does the actual job as follows (check the class diagram as shown in Figure 10-4):

class PortfolioSimulation:

```
"""
Class that perform mean-variance, frontier analysis of a
Portfolio with returns of specified frequency .

Parameters
----------
portfolio_assets: Object,
                Implementation class of PortfolioAssets
                It can be a YahooFinancialsPortfolioAssets,
                MarketStackPortfolioAssets or any custom one

portfolio_optimizer_full_class_name: String,
                                Fully qualified class name of
                                implementation of
                                PortfolioOptimizer
```

CHAPTER 10   PORTFOLIO OPTIMIZATION

```python
"""
_N_SIMULATION_MEAN_VAR = 2000
_N_SIMULATION_EFFICIENT_FRONTIER = 100

def __init__(self, portfolio_assets: PortfolioAssets,
             portfolio_optimizer_full_class_name: str=None):

    self._portfolio_assets = portfolio_assets
    self._load_portfolio_optimizer_class(
            portfolio_optimizer_full_class_name)
    self._mean_var_dist = \
            self._simulate_expected_return_volatility_distribution()
    self._efficient_frontier = self._compute_efficient_
    frontier_path()
```

For now, ignore the function *_compute_efficient_frontier_path*. Function *_simulate_expected_return_volatility_distribution* does the actual job of simulation. Before delving into that detail, we need to know how to generate a batch of weights holding different combinations of assets. These combinations will create different portfolios. We write a special function for weight generation as follows:

```python
import numpy as np

def _generate_random_asset_weight_distribution(self):
    """
    Generate a batch of random asset weight vector of size
    (MeanVarAnalysis._N_SIMULATION_MEAN_VAR, no of assets).
    Weights of each simulation are normalized to make
    their sum equals to 1.
    """
    ri = np.random.randint(100,
            size=(PortfolioSimulation._N_SIMULATION_MEAN_VAR,
                len(self._portfolio_assets.ticker_symbols)))

    norm_factor = np.array(1.0 / ri.sum(axis=1))
    return (ri.T * norm_factor).T
```

CHAPTER 10   PORTFOLIO OPTIMIZATION

I hope you understand that this is not the same as the Monte Carlo simulation we discussed in Parts 1 and 2 (we don't specify any distribution here). Notice that the weights of a portfolio are normalized to make the sum equal to 1. This makes sense, as we always want to divide our investment into parts among different assets. Now we create the function *_simulate_expected_return_volatility_distribution* as follows:

```python
def _simulate_expected_return_volatility_distribution(self):
    """
    Computes expected return & volatility of the simulated
    portfolios with a batch of randomly generated asset weights.
    These weights may not be fully optimal. Only a portion of them
    will give minimum volatility for the portfolio. If plotted
    it takes shape of horizontally lying solid parabola.

    Returns a dataframe of mean-var distribution having
    'Expected Return' & 'Volatility' as columns
    """

    tickers = self._portfolio_assets.ticker_symbols
    weights_batch = self._generate_random_asset_weight_distribution()
    expected_return_volatility = pd.DataFrame()

    # Generates _N_SIMULATION_MEAN_VAR number of data points
    for i_batch in range(PortfolioSimulation._N_SIMULATION_MEAN_VAR):

        # Simulated weights are assigned in the portfolio
        self._portfolio_assets.weights = weights_batch[i_batch]

        means = self._portfolio_assets.expected_return
        var = self._portfolio_assets.volatility

        expected_return_volatility =
                pd.concat([expected_return_volatility,
                        pd.DataFrame({'Expected
                                Return':[means],
                    'Volatility':[var]})],
                ignore_index=True)

    return expected_return_volatility
```

CHAPTER 10 PORTFOLIO OPTIMIZATION

A portfolio data point is defined by (μ, σ^2) where μ is the expected return and σ^2 is the volatility. We can generate 2000 such data points by the above function. It can be tested like the next piece of code (refer to *test_portfolio_optimization.py*) that produces Figure 10-5.

```
import visualization as sv
def test_mean_var_distribution():
    training_set_date_range = ('2017-01-01','2017-01-31')

    yfp = YahooFinancialsPortfolioAssets(tickers=['GM','VZ','WMT'], \
                                    date_range=training_set_
                                    date_range,\
                                     frequency=Frequency.DAILY)

    mv = PortfolioSimulation(portfolio_assets=yfp,
                        portfolio_optimizer_full_class_name=
                'markowitz_portfolio.
                MarkowitzMinVariancePortfolioOptimizer')

    mean_var = mv.mean_variance_distribution
    sv.plot_scatter(data=mean_var, y_name='Expected Return',
            x_name='Volatility', title='Expected Return vs
            Volatility')
```

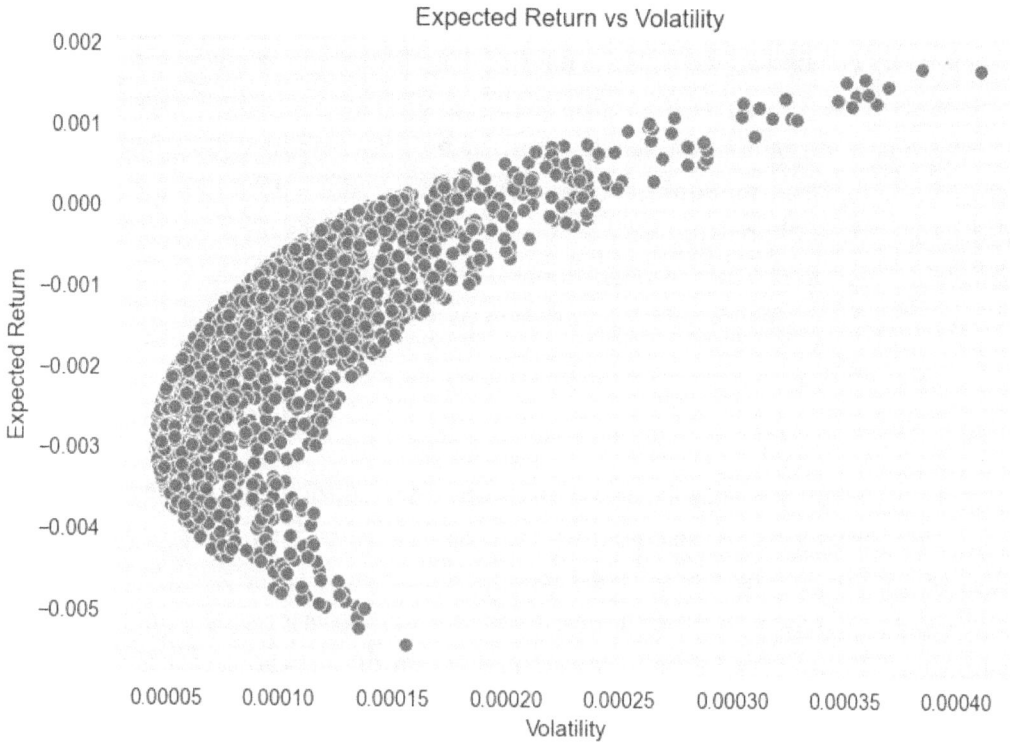

Figure 10-5. *Mean vs. volatility of plot of portfolio with assets: Walmart, Verizon, and General Motors*

Portfolios were constructed with stocks of *Walmart, Verizon, and General Motors* for January 2017, and we considered only daily returns. Figure 10-5 shows that there are 2000 different portfolios with varying combinations of weights. Also, observe the similarity between Figures 10-3 and 10-5.

Minimum Variance Portfolio

An optimal portfolio is mean-variance efficient. In other words, in inefficient portfolios, we can obtain higher returns with lower volatility or vice versa. With risk and return computation techniques in place, we should try finding an optimal portfolio – in terms of asset weights that can provide an optimal return or volatility. Theoretically, many combinations of portfolios can exist with a set of assets. Figure 10-5 already shows such a collection of portfolios, but which one is the optimal? We try finding an answer now.

CHAPTER 10   PORTFOLIO OPTIMIZATION

Every asset of the portfolio may be different than every other one, so intuitively, we can say that tweaking the weights can result in an optimal portfolio, i.e., the right combination of asset returns can produce the desired result. We saw there is a presence of a covariance component between assets in the overall volatility of the portfolio. So, we can exploit that information while determining the optimal portfolio. Covariance is an indicator of mutual price movements of assets, and it is possible to reduce the *risk* or increase the *mean return* by choosing different amounts of assets.

In general, there are two types of portfolio optimization:

- Get minimum volatility with a given expected return
- Get maximum return with a given volatility

Apparently, they may look different, but both can be found using somewhat similar methods. In this context, we discuss the first one, i.e., getting the minimum volatility with a fixed return, and thus, we call it a *minimum variance portfolio*.

One way of achieving a minimum variance portfolio is performing a mathematical optimization in which asset weights are changed to produce the lowest variance. Changing weights adjust the volume of assets, and each one's contribution changes the overall volatility. Some of the asset weights may also go down to zero, indicating a short-selling situation.

We can define the problem statement of finding a minimum variance portfolio like this:

$$\text{Minimize } \mathbf{w}^T \mathbf{C} \mathbf{w}$$

with conditions

$$\mathbf{w}^T \boldsymbol{\mu} = r$$

and

$$\sum_i w_i = 1$$

We try to minimize volatility with conditions of having a specific return and the sum of asset weights being equal to 1. In other words, we want to optimize the portfolio so that it gives the desired return with minimum volatility under those circumstances. Mathematically, it is a constrained optimization problem, and this can be solved through *Lagrange multiplier*.

LAGRANGE MULTIPLIER

It is used for finding maximum or minimum of a function with additional constrains. Suppose finding minimum or maximum of $f(x)$ with constrains $g_1(x) = 0$, $g_2(x) = 0$, .. $g_m(x) = 0$ is equivalent to finding minimum or maximum of *Lagrangian function*

$$L(x,\lambda_1,\lambda_2,\ldots,\lambda_m) = f(x) + \lambda_1 g_1(x) + \lambda_2 g_2(x) + \ldots + \lambda_m g_m(x)$$

$\lambda_1, \lambda_2, \ldots, \lambda_m$ are known as *Lagrange multipliers*. We need to solve systems of first-order equations to get optimal values for $x, \lambda_1, \lambda_2, \ldots, \lambda_m$:

$$\frac{\partial L}{\partial x} = 0, \frac{\partial L}{\partial \lambda_1} = 0, \frac{\partial L}{\partial \lambda_2} = 0, \ldots, \frac{\partial L}{\partial \lambda_m} = 0$$

We can rewrite the constraints as

$$w^T \mu - r = 0$$

$$w^T \mathbf{1}_N - 1 = 0$$

$\mathbf{1}_N$ is a one-dimensional vector of 1 of size N. Lagrange function would look like

$$L(w,\lambda_1,\lambda_2) = w^T C w + \lambda_1 \left(w^T \mu - r \right) + \lambda_2 \left(w^T \mathbf{1}_N - 1 \right)$$

Systems of first-order equations will be

$$\frac{\partial L}{\partial w} = 2Cw + \lambda_1 \mu + \lambda_2 \mathbf{1}_N$$

$$\frac{\partial L}{\partial \lambda_1} = w^T \mu - r$$

$$\frac{\partial L}{\partial \lambda_2} = w^T \mathbf{1}_N - 1$$

Solving the above equations and with linear algebra, it can be shown that optimal value $\hat{w}$ is

$$\hat{w} = \frac{rA - B}{D} C^{-1} \mu + \frac{M - rB}{D} C^{-1} \mathbf{1}_N$$

where

$$A = \mathbf{1}_N^T C^{-1} \mathbf{1}_N$$

$$B = \mu^T C^{-1} \mathbf{1}_N$$

$$M = \mu^T C^{-1} \mu$$

$$D = AM - B^2$$

Fortunately, we can find a closed-form solution to the first-order equation, thus avoiding iterative numerical methods.

With all these in place, we can now focus on putting that into a Python component with a proper design (refer to *optimal_portfolio.py*) as follows:

```
class MinVariancePortfolioOptimizer(metaclass=ABCMeta):
    """
    Meta-class for minimum variance portfolio optimizer
    strategy. It should be implemented fully by the any
    specific algorithm of portfolio optimization
    """

    @abstractmethod
    def fit(portfolio_assets: PortfolioAssets):...
    """
    Runs the portfolio optimization algorithm or any
    formulae provided by this specific optimizer.
    Optimizer should set the _weights variable accordingly
    as output.

    Parameters
    --------
    portfolio_assets: Instance of meta-class PortfolioAssets
    """

    @property
    @abstractmethod
    def asset_allocation_distribution(self):...
    """
```

CHAPTER 10 PORTFOLIO OPTIMIZATION

```
Returns the dictionary of asset names & corresponding weights
"""

@property
@abstractmethod
def optimal_variance(self):...
"""
    Returns the minimum variance of portfolio as
    determined by the optimization algorithm or formulae
"""
```

So far, this design is shown in Figure 10-6.

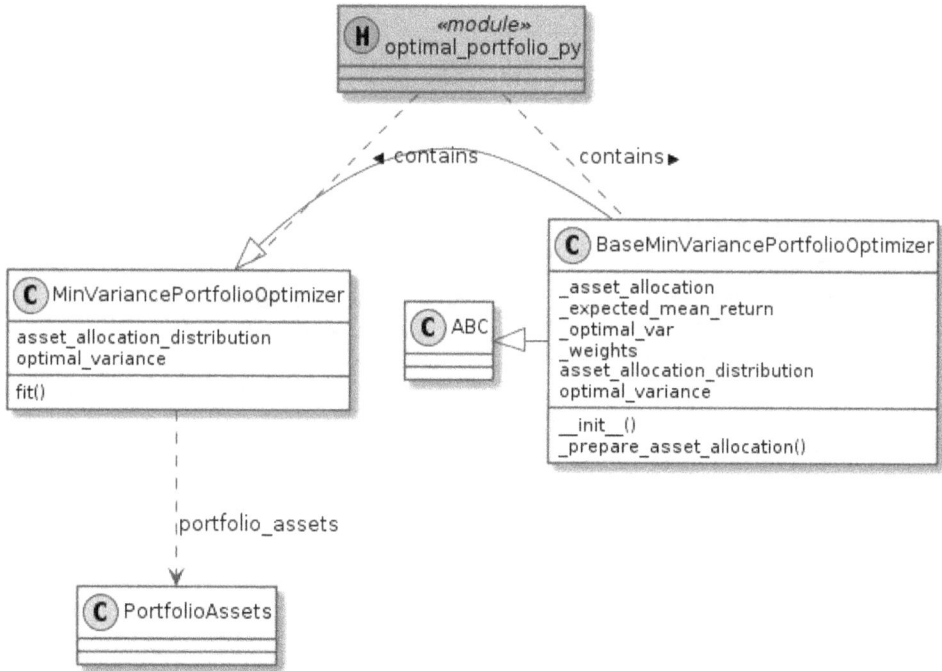

Figure 10-6. *Class diagram for MinVariancePortfolioOptimizer*

Function *_optimize_portfolio,* defined in class *MarkowitzMinVariancePortfolioOptimizer,* uses formulae derived from the *Lagrangian* method and computes weights as follows:

```
import numpy as np
def _optimize_portfolio(self, means, cov, asset_names):
    """
```

373

It computes weight distribution by the formulae,
    w = (rA-B)/D C^(-1) μ + (M-rB)/D C^(-1) 1_N
"""
n_assets = len(asset_names)
cov_inverse = np.linalg.inv(cov) # C^(-1)
u_N = np.ones(n_assets) # 1_N
C_inv_mu = np.dot(cov_inverse, means) # C^(-1) μ
C_inv_1_N = np.dot(cov_inverse, u_N) # C^(-1) 1_N

A = np.dot(u_N.T, C_inv_1_N)   # ⟦1_N⟧ ^T C^(-1) 1_N
B = np.dot(means.T, C_inv_1_N) # μ^T C^(-1) 1_N
M = np.dot(means.T, C_inv_mu) # μ^T C^(-1) μ
D = A * M - (B ** 2)

factor_1 = ((self._expected_mean_return * A) - B) / D # (rA-B)/D
factor_2 = (M - (self._expected_mean_return * B)) / D # (M-rB)/D

self._weights = (factor_1 * C_inv_mu) + (factor_2 * C_inv_1_N)

if self._weights is not None:
    self._prepare_asset_allocation(asset_names)
    self._optimal_var = np.dot(self._weights.T, np.dot(cov,
                                                      self._weights))
```

This component can be tested by creating a portfolio of daily returns and passing it to the fit function like below (refer to *test_portfolio_optimization.py*) as follows:

```
training_set_date_range = ('2017-01-01','2020-12-31')

# symbols of stocks of companies like Google, Meta, Tesla, AT&T, Walmart etc
asset_tickers = ['GM','VZ','WMT','AMD','TSLA','T','GOOG','META']

mp_1 = MarkowitzMinVariancePortfolioOptimizer(expected_mean_return=0.01)
yf_1 = YahooFinancialsPortfolioAssets(tickers=asset_tickers,
                                     frequency=Frequency.DAILY,
                                     date_range=training_set_date_range)

mp_1.fit(yf_1)
```
```

CHAPTER 10 PORTFOLIO OPTIMIZATION

The portfolio consists of eight different stocks of companies like *Google, Meta, AMD,* etc., for 2017-2020 timeframe. We also create another two optimal portfolios having the same set of symbols but with return frequencies as *weekly* and *monthly*, respectively. In all cases, target mean return is set as 0.01. Figure 10-7 shows optimized weight distribution and minimum volatility of each of the three portfolios. The weight distribution of the first portfolio (*daily* returns) looks like this:

```
{'GM': 0.011578929285434886,
 'VZ': 0.27525217452514184,
 'WMT': 1.9225010485242726,
 'AMD': 0.9588844814835566,
 'TSLA': 1.2872702086237637,
 'T': -3.5925850080823984,
 'GOOG': 0.18249690437171293,
 'META': -0.04539873873148344}
```

DISCLAIMER

This book doesn't influence or recommend readers/investors to invest in any specific company's shares. The names of the companies are taken absolutely for experimental purposes, and the results come from publicly available data sources, which will vary with frequency and time. It's solely the reader's responsibility to plan their actions accordingly.

CHAPTER 10 PORTFOLIO OPTIMIZATION

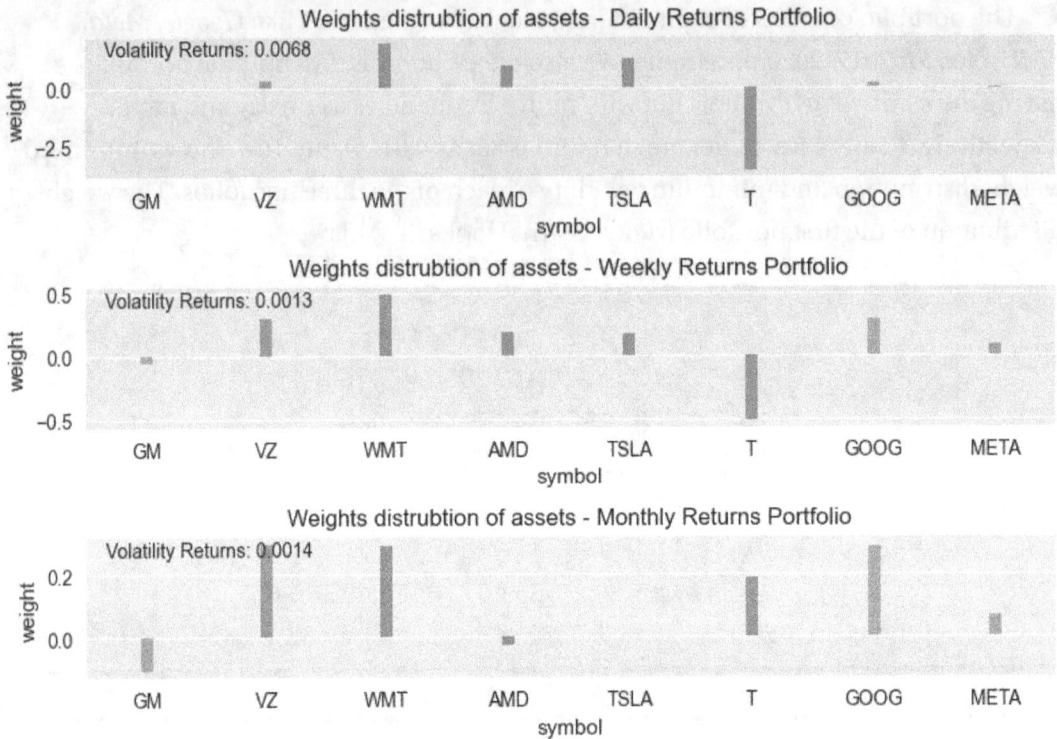

Figure 10-7. *Weight distribution of different portfolios set with various frequencies*

There are negative weights, and some have values of more than 1. But summing up all weights always gives a total value of 1 (approximately, of course !). Now, we get w_i, and with this, you calculate back the number of stocks per symbol using formulae:

$$b_i = \frac{w_i V^0}{S_i^0}$$

b_i is your *investment guideline* as suggested by the portfolio optimizer. It says how many stocks you should buy per symbol for a specified return. You would be knowing initial price of each asset (i.e., S_i^0), initial total investment (i.e., V^0), and of course w_i. This example will simplify it: suppose you have $1000 and want a 10% *weekly* return on it. You are predetermined to invest this $1000 in *Amazon, Tesla,* and *Google* stocks. A *portfolio optimizer* may suggest buying two of Amazon, three of Google, and one of Tesla stocks to have that 10% return with minimum volatility. To get b_i, you may make the necessary changes in the classes *BasePortfolioAssets* and *BaseMinVariancePortfolioOptimtizer*.

Additional Constraints

Figure 10-7 shows the presence of negative weights. In the first portfolio, assets *AT&T* and *Meta* have such values. It happens when you have *short sales* in the portfolio. These assets are not owned by the investor. So, a decreasing asset price will be more profitable here. Having or not having *short sales* in the portfolio is an option which can be included as additional constrain. Recall that we had only two constraints in the portfolio optimization: $\mathbf{w}^T \boldsymbol{\mu} = r$ and $\sum_i w_i = 1$. Restricting short sales will incur an additional constraint: $w_i > 0$. Automatically, this one will restrict each weight to range between 0 and 1, thus making it a real probability. In fact, it is easy to handle the portfolio without short sales. Similarly, there can be various combinations of other constraints. One such example is that investors may additionally think that they will not let any asset weight cross 10%, i.e., $0 < w_i < 0.10$. Adding more and more such conditions makes the optimization process complex, and closed-form solutions for $\mathbf{w}$ may not exist as a result. Moreover, note that there may be many inequalities other than plain *equality* constraints like $\mathbf{w}^T \boldsymbol{\mu} = r$. The traditional *Lagrangian* method works for only *equality*. As a workaround, *quadratic programming (QP)* can be used. It handles all types of constraints together under a single framework where explicit solutions to the problem don't exist.

A typical *QP* problem is defined as

$$\text{Minimize } \frac{1}{2} x^T P x + q^T x$$

with constraints $Gx \leq h$

$$Ax = b$$

Let's start mapping the problem structure into our domain:

$$x = w$$

$$x^T P x = 2 * w^T C w, P = C$$

$$q^T x = 0, q = 0$$

$$G = -I_N \text{ (I is identity matrix)}$$

$$h = 0$$

CHAPTER 10   PORTFOLIO OPTIMIZATION

$$A = [\mu, \mathbf{1}_N]$$

$$b = [r, 1]$$

A few points about the above mapping are as follows:

a) We don't need expression $q^T x$, thus making it zero.

b) Weights should be positive to restrict short sales, i.e., $w > 0$. It can be rewritten as inequality constraint $Gx \leq h$ as $-I_N w \leq 0$ where G and h are the N×N negative identity matrix and $\mathbf{0}$ vector, respectively.

c) Two equality constraints $w^T \mu = r$ and $w^T \mathbf{1}_N = 1$ are combined and held into $Ax = b$. A becomes a concatenated vector of μ and $\mathbf{1}_N$ whereas b is formed with r and 1.

That's all about formulation. You might have noticed that there is an extra one constraint added (positive weight constraint) as compared to the traditional Lagrangian optimization method. You need to plan the necessary changes in these four vectors, G, h, A, and b, to add any more constraints to the problem.

We create a separate class *ExtendedMarkowitzMinVariancePortfolioOptimizer* that extends from *MarkowitzMinVariancePortfolioOptimizer* to leverage most of it. The function *_optimize_portfolio* should only be overridden accordingly to incorporate the required changes as given below (refer to *markowitz_portfolio.py*, the class diagram is shown in Figure 10-8):

```
from qpsolvers import solve_qp
def _optimize_portfolio(self, means, cov, asset_names):
    n_assets = len(asset_names)

    # P of x^T Px. In this case wTCw
    P = np.array(2.0 * cov)

    #  q of q^Tx. q should be zero vector.
    q = np.zeros(n_assets)

    # A of Ax = b. Two constraints wT μ = r & w = 1 are combined here
    A = np.array([means, [1] * n_assets])
```

CHAPTER 10 PORTFOLIO OPTIMIZATION

```
# b of Ax = b. Two constraints wT μ = r & w = 1 are combined here
b = np.array([self._expected_mean_return, 1.0])

# G of Gx ≤ h. It is an identity matrix. It is for w > 0
G = np.identity(n_assets) * (-1)

# h of Gx ≤ h
h = np.zeros(n_assets)

self._weights = solve_qp(P=P, q=q, A=A, b=b, G=G, h=h,
solver="osqp")

if self._weights is not None: # If optimal solution found with
given constraints
    self._prepare_asset_allocation(asset_names)
    self._optimal_var = np.dot(self._weights.T, np.dot(cov,
    self._weights))
```

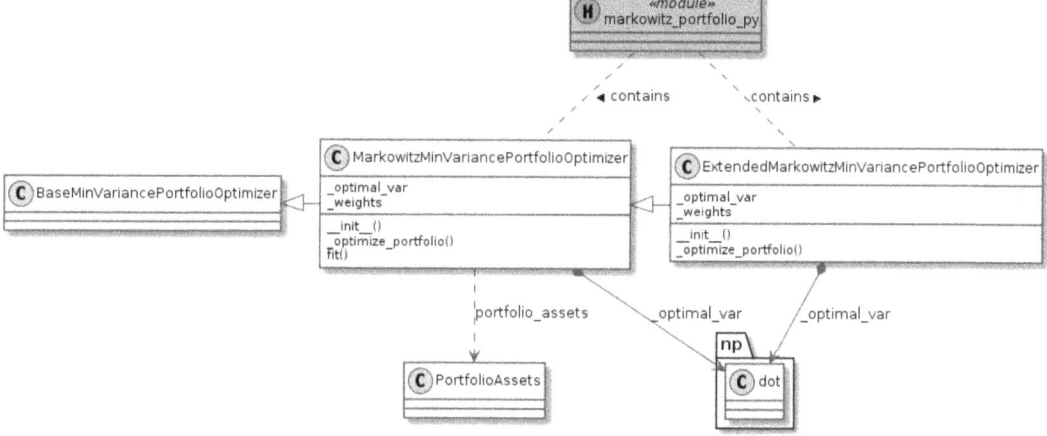

Figure 10-8. *Class diagram for all Markowitz portfolio optimizers*

We can create similar test cases for monthly and weekly, and those give output as Figure 10-9.

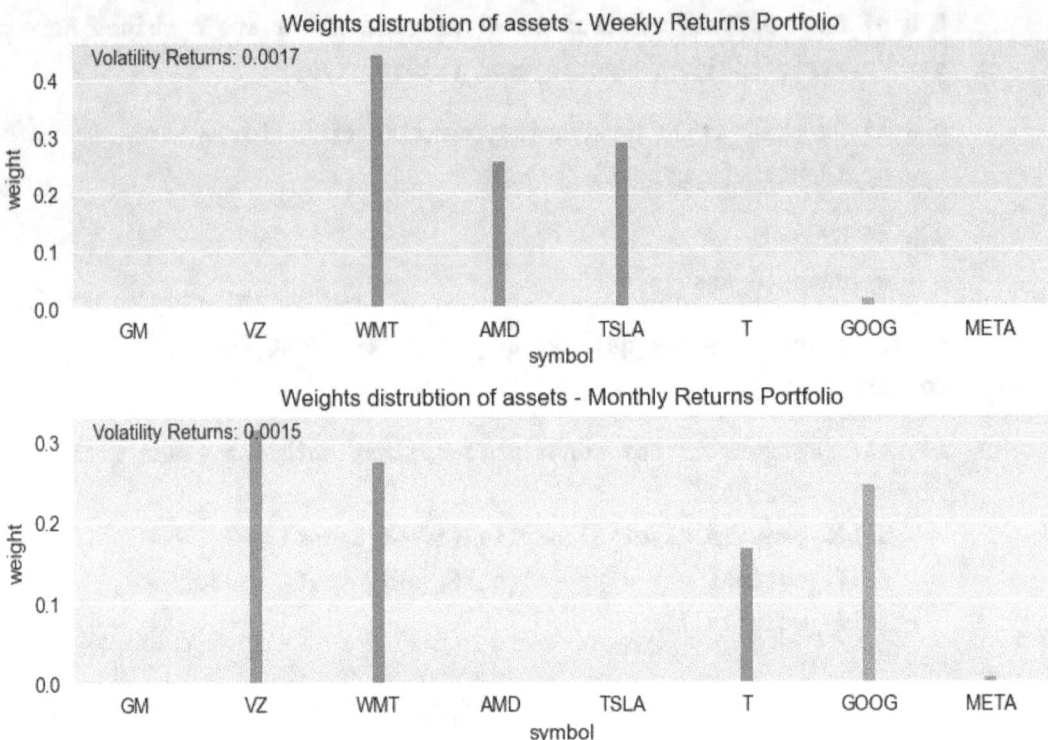

Figure 10-9. *Weight distribution of different portfolios with positive weights that don't allow short sales*

All weights are positive, as shown in Figure 10-9, and range between 0 and 1. It says that you should invest primarily in Walmart, *AMD*, and *Tesla* to get a 1% return for weekly frequency, and for monthly, your choice should be *Verizon*, *Walmart*, *Tesla*, and also *Google*. But, where did weights for *daily* returns go off? Below piece of code below will make it clear (refer to *test_portfolio_optimization.py*):

```
portfolios = []
if mp_1.optimal_variance is not None: portfolios.append(('Daily',mp_1))
if mp_2.optimal_variance is not None: portfolios.
append(('Weekly',mp_2))
if mp_3.optimal_variance is not None: portfolios.
append(('Monthly',mp_3))
```

The portfolio for daily wasn't added as it didn't have the variance computed (its value is none), though we created portfolio optimizers for all three frequencies. It is quite logical. Numerical optimization tries to find a solution in an iterative way, and it may not have the desired result with the given criteria (date range, expected return, frequency). It means that with the stock values of eight symbols for the years 2017-2020, you cannot have an optimal portfolio that gives you a 1% *daily* expected return.

Efficient Frontier

Recall how in Figure 10-3 portfolio simulations trace return volatilities of different portfolios because of varying weights. The objective was to show how weights do impact in two-dimensional return volatility space. The right side of the hyperbola has a plethora of portfolios, and some of them are good ones. Do optimal portfolios exist here? To find an answer, first, we need to know how a portfolio becomes better than others. Suppose we have two portfolios with *mean return volatility* combinations (μ_1, σ^2_1) and (μ_2, σ^2_2). If $\mu_1 > \mu_2$ and $\sigma^2_1 < \sigma^2_2$, then we say that the first portfolio is more efficient than the second one. By *efficiency*, we mean profitability. As discussed earlier, we always seek to invest in portfolios with higher returns with minimal volatility or risk as they are more profitable. In return volatility space, such portfolios lie along with boundary of the hyperbola. Each of them is more efficient than those inside. The boundary itself is known as the *efficient frontier*. Figure 10-10 shows an illustration of it.

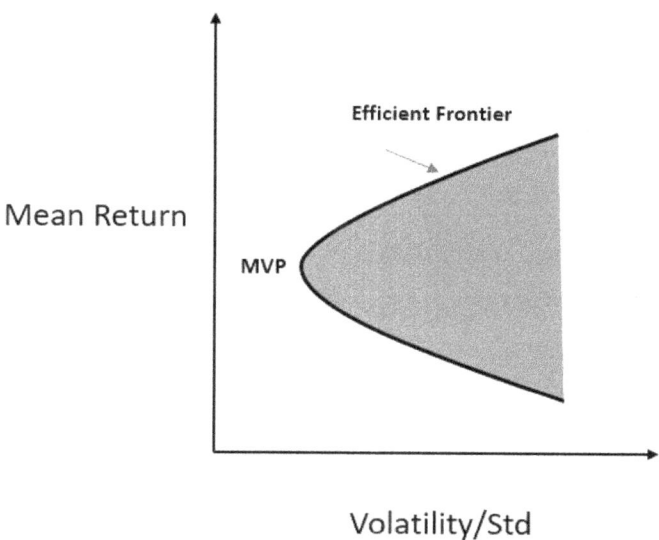

Figure 10-10. *Efficient frontier and minimum variance portfolio (MVP)*

The vertex of the parabola is known as the *global minimum variance portfolio (MVP)*. It has the minimum variance among all possible portfolios irrespective of the expected return. As an alternative definition, a path only above MVP is also considered an *efficient frontier*. The MVP can be obtained by putting $\lambda_1 = 0$ in the Lagrange function $L(w, \lambda_1, \lambda_2)$. It means that when we don't care about the expected return and only want the minimum portfolio volatility, MVP is the solution.

Efficient Frontier Simulation

From the definition, we know that each portfolio point (μ, σ^2) lying on the efficient frontier path is better than the others inside, i.e., their volatility is less than others. We can exploit this criterion to generate the path from the result of mean-variance distribution as done in the *PortfolioSimulation* class. Observe that the path lies within the range of minimum and maximum expected return. Within this range, all portfolios have weights that minimize the volatility.

The algorithm for *efficient frontier simulation* can be summarized in the steps below:

> **Step 1**: Generate a batch of *expected mean return* points within the range of minimum and maximum *mean return* of the entire mean-variance distribution.
>
> **Step 2**: For each generated point taken as *target mean return*, do Step 3.
>
> **Step 3**: Perform *portfolio optimization* with the available optimizer and get the minimum volatility with the *target mean return*.
>
> **Step 4**: Add the *target mean return* and *volatility* in the path.

Return to the class *PortfolioSimulation* where the function *_compute_efficient_ frontier_path* is defined as follows:

```
import numpy as np
def _compute_efficient_frontier_path(self):
    """
    Computes efficient frontier path from the generated
    mean-var distribution. This path is within the range
    of minimum & maximum target means of the mean-var
```

distribution. If plotted, it comes along the
boundary of solid parabola generated by
mean-var distribution.

Returns a dataframe of path having 'Expected Return'
& 'Volatility' as columns
"""
if self._mean_var_dist is None:
    self._mean_var_dist =
        self._simulate_expected_return_volatility_distribution()

efficient_froniter = pd.DataFrame()

Generate a linear space of real numbers of size
            _N_SIMULATION_EFFICIENT_FRONTIER
# within the range of min & max of mean-var distribution
target_means_space = np.linspace(np.min(self._mean_var_dist['Expected Return']),
                                    np.max(self._mean_var_dist['Expected Return']),
                    PortfolioSimulation._N_SIMULATION_EFFICIENT_FRONTIER)

for i_batch in
        range(PortfolioSimulation._N_SIMULATION_EFFICIENT_FRONTIER):
    target_mean = target_means_space[i_batch]

    # Instantiate the portfolio optimizer having expected target
    # mean from the series
    portfolio_optimizer = self._portfolio_optimizer_class(
                            expected_mean_return=target_mean)

    # Run the portfolio optimizer to get the optimal weights
    portfolio_optimizer.fit(self._portfolio_assets)

```
        optimal_var = portfolio_optimizer.optimal_variance
        if optimal_var is not None:
            efficient_froniter = pd.concat([efficient_froniter,
                                           pd.DataFrame({
    'Expected Return':[target_mean],
    'Volatility':[optimal_var]})],
                                           ignore_index=True)

    return efficient_froniter
```

We can test this in a similar way to how we generated the mean-variance distribution. Figure 10-11 shows the simulation's output.

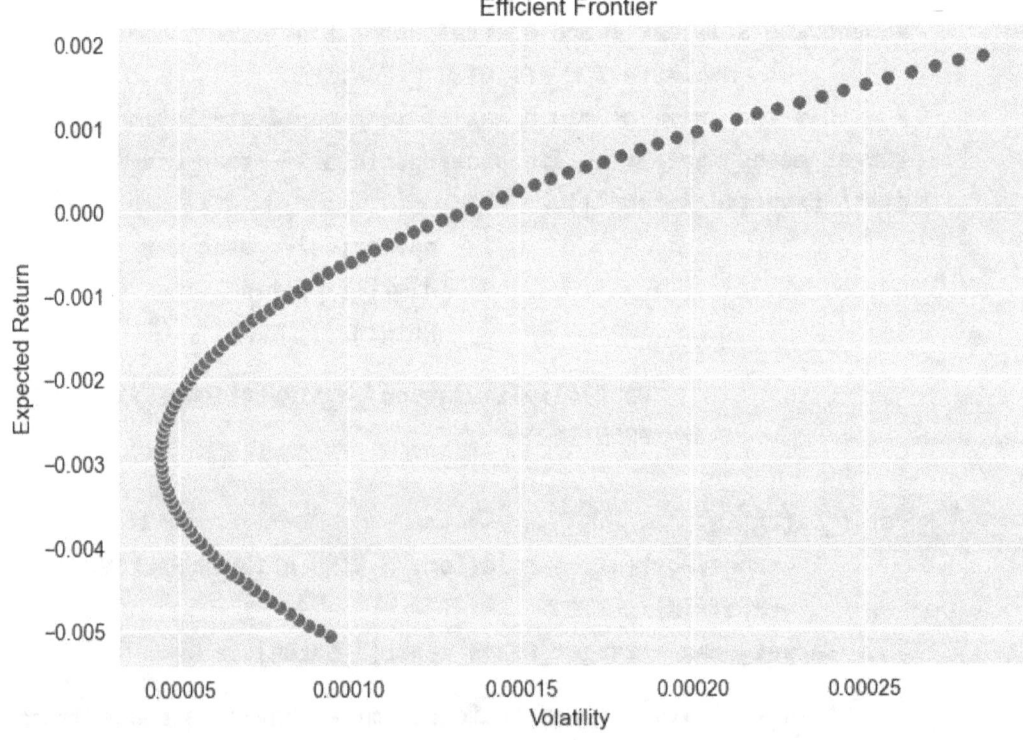

Figure 10-11. *Simulation of efficient frontier*

Recall that while defining the class *PortfolioSimulation*, we had taken one variable named *portfolio_optimizer_full_class_name*, which was used to load the optimizer class at initiation time and leveraged as follows:

```
portfolio_optimizer = self._portfolio_optimizer_class(
                            expected_mean_return=target_mean)
portfolio_optimizer.fit(self._portfolio_assets)
```

Efficient frontier is useful in the analysis of portfolio distribution for investors. Trade platforms can show this insight as a recommendation. But, again, this curve is subject to change upon taking different data frequencies and must be reanalyzed to get fresh insight.

Summary

Most investors prefer managing a collection of assets together rather than individual ones. Such a collection is called a portfolio and may consist of different types of assets – stocks, options, futures, or even other portfolios. A portfolio's variance is determined by the individual asset's volatility, thus providing finer investment control, especially for hedging against bigger risks. Portfolios create an opportunity for investors to diversify their investments into different parts so that the risks originated can be reduced as compared to the same amount of investment in a single asset. To make that happen, models are introduced that can optimize the distribution of assets inside a portfolio.

This chapter introduces the mean-variance theory of portfolio optimization, where both mean and variance are added as constraints to achieve an optimized portfolio. Two separate methods of adding constraints are discussed – one for basic and the other for advanced criteria. The advanced one is suitable for portfolios where investors can switch off the short positions.

Plotting the variance (a.k.a volatility) vs. mean return creates a hyperbolic area, with the border known as the *efficient frontier* and the vertex called *MVP (minimum variance portfolio)*. A Python component for generating such an efficient frontier is introduced that leverages the same portfolio optimization.

Bibliography

[1] Sheldon Ross, *First Course in Probability,* Pearson

[2] Laszlo Matyas, *Generalized Method of Moments Estimation,* Cambridge University Press

[3] Wessel Badenhorst, *Practical Python Design Patterns,* Apress

[4] Charu C. Aggarwal, *Linear Algebra and Optimization for Machine Learning,* Springer Nature

[5] Sandip Mazumder, *Numerical Methods for Partial Differential Equations,* Elsevier

[6] Dimitris Mitsotakis, *Computational Mathematics,* CRC Press

[7] Zhilin Li, Zhonghua Qiao, & Tao Tang, *Numerical Solutions of Differential Equations,* Cambridge University Press

[8] Mark Newman, *Computational Physics,* University of Michigan

[9] Devroye, *Non-Uniform Random Variate Generation,* Springer

[10] Sheldon Ross, *Simulation,* Academic Press

[11] Lintner (1965), *The Valuation of Risk Assets and the Selection of Risky Investments in Stock Portfolios and Capital Budgets,* Review of Economics and Statistics

[12] Modigliani F. & Miller (1958), *The Cost of Capital, Corporation Finance and the Theory of Investment,* American Economic Reviews

[13] Merton (1973), *Theory of Rational Option Pricing,* The Bell Journal of Economics & Management Science

[14] Black F. & Scholes M. (1973), *The Pricing of Options and Corporate Liabilities,* Journal of Political Economy

BIBLIOGRAPHY

[15] Bandi & Nguyen (2001), *On the Functional Estimation of Jump-Diffusion Models*

[16] Bandi & Philips (2001), *Fully Nonparametric Estimation of Scalar Diffusion Models*

[17] Johannes M. (2000), *Jumps in Interest Rates: A Nonparametric Approach*, University of Chicago

[18] Peng Liu (2023), *Bayesian Optimization: Theory and Practice Using Python*, Apress

[19] Avishek Nag (2021), *Bayesian Optimization: A step by step approach*, Towards Data Science

[20] Silverman (1998), *Density Estimation for Statistics and Data Analysis*, CRC Press

[21] Werner Hürlimann (2013), *Improved FFT Approximations of Probability Functions Based on Modified Quadrature Rules*, International Mathematical Forum, Vol. 8

[22] Fang & Oosterlee (2008), *A Novel Option Pricing Method for European Options Based on Fourier-Cosine Series Expansion*, MPRA

[23] Fang (2013), *The COS Method: An Efficient Fourier Method for Pricing Financial Derivatives*, Delft University of Technology

[24] Shreve, *Stochastic Calculus for Finance - II*, Springer

[25] S. G. Kou (2002), *A Jump-Diffusion Model for Option pricing*, Columbia University

Index

A

AcceptanceRejectionMethod, 109, 112, 115
Actual asset price model, 168
Airbnb, stock values, 5, 6
Aleatoric uncertainty, 82
Antithetic sampling, 124, 125, 186
Apple stock price, 82
Asset dynamics, 162
Asset value, 271–273, 346, 356
Asymmetric double exponential distribution, 219–221

B

Backt testing, 178–180
BaseAssetPriceModel, 166, 168, 183–187
BasePortfolioAssets, 359–362
Basic forecasting theory, 144–150
Bayesian method, 158
    aleatoric uncertainty, 82
    dataset, 82, 83
    domain knowledge, 83, 84
    epistemic uncertainty, 83
    Gaussian distribution, 83
    random experiment, 83
Bayesian Optimization, 254
Bayes' theorem, 84–87
Black-Scholes model, 294
    assets, 259
    coefficient, 344
    description, 264
    differential equation, 344
    diffusion model integration, 346–350
    equation, 310
    implicit FDM, 345, 346
    modeling derivatives, 264
    numerical approximation, 345
    options, 260–263
    risk-neutral probability method, 265–284
    self-financing, 345
    stock prices, 265
    See also Greeks
Brownian motion, 136, 140, 141

C

Call value, 281
CDF, *see* Cumulative density function (CDF); Cumulative distribution function (CDF)
CF, *see* Characteristic function (CF)
Change of frequency
    computing distributions, 181–185
    mean path, 181–185
Characteristic function (CF), 62–67, 194, 195, 208
Class diagram, 362
Class function, 168
Class hierarchy, 325, 326
Closed-form estimation, 171, 172
Closed-form expressions, 112
CommonSupremumEstimator, 182
Constraints, 371

Continuous compound interest, 20, 21
Continuous random variable, 47, 48
COS method recovery, 204–213
Counting process, 151
Covariance, 358
Crank-Nicolson method, 338
    coefficient matrices, 339
    heat equation, 340, 341
    stability analysis, 342, 343
    stencil representation, 338
Crux, 168
Cumulants, 203, 211, 225
Cumulative density function (CDF), 102
Cumulative distribution function (CDF), 48

D

Data scientist, 37, 83
Data source adapters, 21, 22
    market stack, 26–30
    Yahoo Financials, 22–26
Debts, 4
Deep learning (DL), 157
DefaultSupremumEstimator, 114, 115
Default supremum implementation, 106, 107
Delta (Δ), 289–294
Density plots, 237
Density recovery methods, 200, 201, 208–211
Derivatives, 4, 16, 17, 49, 98, 160, 195, 256, 309, 311, 312, 316, 337, 350, 355
Determinism, 7, 8
Diffusion model
    backt testing, 178–180
    comparison and improvement, 185–187
    consistency, 157
    financial asset, 157–164
    forecasting system, 177, 178
    Monte Carlo simulation, 173–176
DiffusionProcessAssetPriceModel, 169, 170
Discrete random variable, 44–46, 100
Distributing competing setup, 208
DL, *see* Deep learning (DL)
Domain mismatch, 115
Dynamics recurrence relation, 164–166

E

Efficient frontier, 381
    MVP, 382
    simulation, 382–385
Equity, 4
Euler approximation, 160–164
Events, 39, 97, 116, 126
Explicit method
    Euler's method, 316
    initial & boundary conditions, 317–319
    initial condition, 314
    linear equations, 317
    mesh and grid points, 315
    Python, 320–327
    recurrence relation, 316
    stability analysis, 327, 328
Exponential distribution, 58–60, 75, 97, 99, 112
Exponential likelihood, 76

F

Fast Fourier Transform (FFT) recovery, 201–204
FDM, *see* Finite difference method (FDM)

FFT recovery, *see* Fast Fourier Transform (FFT) recovery
Financial asset price modeling
    log-asset price, 159, 160
    parameter scales, 163
    SDE-based, 158
Financial assets, 360
    portfolio, 17, 18
    stocks, 15, 16
Finite difference method (FDM)
    explicit method, 314–328
    implicit method, 328–337
    partial derivatives, 312
    Poisson equation, 311
    steps, 314
    Taylor series, 311
Forecasting, 213–219
ForecastingProcess, 145, 146
Forecasting system, 177, 178
ForecastResult, 147, 148
Fourier transform, 200, 201
Frequentist method, 85
    MLE, 69, 70
    MSE, 68

G

Gamma (Γ), 294–297
Gaussian density, 112, 113
Gaussian distribution, 60–62, 86–92, 112, 114, 162
Gaussian kernel jump, 239–246
Gaussian log-likelihood function, 77
GBM process, *see* Geometric Brownian Motion (GBM) process
Generalized method of moments (GMM), 81
General Motors stocks, 362, 363

Generic tuples, 113, 114
Geometric Brownian Motion (GBM) process, 160–164
GMM, *see* Generalized method of moments (GMM)
Greeks, 284
    components, 289
    delta, 289–294
    differentials, 284–287
    enum, 286
    functions, 288
    gamma, 294–297
    rho, 304–307
    theta, 297–301
    vega, 301–304

H

Hat function estimator, 104–106, 109, 110
Hyperparameter searching approach, 252–254

I

Implicit method
    decomposed system, 330
    heat equation, 328
    LU decomposition, 331
    Python, 332–336
    stability analysis, 337, 338
    stencil representation, 329
Importance sampling, 126–130, 186
Inception, 37, 38
IndexTimeTransformer, 176
Inference, 158
    Monte Carlo simulation, 173–176
Initial public offering (IPO), 15, 16
Integrals, 141, 142

INDEX

Interest theory
    discrete compound interest, 19, 20
    market movement, 18
    simple interest, 19
Interface, 278, 279
Interquartile range, 251
Inverse method, 100, 101
Inverse transform method, 96, 97
Investment, 358
Ito lemma, 160, 161, 190–192

J

Jump-diffusion model
    CF, 194, 195
    Kou model, 219–231
    Python, 192–194
Jump handling models
    characteristic function, 194, 195
    Ito lemma, 190–192
    Merton model, 195–219
    parametric diffusion, 192–194
    SDE-based models, 189

K

Kernel density estimator (KDE), 235
Kernel method, 158
    approximation errors, 234
    Gaussian kernel, 235
    parameter estimation, 238, 239
    Stochastic process, 239–246
    test function, 236, 237
Kou model
    density function, 219
    forecasting, 228–230
    jump distribution, 219
    parameter estimation, 225–228
    path generation, 221–225
    sampling jumps, 219–221
    stochastic process, 221–225

L

Lagrange multiplier, 370
LCG, *see* Linear congruential generator (LCG)
Linear congruential generator (LCG), 97
Log-asset price, 159, 160
Log-likelihood function, 70, 166
    combinations, 73–76
    density function, 70
    domain restrictions, 72
    Gaussian, 78–80
    template base class, 70–72
LoglikelihoodOptimizer, 212
Log returns, 34

M

Machine learning (ML), 157
Market stack, 26–30
Markowitz portfolio optimizers, 379
Maximum likelihood estimation (MLE), 69, 70
Mean-variance analysis
    class diagram, 362
    computations, 356
    investment, 358
    mean/expected return, 357
    portfolio management, 356
    return, 357
    stock value, 356
Merton model, 225
    parameter estimation, 198–213
    parameters, 195
    path generation, 196–198
MertonProcessAssetPriceModel, 211, 212

Method of moments (MLE), 85
    Bayesian method, 82, 83
    gamma distribution, 80
    parameter estimation, 79
    parameters, 80
Minimum-variance portfolio (MVP), 382
    additional constraints, 377–381
    class diagram, 373
    component, 374
    computation techniques, 369
    covariance component, 370
    distribution and minimum volatility, 375
    first-order equation, 372
    Lagrangian method, 373, 374
    mathematical optimization, 370
    Python, 372, 373
    types, 370
    volatility, 370
    weight distribution, 376
ML, *see* Machine learning (ML)
MLE, *see* Maximum likelihood estimation (MLE); Method of moments (MLE)
Modern portfolio theory (MPT), 355
Moments, 117
    distribution, 54
    population, 54
Monte Carlo simulation, 144–150, 173–176, 367
    definition, 116
    first-order raw moment, 116
    normal distribution, 117
    probability, 117
    probability distribution, 116
    random variable, 116
    standard error, 118
    statistics, 115
    technique, 115

MonteCarloSimulation, 118–122
MPT, *see* Modern portfolio theory (MPT)
Multi-period simple returns, 34, 35
Multiple one-period returns, 33, 34
MVP, *see* Minimum-variance portfolio (MVP)

N

Non-determinism, 7, 8, 37, 38, 40, 95
Non-parametric models, 231–233
Non-recursive model, 171
Normal distribution, 60–62, 112, 117, 165
NoVarReduction, 120
Numerical programming, 11–13

O

ODE, *see* Ordinary differential equations (ODE)
Option nomenclatures, 260, 261
Option value, 271–273
Ordinary differential equations (ODE), 309
OTC, *see* Over-the-counter (OTC)
Over-the-counter (OTC) market, 16

P

Parameter estimation process, 166, 170, 212, 264
    frequentist method, 68–79
    Gaussian distribution, 86–92
    log-likelihood function, 70–79
    use cases, 67, 68
Parameters–likelihood function
    closed-form estimation, 171, 172
    numerical estimation, 166–171

INDEX

Partial derivatives, 312
Partial differential equations (PDE), 311
    Black-Scholes equation, 310
    categories, 310
    Laplace equation, 309
    ODE, 309
    See also Finite difference method (FDM)
Path simulation, 13, 115, 239–246
Payoff function, 16, 17, 262–264
PDE, *see* Partial differential equations (PDE)
Periodic compounding, 20, 21
PMF, *see* Probability mass function (PMF)
Poisson distribution, 55–58, 100, 101
Poisson process, 150–153, 231
Poisson random variates, 101
Portfolios, 17, 18
    collection, 355
    investment strategy, 355
    mean-variance analysis, 356–364
    minimum-variance, 369–381
    simulation, 363–369
PortfolioSimulation, 365
Probabilistic software, 11–13
Probability, 95, 96, 98, 102, 116, 185, 265
    definition, 39–40
    for finance, 40
    financial instruments, 37
    inception, 37, 38
    set-theoretic notation, 41–44
    space, 38, 39
    See also Risk-neutral probability method
Probability distributions, 96, 116, 130
    characteristic function, 62–67
    density functions, 66
    environmental conditions, 48
    functional view, 48
    joint & marginal distribution, 50, 51
    likelihood & and parameters, 51, 52
    moments, 53
    PDF *vs.* PMF, 50
    random experiment, 48
    random variable, 49
    unit length, 49
    variance, 53
Probability mass function (PMF), 48
Proposal density, 112
Pseudo-random number generators, 97
Put-call parity relationship, 263, 267–269
Python, 10, 37, 70, 93, 98, 101, 106, 115, 136, 162, 259, 372
    coding, 21
    enum, 25
    explicit method, 320–327
    implementation, 10, 11
    implicit method, 332–336
    minimum-variance portfolio, 372, 373
    templates in, 192–194
Python-based generic templates, 118

Q

Quantitative finance, 3–5, 7, 13

R

Random values, 271
Random variables (RV), 198, 199
    continuous, 47, 48
    discrete variable, 44–46
    distribution, 98
    examples, 44
    generation, 95, 96
    set-theoretic view, 43
    suitable probability, 96

Random walk model, 133, 134, 136–140
    quadratic variation, 135, 136
    statistical metrics, 134, 135
    stochastic calculus & integrals, 141, 142
Returns, 355, 357, 369
    log, 34
    multi-period, 34, 35
    multiple one-period returns, 33, 34
    simple return, 31–33
Rho (P), 304–307
Riemann integral, 143
Riemann–Stieltjes integral, 141
Risk-neutral measurement, 166–171
Risk-neutral probability method, 345
    call option, 282, 283
    experimental purposes, 268
    integral, 265–267
    interface, 277, 278
    option values, 270–272
    partial view of class, 278–280
    put-call parity relationship, 267–269
    put option, 282–284
Risk-neutral settings
    GBM asset price, 164
    market risks, 164
    PDF & parameters, 164–166
    risk-free interest rate, 164
RMSE score, 178–180

S

Sample space, 39, 116
Sample variance, 121
Scaled random walk model, 136–140
SDE, *see* Stochastic differential
    equations (SDE)
SDE-based model-building, 158
Second-order approximation, 160

Security price, 46
Set-theoretic notation, 40
    independence & conditional
        probability, 42, 43
    probability space, 41, 42
Shareholder, 15
shgo algorithm, 169
Silverman's approach, 251, 252
Simple interest-based assets, 19
Simple return, 31–33
Simulation, 363–369, 382–385
    acceptance/rejection method, 102–116
    change of measure, 98–101
    inverse method, 100, 101
    inverse transform method, 96, 97
    non-deterministic systems, 95
Standard error, 123, 177
Standard normal density, 122
Stencil, 316
Stochastic calculus, 141, 142, 161
Stochastic differential equation, 231
    basic forecasting theory, 144–150
    Euler's method, 143
    integral form, 143
    samples paths, 150
    Weiner process, 142, 143
Stochastic differential equations (SDE), 9,
    118, 130, 141
Stochastic finance, 3, 35, 95, 118, 158
Stochastic process, 7–10, 16, 17, 95, 130,
    158, 159, 357
    call and put options, 276–278
    functions, 273–275
    inception, 131–133
    Kou model, 221–225
    partial view, 272, 273
Stochastic system, 11, 13
Stock exchange, 264

INDEX

Stock market, 4, 37, 39, 40, 55, 97, 172, 187
Stocks, 15, 16
    indices, 18
    option contracts, 16
    options, 16, 17
Stock S&P500 index, 280, 281
Stock values, 31, 178, 356
    fictional company, 48
Stock values, Airbnb, 5, 6
Symmetric random walk model, 134–140

T

Theta (Θ), 297–301
Time-consuming, 97
Time unit transformation, 176

U

Uncertainty bounds, 178, 179
Uniform distribution, 57, 58, 96–98

V

Variance, 53, 95, 119, 165
Variance reduction
    accuracy, 124
    antithetic sampling, 124, 125
    importance sampling, 126–130
VarReduction, 120, 121
var_reduction parameter, 119
Vega (K), 301–304
Verizon stocks, 362, 363
Volatility, 364

W, X

Walmart stocks, 362, 363
Wind movement, 38

Y, Z

Yahoo Financials, 22–26

GPSR Compliance

The European Union's (EU) General Product Safety Regulation (GPSR) is a set of rules that requires consumer products to be safe and our obligations to ensure this.

If you have any concerns about our products, you can contact us on

ProductSafety@springernature.com

In case Publisher is established outside the EU, the EU authorized representative is:

Springer Nature Customer Service Center GmbH
Europaplatz 3
69115 Heidelberg, Germany

www.ingramcontent.com/pod-product-compliance
Lightning Source LLC
LaVergne TN
LVHW080310260326
834688LV00038B/1039